In the Days of the

Northwest Bureau

www.royalcollins.com

In the Days of the
Northwest Bureau

Shi Jie and Si Zhihao

Books Beyond Boundaries

ROYAL COLLINS

In the Days of the Northwest Bureau

Shi Jie and Si Zhihao
Translated by Sun Li and Shelly Bryant

First published in 2023 by Royal Collins Publishing Group Inc.
Groupe Publication Royal Collins Inc.
BKM Royalcollins Publishers Private Limited

Headquarters: 550-555 boul. René-Lévesque O Montréal (Québec) H2Z1B1 Canada
India office: 805 Hemkunt House, 8th Floor, Rajendra Place, New Delhi 110008

ISBN: 978-1-4878-0962-1

To find out more about our publications, please visit www.royalcollins.com.

Editing Committee of *In the Days of the Northwest Bureau*

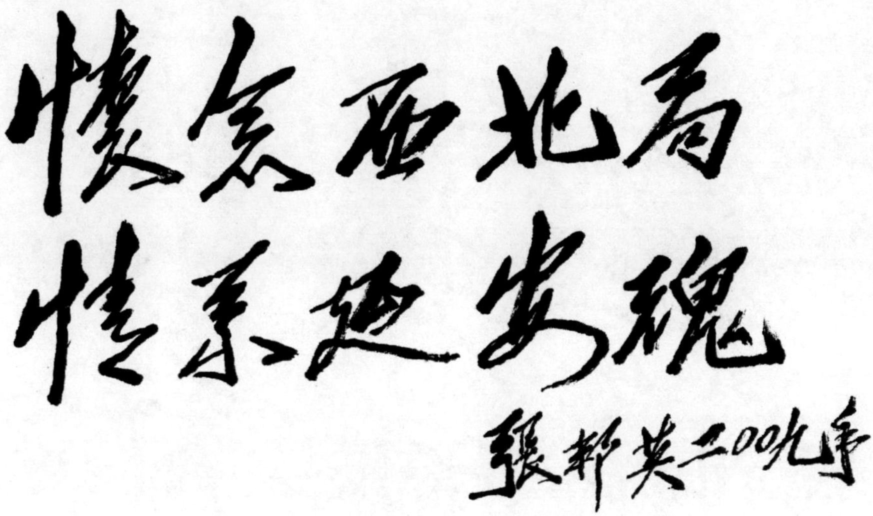

In Memory of the Northwest Bureau and the Spirit of Yan'an

– Inscription by Zhang Bangying, June 2009

西北岁月

王定国

二〇一二年

十一月

Years in the Northwest Bureau

– Inscription by Wang Dingguo, November 2012

Days of Passion and Memory

– Inscription by Ji Shilin, November 2012

The Foundation of the Revolutionary Friendship between Xi Zhongxun and Sun Zuobin

– Inscription by Sun Xiaodong, November 2012

Oil painting: *The Zhaojin Monument, Shaanxi and Gansu*, by Zhang Yadong

Front row (left to right): Liu Jingfan, Yang Chongyuan, Liu Zhidan, Xie Zichang, Gao Gang, Wang Taiji, Zhang Zhongliang, Huang Luobin

Back row (left to right): Gong Fengchun, Wu Daifeng, Hu Yanying, Huang Zixiang, Wang Zhaoxiang, Yang Sen, Wang Shitai, Zhang Bangying, Xi Zhongxun, Tong Fengyun, Li Miaozhai, Yang Qi, Wang Feng, Huang Ziwen, Zhang Xiushan, Chen Xueding, Ren Langhua, Ma Wenrui

Oil painting: *The Paramount Interests of the Party (Mao Zedong and Xi Zhongxun)*,

by Dai Haiyan

Oil painting: *Soviet Sky (Xi Zhongxun in the Shaanxi-Gansu Border Region)*,

by DAI HAIYAN

Traditional Chinese painting: ***Concerted Efforts*****, by Wu Baizhao**

On February 1, 1949, the Shaanxi-Gansu-Ningxia Jinsui Joint Defense Military Region was renamed the Northwest Military Region. He Long (left) served as commander, and Xi Zhongxun (right) served as political commissar (then Secretary of the Northwest Bureau)

Oil painting: *Riding Side by Side (Xi Zhongxun and Qi Xin)*, by Dai Haiyan

Foreword

by Hu Deping

"If it is dark in the east, we'll go to the west, and if it is dark in the south, we'll go to the north." Once the Red Army withdrew from the Central Soviet Area, Hubei, Henan, Anhui, Hunan, Jiangxi, Western Hunan, Hubei, and other base areas and made a strategic shift of a distance of 25,000 *li*, where was it to settle down? Fortunately, under the leadership of the Communist Party, the Red Army found a place to settle down in Yan'an, at the junction of Shaanxi and Gansu, in the northwestern part of China. From that time, the west and the north turned bright, and the Chinese revolution flourished. Mao Zedong's comment regarding a particular area being "in the dark" referred to the regional shift between the Red area of Northern Shaanxi and the soviet area of Southern China, and it was a correct statement.

In the second Civil Revolutionary War, a number of important leaders of the Party, the government, and the army emerged in the Northern Shaanxi Red Army, including Liu Zhidan, Xie Zichang, Gao Gang, Xi Zhongxun, Wang Shitai, Ma Wenrui, Zhang Desheng, Zhang Bangying, Jia Tuofu, Liu Jingfan, Zhang Xiushan, Zhao Boping, Wang Feng, Sun Zuobin, Zhang Mingyuan, and Lü Jianren. During the Anti-Japanese War, almost all of these comrades worked in the Northwest Bureau.

After the Southern Anhui Incident, the national government imposed a military encirclement and economic blockade on the Shaanxi-Gansu-Ningxia border region, and the distribution of funds and military salaries was completely suspended. In a sense, it meant that the legitimate status of the Party, army, and border region would no longer be recognized. The Party's strategic countermeasures were to continue to adhere to the Anti-Japanese National United Front while building the base areas on its own strength and launching the production movement of the Party, the government, and the army, to encourage farmers to set up various work teams, mutual aid groups, and cooperatives, to formulate family production plans, to promote good citizen activities, and to fight against "loafers." A small-scale opera called Siblings Reclaiming the Wasteland vividly showcased the great success of the industrial movement. The region issued the currency of the border region on its own and carried out trade with enemy occupied and Kuomintang controlled areas. Among the items after the Southern Anhui Incident included in Volume 3 of *Selected Works of Mao Zedong*, many are articles and speeches on the Shaanxi-Gansu-Ningxia border region and the tasks assigned to the Northwest Bureau. Renowned articles include "An Extremely Important Policy," "Economic and Financial Issues During the Anti-Japanese Period," and "Organizing the Team." In "Transforming Our Learning," the first article included in the rectification documents, cited the first real case regarding the issue of the currency in the border region.

The Yan'an Rectification Movement began during this period and lasted until the victory of the anti-Japanese war. During this period, the Northwest Bureau held a meeting of senior cadres, and one of the topics discussed was how to summarize the route of the Red Army in Northern Shaanxi. When it came to the line, there were clearly questions of right and wrong, but these were mingled with personal issues as well. Comrade Xi Zhongxun followed the guiding ideology of the Northwest Bureau in summing up his experience and lessons. He was extremely strict with himself and was completely earnest. He said that it was important to remain unconcerned about any personal gain or loss, and that only one thing should be born in mind – "putting the interests of the Party first."

In the northwest battlefield during the liberation war, Peng Dehuai and Xi Zhongxun were the principal and deputy secretaries of the Northwest Bureau of the CPC Central Committee, and they were reorganized twice. Xi Zhongxun played a leading role as Secretary of the Northwest Bureau. Under the leadership of Commander Peng Dehuai, the Northwest Field Army, with its 30,000 soldiers, fought with Hu Zongnan's troops of 250,000 soldiers. Under the leadership of Commander Peng Dehuai, the army grew stronger with each battle, and a large number of captured enemy soldiers were added to the army. At this time, Xi Zhongxun suggested to Commander Peng that the army should engage in the education campaign of "Making Complains and Three Investigation," so as to improve the class consciousness of the soldiers and enhance their combat strength.

Later, Mao Zedong summarized it as an "overhaul of the army," and its experience was introduced across the battlefields of the liberated areas.

After the founding of the People's Republic of China in 1949, Peng Dehuai was the first secretary of the Northwest Bureau of the CPC Central Committee, Xi Zhongxun the second secretary, and Ma Mingfang the third secretary, while Ma Wenrui was the deputy secretary, and Jia Tuofu, Zhang Jiafu, Wang Feng, and Zhao Boping were members of the Standing Committee. The Northwest Bureau cherished the newly founded Republic, which was reflected in their work style, specifically in their persistence, hard work, and plain living, and in their reliance on the masses. In many of his reports, Peng Dehuai said that extravagance and waste were in opposition to the building of the country through diligence and thrift, that self-centeredness was opposed to unified leadership, and that waywardness was resistant to law and order. He noted that extravagance, waste, and corruption were crimes against the people. The founders and pioneering officials were very humble and did not take their feats as merits, and the other officials, officers, and cadres all followed this example.

The northwest region had a vast territory and various nationalities. The Northwest Bureau attached great importance to the cultivation of ethnic cadres and taught them to deal appropriately with religious issues. On February 3, 1950, the first meeting of the Northwest Military and Political Commission presided over by Peng Dehuai unanimously agreed to establish the Lanzhou Institute for Nationalities. The Northwest Bureau actively advocated absorbing advanced elements from ethnic minorities into the Party. Peng Dehuai said that it depended on their consciousness and performance, not just on whether they believed in religion or ate pork, and that counter revolutionaries included both Chiang Kai-shek, who ate pork, and Ma Bufang, who did not eat pork.

At that time, there were many brave, honest Tibetan compatriots in Qinghai and Gansu who lived a nomadic life on the plateau. Their social form was feudal serfdom, and their national and tribal leaders had been cheated by the reactionary regime for many years. They were full of doubt about the new regime and were vulnerable to the provocation of reactionary elements. Taking the Party's ethnic policy as the criterion, the Northwest Bureau enthusiastically and patiently did a good deal of work with the Tibetan leaders and chiefs, especially when it came to settling the rebellion of the Nganglha Tribe in Qinghai Province. After more than ten rounds of persuasion and dialogue, Xiang Qian, head of a thousand households of the Nganglha Tribe, finally surrendered. The CPC Central Committee commended the Northwest Bureau, and Mao Zedong praised Xi Zhongxun, saying, "You are truly powerful. Zhuge Liang captured Meng Huo seven times, and you are more powerful than Zhuge Liang."

On April 27, 1954, the Central Committee of the Communist Party of China decided to remove the Party and government organs at the regional level. In November 1960, the Central Bureaus of the regional governments were restored. My father, Hu Yaobang, worked in the Northwest Bureau at the end of 1964. During his eight years in the General Administration and Organization Department of the Eighth Route Army of Yan'an, he had frequent contact with Chen Zhengren and Zhang Bangying, who were in charge of organizational work in the Northwest Bureau and the Shaanxi-Gansu region, and they became familiar comrades and friends, which is perhaps why I've been invited to write this preface. Partly in memory of the respectable elders in the Northwest Bureau, partly because I grew up on Yan'an millet and should not forget my roots, and partly because I worked under the leadership of Chang Lifu, an old comrade in the Northwest Bureau, for a very rewarding year. Hereby I agreed to the request and offered my part of this history.

February 25, 2013

Preface

The origin of *In the Days of the Northwest Bureau* can be traced back to 2008. Around the time of the Spring Festival, when we visited some veteran comrades in Xi'an, we always heard them recall the people and things associated with the Northwest Bureau, and we were especially curious about their memories of that time. From initial curiosity to later affection, and through their narration, we were greatly touched by the passionate years of the Northwest Bureau of the CPC Central Committee. With the encouragement and request of several veteran comrades, we developed the idea of recording their happy memories of the Northwest Bureau. We considered ourselves lucky, because over the next few years, we genuinely felt the passion and vitality of that era through our interactions with each veteran comrade who had lived and worked in the Northwest Bureau.

Based on the oral materials of the old comrades, this book takes the memories of their work and study in the Northwest Bureau as the main storyline, collating and excavating many important deeds and touching examples that happened during that period. In the process of compiling this book, many veteran comrades said to us affectionately, "You are saving the precious historical materials of the Party. You need to seize the time and persist in doing the work well. We are looking forward to reading the pages of the book as soon as possible." In the past few years, the youngest of the veteran comrades we interviewed reached the age of 83. In the process of compiling this book, some old comrades left us, and they retained their nostalgia for the Northwest Bureau to the end. This made us feel the urgency of publishing this work. If the publication of the book can capture the unforgettable memory and gratification of the older generation who lived and fought in that era, all our work and efforts over the past five years will be of great significance. This is our leading purpose and greatest wish in compilation.

In the process of compiling and publishing this book, we were fortunate to receive help and guidance from Comrade Qi Xin, a revolutionary of the older generation. She read this manuscript very carefully, and with a responsible attitude toward history and in the spirit of seeking truth from facts, she provided valuable insights into the time, place, and characters involved in some historical events. At the end of December 2009, she compiled, printed, and sent us her comments, suggestions, and revisions for each article. This greatly inspired and encouraged us to carry on. We stood in great awe of the history of the Northwest Bureau, and we did not dare be slack in the compilation of the book. Comrade He Zai, chairman of the editorial board, and other members of the editorial board have participated closely in the process of compiling this book and offered clear guidance, which has made the work both rigorous and solemn. Comrade Hu Deping, Hu Dehua, and Ma Ping also offered valuable suggestions for the compilation of this book, out of sincere feelings for the veteran comrades of the Northwest Bureau. Comrade Hu Deping wrote a foreword filled with great affection, which made us cherish all the more the passion and loftiness of the unforgettable years of the Northwest Bureau now as the book is about to be published.

In addition, the relevant departments of the Party history of the Central Committee, the Party History Office of Shaanxi Province, and the Provincial Press and Publication Bureau have also fully affirmed and strongly supported our work. Huan Jie, Vice President of the Party School of the Shaanxi Provincial Party Committee, Cui Xiaomin, member of the Standing Committee of the Weinan People's Congress, Dr. Wang Xiaoyong, of the Shaanxi Academy of Social Sciences, Professor Fu Gongzhen of Shaanxi Normal University, Feng Xiaoli, President of the Humanities Publishing Branch of the Shaanxi Normal University General Publishing House, and editor Deng Wei have done much work in publishing this book. The volume refers to and extracts some precious pictures and writings from other published books, and many comrades and units have given us their selfless help. We would like to express our heartfelt thanks to all.

March, 2013

Contents

Part I

Records of Oral Accounts

My Revolutionary Years with Xi Zhongxun in the Base Area of Shaanxi and Gansu

Zhang Bangying

Born in May 1910, Zhang Bangying was a native of Yao County, Shaanxi Province. He died on June 29, 2010, at the age of 100. He once changed his name to Chang Fangyi. He joined in the revolution in 1926 and the Communist Party of China in 1927. He served as Secretary of the Yao County Committee of the CPC, head of the Organization Department of the Special Committee of the CPC, member of the Revolutionary Military Commission of the Shaanxi-Gansu Border Region, Secretary of the Southern Shaanxi-Gansu Border Region Committee of the CPC, chairman of the Southern Shaanxi-Gansu Border Revolutionary Committee, chairman of the Soviet Government of Guanzhong Special Zone, vice president of the First Session of the Shaanxi-Gansu-Ningxia Border Region, standing committee member of the Central Bureau of the Central Committee of the Shaanxi-Gansu-Ningxia Border Region, standing committee member of the Northwest Bureau of the CPC Central Committee and vice minister of the Organization Department, Secretary General of the Northwest Bureau of the CPC Central Committee, member of the Northwest Military and Political Commission of the CPC, Minister of the Rural Work Department of the Northwest Bureau of the Central Committee of the CPC, deputy director of the Second Office of the Secretariat of the CPC Central Committee, Deputy Minister of the Ministry of Communications of the Central Committee of the CPC, alternate secretary of the North China Bureau of the CPC Central Committee, and Deputy Minister of Civil Affairs. He was a member of the Advisory Committee of the 12th and 13th National Congress of the CPC, the Standing Committee of the First National People's Congress, the Standing Committee of the Third, Fourth and Fifth CPPCC, the representative of the Seventh and Eighth National Congress of the CPC, and special representative of the 14th, 15th, 16th, and 17th National Congress of the CPC.

Editor's note: Recalling the unforgettable years in Northern Shaanxi and Northwest Bureau, at 100 years old, Zhang Bangying showed great enthusiasm and excitement. Although he was unable to easily move around during his interview, Zhang insisted on inscribing the title of the book. This was a recognition of our work and commemoration of the Northwest Bureau.

Xi Zhongxun was one of my old comrades. As early as the great revolution of 1926, he joined the Communist Youth League, and in 1928 he was transferred to the Communist Party of China and engaged in the anti-imperialist, anti-warlord, anti-bureaucratic students' and farmers' movements. I remember that during the period from 1927 to 1928, when I was studying in Xi'an Middle School in Shaanxi Province, Chiang Kai-shek and Wang Jingwei rebelled, and the national revolution began to decline. I learned from Party insiders that he was a student of the Third Normal School in Sanyuan County. He was arrested by the authorities in the struggle with other students against the school's reactionary staff. During his detention, he was firm and indomitable, displaying the character of a Communist Party member. The Party organization decided to turn him into a full Party member, and he was bailed out. Since then, I became familiar with the name Xi Zhongxun, and I learned that he was from Dan Village, Fuping County, Shaanxi Province, practically my neighbor, as his village was only twenty or thirty *li* away from Yao County.

In the autumn of 1932, I returned to my hometown from the army of Yang Hucheng to conduct military movement work. Under the instruction of the Weibei Special Committee of the CPC, I went to meet secretly with Xi Zhongxun, who worked in the special committee of the regiment at Dongguan Stadium in Sanyuan County. At that time, the Party organizations were still conducting underground activities, and the fighting environment was extremely dangerous. In order not to be noticed, we stood by a swing, talking for a short time about the current work and the issues that needed to be given attention. The scene remains fresh in my memory. We started to get to know each other from that time. I also learned that he had done military movement work in the army of Su Yusheng in Gansu Province. Because of the organization issues, the two units we were in entered a battle, and later Xi and Comrade Liu Linpu (who died bravely), along with other members of the Shaanxi Military Commission, led the Liangdang Mutiny. Despite its failure after a few days, it had a great impact on the local area at that time.

In March 1932, Xi Zhongxun and others organized and led a Kuomintang army battalion to launch a mutiny in Liangdang County, Gansu Province. After the uprising, the army was reorganized as the Fifth Detachment of the Shaanxi-Gansu guerrilla group of the Red Army of Chinese workers and farmers, and Xi Zhongxun was appointed Secretary of the CPC team. The picture shows Xi Zhongxun before the Liangdang Mutiny.

In order to develop the farmers' movement and expand the revolutionary area during autumn and winter that year, assigned by the Weibei Special Committee, Xi Zhongxun made use of social relations with villagers and relatives to do mass work in the Zhaojin District of Yao County. He contacted Liu Zhidan and Xie Zichang, the leaders of the Shaanxi-Gansu guerrillas who had operated in the area at that time. Later, Xi arrived in the Soviet region of Weibei and was appointed political instructor of the guerrillas in the Weibei Soviet region. In some villages, the farmers were led to fight against local tyrants and allocate grain, which paved the way for the Second Regiment of the Number 26 Red Army, reorganized from the guerrillas in Shaanxi and Gansu, to establish the Zhaojin revolutionary base area along the border of Shaanxi and Gansu.

In spring 1933, Xi Zhongxun first served as the political commissar of the Shaanxi Gansu guerrilla group, then as vice chairman of the Shaanxi-Gansu Border Revolutionary Committee, and he participated in leading the local people in the revolutionary struggle. At the period of developing and expanding the base areas, Du Heng, the political commissar of the Number 26 Red Army and of the Second Regiment, took a right-leaning approach. Despite the struggle against the enemy, the hard-won Zhaojin Revolutionary Base, and the difficult situation they faced, Du wrongly decided to lead the second regiment out of the base at Zhaojin and to Weihua and Luonan, the central part of the enemy's rule, in hopes of establishing a new revolutionary base. At that time, Xi Zhongxun, Liu Zhidan, and Wang Shitai all firmly opposed to his plan, but Du didn't listen, resulting in failure in Zhongnanshan in just two months after the army went south.

In July that year, the Yao County uprising held by our Party organization, the head of cavalry regiment of Yang Hucheng's troops, Wang Taiji, and the guerrilla group of Yao County (later renamed the Third Branch of Yao County on the border of Shaanxi and Gansu, when I served as the Party representative of the branch) entered the Zhaojin base, where I met Xi Zhongxun for a second time. We were pleased that the cause of the Party and the revolution brought us together again. From that time, we worked together for the establishment of the revolutionary base areas along the Shaanxi-Gansu border, the development of revolutionary armed forces, and the establishment of the Party and of the regime, working together for four or five years.

We met at a time when the Third Branch of Yao County, the remainder of the uprising led by Wang Taiji, and the Fourth Group of the Number 26 Red Army reorganized from the guerrilla forces in Weibei gathered in the base of Zhaojin under the enemy's "encirclement and suppression," and when the Second Regiment

Comrade Zhang Bangying in the 1940s.

of the Number 26 Red Army failed in the south, and the Shaanxi Provincial Party Committee was damaged by the enemy. At that time, many comrades disagreed over the issues of centralized or scattered operations and unified leadership of the army. Because scattered operations could be annihilated by the enemy, in August, under the leadership of the special committee of the CPC, a significant joint meeting of the Party, government, and army was held in Chenjiapo. At the meeting, most comrades advocated centralized action and the establishment of the temporary general headquarters of the Red Army along the Shaanxi-Gansu border and unified command of the operation of these forces. Xi Zhongxun, the executive chairman of the conference, sided with the majority, firmly advocating centralized, unified leadership and opposing decentralized action. He played a vital role in promoting the correct decision-making process of the conference.

In October 1933, Xi Zhongxun was still vice chairman of the Shaanxi-Gansu Border Revolutionary Committee. When our major forces won the victory in Zhanghong Town in Xunyi and continued to forge northward for external operations in Heshui, Gansu Province, with little military strength in the Zhaojin base area, the Xi'an Suijing Bureau of the Kuomintang mobilized a strengthening group to gather thousands of people from all counties to carry out rampant "encirclement and suppression" against the base area of Zhaojin, and they launched a continuous attack against Xuejiazhai. At that time, in coordination with the special committee and the comrades in charge of the guerrillas, Xi Zhongxun rose

In June 2009, Comrade Zhang Bangying and the editor-in-chief of this volume.

up to fight the enemy. He insisted on fighting for several days, and he landed a heavy blow to the enemy. Finally, due to the overwhelming majority of the enemy army, Xi Zhongxun had to withdraw from Xuejiazhai, and the enemy temporarily occupied the base area of Zhaojin. After falling seriously ill for more than a month after the withdrawal, Xi went north to seek the main force. According to the November resolution of the Baojiazhai meeting on the extensive guerrilla war, Xi organized and led the masses to establish a new revolutionary base area with the local staff who had been transferred into the region.

In late February 1934, with a new situation in which our main forces fought against and destroyed many enemy troops and won many battles, the Shaanxi-Gansu Border Revolutionary Committee was formally established in Nanliang, with Xi Zhongxun as the President, to further mobilize the masses, develop the local armed forces, launch guerrilla warfare, eliminate the anti-reactionary forces, and establish the revolutionary regime. Under the leadership of the new special committee of the Communist Party of China, the Party and government leading organs of the Southern Shaanxi-Gansu border region had been established to expand and consolidate the revolutionary base. In November, on the occasion of commemorating the anniversary of the October Revolution in the Soviet Union, the Congress of Workers, Farmers, and Soldiers in the border area of Shaanxi and Gansu was held in Liyuanbao, where the Soviet government was established, and Xi Zhongxun was elected president of the Soviet government. During this period, I was transferred to the special committee of Nanliang, the junction of northwestern Shaanxi and eastern Gansu to do the Party's organization work. The government was stationed in Zhaiziwan. Xi and I worked intensively together again for a while during this period.

From September to November 1935, after the unification of the leadership of the revolutionary base areas in the Shaanxi-Gansu border area and Northern Shaanxi, the Number 26 Red Army in the Shaanxi-Gansu border area, the Number 27 Red Army in the Northern Shaanxi, and the newly formed Number 25 Red Army in the Hubei-Henan-Shaanxi region were on the verge of winning the third encirclement and suppression of the enemy against the Northern Shaanxi base area. The practitioners of Wang Ming's left-leaning opportunist route in the northwest region then launched the "elimination of counter-revolutionaries in the north of Shaanxi" and arrested Liu Zhidan and other leading cadres at different levels of the Party, government, and army in the Shaanxi-Gansu border area. Xi Zhongxun was one of them, and he was in a dangerous situation. Thanks to Chairman Mao and the Central Committee of the CPC leading the Long March of the Central Red Army to Northern Shaanxi, the wrongdoing was remedied in time, which enabled Xi Zhongxun to be released with many other comrades, and thus resolved the revolutionary crisis. Xi Zhongxun suffered greatly during the persecution, but did not waver in his revolutionary morale. Under the correct line of the Party Central Committee represented by Chairman Mao, Xi Zhongxun was even more motivated to work hard.

In January 1936, Xi Zhongxun was assigned by the Party to serve as vice president of the Soviet Government of the New Guanzhong Special Zone, founded on the basis of the former Southern Shaanxi-Gansu border area. At that time, I was doing government work in the area. His arrival at the post allowed us to work together for months in the struggle against the Northeast Army's "encirclement and suppression." After that, he followed the central instructions and launched the Western Expedition. Xi Zhongxun was assigned to serve as secretary of the county committee of Huan County, an impoverished county in Longdong, Gansu Province. In September and October, the Central Committee sent him back to the Soviet region of Guanzhong to work as secretary of the special committee, along

The place where Xi Zhongxun lived in Hegoutai of Nanliang in 1934.

with several cadres familiar with the situation in the Guanzhong Special Zone. At that time, many parts of Guanzhong were occupied by the enemy. In these extremely difficult circumstances, he united the local cadres, relied on the armed guerrillas in all counties and the masses, and persisted in fighting and taking the opportunity to strike the enemy. With the peaceful settlement of the "Double Twelve" incident in Xi'an, the anti-Japanese effort presented a new prospect. At that time, as the chief director of the Organization Department of the new Shaanxi-Gansu Provincial Committee, I accompanied Li Weihan, Secretary of the CPC Committee of Shaanxi-Gansu Province, to Chunyao County, where the leading organ of the Guanzhong Special Zone and the General Political Department of the Red Army was located, to discuss with relevant leaders how to develop the work southward at the opportune time. We stayed in Taoquhe with the special commissar of Guanzhong, listened to several reports from Xi Zhongxun on the basic local situation and new problems encountered in the new situation, and conducted research together, after which we put forward the action plan for the period and were highly commended by Li Weihan. After that, in the new situation,

Comrade Zhang Bangying in 2009.

we worked together for years in the construction and protection of the Shaanxi-Gansu-Ningxia border area.

Xi Zhongxun was a proletarian revolutionary, loyal Marxist, Leninist, and communist who endured long-term testing. He was frank, enthusiastic and sincere, and he was active and energetic in his work. He adhered to the correct guideline, route, and policy of the Party based on the actual situation, and he never hesitated to correct any mistake when it occurred, nor did he hold back his opinions. He took the interest of the Party as his priority and was resilient enough to fit into any situation. He bore in mind the big picture rather than thinking about his personal gains and losses. With a strong revolutionary will, he kept pressing ahead and was never shaken by difficulties or setbacks. He worked hard, along with his comrades and the masses, making great contributions to the establishment of the revolutionary bases and the revolutionary regime, the development of revolutionary armed forces, and the construction of the Party in the Shaanxi-Gansu-Ningxia border area.

With the revolutionary spirit and an excellent ideological and moral character and working style, Xi Zhongxun laid the ideological foundation for his later leadership position as the chief director of the Northwest Bureau, the Party, and the state, and for further liberation of the northwest region and the cause of socialist construction, making great contributions and furthering his achievements. I am greatly impressed by the history of his revolutionary struggle, and I now find it particularly relevant and inspirational.

The Northwest Bureau's Key Role in the Process of Central Decision-Making

HE ZAI

Born in 1919, He Zai was a native of Baoji, Shaanxi Province. He participated in the revolution in 1936, and studied in the Yan'an Central Party School, the College of Marxism and Leninism, the Central Research Institute, and the Anti-Japanese Military and Political University. During the War Against Japanese Aggression, he was engaged in rural investigation and party construction. He served as deputy head and head of the Work Group of Army Expansion and Grain Collection, and as the acting county head. After 1944, he worked as an officer, secretary, and director of the office of the Organization Department of the Northwest Bureau of the CPC Central Committee. After the founding of the new China, he served as secretary and director of the Political Secretariat of the CPC Central Committee and the general office of the CPC Central Committee. After the Third Plenary Session of the Eleventh Central Committee of the CPC, he served as director and Secretary General of the Bureau of Cadre Investigation of the Central Organization Department, a member of the sixth and seventh CPPCC, and standing vice chairman of the Legal Committee. After retirement, he participated in poverty alleviation work and served as the executive vice president of the China Poverty Alleviation Foundation, the standing director of the Old Revolutionary Areas Construction Promotion Association, and a consultant for the Human Rights Foundation. His works include *Glory of Yan'an*, *Mao Zedong and Me*, *The Second Revolution*, *Persistent Loyalty*, *The Rectification of the Cases of Injustice and Falsehood*, and *The Song of Poverty Alleviation*.

Editor's note: At the end of his interview, when He Zai inscribed the four characters "seeking truth from facts" for us, we saw that it was not only the old man's summary of the spirit of the Northwest Bureau, but also his specific expectations of us as we did this job, which was down to earth and free from all empty talk and exaggeration.

I am old now, unable to move around easily. I can hear only a bit, and only if you speak close to my ear, but I'm ready to talk about the Northwest Bureau. There are so many stories about the Northwest Bureau, and it would be impossible to tell them all within a few days or nights. First, it is necessary to make clear that there were three Northwest Bureaus in history. The first was the Northwest Bureau in Yan'an, with Gao Gang as the first secretary, followed by Xi Zhongxun (in October 1945 when Gao Gang was transferred to the northeast and Xi Zhongxun took over until the national liberation). The second was the Northwest Bureau located on Jianguo Road in Xi'an, with Xi Zhongxun serving as Secretary. The third was the Northwest Bureau in the 1960s, when Liu Lantao was in charge. I joined the Northwest Bureau in 1943, mainly in Yan'an, and I was soon transferred from the Northwest Bureau. I think we started the preparation in 1949, and I was transferred in 1950.

It is Important to Write About the Northwest Bureau

Including this one, I have given four interviews about the Northwest Bureau in total. The first group worked to prepare video materials. They went to talk to relevant comrades of the Central Committee, who were very supportive and urged them to work more quickly. At that time, I was asked to introduce them to some old people from the Northwest Bureau, which I did, but sadly some had passed away and didn't get to give their interview. The second group included the adult children of some leaders, including the descendants of Ma Wenrui and Ma Mingfang. The children grew old and intended to write a book and make a movie together about the Northwest Bureau. The third group included those from some counties in Shaanxi, like Fuping County, who related something from the perspective of county records. You are the fourth group.

I have a clear view about the writing: it is necessary to do so, but we do need to keep two points in mind. First, we should get the support and guidance of the relevant departments. Otherwise, a great amount of time and effort will be put into writing a book that may go nowhere, and everyone involved may become frustrated and discouraged. It's good that you plan to write about the Northwest Bureau in three parts. The Party has always attached great importance to the educational influence of the glorious historical tradition of the Party. This year marks the 60th anniversary of the founding of the new China. If relevant leaders and departments can support this project, many problems will be solved. I told the first few groups of interviewers the same thing, and I'm telling you again that this is a very important, critical matter.

Second, after the approval of the relevant departments, there should be a guiding body to assist you. For instance, the Party History Office of the Central Committee should be appointed to assist you, or the Central Literature Research Office should assist you, or the Central Archives should provide you with materials. Even if you work on your own, you should absorb their experience and follow their guidance. You need to work together with those Party history departments to complete such a project, if you aim for it to play a role in publicity and education.

In short, my colleagues from the Northwest Bureau are getting old, and there are fewer old comrades of the Northwest Bureau still living. I am over ninety now, and you may have to take time to interview those elderly people and hear their memories of the Northwest Bureau. It is a preservation of this part of the history. It is very meaningful, and I support this work.

The Northwest Bureau's Key Role in the Process of Central Decision-Making

I have told the other three groups of interviewers that writing about the Northwest Bureau is a meaningful job, because the Northwest Bureau played a key role in the central decision-making process. During the anti-Japanese war, many major policies of the Central Committee were produced in the northwest, or sometimes, Chairman Mao referred to the materials of the Northwest Bureau, and some policies were provided by the Northwest Bureau that way.

The most famous included "The Ten Major Guidelines Governing the Anti-Japanese War," "Strategies Against Japanese Imperialism," "On New Democracy," and "On the Coalition Government" (all of which are the most important articles in Chairman Mao's works), covering "the rational, favorable, progressive" approach to fighting against the Kuomintang. Others involved military issues, such as "The Strategic Issues of the Anti-Japanese Guerrilla War," and philosophical issues like "On Practice and On Contradiction," all arising from Yan'an in Northwestern China. There were also such works as "An Exceptionally Important Policy"

Comrade He Zai in the 1940s.

and "Economic and Financial Issues During the Anti-Japanese Period," which contributed greatly to the base area. Comrade Mao Zedong wrote these after more than a month of investigation and learning from the comrades in the northwest, based on the materials provided by the Shaanxi-Gansu-Ningxia border area and the Northwest Bureau. Many comrades from the Northwest Bureau participated in the process of this writing.

In the winter of 1947, Xi Zhongxun (right) and (from left) Ma Wenrrui, Zhang Bangying, Zhang Jingwu, Li Zhuoran (front), Jia Tuofu, Wang Weizhou, Lin Boqu, He Long, Yang Mingxuan, and others were in Yihe Town, Suide County, Northern Shaanxi Province.

Another indicator of the importance of the Northwest Bureau was the senior cadres' meeting of the Northwest Bureau of the CPC Central Committee, which began on October 19, 1942. This meeting in Yan'an, which lasted more than eighty days, was a crucial one in the history of the Party. Its main task was to summarize the history of the Party and check the work of the Shaanxi-Gansu-Ningxia border area by taking advantage of the opportunity provided by the Party rectification campaign. The Northwest Bureau senior cadres' meeting was an important meeting of the Party, and the most important one in the history of the Shaanxi-Gansu-Ningxia border area. It summarized the historical experience and lessons of the Party in the Shaanxi-Gansu-Ningxia border area, remedied the ideological bias of the Party at that time, unified the Party's leadership, strengthened the Party's unity, and clarified the future missions, thus facilitating the Rectification Movement and the work of the Shaanxi-Gansu-Ningxia border area, and the Rectification Movement of the Party as a whole.

The influential strategies, guidelines, and policies in the anti-Japanese war were all born in Yan'an, which indicates the responsibility of the Northwest Bureau and shows that it played a vital role in history.

The Northwest Bureau Supported the Whole Country, and Vice Versa

In the early period of liberation, the Northwest Bureau received a large number of young students from North China University and the North China People's Revolutionary University from Beijing, all of whom came to support the northwest work. Why were these students assigned to the northwest? I'm afraid not many of the people who were involved in this matter are alive now. The head of the Organization Department of the Northwest Bureau, Ma Wenrui, has departed, and the director of the Northwest Bureau (now Bureau Director) is also gone. Why were such a large number of young people from Beijing invited to the northwest? The reason was that the northwestern region, as an old base, produced three groups of cadres for the entire country.

The first group went to occupy the northeast. I was sent there, and I became a junior captain, then I was called back after the oath-taking meeting at the airport. Gao Gang said that the comrades of the local Party in the northwest needed to stay for the future work in Shaanxi, so I returned from the airport with my backpack. Of those who went to the northeast, there were seventeen Central Committee members and four Political Bureau members. Li Zhuoran, the Publicity Minister,

Chen Zhengren, the Minister of the Organization Department, and Ouyang Qin, the Secretary General, all from the Northwest Bureau, each went to the Northeast in turn. Practically all the cadres were dispatched there, if conditions permitted, and a large number of people were transferred from the northwest.

The second group went to the south. At that time, with the seven consecutive victories in battles in Central Jiangsu Province, a large part of Central and Eastern China was liberated. When the Chen Geng army crossed the Yellow River, another large area in Hunan and Hubei Provinces was liberated, and a large number of cadres were needed there, so many people went from the northwest to the new liberated areas, some even being assigned to Hainan Island.

The third group of people went to Sichuan. He Long led the troops to southwest China to liberate Sichuan. At that time, Shaanxi had not been liberated completely, and a group of cadres from Northwest Bureau were transferred away. How shorthanded was it at that time? In the worst times, the guards of some cadres worked directly as county heads, because there was no one else at that time, and a large number of the liberated land required urgent management.

On April 28, 2009, the editor-in-chief of the book with Comrade He Zai.

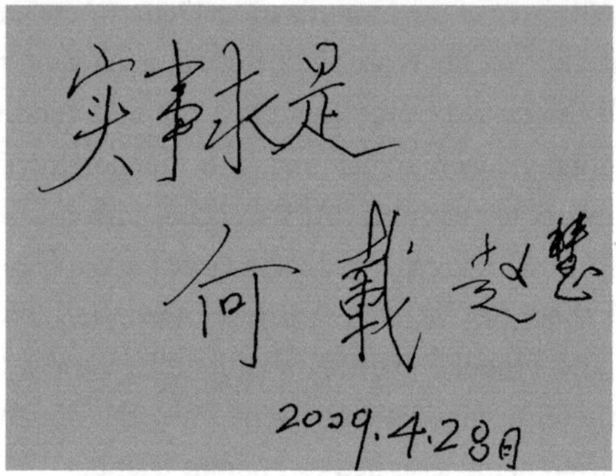

He Zai and his wife wrote an inscription for this book.

The number of cadres generated by the Northwest Bureau was large, and they achieved great things. Many provincial Party secretaries in the northeast, central, and southwest regions were all from the Northwest Bureau at that time, including Comrades Bai Rubing, Wang Pinian, and Bai Dongcai, and many of the local organization ministers and local Party secretaries were transferred from the Northwest Bureau. After the three transfers from the Northwest Bureau, there were not many people left. At that time, Lanzhou in Northwest China was liberated, and so was Baoji, after the battle of Xifu. The Northwest Bureau began to feel the shortage of hands and cadres. At our request, the Central Committee sent us people from three places, North China University (with competent students), the Revolutionary University, and the Zhengding Party School. The Central Committee transferred more than 2,100 cadres to the northwest. I remembered going to Beijing with Cui Guang and Jiang Xibai to make the appeal. To encourage the students to come to the northwest, we also invited the leaders who had worked in Yan'an to do mobilization, including Comrade Lin Boqu, Dong Biwu, and Zhou Yang.

Later, the students to the Northwest China were separated into three teams, taking trains from Beijing to Shijiazhuang. However, the railway after Shijiazhang was not smooth. Sometimes they had to walk down for hundreds of kilometers and arrived at Fenglingdu. Then, they crossed the Yellow River by boat to get to Xi'an.

At that time, it took more than twenty days to train these students in Beijing, and it took another month and three days to get the people to the Northwest Bureau. After arriving in Xi'an, the Northwest Bureau again conducted training. At the training sessions, Xi Zhongxun, Ma Wenrui, and Jia Tuofu of the Northwest

Bureau, along with other leading comrades who didn't go to the southwest, such as He Long, all gave speeches. After training for about three or four months, the cadres were assigned to different parts of the five provinces in Northwest China.

Because the Northwest Bureau first supported the needs of cadres in some liberated areas in the country and then became shorthanded itself after the liberation of the northwest, the Bureau had to ask for help from the central government, which led to a large number of students coming to Xi'an. The Northwest Bureau supported the whole country, and the country supported the Bureau.

Comrades Supporting the Northwest Contributed to the Development and Construction of the Greater Northwest Region

The group of people who went to the northwest from the Northeast China University, the Revolutionary University, and the Zhengding Party School played a key role in all walks of life in economic, cultural, and social construction in the early period of the liberation of Northwest China. Later, some became key leaders at the provincial level.

I remember that Comrade Shao Jiyao was assigned to the Northwest Bureau Research Office at that time. He was educated, active, and hardworking in work. His leaders mentioned this when they talked to me. In short, those comrades were quite competent and highly valued by their leaders.

Another impressive comrade was Zhang Boxing, who was also among the second group of cadres selected by the Central Committee from the Northeast China University to support the northwest. There were more than thirty people in this group. Why impressed? Because at that time, some of them didn't go with the team, as they hadn't settled some of their family affairs. But before those in the first group in Xi'an were allocated, the second batch came, and Comrade Zhang Boxing came from Beijing to Xi'an. Later, he worked in the Organization Department of the Shaanxi Provincial Committee, then successively served as director, organization minister, deputy governor, governor, and provincial Party secretary. He was diligent and down-to-earth, making great contributions to the people of Shaanxi. He is a typical example of the people we worked with, so it makes sense to write about him.

I remember there was a time when I went to Xi'an from Beijing, and before going back to Beijing, I met a cadre from the Suide local committee who said to me, "I was from Northeast China University. You were our captain. I am now Deputy

Commissioner of Suide Prefecture Committee. I didn't know you were here, or I would have visited you earlier." I was in a hurry to rush back, so I only talked to him briefly. That was in the 1980s, and I didn't have the opportunity to go back to those places to see the cadres again. I miss them very much.

Now, it is evident that those comrades contributed a good deal to the northwest. Back then, they were assigned to the general office of the Northwest Bureau, the policy research office, and the organization department. Later, they played a great role in the anti-bullying campaign, the land reform, and the movements against the "three evils" and the "five evils," and they made great contributions to the northwest. A group of cadres was assigned to work in Qinghai, Ningxia, Xinjiang, Gansu, and other places. Some went first to the art troupe of the Party school and later became actors, performing in many excellent films when the film studios were set up. Those comrades made extraordinary contributions at their ordinary posts.

So many young people were devoted to the northwest and achieved tremendously as they worked with the local cadres, which played a great role in the construction of Northwest China. We should put them in the history of the Party in Northwest China. If you write from this point of view, it will be a great article.

There are few people from the Northwest Bureau in Beijing. In the past two years, several have passed away, such as Cai Ziwei, Zhao Shouyi, from the Ministry of Labor, Qin Chuan, Publicity Minister, and those who stayed in the Northwest University and the Party school. They are all gone. Our Organization Department was even worse. Those working in the Organization Department were mostly old in the beginning. Now, even the cadres at the department level can hardly be found. Maybe we can find some in Xi'an. You need to seize the opportunity to finish this book as early as possible, and write it well.

Missing Secretary Xi Zhongxun

MA SONGLIN

Born in 1922, Ma Songlin came from Zizhou, Shaanxi Province. He joined the revolution in 1937 and the Communist Party of China in 1940. He served in the Stenography Department of the Central General Office and of Northwest Bureau, Chengdu Number 784 Factory, and the general office of the Shaanxi Provincial Committee.

As a stenographer of the central office in Yan'an period, I have always had great affection for Secretary Xi Zhongxun. Now, I want to note some memories I have of him for future generations.

A Person Who "Put the Party's Interests First"

I met Xi Zhongxun at the high-level cadres meeting held by Northwest Bureau in 1942, when I was taking minutes for the meeting. In order to prepare for the upcoming Seventh National Congress of the Communist Party of China, the CPC Central Committee held a series of small-scale summaries of our historical experiences and lessons in Yan'an. Here, I will talk about some of the experiences and lessons learned from the meeting held by the Northwest Bureau among high-level cadres.

The central leadership attached great importance to the high-level cadres meetings held by the Northwest Bureau, and Chairman Mao and several key leaders of the Central Committee all provided appropriate guidance. Over the span of a couple of weeks at the high-level cadres meeting of the Northwest Bureau, we talked about the serious harm that the Shaanxi-Gansu border area had suffered from the extreme left-leaning policies.

The meeting was very lively, with the speakers delivering one after another. The victims said many times in their speeches that by following Comrade Liu Zhidan's direction, they had established guerrilla zones to fight against the enemy in areas where enemy rule was weak, where there was less administration, and where there were conflicts between different forces. But the left-leaning people accused them of being "afraid of death, wavering in revolutionary will, and strong in guerrilla habits."

Comrade Xi Zhongxun stood out in his speeches several times. He was open minded and took the overall situation into consideration. He put the interests of the Party first, regardless of his personal gains and losses. He expressed gratitude to the Party Central Committee and Chairman Mao, saying that "if the Party Central Committee and Chairman Mao did not reach Northern Shaanxi, the Shaanxi-Gansu border area would be finished. And if Chairman Mao and the Party Central Committee arrived a few days later, there would be no Liu Zhidan, and no us." Xi stressed that the meeting held by the Northwest Bureau was of great significance. The purpose of the meeting was to summarize their historical experience and lessons, unify their ideological understanding, be united under the correct line of the CPC Central Committee and Chairman Mao, and continue to move forward. It was important that we not consider the slightest personal gains and losses, but only take "the interests of the Party as our first concern," as the purpose of our revolution was to serve the interests of the people.

Chairman Mao praised Comrade Xi Zhongxun at the meeting, saying that Comrade Xi was a good example. What Xi said and did expressed his concern for the interests of the Party, and he always put the Party's interests first. During the meeting in January 1943, Chairman Mao wrote an inscription for Xi Zhongxun on a white cloth of the words, *Putting the interests of the Party first.* As a stenographer, I really benefited greatly during the weeks-long meeting, and I learned much about the history of the Party.

Commanders Peng and Xi Worked Closely Together in the Fight in Northern Shaanxi

On March 16, 1947, Chiang Kai-shek and Hu Zongnan gathered 34 brigades of 250,000 soldiers to attack the Shaanxi-Gansu-Ningxia border area, with the help of Ma Bufang in Qinghai, Ma Hongkui in Ningxia, and the 864 Military Division of Yulin. The army had only six brigades (the 358 Brigade, the Instruction Brigade, the Duyi Brigade, the 359 Brigade, the Xinsi Brigade, and the Police Reserve Brigade) and 30,000 troops in the military division. The enemy's equipment was all American style, while we were equipped with just plain rifles. But there were two good commanders in the northwest battlefield, Peng Dehui and Xi Zhongxun. Their mission was to fight against hundreds of thousands of enemy troops armed to the teeth and to protect the absolute security of the CPC Central Committee and Chairman Mao during the transition to Northern Shaanxi. The task was very challenging. I worked with Secretary Xi Zhongxun of the Northwest Bureau, several standing commissars (Jia Tuofu, Zhang Desheng, and Ma Wenrui), and Liu Jingfan of the border government, in the headquarters of the Northwest Field Army.

Peng and Xi were commanders of the northwest battlefield, and they had a good mutual understanding. Mr. Peng told the commanders on many occasions that we should not be intimated by the enemy's fierce looks and their military equipment, and that in fact, we were stronger than them, as we had the support of the people in the border area. This was the fundamental guarantee for our victory, since we could

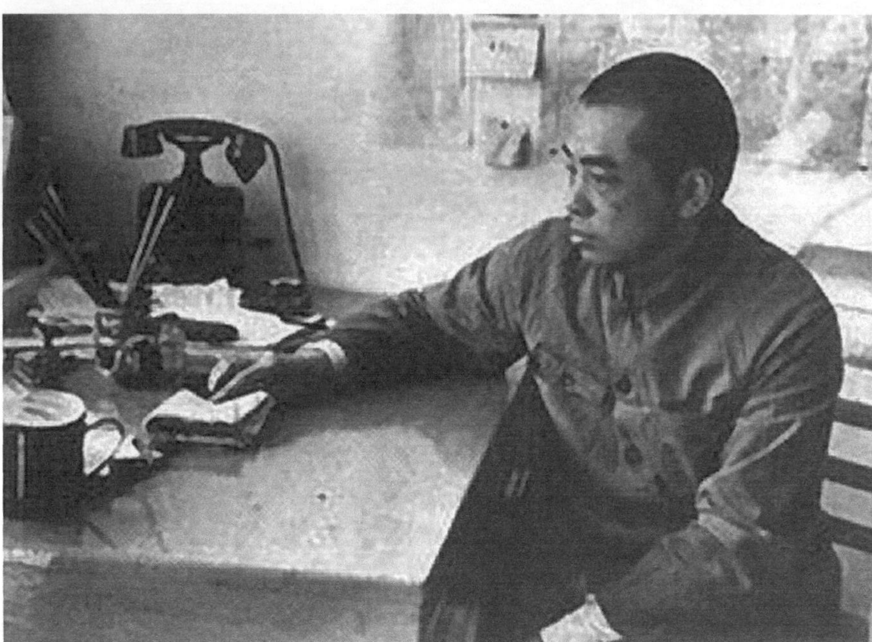

Peng Dehuai in Yan'an.

In March 1947, Peng Dehui and Xi Zhongxun studying the deployment of operations.

exercise the overall strength of the Party, government, military, and people. Peng also said that Xi Zhongxun and others were old comrades in the border area who had deep feelings for the people of the border area, that they were familiar with the geographical situation of the region, that with their support, the enemy would turn out to be a paper tiger, and that we could use mushroom tactics to exhaust the enemy and ultimately defeat them in batches when the time was right for us. Mr. Peng was very pleased to say that he had fought many battles and that this one was the smoothest. He said the commanders would have gone to a lot of trouble, but Xi Zhongxun and the others were a great help, providing detailed information concerning the military and political work, the logistics, the geographical landscape, and the enemy's movements in the operation, so that they only needed to focus on fighting. The commanders were all grateful to Xi Zhongxun for having created such good conditions for our army.

Xi Zhongxun and other old leaders played a role that could not be replaced. The people in the border areas trusted them greatly and felt connected to them. They had a clear understanding of the situation in the border areas, and they referred to the headquarters of the Northwest Field Army as the headquarters of the Party, the government, the army, and the people, which played a vital role in unifying them all. The old comrades in the headquarters worked arduously during the transition. They paid great attention to the political, logistical, and mass work. Everywhere they went, they convened cadres, masses, and Party members, and they held a symposium to publicize the good news of the coming victory, boosting the morale and confidence in that victory. They arranged for the people's livelihood and support for the frontline battle, allowing Peng to concentrate on the military issues. However, the one difficulty that remained in Xi Zhongxun's mind was that the Shaanxi-Gansu-Ningxia border area was largely a poor region, and the enemy blockade and continuous entry into the border area for looting and killing made the people there suffer greatly. This was especially so during the transition, when the civilians and soldiers there had a major problem with their daily provisions, which concerned Xi Zhongxun a lot. Fortunately, the locals had a clear understanding of the issue and volunteered to work together with the local cadres to make proper arrangements. The people there starved themselves to offer all their families' food for the soldiers to combat the enemy. The people of the border area and the army were so closely knit that the army could not survive without the people.

Once at the cadre mass meeting, Xi Zhongxun saw a woman holding a child who was eating a whole bran cake. Seeing this, he felt terribly sad and said tearfully, "My brothers and sisters in the border area, as a 'people's servant,' I should apologize to you. I didn't do my job well, and now such a young child must eat bran cake. This means that you adults can't even afford to eat that sort of plain cake." He was in great pain, and he even cried. Soon, we were all in tears. An old man from among the masses stood up and said, "Secretary Xi, don't feel sad. It is not your fault or the Party's or the government of the border areas. You Party members are all in the same boat with those of us who live here. We know that you worry a lot about the food issue for the soldiers and the masses. We are all aware of the difficulties. No matter how hard it is, we can't let our soldiers fight against the enemy on an empty stomach. We guarantee to provide food for you. Our own food problems will be sorted out. You and Mr. Peng can be assured that you can concentrate on commanding the battle. Only when the bandits are eliminated will the people of the border area have a good life." The old man truly spoke for the people of the border area.

In the same way, Mr. Peng told the commanders on various occasions that the people in the border areas sent their children to the army and sent their food to sustain us. They ate bran to tide them over during times of famine, and if we didn't speed up the elimination of the enemy, we would not live up to their expectations. Such selfless support of the people in the border area really encouraged the fighting spirit of the army commanders. This spirit was clearly shown in several battles during the transition period in the war. On March 25, in the Qinghuabian ambush, we annihilated a total of more than 2,900 enemy soldiers, followed by another 4,000 in Yangmahe on April 14. Headquarters decided that the troops would be put into the mountain area for a short time to rest and reorganize so we could be ready to fight again. At that time, Peng and Xi decided to take the 359 Brigade as the main force and take one platoon from each brigade to pretend to be the main forces, and they would move to Suimi. The enemy mistakenly thought that our main force, the Party Central Committee, and Chairman Mao were going to cross the Yellow River. Hu Zongnan left a division of troops in Panlong, his supply base, and moved all other forces to Suimi to pursue our army, but in fact, our main force had transferred to Panlong. On May 2, the Battle of Panlong began. Because of the enemy's firm work, the battle lasted two days without much progress on our side. Hu's bandits discovered that they had been deceived, and they swiftly turned back to Panlong for fear that our army would take Panlong and they would lose their military supplies. The enemy sent aircraft to bomb, and our soldiers took down two enemy planes with rifles and machine guns. The fighting was fierce.

The site of the Battle of Panlong.

After the three victories at Qinghuabian, Yangmahe, and Panlong, Peng Dehui and Xi Zhongxun sent the Northwest Field Army to attack Longdong and Sanbian from May 21 to July 7, 1947, annihilating more than 4,700 enemy troops and recovering the lost land occupied by the enemy. Pictured is the Northwest Field Army advancing to Sanbian.

Seeing that the main enemy force was coming, the CPC Central Committee and Chairman Mao were very concerned and gave instructions to Peng and Xi. The two commanders talked to the soldiers in the battlefield, asking them whether to attack or withdraw. The soldiers replied in unison to ensure the commanders that they would take Panlong. On May 4, the battle ended, and the enemy's death toll was more than 6,700. In the Panlong base, there were a large number of guns, ammunition, and other military materials, which upgraded our troops' supplies. The soldiers happily said, "Chiang and Hu's transportation captains have provided us with new equipment." The seized flour was sent to the masses.

These "three victories in three battles" were commended by the Party Central Committee and Chairman Mao. On May 14, a celebration was held in Zhenwudong, Ansai. Comrade Zhou Enlai spoke on behalf of the Party Central Committee and Chairman Mao. After the meeting, we pressed on to Longdong and Sanbian, marching swiftly day and night. According to regulations, Peng and Xi were equipped with special horses, but they seldom rode. Instead, they always placed the seriously injured on horseback. They walked along with us, chatting and making jokes, and they never put on airs. They told us that we were only different in the division of labor, but that we were all revolutionary comrades. We felt quite at ease talking with them. They sometimes teased us, too. For example, in March, there was a reporter named Tan who was near-sighted, and after the rain, he always liked to go to bright places. Bright places were often places with more water, so he was often covered with mud on rainy days. The two commanders called him "mud Bodhisattva." Once the Bodhisattva went to urinate. When he came back, Peng noticed that he seemed to be in pain and asked if he was ill. The Bodhisattva replied, "It's not easy to say this. I went to the grass to pee, and I don't know what stung me all over. It's terribly painful." Xi Zhongxun laughed and said, "Mud Bodhisattva, you're in trouble. Take off your pants and let us pull out the poison spines for you." Peng asked, "How did you know that he suffered from a sting?" Xi Zhongxun said, "I fought as a guerrilla in this area and suffered from this before. This scorpion tail grass grows in many places in Longdong and Sanbian. No matter what touches it, it will protect itself by shooting out stingers. Like the sting of wasps and scorpions, the pain can be alleviated only when the stingers are pulled out." We started to pull out the stingers and apply medicine for the Bodhisattva, following Secretary Xi's instructions.

Xi Zhongxun also warned that some places in Longdong and Sanbian were short on water where the masses lived by drinking cistern water (rain and snow water), and the water in some rivers was not drinkable, or it would make the drinker suffer from stomach ailments. In particular, we were told to be careful not to drink the water in the mass's cisterns because they would not have enough water if we did. Peng immediately said that Xi Zhongxun was truly a good guide for our army, as he was familiar with the local people. Peng then gave orders informing the whole army that no one was allowed to drink the water in the mass's cisterns or from the toxic river.

After leaving the area around Yan'an, the enemy could not discern the direction our main force had taken, so they sent out aircraft to scout. Before entering Longdong and Sanbian, we needed to pass some desert areas, which made it hard for us to hide, so we tried to march at night. We had no choice, though, and had to move forward in the desert during the daytime as well. During the day, when we were marching in the desert, we were shot at by enemy aircraft, and we lost some comrades. We were very sad, and we buried our comrades in the field. We stood on the burial ground for a long time, reluctant to leave. With tears of grief, the two commanders comforted us saying, "Don't be sad. We should dry our tears and continue to move forward." Actually, they were more sorrowful than us, and they said nothing all day, quite unlike their usual lively activity during our daily marches. Usually, they acted as facilitators and mobilizers in our team. In order to boost morale, they often asked someone to sing a folk song or a bit of Qin opera. Sometimes they walked up and down to ask about the blisters on one soldier's feet or the healing of another's wounds.

Xi Zhongxun was particularly prominent in his ideological and political work. During the confrontation with Ma Bufang's army at Heshui, Ma's soldiers, strangely enough, preferred death over surrender. In that confrontation, both sides suffered many casualties, which caused the indignation of our soldiers and some commanders. However, headquarters still gave preferential treatment to the prisoners. Many comrades could not accept this, so Comrade Xi Zhongxun held a meeting with the commanders and the accompanying staff to moralize, pointing out that what our comrades saw was the phenomenon, not the underlying part, and that like the soldiers of the Kuomintang, Ma Bufang's soldiers were all working people who were forced to serve in the army. He reminded that the Kuomintang soldiers had fought with our army many times, and they knew our Party's policy regarding prisoners very well, but Ma's soldiers had had fewer fights with us and were not familiar with our policy, so they were cheated by Ma Bufang. Xi mentioned that during the Long March of the Red Army, Zhang Guotao, who had split up with the Central Committee, encountered Ma Bufang's troops and suffered a great loss. Ma had been lying to his soldiers by telling them that the Red Army would take revenge and kill them all if they were captured. Xi said that Ma Bufang's soldiers were thus deceived, and that was why they fought so fiercely against us in the Battle of Heshui. They had been deceived and didn't understand our Party's policies. He said we should not substitute policies for emotion, as Chairman Mao taught us that "policies and strategies are the lives of the Party," and in any case, we should resolutely implement the policies of the Party, which was the absolute guarantee of our victory. He said that if we treated them well and gave them funds to go back to expose Ma Bufang's lies and deception, they would not be so stubborn when they met us again in the battlefield. After hearing Comrade Xi Zhongxun's speech, the commanders and soldiers were all inspired and enlightened, feeling that his understanding and application of the Party's policies indeed set an example for us to follow.

At this symposium, Comrade Xi Zhongxun proposed a new topic and asked for our opinions. He said that since the beginning of the war, our Northwest Field Army had grown in number as we had recruited all the soldiers below the rank of platoon leader from the enemy forces during the three victories in the three battles, and that it was necessary to conduct character training. Xi said that he had had talks with General Peng about carrying out an ideological education movement in the army at the proper time to improve our competence and combat skills, which would be a new military movement centering on sharing (the suffering in the old society and inflicted by the reactionary forces) and the three inspections (class, work, and fighting spirit). Xi asked all the commanders to consider how the Party could better speed up the improvement of the competence and combat skills of our team. Xi asked General Peng for input, and Peng agreed with Xi Zhongxun, saying at the meeting that Xi was a good military advisor for our army.

The Northwest Field Army gathered from Longdong to Yulin in Northern Shaanxi Province to prepare for the battle of Shajiadian. In mid-August, we won a great victory at Shajiadian, killing more than 6,000 bandits of the Number 36 Division of Hu's army and completely defeating the enemy, which was also a turning point for our Northwest Field Army to move to strategic counterattack mode. After the battle, our army was transferred to the Suide mountain area for a period of rest, and we pressed on into the new army ideological education movement in the winter. This new movement was the brainchild of Peng and Xi. When I went with Peng and Xi to a couple of spots for idea sharing and investigation, I was deeply

Xi Zhongxun (left) and Zhao Shoushan (then deputy commander of Northwest Field Army) together.

touched by what happened there. The new and old soldiers, including the cadres, all struggled to share, and they all expected to voice their complaints about the old society and the reactionary forces. They cried out when they were oppressed by the landlords and the reactionary group, their families were destroyed, and their sisters were taken to pay for the debt. They were all determined to beat the landlords and bullies, to defeat Chiang Kai-shek, and to eliminate Hu Zongnan. In the end, everyone was clear that the root cause of the suffering lay in the old society and the reactionaries. Only by eliminating the old evil society, the Chiang dynasty, and the reactionaries could the people be liberated completely, and only the Communist Party could provide the great salvation of the people. The three investigations were carried out on the basis of sharing. Every commander was clear in his mind that the mission of joining the PLA was to fight for the liberation of the oppressed people and to fight for the establishment of the new China. The current mission of the Northwest Field Army was to defeat Chiang Kai-shek and eliminate Hu Zongnan, Ma Wenrui, and Ma Bufang. At the same time, we all had a good understanding of the three inspections, and the core of the three inspections was to check our awareness. In this way, the three inspections involved enhancement of awareness, knowledge, and a fighting spirit. Many people had applied to join the Party. After this new army education movement, the competence and the fighting spirit of the Northwest Field Army was greatly enhanced, and Hu Songnan "helped" to mend our army's weaknesses by providing us with more soldiers and better equipment. We then expanded from 30,000 to 70,000 soldiers.

After the battle of Shajiadian, Chairman Mao went to Yangjiagou, Mizhi County on November 22, to hold the central expansion meeting. In early December, I followed Peng, Xi, and Zhang to the meeting to make a record. From December 7 to 24, at the eighteen day preparatory meeting, several issues were discussed in groups, and the formal meeting was held for four days, where Chairman Mao gave a talk entitled "On the Current Situation and Our Tasks."

After the new army movement, the Northwest Field Army adopted the means of encircling the city in February and March 1948, wiping out one of the main forces, two reorganizers, and five brigades of Hu Zongnan in the Yichuan and Wazijie areas, with a total of 30,000 people. The situation in Northern Shaanxi was then completely changed. At that time, Comrade Xi Zhongxun told me that the CPC Central Committee and Chairman Mao were leaving Northern Shaanxi. As there was no stenographer in the Northwest Bureau, he asked me to stay in the general office to train a group of shorthand personnel for the Northwest Bureau. Xi Zhongxun said the northwest was a poor place, but the people felt connected with us. Not long after, I left the central office and was transferred to the general office of the Northwest Bureau.

Taking Back Yan'an

On April 21, 1948, the news that our army had recovered Yan'an came. Comrades who withdrew from Yan'an were very excited and shouted out in unison, saying that "we are going home." Xi Zhongxun was as excited as everyone else. We had special feelings for Yan'an. After all, the CPC Central Committee and Chairman Mao had lived and fought in Yan'an in Northern Shaanxi for thirteen years. Yan'an nurtured us, and it was the cradle of our revolution. Xi Zhongxun asked Secretary General Cao Liru and me to leave for Yan'an immediately. He asked me to return to Yan'an to visit our brothers and sisters in Yan'an, and to see how badly Yan'an had been damaged by the enemy, especially the places where the Party Central Committee, Chairman Mao, and several standing commissars of the Central Committee had lived.

Xi Zhongxun, Feng Ziying (Xi Zhongxun's driver), Cao Liru, and I rushed back to Yan'an and went to the previous office of Northwest Bureau to have a look. The original office site of the Northwest Bureau was badly damaged by the enemy. We arrived at the headquarters of the Eighth Route Army at Wangjiaping, and comrades of the Yan'an Prefecture Committee went there to meet us. Xi Zhongxun intended to go and see some of the places where the central leaders had lived. The local comrades told us that many buried mines had been left behind when the enemy withdrew, and they were organizing experienced militia to clear the mines. The local comrades and Cao Liru did not think it a good idea for Xi Zhongxun to go around, and instead agreed to report to Xi about the situation in detail the following day. Cao suggested to Xi that in order to speed up the mine clearance and cleaning work, he would not listen to the report, but would go to do the cleaning with the rest. He asked Feng Ziying and me to stay behind, and he told me specifically that before the cleaning of some major former residences, I should not allow Xi to go around to inspect. If anything happened to Xi Zhongxun, Cao Liru would find it hard to report to the Party Central Committee.

I felt it really hard to perform this task. I understood Xi's personality very well, and no one could stop him from doing what he was determined to do. The task Cao Liru assigned me had to be completed firmly, as it was a matter of great concern to the interests of the Party Central Committee. Before day broke that morning, Xi asked Feng and me to go to Yangjialing with him. Feng and I responded that we would not go, and that he should not go, either. Xi asked why we rushed back to Yan'an in advance, then added that he would go on his own if we didn't go with him. I replied that the comrades of the local committee would come to report and that he was not supposed to go until several key former residence were cleaned up. This was the task entrusted to me. Xi was angry, and I was worried. I then said that as all three of us were Party members, we could act as a temporary Party group, voting according to the principles of the Party organization, and the minority would be subject to the majority. This finally worked, and Xi sat on the stool without a word. Feng and I no longer said anything. Xi Zhongxun remained silent for a few minutes, then said that I was smart to think of using this approach to persuade him. When I mentioned the principle of organization, he certainly dared not to violate this discipline. The three of us all laughed. Just then, comrades of the local committee arrived and asked us what was so funny. Xi told them that he intended to go to nearby Yangjialing to have a look and we would not let him go, and that we had prevented him from doing so by using the Party's organizational principles. As a Party member, he had to abide by the Party's organizational principles. The local comrade then reported in detail to Xi Zhongxun the situation in Yan'an after the enemy's occupation. As they gave the report, Xi asked the masses about their current life situation many times, and asked how the local Party committee, county committee, and local governments planned to recover from the war trauma. In this way, he turned his attention to this aspect. He talked with some comrades of the local committee for several days. During that time, Cao Liru returned to Wangjiaping as soon as he finished the mine clearance work. On hearing about the small episode between the three of us, he was pleased, commenting that Xi Zhongxun was a model of abiding by the Party's organizational principles and that we should learn from him. Xi praised Cao for rushing to do the most difficult, most dangerous work, which was always part of Cao Liru's moral character.

On May 1, the army and people of Yan'an gathered for a grand ceremony to celebrate the restoration of Yan'an. Xi Zhongxun greeted the people of Yan'an, publicized the good news of our army's victory in all the battlefields across the nation, and mobilized the people of Yan'an and the border areas to act immediately to heal the trauma of war and launch production campaigns. At the end of the celebration, Comrade Xi again suggested visiting several key former residence, such as Yangjialing, Zaoyuan, and Fenghuangshan, where the leading comrades of the

Central Committee had lived, together with the comrades of the local committee. Accompanied by Cao Liru and the comrades of the local Prefecture Committee during the inspection, Xi emphasized a couple of times that special preservation should be given to the former residences of Chairman Mao and several standing commissars of the Party Central Committee including Mr. Liu, Mr. Zhou, Mr. Zhu, and Mr. Chen, who had worked and lived there for thirteen years. There were clearly many other places to be preserved too, such as the previous sites of Baotashan, the Qingliangshan Central Organization Department, the Central Publicity Department, and other departments, as well as the Central Party School, the Anti-Japanese University, the Women's University, and the Lu Xun Art School. Yan'an was a revolutionary holy land, including the caves in Nanniwan and all the other mountains in Yan'an. Comrades going from Yan'an to other places would wish to come back to see the home that had nurtured them. After the national victory, many at home and abroad would also come to see the revolutionary holy land of Yan'an, and our descendants would come here to pay homage as well.

Xi Zhongxun said that Yan'an had been damaged several times. During the War Against Japanese Aggression, the Japanese bombed Yan'an to a pile to rubble. Since March 11, 1947, the Kuomintang had bombed Yan'an on a large scale with 45 aircraft, dropping 59 tons of bombs, and Yan'an became a desolate place. Lin Boqu, our former head of the Shaanxi Gansu border government, said many times that, after we won the national victory, we must build Yan'an, the revolutionary shrine, into a beautiful garden and make the mountains around Yan'an green, so that the mountain cuttings would become the "Wanhua mountain." This vision and hope of Lin will come about. Chairman Mao addressed the enlarged meeting of the Yangjiagou Central Committee about the former situation and our mission, mentioning that the new China was soon to be born. Shortly after we arrived in Yan'an, the Northwest Bureau and border government personnel returned. The focus of Xi Zhongxun's energy was shifted to the overall work of the five provinces in Northwestern China. Xi was good at combining the central policy and the northwest practice based on the actual situation. Thus, he proposed many new views and suggestions for the land reform, such as the opinions on making policies and correcting the leftist bias in different situations in the old, semi-old, and new areas, approved by the Central Committee and Chairman Mao, and then forwarded to the liberated areas throughout the country.

To Work in Xi'an and Leading the Northwest Bureau

In March 1948, the Northwest Field Army wiped out more than 30,000 people of Hu Zongnan's army in Yichuan and Wazijie. The situation in Northern Shaanxi changed completely. The entire nation shifted to a strategic attack. The Northwest Field Army advanced to Guanzhong, liberated Xi'an on May 20, 1949, and gained control of the area south of the Weihe River. Xi Zhongxun, He Long, Ma Mingfang, and other leaders led the cadres from two counties in the northwest and southwest regions to Xi'an from Wang Jiaping, Yan'an, and Xi Zhongxun asked me to follow them. We arrived at Sanyuan County, and members of the Party underground organization in Sanyuan informed Xi Zhongxun and other leaders about the situation in Xi'an, saying that the main forces of Hu Zongnan had withdrawn from Xi'an, but small enemy units were still in the midst of withdrawing, and they suggested that we should stay for a day in Sanyuan, then go on to Xi'an the next day.

We went into the city from the east gate of Xi'an and saw a couple of individual enemy soldiers running away in a panic. The doors to stores in the city were blocked with bricks, for fear that the enemy would rob them when they retreated. We stayed in the forest of Xincheng the day before entering the city, and after cleaning up (clearing the mines) in several places the next day, we moved to stay in Xingcheng, Nanyuanmen, Beiyuanmen, and other spots. Xi Zhongxun, He Long, Ma Mingfang, and other leaders as well as our entourage stayed in the residence of Wang Youzhi in Jianguo Road, the former Mayor of Xi'an City (now the office of the CPPCC provincial). All the personnel from Yan'an had defensive weapons with us, which allowed us to deal with small groups of enemies, since we had fewer armed forces in the city. The moment we got to the city, we heard the sound of continuous gunfire. Some units of Hu Zongnan's that withdrew to Nanshan fired guns at Xi'an city proper, and Ma Bufang's gangsters in Caotan also fired at the city. The gunfire in the city, especially in the area of Jianguo Road, was constant as a result of the trouble-making from various reactionary organizations and special agents of the Kuomintang. In fact, the sound of guns inside and around the city was constantly heard once we entered.

As soon as Xi'an was liberated, our main forces were transferred to the area south of the Weihe River. Although Hu Zongnan's main force had withdrawn from Xi'an and was ready to enter Sichuan, they were reluctant to leave. As Ma Bufang in Qinghai and Ma Hongkui in Ningxia had entered Guanzhong, they all wanted to use each other's strength to prevent our army from liberating Gansu, Ningxia, and Qinghai, and from going south to Guanzhong. The three forces combined had about 200,000 people, and they intended to attack our Northwest Field Army together, but there were conflicts between them. Hu Zongnan led a direct force of Chiang Kai-shek, while the two Mas' armies were from the local warlord. According to Chairman Mao's strategic policy, we aimed to defeat all three groups, letting none escape.

It was difficult for the Northwest Field Army to defeat these three forces at the same time. Chairman Mao ordered the 18th and 19th Corps to come to Xi'an and instructed Peng and Xi not to attack Hu Zongnan and two Mas' troops at the same time, but rather, to beat one and check the other, annihilating each in turn. Before our 18th and 19th Corps arrived in Xi'an, the Northwest Field Army was preparing a breakthrough movement, a joint attack on Hu Zongnan and the two Mas. It was in this context that we arrived in Xi'an. As soon as we entered the city, we heard the continuous sound of gunfire outside the city. We didn't feel any panic from the enemy guns, as we had come from Yan'an, but the people in Xi'an were very frightened. Hu Zongnan withdrew from Xi'an, but the Kuomintang reactionary special agents and bullies remained. They speculated and hoarded grain and cooking oil to raise prices. The masses were in distress. Various hostile parties spread rumors all over the city, circulating that the Hui people in Xi'an would cooperate with Mas' troops to rush into the city, and Hu and the two Mas would join hands to return to Xi'an.

Our cadres also put forward a variety of suggestions. Some proposed that as Ma Bufang had entered Caotan, we should have taken precautions to prevent the bandits from rushing into the city. Others thought we could temporarily withdraw from Xi'an City. Xi Zhongxun, He Long, and other leaders proposed decisive measures and held a cadre meeting about entering the city. At the beginning of the meeting, Xi Zhongxun said that rumors were flying all over the city, such as those saying that the Hui people were working with Ma Bufang to attack Xi'an City, and he reminded that we should not be misled by the enemy and that the Hui people in Xi'an were our good brothers and sisters and knew our Party very well, and also that they hated the Hu bandits and the two Mas very much. He emphasized that the people in Xi'an had suffered much when encountering the enemy, and that they loved our Party. He continued we could not adopt the proposal some had put forward, suggesting that we withdraw from Xi'an temporarily in case of an enemy attack on the city, as we knew that all the cadres entering Xi'an were the revolutionary seeds that the Party Central Committee and Chairman Mao had cultivated for years in Yan'an, and that if we withdrew from the city, the enemy would seize the opportunity for a massive attack. If our cadres lost, it would be too huge a loss to the Party Central Committee and Chairman Mao. He agreed to the suggestion proposed by some comrades that we should guard against Ma Bufang's impact on the city, saying that in addition, we should take immediate action for the cadres entering the city to go to the streets and publicize the news of our Northwest Field Army's victory in Northern Shaanxi, of Hu bandits having suffered a great blow and planning to escape, and of our Northwest Field Army moving ahead to eliminate all the bandits and the two Mas' troops very soon. He also advised them to spread the news of our consecutive victories in all the battlefields across the nation, of the end of Chiang's reign, and of the birth of New China, noting that they should warn all reactionaries that they were doomed and would be even more cursed if they continued their wrongdoings. And he asked our cadres to tell the people that Chairman Mao had ordered the 18th and 19th Corps of our main forces to get to Xi'an quickly.

Our comrades publicized all this in accordance with Xi Zhongxun's instructions, which greatly encouraged the people. Another of Xi's measures was to have the comrades entering the city work with the local underground Party to launch a large-scale search and arrest of reactionary organizations, bad elements, and Kuomintang agents who had stayed in the city. With these measures, there was no more shooting in the city, and the shops could remove the bricks from their doors and restart business. We did not cook for more than ten days after getting to Xi'an. Rather, we bought steamed buns and salted vegetables on the street to go with hot drinking water for our daily meals. When gunfire stopped in the city, we went and bought what was available for cooking. It was around the Dragonboat Festival, and He Long said we should give ourselves a proper treat. Xi Zhongxun also agreed that we had not yet had a proper meal in Xi'an, but only steamed buns with boiled water, and that when it was close to the festival, we could get some vegetables and meat for our meals. Ma Mingfang said that apricot was in season in Xi'an, and we could get some for the festival.

In mid-June, one of the first troops of the 18th and 19th Corps arrived in Xi'an. They were worn out, being armed with full outfits and having run more than a hundred miles day and night. All the commanders and soldiers were covered with sweat, and their feet were bleeding. They did not stop, but marched through the streets of Xi'an to report to the people. It was a truly touching scene. The local people stood on both sides of the street to welcome them, calling them "blood men" or "sweat men." The rest of the two corps arrived in Xi'an and Xianyang a few days later. By that time, the sound of gunfire in Nanshan and Caotan had stopped, and the public felt safe and reassured.

In May 1948, the Northwest Field Army held the second expansion meeting. Pictured is Xi Zhongxun attending the meeting and making a speech.

In mid-July, the Northwest Field Army wiped out more than 40,000 soldiers in the four troops of Hu Zongnan in the Fufeng and Meixian areas. In Yan'an, the Northwest Bureau and the government officials of the border area arrived in Xi'an in July and August. The Northwest Bureau office was stationed in Yongcun, Jianguo Road, and the border government was stationed in Xincheng. On August 20, Lanzhou was liberated, and more than 27,000 soldiers of Ma Bufang's army were wiped out. On September 23, Yinchuan was liberated, and Ma Hongkui's army was completely destroyed. On September 25 and 26, Tao Zhiyue and Bao Erhan announced an uprising, resulting in the peaceful liberation of Xinjiang.

At this time, the work of Peng and Xi turned to taking over the cities of the five provinces in Northwest China, establishing a new social order, healing war wounds, and carrying out the work of anti-bullying and counterinsurgency, the struggles against the "three evils" and the "five evils," and land reform. Peng served as the first Secretary of the Northwest Bureau and Chairman of the Northwest Military Political Committee, and Xi served as the Secretary of the Northwest Bureau and vice chairman of the Northwest Military and Political Commission. Peng went to the front line of North Korea after staying in Xi'an for a short time. Xi then served as the acting Chairman of the Northwest Military and Political Commission, where he employed collective leadership to make decisions on major issues through discussion within the Standing Committee of the Northwest Bureau and the Northwest Military and Political Commission. (I made records for the Standing Committee of Northwest Bureau.)

Xi Zhongxun had great respect for Zhang Zhizhong, who dealt with many important issues and felt trusted and empowered. After the liberation of the five provinces in Northwestern China, the lingering problem was how to suppress bandits and bullies. In the multi-ethnic areas of Northwestern China, the fight against banditry was often entangled with ethnic and religious affairs. For example, after the Ma Bufang bandits in Qinghai launched a rebellion and were suppressed, the remaining insurgents gathered with Xiang Qian to rebel, turning the rebellion into one led by the leader of a Tibetan tribe. Given this, Xi Zhongxun initiated multiple discussions on the Standing Committee of the Northwest Bureau. Finding ways to properly settle the rebellion of Nganglha tribe was not only important to the liberation of Tibetan compatriots, but also to the work of the Party in Qinghai, and even in the Gansu-Sichuan-Kangzang region and Tibet. At the meeting of the Standing Committee of the Northwest Bureau, it was decided that military preparations should be made and the policy of political struggle should be taken as the main principle in the effort to bring the chief of the Nganglha tribe, Xiang Qian, over to pledge his allegiance to the Party. After more than ten struggles over a span of more than two years, Xiang Qian finally came around. In the disposition of this issue, Xi Zhongxun thought hard and went to great trouble. Chairman Mao said to Xi later, "You're truly good. Zhuge Liang captured and released Meng Huo seven times, and you are more powerful than Zhuge Liang." It was quite a popular story back then.

Xi Zhongxun attached great importance to the investigation and research, which was his consistent ideological and working style, and he also demanded the staff of the organs to do the same. After the liberation of Xi'an, when the office staff of the Northwest Bureau had just arrived in Xi'an, he asked the staff to go and make an immediate investigation and study of the issue, and he asked Zhao Shouyi and me to find out more about the situation in Xi'an's factories. There were few factories in Xi'an back then, apart from the Dahua Yarn Factory, the Flour Factory, the Power Plant, and a few others. During the investigation, we found many issues. Labor relations were very tense, and the workers talked about the problems that needed to be solved.

When Zhao and I finished the investigation, Xi asked us to survey about the prostitutes in Xi'an city. I shook my head and said I didn't want to go. Comrade Xi read my mind. He said, "Aren't you brave? After the first battle at Qinghuabian, when the prisoners above the rank of platoon needed to be escorted to the safe areas, Zhao Huaibi and you were asked to lead some comrades of the mass troupe to escort them, as we were running short of our main forces. Didn't you accept the task bravely? When you had gone, I was quite worried, fearing something might go wrong with the escort because those prisoners, including the brigades, were as strong as tigers. I was relieved only when I saw you had come back. Now, what should you be worried about? These prostitutes are our sisters who have suffered more than anyone. I've heard there are quite a few brothels in Xi'an, with a large number of prostitutes. It is a disease of the Kuomintang's making in the old society. We should try to pull them out of the mire as early as possible. You're doing what a Bodhisattva would do. When you learn the situation, we can put forward proper measures to save them from the fire."

Hearing this, Zhao and I accepted the task and went to conduct the investigation immediately. When I went to the gate of Kaiyuan Temple, a brothel, I heard the madame calling to welcome the guests. Many prostitutes came out. Zhao and I said in unison that we were there to visit relatives and she could go to about her business. When the prostitutes who stood in the courtyard heard that we were visiting relatives, they looked at us to see whom we were looking for. We asked all of them to go into the room and be seated, then told them that they were all our relatives and we would like to chat with them like family members. During the conversation, they cried and shared their experiences with us. Most had been bought there and were beaten many times if they refused to entertain guests. After the talk, we did in fact feel like a big family. They gave us detailed information about the situation and helped us to lay a good foundation for further investigation. To get first-hand detailed information about the brothels, we went to Baojixiang, Minleyuan, Babakeng, and a couple of other brothels in Nanyuanmen to conduct the investigation and put forward our suggestions on addressing the problems. After reviewing our investigation report, Comrade Xi Zhongxun phoned Chang Lifu, Secretary General of the Military and Political Commission, and required the general office of the military and political commission to convene the public security, civil affairs, health, finance, women's federation, and other departments to make specific arrangements and take immediate action. In this way, the brothels in Xi'an were completely banned. We then put the suffering sisters in several places to cure their venereal diseases and to help them to start a family. This was very welcome at that time, and everyone praised the Communist Party.

Comrade Xi Zhongxun Transferred from Northwest China

In September 1952, when Comrade Xi Zhongxun was appointed Minister of the Central Publicity Department and deputy director of the Committee of Culture and Education of the Government Council, the major leaders of the five provinces in Northwest China held a small business meeting in Zhiyuan, Xi'an. At that time, Secretary General Wu Kaizhang of the Northwest Bureau asked me to take notes. At the symposium, the leaders of five provinces said they would be reluctant for Xi Zhongxun to leave the northwest. They asked if he wanted to leave people in the northwest, to leave the comrades and workmates with whom he had worked for years, and why he didn't apply to the Central Committee and Chairman Mao to stay in the northwest since the people and comrades of the five provinces didn't want him to go. Xi replied in a serious tone, "Honestly, I do have deep feelings for the people of the northwest. I really don't want to leave them or any of you who I

Right of the person holding the child, Secretary General Wu Kaizhang.

have known for years. I earnestly reported to Chairman Mao about my concerns, saying that with my experience and competence, how could I take the leading role in cultural education and publicity work for the whole country? Chairman Mao told me that snakes look terrible, and the reason why Indians play with snakes so well lies in their true modesty in following the laws of natural things. Any work can be done well in this way. I understand Chairman Mao's decision to send me to practice my new job, and I hope that comrades, especially the people, of the five provinces, can understand that. I will start afresh and learn from the insiders according to Chairman Mao's directions, and I will try to become familiar with the new work as quickly as possible. I also hope that you will bear in mind the features of the five provinces and the actual situation of the multi-ethnic groups in your future work, respect ethnic customs and religious beliefs, get along well with the leaders of all nationalities and religions, seek truth from facts, and be frank with them. You need to respect those outside the Party organization, cherish them, unite them, and listen to their opinions with an open mind, so as to allow them to feel trusted and empowered. The northwest region is a poor place where the local people have many difficulties in their daily lives, especially in the old districts. We should work to solve the problems related to their basic necessities. We have been working together for years. You all know me. I am a straightforward person. I am realistic, honest, and frank, both inside and outside the Party. We can be straightforward with each other and point out each other's mistakes directly. This is the principle of getting along with one another. This may be my lack of leadership. I have many weaknesses, and I hope that you will be more critical and strict with me."

During the discussion, it was agreed that Comrade Xi Zhongxun was open-minded, fair, upright, modest, prudent, generous, and approachable, and he was always thinking for the interests of the Party and the public. Everyone was willing to approach him and enjoyed speaking to him. He was very caring toward the cadres, but also strict with them. If they did something wrong, he was harsh and critical. When they recognized their mistake and corrected it, he was very pleased. He never found excuses for himself or others, which was his distinctive strength, so he had many intimate friends. He enjoyed great prestige. The people, cadres, leaders of all nationalities and religions, and members of other parties in the northwest were reluctant to let him leave the area. I had worked with him for years and was all the more reluctant to let him go. He had a truly good moral character, one I hope to follow always.

Unforgettable Last Meeting

In 1989, Comrade Xi Zhongxun returned to Xi'an and stayed in the People's Mansion. Since he was transferred to the Central Committee in 1952, he had served as Minister of the Publicity Department of the Central Committee, deputy director of the Committee of Culture and Education of the State Council, Secretary General of the State Council, and vice premier of the State Council. We had not met for thirty years. In the hard years in Yan'an, from the period of war to the liberation of Xi'an, I worked with him, mainly making records for him. After he was transferred to work in the Central Committee, I often thought about him and about the help he had given me. After he left the Northwest Bureau, I was transferred to a national defense plant to work from 1954 until 1963. During this period, I went to Beijing for meetings a couple of times. I always planned to visit him when I went to Beijing, but I thought he was too busy with his work for me to disturb him, so we didn't meet. In 1959 and 1962, Peng and Xi were criticized and attacked, labeled as the so-called "black lines" in Northwest China. In order to eliminate the poison of the "black lines," I was assigned to expose their problems. I was deeply impressed by Peng and Xi's moral character, showing respect for them, so I was implicated, which made it more difficult for us to meet.

Ma Songlin (second from the right) and his wife Comrade Ma Shufang, with Comrade Xi Zhongxun in Xi'an.

Ma Songlin and Wen Guiting (Mrs. Wu Kaizhang), President of Northwest Bureau Children's Hospital, in Jinan, Shandong Province.

Ma Songlin and Comrade Qi Xin.

In 1989, Xi returned to Xi'an. I was eager to see him as soon as possible, but I heard that many people had gone to visit him, and I was afraid that he would be too tired to receive more guests. On the last day before he left Xi'an, I made contact via Secretary General Liu Wanxing (the one appointed by the Provincial Party Committee to receive Comrade Xi Zhongxun). I was later teased and criticized by Xi, who immediately called me and said angrily, "You're quite a character and have forgotten all about me, but I always think about you. We are revolutionary comrades. You should not forget that in Yan'an we fought hard day and night on the front line of Northern Shaanxi. Over the past thirty years, I've asked around and knew that you went to the national defense front and had various opportunities to come to Beijing, but I've never seen you. I also heard that you suffered a lot because of your ties with us, and I was afraid you harbored some resentment. Let's meet and have a good chat. I will arrange a car to pick you up." So I went to the People's Mansion with Zhang Zhenbang, Zhou Chunyi, and my wife to visit Xi.

We arrived at the People's Mansion, and Xi and his wife, Qi Xin, welcomed us very warmly. It had been a long time since we met, and we had so many things to talk about. Mr. Xi talked about his return to Xi'an during the Cultural Revolution in 1969. The rebels took him to Xi'an for a long period of brutal struggle.

Someone did a video record of our meeting. Mr. Xi suggested that they also take pictures for us and give each person a photo. We didn't leave until 11:00 am, so that he could rest for a while and get on with his journey in the afternoon. Mr. Xi and his wife, Comrade Qi Xin, sent us to the door and shook hands to say goodbye. I never imagined that this meeting would be the last farewell. On May 24, 2002, when Ma Shufang, my wife, and I heard the news of Mr. Xi's death on television, we were very sad to lose a good leader and a good brother. We wept and mourned for a long time.

Following Mr. Xi for Twenty Years

ZHANG ZHIGONG

Zhang Zhigong, from Shaan County, Henan Province, was born in 1927. He was the former director of the general office of the United Front Department of the Central Committee. He served two stints as Comrade Xi Zhongxun's secretary. From March 1950 to 1964, he was transferred from the Northwest Working Committee of the Youth League to the Northwest Bureau of the CPC Central Committee to work as secretary for Comrade Xi Zhongxun, and from April 1978 to May 1984, when Xi Zhongxun served as Secretary of the Guangdong Provincial Committee, Zhang once again worked as his secretary.

Editor's note: The author Zhang Zhigong was Comrade Xi Zhongxun's secretary, working for him for twenty years. This article was originally published in *Xi Zhongxun's Revolutionary Career*. Zhang made some modifications and supplements for its inclusion in this book, and the editor selected relevant historical photos in memory of Comrade Xi Zhongxun.

Time flies. Looking back on the time I worked for Xi Zhongxun, my previous leader, I can't help but think about a lot of things, which really stuck with me and make me emotional.

In March, 1950, I was transferred to the Northwest Bureau of the CPC Central Committee from the Northwest Committee of the Youth League in Xi'an to serve as secretary to Comrade Xi Zhongxun until 1964. Due to the partisan struggle in 1962, Comrade Xi was wrongly accused of being one of the "anti-Party members," and he was then transferred to Luoyang, Henan Province. My family was relocated to Jinan, Shandong Province. From then, we were apart for fourteen years. In April

1978, when he served as Secretary of the Guangdong Provincial Committee, Xi transferred me to continue to work as his secretary until May, 1984. I am deeply grateful to him for his great trust and care for me. My growth was closely linked to his teaching and guidance.

Over a span of twenty years, he was transferred many times, his posts ranging from Secretary of the Northwest Bureau of the CPC Central Committee and Vice Chairman of the Northwest Military and Political Committee to Vice Chairman of the Committee of Culture and Education of the State Council, and from the Minister of the Central Publicity Department, Secretary General of the State Council, and Vice Premier to member of the Central Political Bureau and Vice Chairman of the Standing Committee of the National People's Congress. No matter how his posts or positions changed, I always addressed him as Secretary Xi. For twenty years, he was my leader, a good Secretary in my mind, and my mentor and friend. We established a deep friendship through the revolution. His children called me Uncle Zhang from the time they were young. When they grew up and started working, they still called me Uncle, like I was a member of the family. Those twenty years were times of intense fighting, and also of continuous learning and progressing in close cooperation with Secretary Xi.

My duty as his secretary was initially to send and receive messages, copy documents, handle letters from the masses, and receive visits, and later to be responsible for his daily life and security and be involved in drafting documents. Over the years, I keenly felt his loyalty to the Party Central Committee and the cause of the Party, his high sense of responsibility for his work, and his consideration for the cadres and the people.

Treating People with Sincerity and Friendliness

Xi was always honest and generous with people. In the northwest, the central government, and Guangdong, he made many friends from all walks of life, including many famous people outside the Party, such as Zhang Zhizhong, Fu Zuoyi, Zhang Xiruo, Deng Baoshan, and the top figures in ethnic minority communities and religious circles, such as the Tenth Panchen Lama, Huang Zhengqing, and Geshe Sherab Gyatso. Xi was honest and frank with them, going through thick and thin and sharing both glory and gloom as friends. He was acclaimed as a model of United Front work, from which his charisma emanated.

Mr. Qu Wu, the former chairman of the Central Committee of the Civil Revolution, was from his hometown in Shaanxi Province, and they were old friends. One time when visiting Xi, Qu was barred from getting in, as the new guard did not recognize him. Upon going in, Qu said to Secretary Xi in an ironic tone, "Your mansion is really as hard to get into as a royal palace." Secretary Xi was quite at a loss about where that comment had come from. When he learned what had happened, he immediately apologized to Qu, and they both laughed it over.

At the beginning of the founding of the new China, Mr. Yu Xinqing, a non-Party member, served as the Director of the Ceremony Bureau of the Central People's Government, and later as the Director of the Bureau of Affairs of the State Council and Vice Secretary General of the Standing Committee of the National People's Congress, and he worked with Secretary Xi for years. They had great respect for each other. In the autumn of 1958, Mr. Yu Xinqing, along with Xu Ming, Secretary to Premier Zhou, and Ding Naiguang, Deputy Director of the Secretary General Office of the State Council, visited several provinces in Northwest China, and they

During the war of the Northwest Liberation, Xi Zhongxun went deep into the masses to mobilize them to prepare for war.

went all the way to the grassroots level, held meetings and discussions, listened to reports, and visited industrial and agricultural production sites. Secretary Xi frowned on the boastful, rash work style prevalent during the Great Leap Forward, the great steelmaking, and the people's commune movements. He put forward many constructive opinions on local work while criticizing the brash progress and recklessness.

A close comrade of Secretary Xi did not stay in close contact with him as a result of their disagreement on some issues. Despite this, always generous and accommodating, Secretary Xi never said a nasty word about the other, but rather always talked about his strengths and merits. When the comrade died, Xi went to his funeral to mourn and convey condolences to his family members, and he helped out with the corresponding affairs. Talking about Secretary Xi, those both inside and outside the Party always mentioned the long-cherished friendship nurtured through their cooperation with him, and they all extolled him as a great leader.

Care for the Cadres and Get Close to the People

Xi was considerate and concerned about the cadres. His criticism of any comrade who made mistakes was severe, but always offered with genuine concern and sincere help.

When comrades were hospitalized, whether they were his co-workers or subordinates, Xi would take time to visit and comfort them, no matter how busy he was at work, conveying the care and concern of the Party, and everyone felt loved and cared for. Xi got along well with the masses who were willing to talk to him honestly without hesitation. When his former comrades and colleagues and the cadres and masses at the grassroots level arrived in Beijing or Guangdong, Xi always managed to meet them cordially. For those who had financial difficulties, especially those from the old revolutionary areas who had contributed to the revolution, Xi bought the train tickets and sent them to the railway station, giving them proper subsidies. He saw it as an excellent opportunity to keep close contact with the masses and understand the local situation. The masses praised Secretary Xi for his easy-going, approachable work style. In the period of the revolutionary war, Xi led the army to victory, and he led the democratic revolution in Northwest China in the early period of liberation because of his character and solid support from the masses, along with the appropriate strategy, tactics, and central policy.

Plain, Simple Farmer

Born in a farming family and working in the fields as a child, Secretary Xi knew the hard work of farming and had developed the habit of being thrifty since he was a child. He lived a simple life and never cared much about clothes and food. He had several sets of woolen clothes, which he wore only when meeting foreign guests and participating in major political activities. He usually wore cotton clothes and shoes, or a plain T-shirt in summer. For his tattered underwear and trousers, he'd mend and wear them rather than throw them away. As to his eating habits, he followed the northwest people, taking mainly noodles, dumplings, and vegetables. He was not particular about food at all, and fish, shrimp, and other seafood were rarely seen on his table. For decades, he lived this sort of plain, simple life.

From the 1950s to the early 1960s, Secretary Xi, like Chairman Mao and Premier Zhou, was paid at the third-level wage, 404.80 yuan a month, and his salary income and expenses were managed by me, his secretary. Every expense, even if it was only a few cents, was accounted for. He often told his children to live a thrifty life and not to spend money frivolously. The family's monthly expenses on meals and children were only slightly over 100 yuan, which remained at a lower consumption level than most national leaders at that time. He asked his family members to practice strict frugality, but he was generous with his friends. In the 1950s, some of his previous Red Army comrades, co-officers, and landlords often went to visit him in Beijing, some invited and others going on their own initiative. Secretary Xi earnestly welcomed all of them, inviting them to dinners and making arrangements for their visits and sightseeing tours. Secretary Xi had many friends and was very hospitable, and a large part of his salary went to the reception of his friends.

Secretary Xi had enjoyed physical labor since he was a child. He was capable of various farming tasks, such as rolling, planting, plowing, and raking. He was later engaged in the revolution, but he still kept some of his farmer's habits. There was a spare plot in the courtyard where he lived, and he led the staff to reclaim it and plant vegetables. He fertilized and watered the soil on his own. Though sweating and suffering from a sore back, he enjoyed the work greatly.

Strict Family Education

Secretary Xi was a devoted revolutionist. He devoted most of his life and energy to the cause he fought for. While focusing on his work, he had great attachment to and affection for his wife and children. On March 1, 1949, he and his wife Qi Xin's first daughter was born in Qiao'ergou, Yan'an. Qi Xin's mother, Deng Yaozhen, said, "Since your daughter was born in Qiao'ergou, you could name her Qiaoqiao." At that time, Secretary Xi was attending the Second Plenary Session of the Seventh Central Committee of the Communist Party of China in Xibaipo. He was very happy to receive a telegram about his daughter's birth. Back in Yan'an, he happily held his daughter in his arms and looked at her young face, smiling broadly. After work, he often held little Qiaoqiao in his arms. Once she urinated all over him, and he said with an indulging smile, "Baby's urine doesn't stink." Qiaoqiao was smart even as a child, and Secretary Xi cared a great deal for her. When Xi retired in his old age, Qiaoqiao was working as the director of the Administration Office and of the Foreign Affairs Office (division level) of the armed police headquarters. As a filial daughter, she resolutely gave up her official career and took care of her father for over ten years.

Xi's second daughter was born in Xi'an, and was thus named An'an. She was very close to her elder sister Qiaoqiao. His two sons, Jinping and Yuanping, were chubby, strong, and adorable when they were little, and thus very popular. Secretary Xi was busy with official affairs, but he always tried to accompany his children as much as possible in his spare time. At that time, recreational activities were quite limited. When the children came home from school on weekends, they would wrestle and play with their father. This was the happiest and most relaxing time for Secretary Xi. Like any other father, he liked to tease them, and when they were teased to tears, he would hurry to comfort them. When enjoying quality time with his family, Xi would behave like a carefree child himself.

Secretary Xi loved his children, but he never indulged them or allowed them to develop bad habits. On holidays, when he was not busy with work, he would take his children to the park, to his friends' gatherings, or to shops. Sometimes the kids clamored for new toys, but Secretary Xi never bought any for them. When they got angry with him for refusing to do so, he would patiently explain to them why he did so. He never allowed anyone else to buy the toys or give them gifts either. His children were very studious, especially fond of reading comic books and storybooks since they were young. When visiting bookstores, Secretary Xi often asked me to buy many books of this sort. Upon receiving the books, the kids would read, eagerly and fondly, thus acquiring basic knowledge in various subjects, ancient and modern, domestic and global.

Secretary Xi was diligent and thrifty all his life. He taught his children to form the good habit of thrift from their early age. With his influence, his family members were extremely frugal, beyond what most would imagine. To save water, every time Secretary Xi took a bath in the bathtub, he would ask his two young sons to take a bath in it after him, and then use the water to wash their clothes. He thought saving every drop of water was as important as saving every piece of grain. What's more, when he and his children dined together, he often quoted the famous Tang verse, "Who knows how hard-earned every piece of rice on our plate is," to teach

In 1958, Xi Zhongxun and his sons Jinping (left) and Yuanping (middle).

the children to pick up the rice grains that fell on the table or the ground and eat them. No waste was allowed in his family.

This virtue of thrift was passed down in the family. His children's clothes, shoes, and socks were "relayed" in turn, with the elder sister passing down to the younger ones, with some mending. When the clothes, shoes, and socks of the elder sister Qiaoqiao were passed down to Jinping and Yuanping, the boys were reluctant to wear them for fear of being laughed at by their classmates, because the shoes had flower patterns. Secretary Xi had the shoes dyed in black with ink. In order to help the children develop the good habit of independence and economy, the four of them all boarded in the Bayi Primary School and only went home once a week. They had little pocket money, just the 12 yuan meal fee and their bus fare. Children are naturally fond of snacks and fun. Sometimes, in order to watch movies or buy some popsicles and other snacks, they spent the money from the bus fare, and thus had to walk home. Sometimes they were too tired to walk, so Qiaoqiao took her younger brother and sister by the hand and insisted on walking to the next stop before getting on the bus, because the fare was calculated according to the number of stops. The children thought that it was not a good way to use the money saved from the bus fare for watching movies and buying popsicles, so they asked me for

On May 29, 2010, Comrade Zhang Zhigong wrote an inscription for the book.

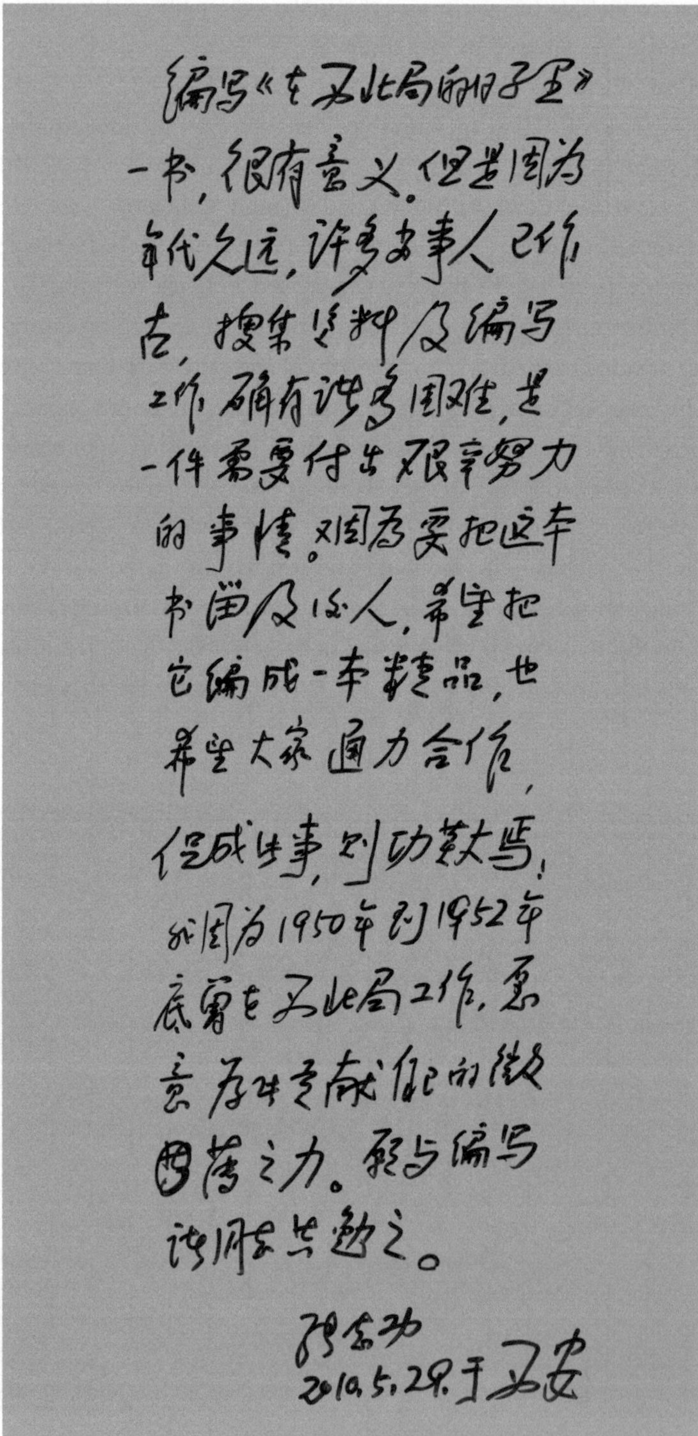

编写《在西北局的日子里》一书，很有意义。但是因为年代久远，许多当事人已作古，搜集资料及编写工作确有许多困难，是一件需要付出艰辛努力的事情。我认为要把这本书留及后人，希望把它编成一本精品，也希望大家通力合作，促成此事，则功莫大焉！我因为1950年到1952年底曾在西北局工作，愿意为此贡献自己的微薄之力。参与编写诸同志共勉之。

张勃兴
2010.5.28.于西安

money. Although it was only a few cents, I had to keep accounts and send them to the secretary at the end of the month.

Secretary Xi taught his children not to enjoy any privileges. Having graduated from primary school, Qiaoqiao was admitted to the Beijing Middle School in Hebei Province. Although the school was only one bus stop away from home, to get his daughter to mingle with her classmates, Xi insisted that she live on campus to eat, live, and study with her classmates. Back then, the diet and lodging conditions of the school were very poor, and coarse grains accounted for 70% of the diet. At that time, Secretary Xi served as Vice Premier of the State Council, and his name often appeared in newspapers. Xi was not a common surname, so it reminded Qiaoqiao's schoolmates and teachers that she was Vice Premier Xi's daughter. Secretary Xi was worried that others would take note of the identity of his daughter, so he asked his daughter to change her surname and follow her mother's, and the status of her family background was also changed from "revolutionary cadre" to "employee." The name Qi Qiaoqiao is the one she uses to this day.

Secretary Xi often taught his children to rely on their own skills and competence to make a living, and he encouraged them to go to harsh places, grassroots units, and places where competent people were most needed for economic construction. It was precisely because of the strict education of Secretary Xi and his influence upon the family that his children were very independent and self-reliant. They have withstood tests in both adversity and prosperity and have become useful members of the Party and the country.

Fun and Diversity in Life

In addition to working diligently, Secretary Xi had many hobbies and enjoyed a diverse life. He liked to dance and often went to parties on Saturday nights, an activity good for physical and mental health, which helped to relieve fatigue and enhance work efficiency. He was always in a good mood, high spirits, and full of energy, and he always continued participating in the activity. At that time, recreational activities were relatively monotonous, so many central leaders often attended dances to relax the mind and strengthen the body, as well as to mingle with the masses and chat with them in a casual setting.

In the 1950s, due to his work at the Central Publicity Department and the Committee of Culture and Education of the Government Council, Xi had more opportunities to watch art performances, and he developed an interest in Beijing

Opera and local operas such as Henan, Shaoxing, and Cantonese opera. He had a unique love for Qin opera in his hometown, and he was close to many actors in the theater community, especially with the famous performing artists such as Mei Lanfang, Cheng Yanqiu, Shang Xiaoyun, Xun Huisheng, Chang Xiangyu, and Hong Xiannü. Xi and Premier Zhou were good friends with Cao Yu, a well-known dramatist and President of the Beijing People's Art Theater, and he had frequent contact with several renowned directors and major performers of People's Art Theater. When there was a new play on, the couple was often invited to the show, and Xi was always pleased to go. During his stay in Shenzhen in his late years, he always listened to tapes of many folk songs and operas with great interest, alongside watching them on TV. He could never get enough of them.

Secretary Xi paid great attention to exercise. He said that if one did not have a strong body, it would be hard to do a good job and live a happy life. During his delegation to Luoyang, he insisted on walking dozens of miles twice a day. When he lived in Jiaodaokou of Dongcheng District, Beijing, the central government reformed the security system and removed his guard, so I went on and off duty with him. To exercise, on his way back and forth between his residence and the Zhongnanhai office, he would walk through Beihai Park and look around as he passed by. He usually walked for half an hour, sweating, but also feeling refreshed. He also learned *taiji*, but failed to follow through.

Throughout the decades of revolution, Secretary Xi had gone through days of storms and billowing waves, and also fine days of peaceful, sparkling waves. There were lessons from the failure of mutinies and the joy of winning the war. There were perplexity and confusion in times of sudden twists of fate, humiliation, and torture, and even imprisonment, as well as fearlessness in overcoming difficulties, fighting courageous fights, holding onto truth, and staying on the revolutionary course. There were sorrow and agony through ups and downs and thick and thin, as well as the joy of being loyal to and worthy of the Party and the people, being admired by the masses, and being successful in his career.

Looking back to Secretary Xi's revolutionary career, he was modest, prudent, hardworking, and plain, open and upright, honest and straightforward, loyal to the Party, united with the masses, caring for the cadres, seeking truth from facts, opposing the extreme left, upright, and doing things in a decent way. All this emanated throughout his career and life like a sparkling line.

Recalling the Days When Huang Zhi and Xi Zhongxun Worked Together

Shi Hong

Born in 1921, Shi Hong was from Qinyang, Henan Province. She joined the revolution in July 1937 and the Communist Party of China in December that same year. She went to Yan'an in 1938, where she studied at the Women's University, then at the Central Party School. She worked as the director of the Yan'an Primary School and the principal of the Xi'an Primary School and Middle School. After the founding of the new China, she served as second-level inspector of the Ministry of Finance and Trade of the Central Committee, inspector of the Organization Department of the Northeast Bureau, deputy director of the Political Department of the Material Bureau of the Northeast Bureau of Economy and Trade, deputy director of the Shenyang Foreign Trade Bureau, and deputy director of the Shaanxi Committee Economic Trade for Foreign Countries. She retired in 1983.

Editor's note: Comrade Shi Hong was the first old comrade of the Northwest Bureau we interviewed in Xi'an. Her trust in us and affirmation of our work was a good start for our trip to Xi'an, which strengthened our determination to do a good job on this project. Her deep feelings for the Northwest Bureau helped us realize the significance of the book and the responsibility we had taken on.

The old site of the Northwest Bureau in the Yan'an period was on the south side of the Yan'an border government, beside which there were several caves, all nestled close together. At the time, we lived in the caves. Xi Zhongxun, Secretary of the Northwest Bureau, Ma Wenrui, the Organization Minister, and Secretary General Chang Lifu were also there. I heard that some kids, probably Ma Xiaowen, the eldest son of Ma Wenrui, wanted to go back to restore the caves. He's now in Beijing and could have retired. When they went back to see the old site of the Northwest Bureau and saw the caves where they lived when they were young, they were reminded of the old days and thought of restoring the caves to preserve them for posterity.

The Impression of the Northwest Bureau

Now, when I think back to the Northwest Bureau in those days, the most impressive thing is that the relationship between the upper and lower ranks was quite harmonious. There were no gaps, and everyone was happy to work. I often went to Secretary Xi Zhongxun's house, taking what I liked to eat as if it were my

The old site of the Shaanxi-Gansu-Ningxia border government.

home and feeling quite at ease talking to him about what was happening at work. He would correct me immediately if I said something wrong, and he agreed to what I said if I was right. It was not just Secretary Xi who worked like that. The newly established Provincial Party Committee all worked in the same way. Ma Wenrui was Secretary of the Shaanxi Provincial Committee, and Yu Mingtao was Governor of Shaanxi Province. We lived within walking distance, and I often went to their residences to talk to them about work.

In addition, the cadres often visited the grassroots units. For example, Chang Lifu often visited the grassroots units, carrying his medicine can. Because he was not in good health, he had to carry the medicine can with him and work hard, despite his illness. Chang Lifu often said, "There is nothing wrong with me taking my medicine can to the grassroots, as it allows me to continue with my work. I take medicine at night and work in the daytime, and with the work done and the illness treated, isn't that a win-win result?" That was the working style of the Northwest Bureau, focusing on the work and sacrificing the self for the general good.

Recalling the Days When Huang Zhi and Xi Zhongxun Worked Together

The earliest site of the Northwest Bureau was in Yan'an, but I can't remember exactly which year it was founded. At that time, I worked in the Suide County Committee. My husband, Huang Zhi, was the president of the *Suide Daily Newspaper* at that time, and he later worked in the United Front Department of the Suide Special Committee as deputy minister. Xi Zhongxun worked in the Special Committee of Guanzhong and later transferred to Suide as the Party Secretary. When he arrived, my husband began to serve as Secretary General of the Suide Special Committee, drafting documents and writing reports for Xi Zhongxun. In 1945, Xi Zhongxun was transferred to the Northwest Bureau as second Secretary, with Comrade Peng Dehui serving as first Secretary of the Northwest Bureau (after the liberation of the country, at the Xi'an Northwest Bureau). Xi then transferred my husband to the Northwest Bureau, where there was a good deal of mutual understanding between them, and they worked very well together. Secretary Xi Zhongxun usually briefed him on a central idea and a general meaning, and my husband would write and complete the articles based on Xi's ideas.

When Secretary Xi Zhongxun was transferred to the Central Committee in 1952, he was separated from Huang Zhi, who remained in the Northwest Bureau to work, as the Bureau did not want him to go. From 1944 to 1952, including the

In October 1950, Xi Zhongxun reviewing the documents while in charge of the work of the northwest Party, government, and army, with Huang Zhi, director of Policy Research Office of Northwest Bureau (right).

periods in Suide and the Northwest Bureau, my husband worked for Xi Zhongxun for about ten years, serving as Secretary General at the Suide local committee and Secretary and Director of the Policy Research Office in the Northwest Bureau of Yan'an. The Policy Research Office was established after Liberation, and he served as its director.

In 1949, the Northwest Bureau was moved to Yongcun, on Jianguo Road in Xi'an. During this period, my husband drafted many documents for Secretary Xi.

Secretary Xi was brilliant, who particularly excelled at grasping the gist of things. For example, he could articulate in a clear, logical way the theme and supporting items of a matter, and my husband would draft the document based on his ideas and on the other documents distributed by the central and local governments. I remember that shortly after liberation, everyone was very busy and worked overtime because of the lack of labor. At that time, most of the documents sent from the Northwest Bureau to the central government and the other regions were drafted by my husband.

Chang Lifu was previously the Secretary General of the Shaanxi-Gansu-Ningxia border government. As he and my husband were both engaged in paperwork and writing, they had frequent contact. Sometimes in writing, the two would share views with each other. When they got stuck in their writing, they simply put it aside and picked it up to work on it together again the next day. I heard about these things from Chang Lifu. Later, Chang served as the Deputy Secretary General of the State Council. After he retired, he returned to Xi'an, where he passed away several years ago. My husband had died earlier, and he and Ma Wenrui together wrote a memorial poem for him.

Most of the articles in *A Collection of Xi Zhongxun's Works* were drafted and sorted out by my husband under the guidance of Xi Zhongxun, mostly including reports and speeches. It also includes some speeches Xi Zhongxun made in Guangdong and after Reform and Opening Up, which were not written by Huang Zhi.

After the toppling of the Gang of Four, Xi Zhongxun returned to work, and he later went to Guangdong to work with Yang Shangkun. Xi Zhongxun served as Secretary of the Guangdong Provincial Committee and Yang Shangkun as its Deputy Secretary. Xi hoped that my husband could go to work with him as usual. My husband was still in good health, but he didn't go, because my husband was from Guangdong, having family members there, and he was afraid that they would ask him for favors. At that time, we were still in the Northeast Bureau, living in Shenyang. During that period, my husband was Secretary of the Shenyang Municipal Party Committee. Later, when working as Secretary of the Shaanxi Provincial Party Committee, Ma Wenrui asked my husband to go there, if he would not go to Guangdong. We then went from the northeast to the northwest.

Recalling My Work

Actually, I worked in the Northwest Bureau for a short time, only in the period of the Shaanxi-Gansu-Ningxia border government. Later, when the Northwest Bureau moved to Xi'an, I did not work there. The reason behind it had something to do with Ke Hua.

Ke Hua worked in the Publicity Department of the Northwest Bureau and was later appointed as ambassador to the UK. Ke and my husband both came from Guangdong, so they were familiar with each other. When the Northwest Bureau was relocated to Xi'an, Ke Hua knew that I had been a teacher and director of the primary school in the Shaanxi-Gansu-Ningxia border area and had also worked as headmaster. When he worked as Director of the Publicity Department of the Xi'an Municipal Committee, he asked me to go there to work in a primary school in Xi'an, Kaitongxiang Primary School, to set a model for the rest of the schools there to focus on education.

I worked in that primary school for several years and was later transferred by the Education Bureau to Juyuan Middle School to serve as principal. I said that I was afraid I was not competent enough for the job, so I was told to work and learn. I was assigned a teaching director and an administrative director to work with me as a team. The three of us worked very hard, and doing overtime was the norm all year round. I remember that there was a time when we didn't leave our office until late in the afternoon on the Chinese New Year's Eve. The workload was very heavy at that time, and apart from teaching, we had a special, important task that involved

On April 3, 2009, the editor-in-chief of this book interviewed Comrade Shi Hong and took a group photo. Shi Hong is in the middle.

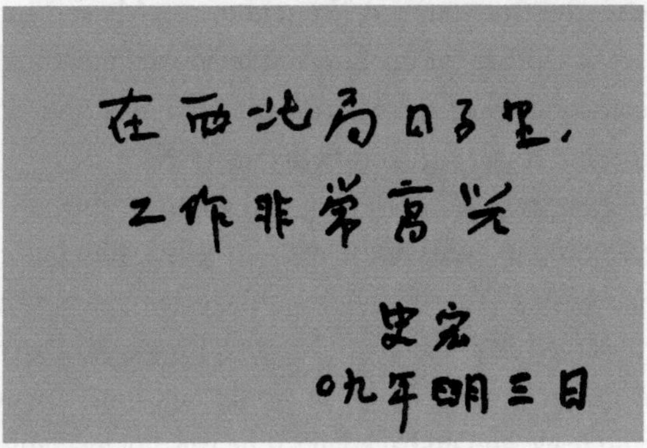

Comrade Shi Hong's inscription for this book.

conducting investigations to locate hidden secret agents. The work was particularly tense. I was in good health at that time, and others said I worked like an ox. Even when I was pregnant with my youngest son, I worked late before returning to the Northwest Bureau residential quarters. Once, I walked past a hospital that practiced traditional Chinese medicine on the way back home, so I went in and did a medical check. After the examination, the doctor told me that because of poor positioning, I needed to induce labor and have the baby ahead of schedule. So I did.

I say all this to let you know that the work was quite stressful back then, doing both teaching and investigation at the same time. But to do a good job, we had to mobilize and organize the masses. This was the experience, which I have summarized in my work.

Secretary Xi Zhongxun in My View

Secretary Xi Zhongxun in my view was not only approachable, but also helpful. There were two things that impressed me most, the cloth he gave me and the dinners I had at his home.

Secretary Xi Zhongxun was warm with people. He was also very concerned about the family members of the ordinary Northwest Bureau staff like me. I remember when we were in Suide, we had our elder son, Huang Dashu, with us. Xi was even concerned about such a small child. At that time, my son was going to school, but the living conditions were harsh, and he didn't have decent clothes to wear. I didn't know how Secretary Xi got a piece of white silk with a pattern on it.

"Take it to make clothes for your son," he said to me. My son and I were thrilled. Later, I made a set of clothes for my boy, and he looked great in that. We were all pleased. When someone asked me where I got such beautiful clothes, I was very proud to tell them that it was a gift from Secretary Xi.

Secretary Xi Zhongxun was easygoing and approachable at work and in daily life. You could even drop in at his house without telling him beforehand. We went to Xi Zhongxun's and Ma Wenrui's houses quite often in a very casual way. Later, when Ma Wenrui served as Secretary of Shaanxi Provincial Party Committee, we went to his house from time to time. He would talk to us about work if he had time, and we would leave and go back later if he was not available. As I worked in the Shaanxi Foreign Economic Office at that time, I occasionally went to report to him on my work, or to ask for advice, or even just to check with him if I was right about a particular thing. Both leaders were straightforward, giving praise or criticism based strictly on facts.

Secretary Xi had an excellent reputation among the masses. He worked hard and was quite efficient and straightforward, taking care of both his work and leisure activities. For example, if he needed to summarize his work and prepare a report the next day, Secretary Xi would go dancing as usual, but before going, he would tell my husband the gist of what needed to be included in the report. The next day, my husband would put the finished report on his desk. Xi Zhongxun was always very pleased with the report, as it followed his thoughts without mistakes. My husband usually wrote at night, and he put it on Xi's desk the next morning.

I will not talk too much about Secretary Xi Zhongxun. He impressed me greatly, as he treated his workmates like his own family members. He was quite a young, promising leader, only 39 years old when transferred to the central government, and 46 when he worked as the Vice Premier. It was amazing.

Secretary Xi Zhongxun lived a simple life. When he was Secretary of the Guangdong Provincial Party Committee, my husband and I went back to Guangzhou. He invited us to his house for dinner and said he had prepared a big plate of *guokui*, a Shaanxi specialty. He liked noodles, *guokui*, and vegetables. Fish and shrimp were rarely seen on his table. He found it acceptable if the dishes were tasty and paid little attention to the nutritional balance. He basically followed the living habits of the northern people, and he didn't bother too much about clothes, either. He had several woolen Zhongshan suits, but he only wore them when meeting foreign guests and participating in major political activities. Otherwise, he was mostly dressed in cotton clothes and shoes. If the clothes were tattered, he would have them mended and continue to wear them, rather than throw them away.

Sorrow in Cao Liru's Sacrifice

Now when I recall the people and things in the Northwest Bureau, one person I feel quite sorry for was Comrade Cao Liru, Deputy Secretary General of the Northwest Bureau. In the winter of 1949, when Comrade Cao Liru was ordered to assist Comrade Wang Zhen in Xinjiang as the main leader of the government, a car accident took his life. The news came as a great shock to the cadres and people in Northwestern China. People mourned the Party's loss of a loyal communist soldier and an excellent leading cadre. Whenever I recall him, I feel an endless sorrow inside me.

How did all that happen? After the liberation of Xi'an, Cao Liru went to Xi'an with the Northwest Bureau. He was very happy because his guard had learned to drive, so he asked the guard to drive him and Ma Wenrui to inspect the work. Unfortunately, they had a car accident at Baqiao in Xi'an. Cao Liru was seriously injured, and Ma Wenrui was less seriously injured. They were rushed to the Fourth Hospital[1] of the city, a hospital run by foreigners. It was advanced and well-equipped, but Comrade Cao Liru died as a result of the serious injury. He said to Ma Wenrui, "Minister Ma, I'm sorry that you were injured."

Today, there is a mausoleum for Xi Zhongxun in Fuping County, Shaanxi Province, which has some historical information about him. What you're doing with this book is quite meaningful, and you must do it well.

1. Previously the Xi'an Guangren Hospital.

Growing Grain for the Northwest Bureau

ZHANG ZHENBANG

Born in 1917, Zhang Zhenbang was from Yanchuan, Shaanxi Province. In 1944, he joined the Northwest Bureau, serving as the chief of the general affairs section of the Bureau in 1949. He was in charge of food production, and he made tremendous contributions to the development of the Northwest Bureau in difficult times. He later worked as Deputy Secretary General of the General Office of the Shaanxi Provincial Committee and other posts.

Editor's note: Comrade Zhang Zhenbang, at 92, was still in high spirts and had a clear mind. Recalling the years of work at the Northwest Bureau, he obviously felt very attached to and nostalgic for that time.

My hometown is in Yanchuan, Shaanxi Province. It is a good place, with a long history and a deep cultural heritage. It is known as "a home to culture." Yanchuan was one of the earliest counties in Shaanxi in which the Party launched its revolutionary activities and built Party groups. It was the central county of the revolutionary base area in Northern Shaanxi and the border area of Shaanxi, Gansu, and Ningxia. The armed struggle, land reform, democratic construction, stretcher transportation, and mutual aid production were carried out with great enthusiasm and on a large scale. The people in the area accepted revolutionary thought early on and made great contributions to the cause of the revolution. Perhaps I was influenced from childhood by this kind of folk custom, and that led me down the revolutionary path.

First Entry into the Northwest Bureau

I arrived at the Northwest Bureau in 1944, when Gao Gang was serving as Secretary. Although the Central Committee decided as early as May 1941 to merge the Northwest Working Committee of the CPC Central Committee, established early in 1939, with the Central Bureau of the Shaanxi-Gansu-Ningxia border area to form the Northwest Bureau of the CPC Central Committee (then located in Zhangya Village, north of Yan'an City) and to unify the work of the liberated area and the Kuomintang ruled area in Northwestern China, we were used to referring to it as the Shaanxi-Gansu-Ningxia Border Work Committee. Not long after, the Central Committee decided to restructure the Northwest Bureau. In the second year after I arrived at the Northwest Bureau, in 1945, Comrade Xi Zhongxun was appointed by the Central Committee and served as Secretary of the Northwest Bureau, while Gao Gang was transferred to the northeast to preside over the work there.

Shortly after I joined the Northwest Bureau, it began to move frequently. In March 1947, the Northwest Bureau evacuated Yan'an and moved to Northern Shaanxi. On April 21, 1948, our army recovered Yan'an, and in mid-May, the Northwest Bureau organs were moved back there. There was a place called Huashiyabian in Nanguan, Yan'an. Before moving to Northern Shaanxi, the Northwest Bureau was located there. I also lived in that place. It was all earth caves, and a two-story building was built behind them, with a kitchen beside it. Leading comrades like Xi Zhongxun dined upstairs.

At that time, we cooked in large, medium, and small pots. The large ones were for the staff of the general organs, the medium ones were for the cadres at the level of the department, and the small ones were for Xi Zhongxun and other leading comrades. At that time, Ouyang Qin (member of the Eighth CPC Central Committee, member of the Standing Committee of the Fifth National People's Congress, and vice chairman of the Fifth CPPCC) was Secretary General, and he came from the southern area. Yuan Fuqing (the chief executive of the People's Government of Hunan Province), was a veteran cadre of the Long March. Liu Wenyu, deputy director, was from Northern Shaanxi Province. Those comrades ate from the small pots. In fact, the staple food was rice or noodles, regardless of whether it was cooked in big, medium, or small pots, though the things made in small pots might be cooked in a slightly more refined way. On June 14, 1949, the Northwest Bureau moved from Yan'an to Xi'an, and the office was in Yongcun, on Jianguo Road in Xi'an.

Growing Grain Was a Major Issue

When we first arrived at the Shaanxi-Gansu-Ningxia border area, the most common problem was the shortage of food, and we were not adequately fed. At that time, the Shaanxi-Gansu-Ningxia border area was a region with relatively underdeveloped productivity and a poor economy. In addition, the outbreak of the self-defense war in the border area and the Kuomintang reactionaries strengthened the blockade of the border area, making it a very difficult time in the base area.

Yan'an was facing the most difficult period since 1939. Due to the Japanese invasion, the blockade, and disasters brought by the Kuomintang, the government of the Shaanxi-Gansu-Ningxia border region, the central government of the Party, and the army faced unprecedented difficulties in their supply of food and clothing. At that time, the Kuomintang not only broke many agreements reached by the KMT and the Communist Party, but also stopped providing supplies to the Eighth Route Army and the New Fourth Army, and they seized all the materials donated by overseas Chinese to Yan'an. In particular, they banned the transportation of cloth, food, salt, and medical supplies to Yan'an and imposed a strict blockade on the border area. At the critical point, the central government reviewed the situation and changed the financial policy from "seeking foreign aid and the recuperation of the people" to "self-sufficiency in production." In December 1938, the Central Committee of the Communist Party of China issued for the first time the instructions on the "extensive production campaign" to the army and civilians in the base areas to ensure the self-sufficiency of material supply in various regions. In February 1939, the Central Committee of the Party and the government of the Shaanxi-Gansu-Ningxia border region held a production mobilization conference in Yan'an. Mao Zedong called on all the people to "do their own work, put forth their own effort, and work hard to overcome difficulties" and vigorously carry out production campaigns.

In this context, I joined the Northwest Bureau and was in charge of production from that time, serving as chief of the General Affairs Section. Life was hard then. Ordinary people and leading cadres all lived in the caves, two people in one cave, working and living in the same space. After a period of hard work, our effort satisfied Secretary Xi Zhongxun, as later everyone had enough rice for meals, which was an extraordinary achievement at that time.

Because I was in charge of logistics, I got to know Comrade Wang Zhen, the commander of the 359 Brigade. In 1941, Wang Zhen led the 359 Brigade to cultivate the land for farming in Nanniwan. Later, when I worked at the Northwest Bureau as the chief of the General Affairs Section, he called me and asked me to go there to grow grain. They had reclaimed a good deal of land for us to grow grain. Comrade Wang Zhen was a member of the Northwest Bureau, and he was famous in Northern Shaanxi Province. Everyone privately called him "Beard Wang," as Comrade Wang Zhen would leave his beard unshaven after receiving an assignment for battle or construction until the task was completed. Mao Zedong, Zhu De, Peng Dehuai, He Long, and other people gave him the nickname "Beard Wang."

Actually, many people were familiar with Nanniwan, but why did our regular troops go there to reclaim wasteland and cultivate farmland? During the anti-Japanese war, there were serious economic difficulties in the base area. When the Red Army arrived in Northern Shaanxi after the 25,000-*li* Long March, the Party Central Committee based the camp of the anti-Japanese war effort in Yan'an. The Loess Plateau in Northern Shaanxi was barren and had a sparse population, which made it hard for average people to survive. How could the revolutionary forces of the Chinese people expect to survive and develop under the blockade of the Kuomintang, then? In order to break the economic blockade in the Shaanxi-Gansu-Ningxia border area and overcome the difficulties of the army supply, Chairman Mao and the CPC Central Committee issued a call to "rely on ourselves for subsistence and survival." The 359 Brigade, led by General Wang Zhen, went to Nanniwan to cultivate and open up the wasteland. The people of the border area carried out a vigorous mass production campaign, which finally solved the problem of the food supply and made an indelible contribution to the development of the revolutionary cause.

From the end of 1940, the 359 Brigade was stationed in Nanniwan, where it carried out a large-scale production campaign for self-sufficiency in production, aiming to lighten the burden on the people. From 1941 to 1943, the 359 Brigade handed in 10,000 *dan* of grain to the border government every year. In the mass production movement, they not only focused on agriculture as the main sector, but also developed other sectors. They opened thirteen textile, leather, and paper mills in succession, established the salt industry, local products, transportation, and other companies, and ran hotels, shops, military cooperatives, and various processing workshops, building a multi-level production and management form with consideration of both the military and civilians, and of both public and private interests. At the senior cadres meeting of the Northwest Bureau of the Communist

In 1942, Mao Zedong met the cadres of the 359 Brigade Wang Zhen (second from the right in the front row), Wang Enmao (the second on the left of the front row), Zhang Zhonghan (fourth from the right in the rear row), Zeng Di (the first on the left of the front row), and others.

Party of China in February 1942, the 359 Brigade was hailed as a banner of the border area mass production movement. Chairman Mao Zedong spoke highly of the brigade as "pioneers of economic development."

In the large-scale production movement, the 359 Brigade conducted large-scale military training at the same time. It then launched the Rectification Movement after the spring sowing in 1943, which ensured and facilitated the completion of military training and production tasks.

Recalling Secretary Xi Zhongxun

When I was in the Northwest Bureau, the work style of the whole department was very strict. We could talk about work and business, but there was no casual chatting at all. Secretary Xi Zhongxun set an example for us to develop these habits and styles. Even today, I always tell the young people around me that Comrade Xi

Zhongxun's firm Party spirit, hard-working, plain living style, and approachable work style left a deep impression on the Party, government cadres, and the masses at all levels. In the people's minds, this young secretary, who was only in his 30s at that time, was not only great in his vision and strategic thinking, but also firm in holding to principles and flexible enough in practical work. He was good at investigation and research work and open to others' views and suggestions when making decisions. His work style and method are worth learning.

Comrade Xi Zhongxun played a vital role in the Northwest Bureau. After the Long March, when the Red Army arrived in Yan'an, Gao Gang was Secretary and Xi Zhongxun was Secretary of the Guanzhong and Xi'an Working Committee. Later, Comrade Xi Zhongxun served as Secretary of the Northwest Bureau and presided over the Bureau's work. He not only made great contributions to the development of the northwestern region, but also provided valuable experience for the development of the national work at that time.

In the work of the Northwest Bureau during the period of the restoration of the national economy after the War of Liberation and the founding of the new China, Secretary Xi Zhongxun attached great importance to the study of Marxism, Leninism, and Mao Zedong Thought. He was good at proceeding from reality, combined the guidelines, principles, and policies of the Central Committee with the reality of the northwest, and carried out a series of fruitful work. First, during the land reform, Chairman Mao attached great importance to Xi Zhongxun's report on the work in the old liberated areas of the Shaanxi-Gansu-Ningxia border region, which he wrote to the Northwest Bureau and the Party Central Committee. He put forward a host of suggestions on making policies based on the different situations of the old, semi-old, and new districts, correcting the left-leaning bias, and remedying the extreme left-leaning mentality. In addition, according to Chairman Mao's instruction that the Shaanxi-Gansu-Ningxia border region should "serve as a model and an example for the entire nation" to "promote national democratization," Secretary Xi Zhongxun and the Northwest Bureau were resolutely engaged in the construction of the democratic regime. Further, the Bureau adopted correct policies and strategies to launch an effective fight against bandits and bullies in the northwest ethnic minority areas. The Bureau also prepared a large number of cadres for the liberation of the northwest, which was a big issue for the Bureau. Due to the rapid development of the situation in Northwestern China, a large number of competent cadres were urgently needed in the revolutionary team. The Northwest Bureau took measures to send capable, respected comrades to serve as provincial leaders, vigorously improve the ideological and professional level of in-

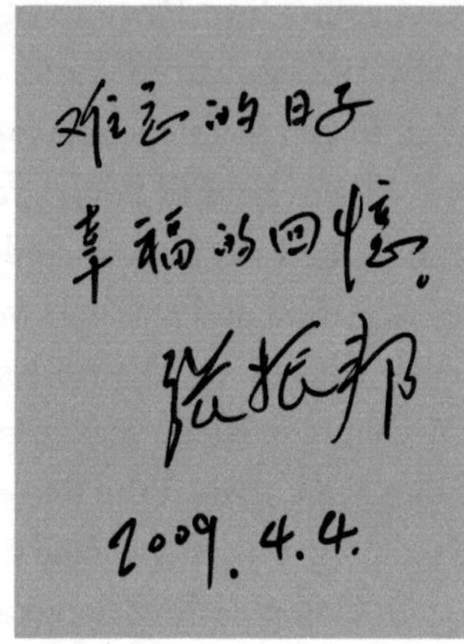

On April 4, 2009, Comrade Zhang Zhenbang wrote an inscription for this book.

service cadres, train and promote young intellectual cadres, turn the army into a working team, strengthen the Party construction in the new area, adhere to serving the people, follow the mass line, and seek truth from facts. Xi Zhongxun and other cadres of the Northwest Bureau contributed greatly to the victory of the revolution.

In addition, Secretary Xi Zhongxun not only did well in his work, but was very approachable and concerned about us in daily life. Back then, the colleagues in the Northwest Bureau all had a good relationship. I loved playing basketball, and I often played with my workmates in the court under the cave where we lived. I also loved playing mahjong. At that time, Secretary Xi Zhongxun often called me from upstairs to play mahjong. And I was always happy to go, and I never felt uneasy or awkward playing with a leader like him. I didn't feel that way at all. Sometimes during my break, I went to watch Xi Zhongxun and his old comrades playing. When playing the game, Xi Zhongxun, who was very quick witted, often secretly took a tile from those already played and shouted, "I won!" Because of their poor eyesight, the others didn't know he was cheating. They all played happily, like innocent children.

At that time, we had some recreational activities after work. Everyone could dance, men and women, young and old. On the weekend, there was a small building in the Northwest Bureau, where everyone could go to dance. Secretary Xi Zhongxun loved to dance, and he danced very well. He often asked us to dance. Secretary Xi danced every Saturday night to keep fit. In addition, many central leaders liked to participate in this activity, and they took it as a gathering place to mix with the masses. From this, we could see how Xi Zhongxun was concerned for the masses and the cadres and had a good relationship with them.

Secretary Xi Zhongxun's excellent work style of holding onto the Party's policies with revolutionary courage and prudence, and his capability in uniting cadres in a humble manner and in caring for the intellectual cadres from other areas were highly commended by many comrades. At that time, as the deputy political commissar of the Northwest Field Army, Xi had great respect for Peng Dehuai. They were close and would naturally reach an agreement on major issues, which allowed them to win great victories in the military struggle and high praise from the Party Central Committee.

(Postscript of this interview: At the end of this interview, Mr. Zhang Zhenbang happily wrote an inscription for us. He said, "I am the oldest person alive among the cadres of the Provincial Party Committee. There is no one else. There is also a former female director who is one year older than me. She is 93 and I am 92, and we old people are very happy and content that you can dig into this period of history and preserve it. I hope to see your book published as soon as possible.")

Following Mr. Xi for Eight Years

SUN BINGWEN

A native of Qinyuan, Shanxi Province, Sun Bingwen was born in 1925. He joined the Red Army in July 1937, and arrived in Yan'an in 1938. He was a young captain then. From 1944 to 1952, he served as Xi Zhongxun's guard.

Editor's note: Mr. Sun Bingwen was a guard of Comrade Xi Zhongxun during his work in the Northwest Bureau. Through his interview, we gained a close understanding of Comrade Xi Zhongxun's work and life in the Northwest Bureau at that time. His experience is valuable for helping future generations understand the people and things of that era.

Unforgettable Yan'an, Unforgettable Nanniwan

My hometown is in Qinyuan County, Shanxi Province, which was under the administration of Central and Southern Shanxi Province. I am 86 years old now, and in September 1937, I went to Yan'an from Shanxi to join the revolution. In another two months, I will be an old member of the Red Army. When I first joined the revolution, I was only 13 years old, just a child. I was a publicity member in Linfen. Because I was small in size, I was lifted onto the horse when I went out to work, and I had to be helped off when we had a break. Later, someone asked me to go to Yan'an. At that time, I didn't want to go, because I wanted to stay in the army and do publicity work. Then I was told, "Go and you'll see Chairman Mao and Commander-in-Chief Zhu." I thought, "Oh? If I can see Chairman Mao and Commander-in-Chief Zhu, I'll go." So I went to Yan'an.

Having arrived in Yan'an, I first worked in the publicity office of the Yan'an Anti-Japanese University,[1] then was transferred to the enemy's rear region, where I entered the Jinchaji military area and reached Yi County and Tangshan, Hebei Province. There, I went to work in the army. The army I served had formerly been Yang Hucheng's army. We fought the battle presented in the film *Five Heroes of Langya Mountain*. Later, I joined the "hundred-regiment war" with the army. Because I had been in the army since I was a child, I had never been to school, and I didn't know many words, so I always reminded myself to strengthen my studies. In 1943, I went to Yan'an again. At that time, the Organization Department of the Northwest Bureau selected some of us, sending us first to Nanniwan, and then to the Northwest Bureau. Gao Gang was the main leader of the Northwest Bureau then.

When I first got to the Northwest Bureau, I happened to encounter three anti-Communist upsurges launched by KMT diehards, which carried out military encirclements and economic blockades on the Shaanxi-Gansu-Ningxia border region. The border region faced extremely serious financial and economic difficulties. There were almost no clothes, shoes, or socks, and no edible oil and vegetables. Food was hard to come by. I remember that in the face of these difficulties, Chairman Mao had a wonderful remark. He said, "Are we going to starve to death, be dismissed, or work on our own to survive?" No one was in favor of starvation or dismissal, so we worked together to get it done. That was our answer.

At that time, under the leadership of the Party Central Committee, the Northwest Bureau, and the border region government, the army and people in the Shaanxi-Gansu-Ningxia border region launched a vigorous mass production movement. From Chairman Mao, Commander-in-Chief Zhu, and other leading comrades of the Central Committee to every individual cadre and soldier, we all went to cultivate the wasteland for farming or spun thread and planted vegetables. Heroes and model workers on all fronts kept emerging.

At the beginning of 1943, the Party Central Committee and Chairman Mao called on us to work for self-sufficiency, aiming to have enough food and clothing within a year. This call received a positive response from the military and the

1. The Anti-Japanese University, the short name of Chinese People's Anti-Japanese Military and Political University, was established in June 1936 in Wayaobao, Northern Shaanxi Province. At that time, it was called the Chinese People's Anti-Japanese Red Army University. In 1937, the Kuomintang and the Communist Party established the policy of their second cooperation. The Anti-Japanese Red Army University moved to Yan'an and changed its name to the Chinese People's Anti-Japanese Military and Political University.

people of the border region, and the various systems promptly set off an upsurge in the production campaign. By the end of 1943, the border region was more than self-sufficient in its grain production. Its industry was greatly developed, and in providing a variety of daily necessities such as shoes, socks, soap, and toothbrushes, we were basically self-sufficient. The military and people in the border region spent the most difficult financial year, smashed the Kuomintang's economic blockade, consolidated the border region, and at the same time, played an exemplary and inspiring role in the production and construction of all anti-Japanese base areas in the country.

Two Encounters with Chairman Mao

I followed Mr. Xi and lived with him in Zaoyuan as his guard. One day I happened to meet Chairman Mao, and I quickly saluted him. Chairman Mao saw me and asked, "What's your name, kid?" I answered, "Sun Bingwen." He said, "Where are you from?" I replied, "Qinyuan, Shanxi." Chairman Mao said, "Oh, you are from Qinyuan. Qinyuan is a heroic city with heroic people." I was thrilled to have seen Chairman Mao in person and spoken to him.

In the second or the third year after Mr. Xi was transferred to Beijing, I went there to visit him. A chief of the photography department asked me to take some photos in Beijing as a souvenir. I said I couldn't, as I didn't know how to develop the film after I took them. The chief of the photography section was very nice. He said, "Don't worry. You simply go and take the photos and give me the film, and I'll develop them for you." Later, when I went to deliver the film, I met Chairman Mao a second time. Chairman Mao saw me from a distance and said, "It's Sun Bingwen, from Qinyuan, Shanxi." I quickly replied to the chairman, "It's been many years. Do you still remember me?" He replied, "How can I forget, kid?" I will never forget those two encounters with Chairman Mao.

Cherishing the Memory of the Respectable Mr. Xi

After Japan surrendered in 1945, I followed Mr. Xi, working for him for eight years, from 1945 to 1952. After the dismissal of the previous Northwest Bureau, I did not go to Beijing. After the Cultural Revolution, Mr. Xi went to Guangdong to work, and later to the central government. He came to Xi'an in 1989, and my son took me to see him in the People's Mansion. I was very excited to see both Mr. Xi and Comrade Qi Xin.

I remember that in 1947, Hu Zongnan attacked Yan'an, and we set up the First Field Army. Peng Dehuai was the commander and political commissar, and Xi Zhongxun was the vice political commissar. Under their leadership, it took us a year to restore Yan'an in 1948. In the process, I was most impressed by two things.

One was the Battle of Panlong. At that time, we had been fighting for days. The enemy was always on the highest mountain, but we just couldn't break through. There were enemy planes constantly flying in the sky, circling and dropping bombs on our side. I picked up my machine gun and started shooting at the planes. I did in fact hit one. Later, the army marked it as my contribution. Thinking back now, I find it was really a hard time for us back then.

At that time, there were only four people at home. Mr. Xi came back to stay for about ten to twenty minutes, then left in a hurry. He didn't tell us when he left. Even though I was his guard, I didn't know about it. So, I leaned against the door to stand guard and dozed off, as I hadn't slept for a few nights. Xi didn't have the heart to wake me up when he went out, but he kicked me when he came back. It was not easy. When fighting any battle, he didn't sleep for a few days. This spirit always touched me.

Another thing was the Rectification Movement and land reform. When I got to the Northwest Bureau, the Rectification Movement had just started. At that time, the leftist inclination was very strong. Chairman Mao transferred Mr. Xi to the Suide Prefectural Party Committee. During the land reform, the left-leaning tendency was very serious. The poor and lower middle farmers were united on our side, but they were also dealt with at that time. At the land reform conference held in Yangjiagou and Mizhi, Mr. Xi pointed out that the middle farmers were on our side, and they were commonly referred to as the part of poor and lower middle farmers. It would be wrong to take land from them. After hearing the report from Mr. Xi, Chairman Mao gave instructions that the rich farmers and landlords should be overthrown, but the middle farmers should be united. Later, because Mr. Xi was doing a good job in land reform, Chairman Mao wrote a special banner for him, which read *Model of Policy Implementation*, and gave it to Mr. Xi. I took it home for him.

Mr. Xi was very dedicated to his work. He could sit all day and work continuously without moving or stretching. Later, I made a special ping-pong racket for him. At noon, I asked him to rest, and he played table tennis outside with the secretary. I said he needed to exercise or his health would decline. There was a time when Mr.

Xi was sick and still had to ride to another place for work, so I held a watch in my hand and kept checking the time. When it was time for him to take medicine, I reminded him to stop and take it. If he refused to, I forced him.

When Yan'an was restored, I wanted to go for study. Mr. Xi told me not to. I said that I couldn't read properly without recognizing the characters, and that I'd go to that Yan'an Middle School for study and when he needed me, I'd go back. Later, after less than a month into my studies, Xi's horsemen came and asked me to go back. It turned out that the Second Plenary Session of the Seventh Central Committee was to be held. Mr. Xi planned to go to Xibaipo for a meeting, and he wanted to take me with him. When we drove past Pingyao in Shanxi Province, I said excitedly, "That's my home, just on that mountain. When we go up, you can see my home." Since I had joined the army, I hadn't been home. It had been many years. "That's good. When you come back, you can go home to have a look," said He Long, who was with us. I was excited and moved. After the meeting in Xibaipo, we first went to Shijiazhuang, and then to Tianjin. The Secretary of the Tianjin Municipal Party Committee gave us some loudspeakers to broadcast from a big truck. Because we needed to send the goods back to the Northwest Bureau, I didn't go back home. I had to wait until the goods were sent to Yan'an. Unexpectedly, the next day after I returned to Yan'an, I was told to go home, along with a soldier on horseback sent to accompany me. I rode a mule from Yan'an to Pingyao in Shanxi Province, and we walked for more than two days. "You don't need to go further. My home is over there by the mountain," I said to the horseman when we got close to my hometown. That's how I went back home. When I got home, my family members did matchmaking for me in my hometown, saying that I hadn't been home for more than ten years, but that I'd go home more often if I had a family there. So I got married. Later when Xi'an was liberated in June 1949, I didn't go back to Yan'an, but went directly to Yongcun. Once I met Mr. Peng, who said, "You should not stay here. Go to Lanzhou, as the troops are there and you can go and learn." I told him that my family was here, including my children. He said that in that case, I should stay put.

The Teaching of Mr. Xi Lasted My Whole Life

Mr. Xi was very concerned about his subordinates, both at work and in life, but acquaintances never thought of asking him for favors. Xi treated the masses on

In June 1949, Comrade Xi Zhongxun was appointed third Secretary of the new Northwest Bureau of the CPC Central Committee.

an equal basis. When some of the young people from the Northwest Performing Troupe went to visit him in Yongcun, Jianguo Road, Xi'an, Xi stood up and said, "I'll make tea for the masses." He poured water from a thermos for each in turn. He was so approachable, without putting on airs at all. I was greatly impressed.

When asked if there was anything that I needed help with, I said there was nothing, and that I could handle things on my own, as I had always borne in mind the quote, *Devoted to the people and seeking no fame or fortune.* This was a line from Comrade Liu Shaoqi's "On the Character of Communist Party Members." It was embedded in my mind, and it was unimaginable to me to work for my own interests or for fame and fortune, as it is to this day. When the Northwest Bureau was closed down in 1952, Li Wanchun, who was in charge of personnel, asked me how much salary I would set for myself. I asked him to make the decision. Later I learned that the minimum level for people like me was 18, and I asked him how much it was for level 18. Li told me it was 92 yuan. I replied that he could set mine at level 18. Later, I learnt that I was given an extra 100 yuan to help me take care of my family, because I had started working at an early age. I didn't accept the extra 100 yuan. From Tongchuan to Xi'an, my salary remained at level 18. I supported nine people in my family (three parents and four children) with a salary of slightly over 90 yuan.

In 1954, the Northwest Bureau was closed down. Previously, our welfare had been based on the supply system, and later, when the new policy was implemented, my wife's salary couldn't support the family, so I went to work for two years in Baoji, where labor reform was continuously conducted. From there, I went to Tongchuan for more than twenty years. In 1981, Ma Wenrui transferred me back to Xi'an, and I retired here.

I will never forget the days at the Northwest Bureau, especially the eight years following Mr. Xi. That was the experience I'm most proud of.

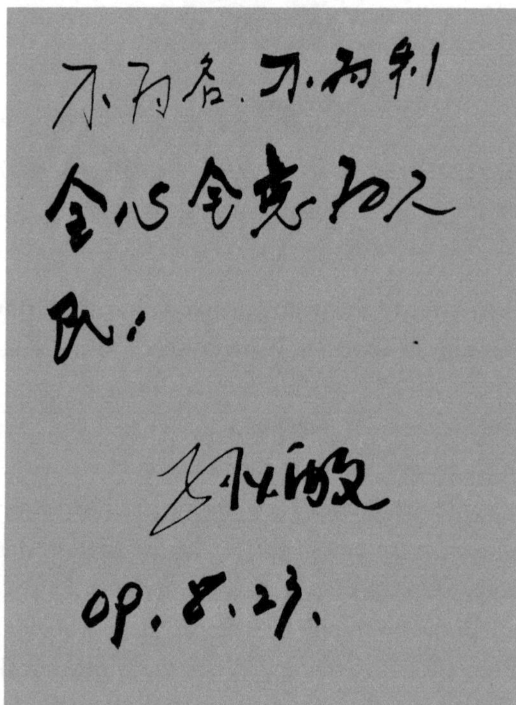

On August 23, 2009, Comrade Sun Bingwen made an inscription for this book which reads, Devoted to the people and seeking no fame or fortune.

Northwest Bureau: A Beautiful Memory in My Life

Shao Jiyao

Born in 1927, Shao Jiyao was a native of Xifeng City, Liaoning Province. From 1947 to early 1949, he was engaged in the underground organizations of the Work Department of the First Division of the Liaoning-Jilin Military Region and the Third Division of the Beiyue Military Region. He joined the Communist Party of China during that period. He went to the North China University for studies in the early days after the liberation of Beijing, and upon finishing his studies, he was dispatched to Xi'an by the Northwest Cadre Team set up by the central Organization Department to participate in the democratic reform and construction of the five provinces and regions in Northwestern China. After that, he was sent to the Policy Research Office of the Northwest Bureau for research work. In December 1954, when the Northwest Bureau was closed, he began teaching in Northwest University and was employed as a visiting professor by Kyoto University and other overseas universities.

Editor's note: In the interviews in Xi'an, Professor Shao Jiyao and his wife accompanied us to interview every one of the old comrades, and they even took the trouble to check the route for us ahead of time, so that our interviews would be much smoother. Seeing the selfless dedication of this elderly couple, we had no reason to slack off. Only by doing our best to work on this book could we live up to their expectation.

In retrospect, my life trajectory has been quite tortuous, full of both joy and woe, but overall it's been quite satisfying. In particular, the time working at the Northwest Bureau can be said to be the happiest and most fulfilling years in my life. The care of the leaders and the help of my colleagues are so memorable that I am immersed in that beautiful memory when I think back today.

The Tense, Repressed School Time

I was from Shandong, and my father moved the family to Northeastern China. I went to primary school, middle school, and university in Northeastern China, all of which was then under Japanese rule. Later, after the anti-Japanese war, the Kuomintang took over the northeastern region and sent a large number of people there to manage the area, people the Kuomintang called receivers, but I called "robbers," because they began seizing property the moment they arrived, taking foreign buildings, beautiful women, and gold bars. That's why I referred to them as "three thefts."

I couldn't understand what they did, and I thought to myself, "How can they treat their own people like that?" Those people had suffered under Japanese rule for fourteen years, and they were disgusted by what the KMT soldiers did. When the KMT army arrived in Shenyang, we all took out our own blankets and overcoats to cover the wounded to keep them warm. At that time, we felt that the country was liberated and would be stronger. But in the end, I felt that we had driven away a pack of wolves only to welcome a tiger. This experience prompted me to later join the Communist Party without any hesitation. In 1947, I started working underground for the Party.

By 1948, there were plans to move the Northeast University established by Zhang Xueliang to Beiping. At that time, the Kuomintang ruled by severe suppression, and they launched a winter camp in the university, requiring all students to participate. It was actually an organization to require the students to follow KMT rule. Later, some students planned to escape, and when Chu Xichun, a KMT official, learned this, he gnashed his teeth and said that he would root them out. He aimed to take a three-step measure against the students, catching, imprisoning, and killing them, and thereby eradicating the perceived threat. For this reason, the students opposed moving the school to Beiping. Having learned of this situation, I immediately reported to my direct superior Comrade Ni Xueyuan, Minister of the First Army Division of the Liaoning-Jilin Military Region.

Hearing my report, the Minister of Urban Engineering asked me to return to Shenyang immediately to convey his instructions. He said that where the school was moved, there we would go and fight to the end. Having done this, I went to Beiping, where my new leader was Feng Peizhi, the Minister of Urban Engineering of the Third Army Division. At that time, I studied at school during the day and engaged in the underground activities in the evening. I was stressed and tense all day long.

Recently, there was a drama entitled *The Battle in Beiping* on TV. I was moved when watching it. I even shed tears when I saw some of the scenes, because the struggle back then was truly fierce, and one of the fronts was the work of the underground personnel. In fact, the underground Party organization was already quite strong by then.

In brief, speaking of the period of Japanese rule and later KMT rule, I felt very depressed and frustrated. It was because of my previous experience that I was determined to combat the enemy later in my life.

Happy Moments in the Northwest Bureau

I remember on February 3, 1949, after the liberation of Beiping, Northeast University moved back to Shenyang. Originally, the university hoped that I would go back to Shenyang, but as there was business to deal with in Beijing, I went to North China University to give lectures there. Then the Northwest Bureau came to mobilize the students to go to work in the northwest. They went to North China University and formed a Northwest Cadre Brigade of more than 2,100 people recruited from three schools. In the summer of 1949, they left Peiping for Xi'an.

The team was divided into three groups. The first group was led by Comrade He Zai, the second group by Comrade Cui Guang, and the third group by Comrade Jiang Xibai. At that time, I was the instructor of the second squadron of the third group, and I escorted the students to the Northwest Bureau as a school cadre. When I arrived in Xi'an, the organization asked me to stay, and I thought I could do something useful there. Later, it happened that a Hui People's Brigade was set up, and I was asked to talk to them, live with them, and offer them some guidance. Later, I was assigned to the Policy Research Office of the Northwest Bureau, which was divided into three sections, the rural section, which was a large one, the urban section, the smaller one where I worked, and the reference section. Comrade Huang Zhi was the director of the Policy Research Office. To be honest, I didn't know

Shao Jiyao at the foot of a slope in Yongcun in 1949.

what the Northwest Bureau was at that time. It was only later that I heard people say that it was a leading organ.

After I got to the Northwest Bureau, I felt like a different person. The previously tense, depressing days were gone. I was genuinely happy to work in the Northwest Bureau, where I felt that the days were brighter, the sky broader, and the mood lighter. This was probably because the colleagues and leaders around me were exceptionally nice. From Secretary Xi Zhongxun and Director Huang Zhi to all my other colleagues, everyone was kind and warm, striving for the common ideal of working hard and making contributions to the motherland. Life in those days was very simple and pleasant. In such an environment, how could I not feel relaxed? I loved working there, no matter how tiring it was. As the saying goes, one is always ready to give one's life to what is worthwhile.

Recalling the Respectable Mr. Xi

Mr. Xi was a very down-to-earth person. He showed great care for his subordinates, his guards, and his attendants, not to mention other ordinary people. One example of this was that Xi had the habit of listening to the radio in the morning, and one day when he heard on the radio that a 17-year-old boy was about to be shot, he immediately told his secretary Zhang Zhigong to go and get Ma Xiwu, who was then president of the Supreme People's Court of the five northwest provinces. When Ma arrived, Mr. Xi inquired about the broadcast he had just heard and asked what wrongdoing the boy had committed, saying that the boy was only 17, and it was a matter of life and death, not a trivial thing, so we needed to be prudent. Later, when things were sorted out at last, the boy was saved. This incident shows that Mr. Xi was very sensitive and sharp. He was always concerned about the ordinary people and was determined to figure out whether a boy should be brought to justice or sentenced to death.

On February 19, 1949, a group photo of the staff of the Policy Research Office of Northwest Bureau.

Mr. Xi was always concerned about the life of the people. Once Mr. Xi went out without taking his guards with him. He lived in Yongcun, so he went to the city wall to the south of Yongcun. Seeing the refugees from Henan Province digging holes under the city wall, he felt terribly sad. His security guards were anxiously going around looking for him, and when they found him, he was squatting, talking to the refugees. That's why I say that Mr. Xi was a civilian official, or "a servant." As a servant or a civilian official, Mr. Xi was a respectable leader to the core.

When we were in the Northwest Bureau, we often organized dances or watched movies on Saturday, which was all the recreation we had at that time. Every time I organized a dance, Mr. Xi was quite enthusiastic. At first, I was a bit confused about why Secretary Xi loved dancing so much. At the party, I learned that Mr. Xi danced with anyone, young or old, male or female, and chatted with them while he danced. I then realized that he seemed to be dancing, but he was actually learning about the actual situation and people's thoughts in a more casual setting. This way of getting to know what was happening in the real life of the average people greatly touched and impressed me.

Mr. Xi was strict with the cadres, and yet greatly respected them for their ideas. Once I was sent to the factories for research and survey. I went to the Caijiapo Textile Mill near Baoji. The Secretary of the Party Committee and the director of the mill came to receive me and asked me what I needed. I told them that I was there to learn and that my identity as an investigator from the Northwest Bureau should be kept secret. I asked them to help me with these two things. They agreed, and I went to the frontline production and to all the workshops and departments. I made friends with the workers, learned about their situation, and learned from them as well. I wrote a research report based on what I had learned. When the report came out, Director Huang Zhi said that it was very good and should be sent to Secretary Xi. Having read the report, Secretary Xi called Secretary Zhang Zhigong and asked him to find out who wrote it. Director Huang Zhi, two other comrades, and I were playing carom at the time. That was our favorite game back then, as we didn't know how to dance. Zhang Zhigong came and asked who had written the report. Director Huang Zhi pointed at me with his pole and said, "Mr. Shao."

When I got to his place, Mr. Xi pointed to a spot in the report and asked me if there was something not quite clearly stated there. Reading it, I replied that I found it acceptable and suggested not modifying it. In the end, after he read it a couple of times, Secretary Xi took my suggestion. This research report was submitted to the CPC Central Committee and distributed to other parts of the country by the

Central Committee. The report was entitled "Opinions of the Northwest Bureau on Democratic Reform of Industrial Enterprises." When the report was officially issued, I had a great sense of achievement. It was not because the report was sent to the Central Committee, but because I recognized how seriously Mr. Xi took such small matters and how prudent he was when identifying something unclear. He was such a major leader and did not need to personally check every detail in a report presented by the Northwest Bureau, but he took the trouble to check with the author. I was deeply moved and was pleased to work under such leadership. For me, it was a great encouragement.

I think one of the biggest characteristics these leading comrades in the Northwest Bureau, including Mr. Xi, shared was prudence. Prudence was a top priority, and rashness was by no means acceptable. At that time, the situation in Northwestern China was particularly complicated. Mr. Xi had done a lot of work and achieved remarkable things involving ethnic issues, industrial and commercial enterprises, capitalists, and other matters, especially on ethnic issues.

At the beginning, I didn't quite understand Mr. Xi's approach to ethnic issues. I remember that when the Panchen Lama Bainqen Erdini traveled to Beijing for a meeting and needed to stop by Xi'an, Mr. Xi asked the relevant departments of the Northwest Bureau to meet him and arranged for him to stay in the courtyard of the Northwest Bureau. I couldn't figure out why Mr. Xi attached so much importance to him. I realized that Mr. Xi thought that the issue of national unity was of great importance, which was part of the United Front work at the top level, and it needed to be carefully dealt with. But not all national issues were the same. For example, for Ma Hongkui and Ma Bufang, the diehards and extreme reactionaries who refused to cooperate no matter what, Mr. Xi was never soft or hesitant in handling them. But for those who were likely to be won over, Mr. Xi always did his utmost to persuade them. There was a tribal leader in Qinghai, Xiang Qian. He was captured and released by Mr. Xi several times, and Xi didn't give up until he finally succeeded in winning him over, which had a great impact at that time. When he was in charge of the United Front work in the Central Committee, Mr. Xi achieved remarkably and understood properly the big picture, which greatly enlightened me.

Mr. Xi cared for the cadres and mingled with the masses. Zhang Zhizhong, a cadre of the Kuomintang, finally became good friends with Mr. Xi. When Mr. Xi was wronged, Zhang Zhizhong visited him every year and sent him New Year's greetings. Not only Zhang Zhizhong, but also many other people, including high-ranking KMT officials, kept contact with Mr. Xi, as he was very open-minded and tolerant.

Other Leaders of the Northwest Bureau

When I was working in the urban group of the Policy Research Office of the Northwest Bureau, my workload was quite heavy. Basically, all urban issues were within our scope of work, such as taxes and industrial and commercial enterprise transformation. As a result of the great pressure from my work, irregular working hours, and limited materials, I suffered from stomach ailments. It was slightly better at other times, but was especially severe in summer. I remember that once at a meeting on a hot day, when there was a big crowd and no air conditioning, I had to cool down with an electric fan, but it was of little use. In less than twenty minutes, I felt very sick and wanted to vomit. Seeing this, comrade Pu Anxiu, the wife of General Peng Dehuai, who was temporarily responsible for organizing the investigation team, immediately asked someone to take me to the hospital. It was not easy to get a car at that moment, so she made prompt arrangements, as General Peng had gone to Taoyuan for a battle. Finally, I was sent to the Central Hospital

Peng Dehuai and his wife Pu Anxiu in Zaoyuan, Yan'an.

(now the Second Hospital) in General Peng's car, where I was treated and cured.

Comrade Pu Anxiu was a nice person and cared greatly for us young people. She took good care of General Peng as well. I remember that shortly after Mr. Xi went to serve the Vice Premier of the State Council, General Peng had just come back from the Korean battlefield to report to Chairman Mao. Mr. Xi called Pu Anxiu during a break and asked her to immediately take a plane to Beijing. We learned of it when Mr. Xi was arranging it, and we thought there must have been something urgent. Later, I learned that it was specially arranged by Mr. Xi so that General Peng and Pu Anxiu could meet as quickly as possible. Upon meeting, General Peng asked Pu, "How come you're here?" She said, "Secretary Xi asked me to come for something urgent." General Peng told her, "Go back right away." So Pu Anxiu immediately returned to Xi'an. I was wondering then why she returned so soon. Having learned of the back and forth of the thing, I was quite impressed first by Mr. Xi, who was very considerate and concerned about his colleagues, and then by Pu Anxiu, who, as a highly competent college graduate, was so thoughtful, caring, and extraordinarily understanding.

During my time at the Northwest Bureau, another person who had a huge influence on me and helped me greatly was Huang Zhi, director of the Policy Research Office. Huang helped me grow more competent with work, giving me just the proper amount of pressure. I was truly thankful to him. Sometimes I told Xiaowu (Comrade Huang Zhi's son) that Huang Zhi was a very affectionate person, treating his subordinates like his own relatives, and that I had many mentors, but the most influential one was Huang Zhi, who taught me in every area of life – not merely in my professional career, but in how to live as well.

Those old cadres genuinely cared about their subordinates, and I was deeply moved. Before the Northwest Bureau was closed down, Mr. Huang and other comrades went back to Beijing. At that time, I was being investigated as a spy for hostile forces in China. Mr. Huang came to me and said, "Mr. Shao, the district office has been closed down, you know. We will go back to Beijing first. You have business here you need to deal with, and you will return to Beijing when things are settled. We will wait for you." This was exactly what he said, and he did not believe I was a spy. Otherwise, he would not have said that. He asked me to cooperate with the investigation. At that moment, all I knew was to work hard, being completely unaware of what was going on.

Even today, I think that Mr. Huang contributed greatly to the Policy Research Office of the Northwest Bureau. My evaluation is that he was the eye of the Northwest Bureau.

On April 10, 2009, a photo of Shao Jiyao and his wife Ai Liping.

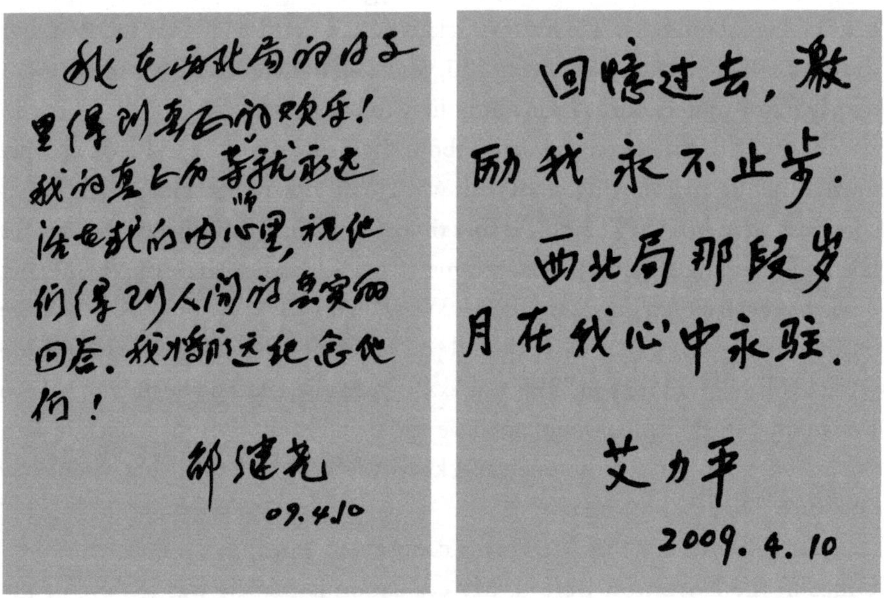

Shao Jiyao and Ai Liping wrote inscriptions for this book.

Days after Retirement

I retired at the age of 65. After that, I was relaxed. In 1985, I went to Japan as a visiting professor, then came back, and later went to Japan to work as a foreign researcher at Kyoto University. I set up the first Japanese major in Northwest University, which took a good deal of effort. With the help of all involved, we finally completed the task, producing a group of hard-working students. I like young people very much. Among the students studying in Japan, some have been assistants to the presidents of Japanese universities. They are all excellent staffs, and I am very pleased.

I have worked in Japan for more than ten years, mainly on China issues under the academic environment and conditions in Japan. My main topic focused on the needs of China's macro- and micro-economy, and on a "harmonious society," which is a really good philosophy, in line with the traditions of Chinese culture.

I think it's very good for us to do the work at this time, so I hope to contact the old leaders and my colleagues from the Northwest Bureau soon to talk about it and leave some memorials, as there are not many old comrades from the Northwest Bureau. It's a very meaningful job.

Recalling Secretary Xi Zhongxun

MA SHUFANG

Ma Shufang, a stenographer in the Stenography Department of the Northwest Bureau, attended many important meetings with Xi Zhongxun and other leading comrades. She was mainly responsible for recording and sorting out the leaders' speeches.

Editor's note: Comrade Ma Shufang is an old comrade of the Northwest Bureau whom we had been looking for so we could interview her, but we failed to find her. Later, we were introduced by Mr. Zhang Ke and his wife Zhang Yuying, and we had the honor to interview Ms. Ma. As a member of the Stenography Department of the Northwest Bureau, Ma Shufang was mainly responsible for recording and sorting out the leaders' speeches, and she told us about the main work of Mr. Xi during that period.

The Northwest Bureau had a Stenography Department in the 1940s and early 1950s. There were more than ten stenographers who made records of the leaders' speeches, and I was one of them. At that time, there was no written manuscript of the leaders' speeches, but merely a simple outline. It was all recorded by the stenographer. Through my work, I was able to be in contact with leaders of the Northwest Bureau such as Secretary Xi Zhongxun.

Excelling at the United Front Work

At that time, Comrade Xi Zhongxun was third Secretary of the Northwest Bureau, and General Peng was responsible for the overall work, more focused on the work of the Northwest Military and Political Commission. Secretary Xi was responsible for the major work of the Northwest Bureau, and he had a heavy workload. Secretary Xi's speeches were vivid and practical, and always easy to follow. Everyone loved to listen to him talk. The meeting venue was always quiet, and even those who were criticized were convinced. Leaders at different levels, from county to province, all trusted him and talked to him if they had any problem or difficulties. Xi was very understanding. At that time, the five provinces in Northwest China had just been liberated and needed development. The northwest region was also a multi-ethnic area, where religious and ethnic issues were particularly prominent, and if there was even the slightest oversight, problems would arise. Secretary Xi was good at combining the central policy and the northwest practice based on the actual situation. He put forward many new views and suggestions on the issue of land reform, such as creating policies and correcting the left-leaning bias in different situations in the old, semi-old, and new districts. His approach was affirmed by the Central Committee and Chairman Mao, then forwarded to the liberated areas throughout the country.

Secretary Xi made special contributions to the handling of national issues and the issue of solidarity with people outside the Party. He emphasized that the top figures of democratic parties and religious circles should meet with each other honestly and do in-depth, meticulous work based on facts. He united the Panchen Lama, Geshe Sherab Gyatso, and democratic people very well. In order to facilitate the Panchen Lama's work, Xi had a small building set up for him in the fifth lane of Jianguo Road, Xi'an. In the early days of liberation, there was a Nganglha rebellion in Qinghai. In order to win over Xiang Qian, the chief of a thousand households, after two years and seven months of work, Xi negotiated on seventeen different occasions and finally won him over. Chairman Mao praised Xi, saying, "Xi Zhongxun is good, better than Zhuge Liang, who captured and released Meng Huo only seven times." It was a widely spread remark at that time. That the newly liberated northwest region was able to have a stable situation was inseparable from his work.

In September 1952, Xi was transferred to work at the Central Publicity Department. When the main leaders of the five provinces in Northwest China saw him off, he emphasized that the officials should pay attention to national

Stenographer Ma Shufang (right) and Zhang Shiying in Northwest Bureau in 1948.

issues, respect democratic people, and take care of them and listen to their opinions. His own efforts reflected that the United Front of the Party worked anytime and anywhere, and one example of that was Zhang Zhizhong, Vice Chairman of Northwest Military and Political Commission. When General Peng went to the DPRK, the work of the Northwest Military and Political Commission was presided over by Comrade Xi Zhongxun. To grant Zhang the right and power to work, Xi often asked Zhang for advice to maximize his role. Xi asked Zhang to deliver some major lectures, and Zhang was very pleased, speaking highly of Xi's work style, way of doing things, and approach to people.

Strict with Work and Caring for the People

Another point that impressed me was that Secretary Xi was good at work, and he balanced work and leisure activities very well. He liked to play carom with other comrades during his break, and he always walked side by side with other comrades when walking. I could often hear his hearty laughter. Although he was very busy with his work, he could still keep small things in mind. Because of our work, we often went to meetings in his car to take notes. Once, after a meeting, he had another activity to attend. He took me and another stenographer to the intersection of Xiwu Road. In order not to disrupt his work, we walked back to the office to sort out the records. That was part of our work, taking notes during the day and sort them out at night, so as not to hinder the next day's work. The next day, when Secretary Xi saw me from afar, he called out, "Ms. Ma!" I hastened to ask Secretary Xi what had happened. He said, "How did you get back last night?" Hearing my reply, he said, "I forgot that you needed to transcribe after taking the notes. I'm truly sorry." I didn't expect Secretary Xi to take this trivial matter into consideration. I would never forget his style of caring for subordinates.

Although Secretary Xi put on no airs in what he said or did, he was very strict with work and did not allow any carelessness. My husband, Ma Songlin, made a record for the Standing Committee of the Northwest Bureau. Once, when the Standing Committee held a meeting without a record, Secretary Xi got angry and

When the Northwest Bureau first distributed cotton clothes, Ma Shufang (first from the right) took a photo with her colleagues in those clothes.

In 1993, four generations of stenographers gathered at the Dayan Pagoda.

In September 2003, a group photo with Comrade Qi Xin (from left: Ma Shufang, Qi Xin, Ma Songlin).

criticized him severely. After the meeting, when Xi learned that it was the General Office that had not made the proper arrangement, he immediately apologized to my husband.

When Secretary Xi came to Xi'an in 1989, my husband, Secretary General Zhang of the General Office of the Provincial Party Committee, and Director Zhou of the Publicity Department went to the People's Mansion to see him. He was very enthusiastic and talked about many things from the past. He mentioned the episode in which he had criticized my husband. He went back to his secretary and said, "Look, I also criticized them. I hope you can understand." Finally, we took photos with Secretary Xi and Comrade Qi Xin, leaving a permanent commemoration.

The Path I've Taken

ZHANG KE

Born in 1928, Zhang Ke came from Yan'an, Shaanxi Province. He joined the revolutionary work in 1941, worked and studied in the accounting training class of the Border Construction Department of the Six District Cooperative of Yanchang County from 1941 to 1945, and was transferred to the Northwest Bureau of the CPC Central Committee as the accountant of the Departments of Production and Auditing from 1945 to 1950. He joined the Communist Party of China in September 1947. After that, he served as chief of the finance section of the Northwest Petroleum Administration Bureau, deputy director (deputy division level) of the Northwest Engineering Administration Bureau (military level), chairman of the Xi'an Association for Science and Technology, and member of the Standing Committee of the 7th and 8th CPPCC Committee of Xi'an. He retired in 1994.

Editor's note: The nearly two-and-a-half-hour interview with Comrade Zhang Ke was the longest one in our trip to Xi'an. Even so, he seemed to have a lot more to say and remained eager and excited when talking about the Northwest Bureau, which showed his nostalgia for his time at the Northwest Bureau.

It is a good thing to organize the compilation of *In the Days of the Northwest Bureau*. Many of the veteran cadres in the Northwest Bureau are already gone, such as Xi Zhongxun, Liu Zhidan, Ma Wenrui, and Jiang Xibai. Therefore, it is very important to record this period of our history with your work, because we shouldn't forget history.

Looking back on my days in the Northwest Bureau, it is fair to say that the Northwest Bureau helped me grow. I didn't truly mature until I got to the Northwest Bureau, because it was there that I attained the truth of revolution and a good deal of knowledge and came to better understand society. In a sense, the Northwest Bureau was my home.

On the Path to Revolution

When I finished primary school, the CPC Central Committee launched two major movements in Yan'an, for rectification and mass production. It mobilized cadres to learn Marxism and Leninism and rectified the Party's work style. It also mobilized the Party, government, army, people, and schools in the border region to carry out various productive activities to meet their basic needs. I was thirteen years old and was already seen as an educated person in the local area, though I had only finished primary school. At that time, the Cooperative of Six Districts of Yanchang County had just been established and was urgently in need of workers. Guo Yukui, director of the Red Army and Cooperative of Northern Shaanxi, recommended me to work in the Cooperative of Six Districts of Yanchang County. When I got there, I first did chores, such as carrying water, sweeping the floor, and helping to cook. A few months later, a disabled Red Army soldier named Zhao Shengcai was transferred to our place, and he was responsible for carrying water and cooking. I was then asked to help the deputy director collect money and do the bookkeeping.

In 1943, the Construction Department of the border region government started an accounting training session for the county cooperatives in the valley south of Baota Mountain in Yan'an. The director sent me there to learn how to improve the bookkeeping method and abacus. Wang Yingyuan (former director of the Shaanxi Provincial Bureau of Materials) and Shi Zizhu (former director of the Shaanxi Provincial Bureau of Taxation) were my classmates with whom I studied, and we kept in touch. When the training session ended, we went to the Dongguan sub-district of Yan'an to go through the procedures and return to our previous units. I went back to the Six District Cooperative to work as the chief accountant. At this time, the border region government mobilized the masses to raise funds and become shareholders, set up supply and marketing cooperatives and mule teams to transport salt, and opened restaurants, farms, and rice noodle workshops. The Cooperative of Six Districts also renovated the headquarters, purchased cotton, traded local cloth, and distributed dividends to the masses at the end of the year, creating a prosperous scene. Commander Wang Zhen also personally inspected our cotton-for-thread work.

After several years of hard work, the Party, government, military, and school units in the border region largely met the public demand for necessities, steadily achieved the goal of "relying on one's own for food and clothing," and greatly improved the people's lives. In this process, I embarked on the revolutionary road as a student.

Transferred to the Northwest Bureau as an Accountant

When Japan surrendered in 1945, the army and people in the border region cheered and celebrated the victory. At the same time, a large number of military and political cadres were sent to work in the northeast, Northern China, and other places. At that time, I also wanted to go. It happened that Zhao Fumin, from the Northwest Bureau of the CPC Central Committee, who had opened a shop in Ganguyi, said that the Production Department of the Northwest Bureau was recruiting accountants and recommended that I go. Zhao Xinmin, head of the production section of the Northwest Bureau, personally went to the cooperative to learn about my situation. He sent a letter to transfer me to Yan'an and assigned me to the Qilipu transportation station as an accountant. Soon after, Zhang Ge, the accountant of the Production Department, was transferred to the executive department of the Beiping Military Mediation Office, which Ye Jianying joined on behalf of our Party. So I was transferred to the Huashibian production department to assist Shao Zhengxing (former head of the Logistics Department of Lanzhou Aerospace) in the accounting work.

At that time, the major task of the Production Department was to manage trade and commerce and provide funds for the United Front expenses of the various organs. There were shops in Yan'an, Sanbian,[1] Suide, and Liulin of Shaanxi Province, and camel teams transporting salt in Dingbian. In addition, the production section often performed some special tasks. At the time of the liberation of Zhangjiakou, Captain Liang Ruiying was dispatched to take the transport team to carry booty such as woolen cloth, seafood, and long and short guns, and Liu Xianrui was sent to escort leading cadres to Handan and other places.

1. *Editor's note:* Jingbian, Anbian, and Dingbian in the Yulin area of Shaanxi Province were collectively referred to as Sanbian.

At that time, we got involved in transportation. There were many teams, such as mule teams, horse teams, and even camel teams, with sufficient funds. The environment was good for rapid development. The main resource of the border area was salt, and there was a salt pool in Sanbian. There were no other resources, and the three other treasures of this area included sheepskin, wool, and licorice (the latter used in traditional Chinese medicine).

Back then, trade depended on using one's own channels to find someone to trade with. I took goods to the border of Lingqiu. I didn't know how to trade, so I asked others how they did it. They told me to go to the bottom of the hillside and tie my horse to the side, as there were two earthen caves on the hillside where I could trade with local KMT officials. They said that the KMT's people were all desperados who came in plain clothes with guns and ammunition. They went to the cave on the hillside and agreed that I would give them the goods they needed and they would give me the guns and ammunition. I was also told to run away immediately after the transaction, or I would be in trouble if they took the goods and refused to offer me the guns. At that time, I was afraid, and they were afraid, too. There were also other people who went to the edge of the Yellow River to trade with the KMT soldiers, especially in summer. With two white gourds in their hands, those people swam across the Yellow River to trade. You may ask why we did so at that time. It was because we were short of materials, and paper notes would not be accepted if we printed them on our own. But we had to fight the battles and couldn't do so without weapons and other materials. There was no other way.

Later, all the tasks of the production department were well completed. During the Spring Festival of 1945, on behalf of the leaders of the Northwest Bureau, Secretary General Cao Liru invited the cadres of the production department to dinner in the chief's restaurant, offered a toast to everyone, and encouraged us to put forth persistent effort. We were greatly encouraged.

During our time working at the Northwest Bureau, the material conditions of Yan'an were very poor, but the people were full of energy and passion and actively engaged in various recreational activities and sports. All the organs organized basketball, volleyball, and other ball games on weekends. In the small auditorium of the Northwest Bureau, a dance was held every Saturday, where Secretary Xi Zhongxun and Minister Ma Wenrui would take the lead in the dance, and Liu Shaoqi, General Zhu, and other central leaders also attended. At that time, there were no electric lights, and the party was lit by a steam light, which was very bright. Both men and women in the government organs, regardless of their age, position, or performance, participated actively in the dance. There were a lot of people immersed in the lively atmosphere. At that party, I saw that Secretary Xi Zhongxun was very active and approachable, chatting with different people.

Withdrawing from Yan'an and Moving to Northern Shaanxi

At the beginning of 1947, Chiang Kai-shek gathered up his personnel and attacked Yan'an and Shandong. Among them, Hu Zongnan's army with its 230,000 soldiers attacked Yan'an. The situation became very tense. On March 8, a meeting mobilizing ten thousand people to defend the border area was held in Nanguan. Commander-in-Chief Zhu De, Vice Chairman Zhou Enlai, and Comrade Lin Boqu made speeches and conveyed Chairman Mao's instructions, telling us that we had to abandon the illusion of peace and be prepared for war, and that we should stand firm, not leaving a single piece of grain to the enemy. At that time, we decided to give up Yan'an, and many cadres couldn't accept it. Later, it turned out that the Party Central Committee had made a very wise decision.

At that time, Secretary Xi was transferred to the frontline headquarters and began to organize the Northwest Field Army. Mr. Peng was then commander of the Northwest Field Army, and Secretary Xi was the political commissar. They worked together very well. Although it was called a field army, there were actually not many troops. In Yan'an, there was the Instruction Brigade, New Fourth Brigade, and 358 Brigade, while the others were police brigades. In Yan'an, there was Police Brigade 1, Police Brigade 2, and Police Brigade 3, with a total of less than 20,000 people, while the Kuomintang troops were said to number 230,000 to 250,000 soldiers, at least ten times more than ours.

On March 11, the KMT troops led by Dong Zhao and Liu Kansuo attacked Yan'an from two sides at the same time. The Instruction Brigade officers and soldiers stood to fight for seven days and nights and completed the task of covering the smooth transfer of the masses from Yan'an. Xue Fuxian and I left Yan'an one night after the enemy's heavy bombing, and we went to Zhenwu Cave in Ansai to take care of the supplies there. We stayed for two days at Zhenwu Cave. From behind, people said that the enemy was chasing very closely, so we had to keep moving westward right away. One night, we had to cross a river. It was not a big one, but it was dark and cold in Northern Shaanxi in March. There was a layer of ice on top of the river, over which there was no bridge. We had to cross the river by stepping on the stones, and when those in the front fell into the river, water splashed onto the stones and formed ice. When those following them stepped on the stones, they slid into the water. My shoes, socks, and trousers were all wet and icy. It took us a day and a night to get out.

Most of the people of the Northwest Bureau withdrew to the rear along the Yellow River. I didn't know where the organs of the Northwest Bureau were moved to at that time. I followed a command organization in the Shaanxi-Gansu-Ningxia border region to deliver materials to the front line. At that time, the materials of the government organs were first buried in the countryside, and after two victories, they were dug out to be exchanged for money to buy vegetables, salt, and oil.

Commander-in-Chief Peng and Political Commissar Xi led the three battles and won three victories, defending the Shaanxi-Gansu-Ningxia border region. The first battle at Qinghuabian was a big ambush, in which Wang Zhen's 359 Brigade was transferred there and completed a nice, swift defeat. The second was at Yangmahe, and the third was at Panlong, which was the Kuomintang's "huge warehouse" to store the "foreign noodles" from Xi'an Flour Mill and the "foreign cloth" from Xi'an Textile Mill. At that time, our troops were worried about having no winter clothes to wear, but we all got clothes after the battle.

The three battles and three victories quickly reversed the situation, shifting from internal operations to external operations in enemy occupied areas. After the victory of the three major battles, a celebration was held in Zhenwu Cave. At that

In March 1947, Peng Dehuai (second from left), Xu Liqing (first from left), Xi Zhongxun (third from left), and Zhang Wenzhou (fourth from left) investigating the battlefield in Qinghuabian.

time, the KMT still occupied Yan'an. We held a meeting in Zhenwu Cave, eighty or ninety miles to the west of Yan'an. Vice President Zhou Enlai attended the meeting and delivered a speech. At that time, Chairman Mao was still in Northern Shaanxi. During the guerrilla battle that lasted more than a year, the first of the four field armies suffered the most. Because of the backward economy and inconvenient transportation, the frontline materials were transported by donkey. Each donkey carried two boxes of mortar shells, and soldiers carried dry food to feed the donkey. They all walked at night. During the day, they were attacked by enemy planes. It was very difficult to win a battle at that time. Commander-in-Chief Peng and Secretary Xi quickly reversed the situation in Northern Shaanxi with three major battles against the much stronger enemy. This was a great contribution.

The three victories in the three battles and the subsequent attack on Yulin were very inspiring, but we knew the conditions under which our troops won. The biggest problem was that there was no food, and there was a severe shortage in the food supply for the army. I remember when we attacked Yulin for the first time, we still had something to eat. When we attacked Yulin for the second time, we had nothing at all. We ate all kinds of pumpkin vines and buckwheat stalks. I watched with my own eyes as people fell over, starving to death as they walked to Yulin. At that time, the food served in the Northwest Bureau was not much better. Everyone ate black beans, which were originally meant for animal feed. As the food was supplied to the frontline troops, what was left was black beans. After cooking, the pot was full of black water. After our meals, we all had a swollen belly, and we were too uncomfortable to sleep through the night.

Restoring Yan'an

Our army attacked Baoji in 1948, forcing the enemy to flee Yan'an and Luochuan. Yan'an was restored on April 22, 1948, which was of great political and historical significance. In a situation where the enemy army was ten times as large as ours, we eliminated more than 100,000 of their soldiers in slightly more than a year. The enemy retreated without fighting, and Yan'an was restored to the hands of the people. The balance of power between us and the enemy shifted.

After the restoration of Yan'an, the Northwest Bureau and the border region government soon returned from the Yihe, Suide area. Secretary Xi returned to Yan'an early with his secretary, drivers, and guards. By then, we had seized a small jeep provided by the American government to the Kuomintang, so Mr. Xi came back by car. On returning to Yan'an, Xi said anxiously, "I'm going to Yangjialing and Zaoyuan to see the place where Chairman Mao lived." Cao Liru told him not to go, as there were still hidden enemies. Later, he sent guerrillas to flush out the enemy before Secretary Xi went there.

The liberation of the Northwest went fast, and the final key battle was at Fumei, where Hu Zongnan was defeated. In July 1949, after the Northern China troops entered Shaanxi, it was reorganized into the Northwest Field Army, with a total force of 12 corps and 340,000 people. Hu Zongnan's mobile troops, with only just over 70,000 people, gathered on both sides of the Weihe River, and Ma Bufang's and Ma Hongkui's troops in Qinghai and Ningxia, with more than 80,000 people, gathered in Liquan and Qianxian. The conditions for our decisive battle were ready, and we decided to separate and annihilate Hu's and the two Mas' troops. On July 12, 1949, our army launched an overall attack. After two days of fierce fighting, we annihilated four enemy corps, more than 43,000 people in total, liberated eight counties and towns, and took Baoji, ending Hu Zongnan's twelve year rule in Northwestern China. Our army then took advantage of the victory and destroyed the main force of Ma Bufang in Shenjialing, Lanzhou, which he had run for more than forty years in Qinghai. Lanzhou was liberated on August 26, Xining on September 5, and Yinchuan on September 19. Under the direct leadership of Commander-in-Chief Peng, after two and a half years of fighting, we finally liberated the northwest, and those great achievements will remain in the annals of history.

Moving to Xi'an with the Northwest Bureau

On May 20, 1949, Xi'an was liberated, and the Northwest Bureau moved to Xi'an and conducted structural reorganization. Peng Dehuai, He Long, and Xi Zhongxun served as the Secretaries of the Northwest Bureau. Later, He Long was transferred to the southwest, and Commander-in-Chief Peng was transferred to resist US aggression and aid Korea. Secretary Xi was then serving as the Second Secretary of the Northwest Bureau, and he actually presided over the overall work.

At that time, the liberation of cities went swiftly, and it brought many problems. Public security was poor, and ethnic issues were complicated. In particular, there were many ethnic minorities in Northwest China, such as the Hui and Tibetan people. In addition, the scatter KMT troops were lurking and engaged in sabotage maneuvers from time to time. Public security became a serious issue as a result. To maintain public order, Secretary Xi sent out a number of cadres. At that time, we said that those cadres were transferred one after another, just like cutting leeks. Through a large number of expatriate cadres, social order was steadily restored.

After I got to Xi'an with the Northwest Bureau, I spent most of my time traveling on business. At the beginning of 1950, in order to meet the needs of developing automobile transportation industry in Northwest China, we prepared to set up the Automobile Transportation Bureau. At that time, the Soviet Union provided us some vehicles, and we were asked to go to the northeast to make contacts to receive them, so we were led by director Zhao Xinmin of the Administrative Department to the northeast. In addition, we also went to Shanghai and Tianjin to purchase office supplies, such as pencils and pens. At that time, Shanghai's Jinxing pens were very famous, so we purchased some for the section chiefs and directors of the Northwest Bureau. And we bought a Parker pen for Secretary Xi. When I sent it to Secretary Xi and asked him what color he preferred, he asked his wife Qi Xin to choose one for him. He was very pleased with the pen.

Northern Shaanxi Saved the Central Government and Vice Versa

It was fair to say that the central government saved Northern Shaanxi, and vice versa. Why do I say this? When he led the Red Army on the Long March all the way to Gansu, close to Shaanxi, Chairman Mao did not know where to go. At that time, he only knew that he was going to the north to combat Japan, but no one knew where to go. Later, someone picked up a Kuomintang newspaper, which mentioned Liu Zhidan and a base area in Northern Shaanxi. They went to report to Chairman Mao that we still had a base area in Northern Shaanxi, and Liu Zhidan was the leader. As Jia Tuofu was a native of Northern Shaanxi and had been with Chairman Mao on the Long March, Jia and others were later asked to report on the situation. After this inquiry, Chairman Mao knew that there was still a base area in Northern Shaanxi, and there were two forces, one from the central government and the other from the local government, namely, those of Liu Zhidan and Xi Zhongxun. Having learned about the situation, Chairman Mao led the army to Northern Shaanxi. At that time, there were no base areas in other parts of the country. During the Long March of the Red Army, there were

In 1936, the Guanzhong Special Committee was established, and its organ was based in Malan (Majiabao Village). Jia Tuofu and Xi Zhongxun each served in turn as Secretary of the Special Committee.

100,000 people. In the first battle of the Xiangjiang River, 40,000 people were lost and 40,000 to 50,000 remained. When Chairman Mao entered the Shaanxi-Gansu-Ningxia border region, some said he had 7,000 people, while others said he had 3,000 people, but either way, there were not many left. Chairman Mao remarked at that time that although there were only a few thousand of us, we were all the seeds of the Red Army, and we were the most capable. Upon arriving in Northern Shaanxi, Chairman Mao heard that Liu Zhidan and Xi Zhongxun had been arrested, and he immediately sent four or five people, including Jia Tuofu and Wang Shoudao, to talk to those arresting the pair and asking them to release the prisoners. Later, Chairman Mao sent Zhang Wentian and others to Wayaobao, and he finally rescued Liu Zhidan and Xi Zhongxun. It is fair to say, then, that the central government saved Northern Shaanxi, and in the meantime, the Northern Shaanxi base area became the foothold of the Long March and the starting point of the anti-Japanese war, because the army on the Long March did not know where to go. It was in Northern Shaanxi that it settled in, took root, and thrived. In the end, Chairman Mao led the army to win the national victory in Yan'an, so it was also true that Northern Shaanxi saved the central government. In 1948, when crossing the Yellow River, Chairman Mao said that he would not forget Northern Shaanxi, and he would always remember the millet and potatoes there.

Secretary Xi in Memory

Secretary Xi was a veteran leader of the Northwest Bureau, a forerunner of the revolution, and one of the founders of the Shaanxi-Gansu Border Base and the Northwest Workers' and Farmers' Red Army. Secretary Xi came to the Northwest Bureau around October 1945. I was transferred there between September and October in 1945. When Secretary Xi first arrived, we lived in Huashibian, Nanguan, Yan'an, where there was a bumpy mountain road. When Secretary Xi went to the Central Committee for a meeting, he took a type of car which we called double-row seats. At that time, we didn't need to see the car before knowing it was Secretary Xi coming, because the road conditions were really bad, and the car was not in good shape either, so the noise it made was loud and clear.

Looking back, I think Secretary Xi correctly implemented the principles, lines, and policies of the Party Central Committee in the Agrarian Revolution, the War of Resistance Against Japanese Aggression, the War of Liberation, and in the land reform and democratic reform after the liberation of the country.

Later, Secretary Xi went to work at the State Council and made great contributions there too. At that time, he was Premier Zhou Enlai's right-hand man. As we all know, among the leaders of the Central Committee, Secretary Xi was the youngest, most promising, lively, approachable, and always mingling with the masses. He impressed us greatly in many aspects. As I see it, Secretary Xi made outstanding contributions in different historical stages, and he was diligent and dedicated. During the period in Northwest China, I think his greatest contribution was the defense of the South and North Gates.

The defense of the South Gate referred to the fact that Secretary Xi served as the Secretary of the local Party Committee of Guanzhong. The situation in this area was complex at that time, which mainly involved combating the Kuomintang. There were many other tasks in the military, politics, the United Front, mass work, and the establishment of political power. At that time, the KMT "eliminated and suppressed" Jiangxi five times, and the Shaanxi-Gansu-Ningxia border area at least three or four times, so the struggle against the enemy in the border area was quite intense. The key period was July 1945, when at the height of the KMT's anti-

Communist Party movement, troops were sent to seize the Malan area. We fought for seven days, but failed to defend it. After the area was occupied, Chairman Mao gave an order to Xi Zhongxun to take it back. Secretary Xi, Deputy Commander Zhang Zongxun of the Yan'an Joint Defense Command, and Vice Commander Wang Shitai organized the troops of the Shaanxi-Gansu-Ningxia border area to take it back. After our victory, Chairman Mao was very pleased, because it protected the South Gate of Yan'an, the revolutionary holy land.

The defense of the North Gate referred to a time in 1943, when Mr. Xi was transferred to Suide as the Secretary of the local Party Committee. He was transferred because the 22nd Army of the Kuomintang occupied Suide for a long time and supported Hu Zongnan in frequent attacks on the border area. At that time, the KMT Commissioner in Yulin was He Shaonan, who was an extreme anti-Communist and always stirred up trouble for us. Suide was the site of political power for both the Communist Party and the KMT, and home to the county governments of the KMT and of the Communist Party. The county government of the KMT was set up in the county, and the county government of the Communist Party was set up in the town. At that time, the KMT occupied the areas from Hengshan to the west of Suide, and there was frequent friction. In this context, Chairman Mao asked Xi Zhongxun to go to the Suide local committee, where things were very complicated, involving the Kuomintang, Yan Xishan, and local anti-Communist forces, so that we should combat "encirclement and suppression" while engaging in United Front work. Secretary Xi did a good job when he went there. A typical example was his planning for Hu Jingduo's uprising in 1946. The deputy commander of security in Yulin was Hu Jingduo, whose brother was the deputy commander of the KMT 22nd Corps, which was an important KMT force in Yulin.

At that time, under the direction of Chairman Mao, Secretary Xi began to do the work in the summer. Zhang Siyuan was the head of the United Front Department of the Suide local committee, whom I was not familiar with. Secretary Xi did Hu Jingduo's work through the local underground party. Xi sent Fan Ming in disguise to meet Hu Jingduo, recalling life in the latter's hometown and explaining the current situation, and then Fan reported back to Xi Zhongxun, who asked the Central Committee for approval to send Fan Ming again, disguised as an officer of the KMT to discuss with Hu Jingduo about where and when to rise up. Later, Hu Jingduo revolted, with our initiative, which laid a solid foundation for defending the North Gate of Yan'an. After Hu Jingduo's uprising, his brother, the deputy commander of the 22nd corps of the KMT, led the troops to pursue them from

Yulin, and he was defeated by the troops we had already deployed. His brother didn't even get to mount his horse or wear his coat. He simply ran, carrying his gun. Later, when we saw the officers of the KMT coming to the Northwest Bureau, Secretary Xi Zhongxun received them in person. We didn't know why they were there, and we found out later that the KMT officers came to the Northwest Bureau after their uprising to apply to join the Communist Party. Everyone felt it was like a myth, and they praised Secretary Xi for being so capable as to win over all the KMT security commanders.

When the Northwest Bureau moved to Xi'an, I often met Secretary Xi, but I knew he was very busy after he arrived in Xi'an. At that time, the Northwest Bureau held frequent meetings, such as the meeting on the cultivation of young cadres, or one explaining the meaning and significance of United Front work to the cadres and staff of the organs, the United Front work meetings held by the Ministry of the United Front, and the Youth and Women's Congresses. In brief, there were many meetings, and Secretary Xi was extremely busy. We sometimes saw him pacing near the desk outside the office, and at first we didn't know what he was doing. We later learned that this was how he thought through things.

On April 4, 2009, the editor-in-chief of the book with Comrade Zhang Ke.

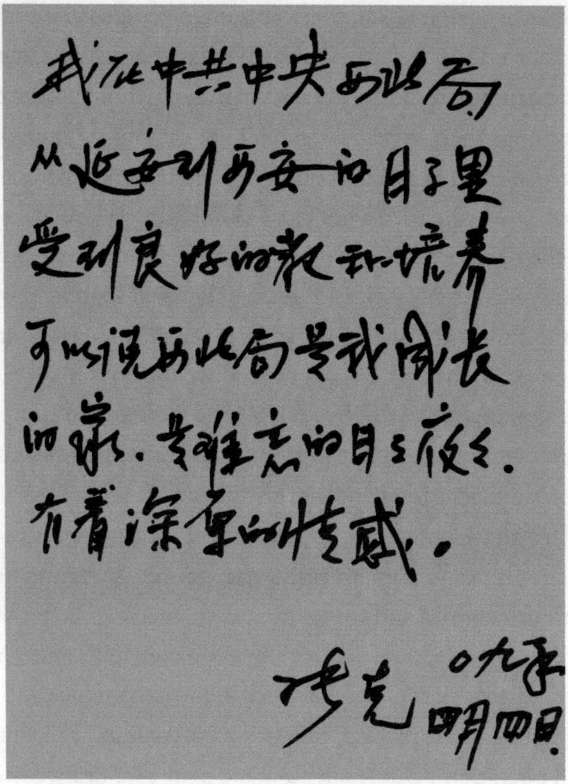
我在中共中央西北局
从延安到西安的日子里
受到良好的教和培养
可以说西北局是我成长
的家。是难忘的日日夜夜。
有着深厚的情感。

张克 〇九年
四月四日

Comrade Zhang Ke writing an inscription for this book.

I have deep affection for the Northwest Bureau. I started working at the age of 13 and joined the Bureau at 16, when I literally didn't know a thing. Later, I studied the relevant theories under the education of the Northwest Bureau and came to understand the purpose of the revolution. It's fair to say that the Northwest Bureau was like a big family, where I was properly trained to grow into a national cadre. I will never forget my time at the Northwest Bureau. It was the most precious time of my life.

On the Historical Role of the Production Section

The Northwest Bureau of the CPC Central Committee was the leading organ of the Party. Why should a department named the Production Section be set up? Many comrades don't know, so I will briefly describe the situation as I remember it.

During the anti-Japanese war, the Kuomintang imposed a military siege and economic blockade on the Shaanxi-Gansu-Ningxia border area, which made both military and civilian life in the border area extremely difficult due to the shortage of food and clothing. There were no vegetables or oil, and no shoes for the soldiers. It was difficult to survive in 1942. In order to keep the enemy from straining us to death, Chairman Mao proposed a policy of "developing the economy and ensuring the supply" at the high-level cadres meeting of the border area, pointing out that the financial and economic work in the area centered around the issue of living expenses and the supply of the enterprise funds for tens of thousands of soldiers, the Party, and government staff. In order to reduce the burden on the people in the border areas, it was necessary to carry out a mass production campaign. All units were to do their own work and put forth effort to be self-sufficient and meet the requirements of "sufficient food and clothes."

At the call of the Central Committee, the Party, government and military organs, and schools responded warmly. The border government immediately established various factories and workshops, such as a soap factory, a quilt factory, a textile factory, a shoe factory, a Malan grass paper mill, and a match factory, and it produced various necessities for daily life in accordance with the principle of "integrating public and private, military and civilian." All units established production and operation institutions to make plans, set tasks, divide targets, and hold contests to mobilize the personnel of the unit to get engaged in production activities, cultivate wasteland and plant vegetables, raise pigs and grind tofu, and make rice noodles. We would do anything possible to overcome difficulties and complete tasks. In addition, it also required that everyone in the agency find various ways to turn in a certain amount of millet every year. At the end of the year, the system held a conference for rewarding the heroes of labor, and among them was the famous worker Zhao Zhankui and the farmer Wu Manyou, who set excellent examples.

The Northwest Bureau took the lead in establishing its own business organization, the Production Section, to work in the mass production movement, and it acted independently under the leadership of the Secretary General and the administrative department. It was mainly engaged in business and trade to provide living and business funds for the organs.

1. The Personnel of the Production Section and Its Subordinate Business Units

The leaders attached great importance to the staffing of the Production Section, and they selected a group of highly competent comrades as the backbone, mostly veterans of the Red Army and the cadres of the veteran Party members. Comrade Zhao Xinmin, chief of the section, was a veteran cadre who joined the Party with Liu Zhidan in Yulin Middle School. More than ten cadres and communication personnel, cooks, and the service staff joined in at different times, including Zhang Ge, Zheng Xing, Li Handou, Zhang Hui, Chang Junqing, Zhan Shengxian, Liang Ruiying, Liu Xianrui, Jia Zhongwu, Ren Ruiting, Gao Zhonghuai, Fan Ziying, Xiao Sheng, and Zhang Ke. The Production Section set up accounting, cashier, storage, procurement, business, and other posts, which were taken on by those comrades. Cadres in the Production Section, regardless of their position or qualifications, took whatever jobs they were assigned seriously with a high sense of responsibility, putting forth concerted efforts to achieve the common goal.

In the Yan'an era, the subordinate business units of the production section included the New Market Consumer Cooperative, Nanguan Big Production Inn, Qilipu Mule and Horse Shop and Transportation Team, Ansai Zhenwudong Department Store, Suide Trade Station, two stores in Qikou and Liulin Town, Shanxi, the Jingbian Trade Station, and the Camel Salt Transportation Team. Under the special circumstances at that time, the business mode was mainly folk trade in Shanxi, Inner Mongolia, and other border areas of the KMT and Communist Party, and it involved going to various places to participate in material exchange conferences. Because of the flexible operation mode and the broad range of activities, the business enjoyed rapid development, and the annual profit generated by each business unit, as the economic source of the Northwest Bureau, ensured self-sufficiency in the supply of the organs.

2. *Primary Office and Daily Supplies Provided by the Production Section to the Bureau*

Office supplies such as paper, pencils, printing machine, carbon paper, and ink were purchased from enemy-occupied areas. Daily supplies such as towels, toothbrushes, soap, matches, and kerosene lamps were things that were not in ready supply in Yan'an.

There was also personal production by the organs for items such as cotton yarn, twist wool, wool gloves, and socks. In 1948, the winter was exceptionally cold. The Production Section bought one pair of felt shoes from Sanbian for each member of the staff.

The expenses for some special cases were also settled by the Production Section. For example, the funds and articles needed for the cadres to be dispatched to the northeast and other places and the clothing supplies transported back from the enemy-occupied areas fell under this category. It is also worth mentioning that after the surrender of Japan, a large number of cadres were transferred to other places. When the Production Section sent a transport team to accompany the cadres' families to the northeast, it coincided with the first liberation of Zhangjiakou City. When the transport team returned, it brought back a large number of spoils, including items like squid and sea cucumbers, which were handed over to the canteen as a special treat. There was also much woolen cloth, textiles, and more than a dozen long and short guns, which added many items to the Production Section's supplies and improved the life of the people in the organization.

The Party fees of the Northwest Bureau, mainly gold, were also provided and managed by the Production Section. Because the currency of the border region could not be circulated elsewhere, the special fees were mainly used for United Front expenses (later, urban work expenses), which were classified. These payment were made with the signature of Secretary Xi Zhongxun.

In brief, the Yan'an Production Section had acquired abundant funds and materials by 1945, which became the pillar of the supplies for the organs, helping the Northwest Bureau through the most difficult time and ensuring the Northwest Bureau's "self-sufficiency and sufficiency in food and clothing," which played a positive role in furthering its work in various fields.

These achievements were mainly due to the attention and support of the leaders, especially the selection and assignment of competent cadres to the production section. They worked hard and selflessly, and they strove to complete the task without any concern about fame or fortune.

3. The Production Section Stuck to Its Duty During the Transition Period

In 1947, the Kuomintang launched a large-scale attack on Yan'an. In order to lure the enemy deeper into our territory, the Party Central Committee decided to take the initiative to withdraw. During the evacuation, many cadres of the Northwest Bureau went with Secretary Xi, Ma Mingfang, Ma Wenrui, and other leaders of the army. The logistics personnel and their families moved to the Qikou defense line in Shanxi. Only Secretary General Cao Liru, armed with the radio transmission device, and a few staff members stayed in Northern Shaanxi. At this time, all the business of the Production Section stopped, leaving more than ten transportation teams to follow the organization's team in Northern Shaanxi. If there was an emergency evacuation, first we swiftly transferred the materials to Zhenwu Cave in Ansai at night. The enemy entered Yan'an and chased us westward. Along the way, we buried the materials in a village. Then we caught up with the organization team and stopped at Baimiaocha. During this period, the scattered personnel of the Northwest Bureau arrived one after another. One day, the secretary general held a border region meeting in a mountain hideout. Unexpectedly, Premier Zhou and Comrade Lu Dingyi came to the meeting. Premier Zhou shared with us the situation in the war and required that "the governments at all levels in the border region remain where they are, in districts or counties, to organize guerrilla units and lead the masses to carry out the guerrilla war." On this basis, the Northwest Bureau left this team behind and formed a commanding body for the Party's work in the wartime border region. The leader of the Production Section decided that Comrade Xiao Sheng and I would lead the transportation team to follow the command organ to transfer. Our task was to deal with the materials while marching and provide funds for the organ. Xiao Sheng and I did all we could, acting immediately. Every day, we carried a cigarette box and set up a cigarette stand at the intersection of Baimiaocha to sell cigarettes.

We stayed at Baimiaocha for more than a month. One night, we were told to set off immediately and transfer overnight. We lost contact with the front troops when we climbed the mountains and went down the gullies along the winding trails. In the heavy rain, we wore wet clothes as we marched for two days and two nights. Everyone was exhausted. During the day, the enemy planes bombed us. Once when a mule was scared and ran away, I went to catch it and was almost hit by a bullet. Another transporter was hit on the head by a cartridge magazine dropped by the enemy. Exhausted and worried, we finally got in touch with the front troops and went eastward to Matigou for a break. From then, when the team stopped for a break, Xiao Sheng and I carried the materials that could be traded to the market at the entrance of the village for sale, and the money we earned was handed over to the authorities for emergency use.

Before the Battle of Shajiadian, our superiors gave an urgent notice telling us to move to the east of Suide. The moment we stopped at Xuejiaqu near Yihe, Xiao Sheng and I were told to cross the Yellow River immediately. We took the transport team, loaded the supplies, and crossed the mountains to the bank of the Yellow River. Because there were many people crossing the river and few boats, we had to stay and wait. Later, due to the heavy rain at night, the boat could not ferry us, and we had to hide under the rocks the whole night. The next morning, we crossed the river and went back to the Production Section stationed in Xiwan Village, Qikou. We handed in the materials and went through all the procedures.

Although it was a dangerous, arduous trip, we managed to fulfill our duty and successfully completed the task.

In Xiwan Village in Qikou, Shao Zhengxing, Li Handou, Xiao Sheng, and other comrades were transferred to the army, and I took over the accounting of the Production Section. After the victory of the Shajiadian battle, Secretary Xi Zhongxun and other leaders returned to the Northwest Bureau, and then to Xuejiaqu near Yihe. The Yihe Meeting held in October conveyed the gist of the central land reform conference. The staff of the Production Section went to the meeting, and Comrade Jia Zhongwu and I stayed behind at Qikou to go back and forth between the two spots.

After the restoration of Yan'an in 1948, the Northwest Bureau immediately returned to Wangjiaping, where the former Central Military Commission was stationed. At this time, the head of the organ, the Organization, Publicity, and United Front Ministries, and the Secretariat, Confidential, and Administration Departments were soon settled. The funds for the organs were temporarily provided by the supply department of the Joint Defense Command. The Northwest Bureau was responsible for the supply of the mass organizations and the performing troupe of the Northwest Bureau and its affiliated Party-civilian system, and a specialized auditing section was set up. At this time, the Production Section had just three people to assist the auditing section. The Production Section had completed its historical mission by this time. The work of the Northwest Bureau was mainly to prepare for the liberation of the northwest, especially for the task of taking over a city as big as Xi'an. It started to move to Xi'an in May.

When the Northwest Bureau was in Yan'an, many cadres of the Red Army of workers and farmers in the production and logistics sections of the organ, unknown in their ordinary posts, worked diligently and tried every means to do good jobs despite the dirt and the fatigue. One example was Comrade Lin Fengchun of the Long March Red Army, who was born in Fujian. He was responsible for slaughtering pigs and supplying pork to the canteen in the Shi'an Cave by the river at the foot of Huashibian Mountain. He introduced me to the Party on the way to Northern Shaanxi. In 1947, the Northwest Bureau held a meeting in Yihe. At that time, Northern Shaanxi was on the verge of having nothing to eat, and the people in the organs ate boiled sorghum and black beans with plain water. Lin went to the Goulan and Wuzhai Mountain areas of Shanxi Province to buy pigs for the conference, traveling a distance of hundreds of miles, and he rushed back to Yihe. In 1949, when the Northwest Bureau entered Xi'an, Lin worked as an

The former site of Huashibian of the Northwest Bureau of the CPC Central Committee in Yan'an.

administrator in the canteen catering to cadres. He was single at that time, and later married someone who had a hard life. Soon after his marriage, he died of illness, leaving no children.

Another example was Xiang Daming of the Long March Red Army, who was raising pigs outside the city in the early days of entering Xi'an. He ran back and forth every day, carrying the swill from the canteen. The Organization Department allowed him to dine with the mid-level cadres. He was afraid that others might mind his dirty clothes, so he never sat at the tables or on the stools of the canteen, but always squatted outside the canteen to eat. He remained single all his life and departed us two years later.

There were many other great comrades in the Northwest Bureau who died years ago. They worked hard for the cause of the Party and devoted all their lives to the Party. I feel sad when I think of them. In order to commemorate the 60th anniversary of the founding of the new China and their great achievements, we should put a few words here in their memory. We should always keep them in mind.

Most of the comrades in the Production Section during the Yan'an mass production movement have now passed away. On the 60th anniversary of the founding of the People's Republic of China, this article is to commemorate the memory of those who made contributions in that exceptionally difficult era.

Forever in Memory

Zhang Yuying

Born in 1932, Zhang Yuying was a native of Jiaxian, Shaanxi Province. In 1946, she was admitted to Mizhi Middle School and was later transferred to work at Yan'an University, where she was assigned to the Stenographer Department of the Northwest Bureau Secretariat of the CPC Central Committee in 1948 and served as director of the Party Committee Office of the Shaanxi Provincial Architectural Design Institute.

Editor's note: When working in the Stenographer Department of the Northwest Bureau Secretariat of the CPC Central Committee, Comrade Zhang Yuying went to multiple meetings with the leading comrades of the Northwest Bureau. She still has deep affection for these leading comrades even today. The article "Forever in Memory" is her commemoration of Secretary Xi Zhongxun.

Secretary Xi Zhongxun was my most revered revolutionary senior, an old leader, and a good secretary. He was the founder of the soviet in the Shaanxi-Gansu-Ningxia border area, and one of the leaders of the base area and the Workers and Farmers' Armed Forces in the border area. He served as Secretary of the Northwest Bureau of the CPC Central Committee for eight years after he went from Yan'an to the Northwest Bureau. He was promoted to Vice Premier of the State Council when he was transferred to the Central Committee. He was a competent, reliable assistant to Premier Zhou, but no matter how his position changed, Xi was always the great Secretary in my heart. Today, when they mention Xi, senior comrades always address him as Secretary Xi, which feels more familiar to them.

On the occasion of the 60th anniversary of the founding of the new China, I started to miss Secretary Xi even more. I was deeply impressed by his noble character, including his infinite loyalty to the Party, his integrity, his seeking truth from facts, his modesty and prudence, his solidarity and care for comrades, his adherence to principles, the way he took the overall situation into consideration, his integrity and honesty, his selflessness, and the way he avoided leftist extremes and humiliating others. He correctly implemented the Party's line, policies, and principles, putting the revolutionary interests above all else. Secretary Xi's life was a revolutionary one, a life of fighting, devoted and dedicated to the cause of the Chinese revolution, socialist construction, and Reform and Opening Up. His achievements will forever be recorded in history as an example for future generations to follow.

Secretary Xi paid special attention to the cultivation and education of cadres and the construction of the Party. After the restoration of Yan'an in 1948, preparations for the takeover in the liberation of Xi'an and the northwest provinces were carried out very intensely, especially in the expansion of the cadre team and intensification of training. Secretary Xi went to the Party school to lecture the candidates, and he paid particularly close attention to the study of the on-the-job cadres. Shortly after moving back to Yan'an, the Northwest Bureau set up a shorthand training class and a training team of the key personnel, and they brought in a large number of young people. Fortunately, I was selected from the school affiliated to Yan'an University when I was not yet 17, and I entered the shorthand training class. The training was so intense that I practiced in my spare time in the morning and evening as well. We learned both professional technology and political theory. As a result, in a short time, we young people acquired professional technology, enhanced our ideological and political theory, and were immediately assigned to the positions in need of competent people, so that we could play a good role in our respective posts. Because of the specificity of the work, the organs paid close attention to the development of the Party and League organizations. Among the ten new comrades in the shorthand training class, four of us League members had not yet joined the Party. The leaders and comrades were very concerned about our progress and training, and with strict requirements, they designated that the study documents be read within a certain time limit, and we had to report our work and study on weekends, where sincere criticism and self-criticism were held among the comrades, with our progress being confirmed and weaknesses identified. There were strict procedures for developing Party members, which had to be handled according to the Party constitution. Candidates under 18 years old could not be accepted, even if they were qualified, so the four of us did not go through the Party entry procedures until January through March 1949, because we were not old enough until then. I remember that the preparatory period was different based on our different backgrounds. It was half a year for those from poor or tenant farmers, and a year for the rest. There was a Party joining ceremony for the new Party members. Comrade Guo Enlai and I joined the Party at the same time, together with another four from other departments. On the night of March 9, 1949, the solemn oath-taking ceremony was held for six new Party members. Director Cai Ziwei presided over the meeting, and comrades from the Organization Department also attended. The meeting room was full of people, some squatting on the ground. In addition to the oath taken by the new Party members in front of the Party flag, there were also speeches made by the leaders and the representatives of the veteran Party members, to encourage the new comrades who had just joined and to outline the direction and requirements for our continuing efforts. At the oath-taking ceremony, the new Party members nominated me to speak on behalf of all. This meeting was educational for me and a lively Party lesson for other comrades who participated in it. On March 10, I attended the first League Congress of the Shaanxi-Gansu-Ningxia border area. When I put down the characters "Communist Party member" on the registration form for the first time, I was extremely excited. I will never forget it for the rest of my life.

Xi'an developed rapidly after Liberation. The five provinces in Northwestern China were each liberated in turn, and all industries were yet to develop. There were many tasks in the work, including taking over the cities of the five provinces in the region, establishing the new regime, healing the war trauma, developing production, suppressing bandits and bullies, and establishing a new, stable social order. Secretary Xi had a heavy burden, and cadres in all areas were in shortage. Xi required the training of cadres, as early as possible, to improve their working competence so as to meet the needs of development. The relevant departments soon set up secondary schools for workers and farmers, literacy training schools, and various professional and technical training seminars. The Northwest Bureau also set up Russian learning seminars and literary training seminars, and we did all the studies in our spare time. Secretary Xi spot checked and corrected the work of comrades all around. The atmosphere of learning in the institutions was very strong, presenting a vigorous, positive scene. Secretary Xi was particularly concerned about the growth of young people. Most of the comrades of the youth team (responsible for the daily life of the head of the organs) were teenagers from Yan'an who did not have much schooling or education. To nurture those young people into a workforce, the institutions sent them in batches to temporary secondary schools, which created good learning conditions for them. Everyone studied hard and achieved success. Some of them later became college professors, others engineers of state-of-the-art technology of national defense, and still others took the leading role in specific fields. All of them lived up to the expectations of the leaders.

At that time, the work at the organs was very busy and in need of labor. In order to elevate the cadres' competence in their theoretical, cultural, professional knowledge and work, the leaders of the Northwest Bureau decided to transfer more than ten department cadres to Beijing University for study, while sending the veteran cadres of workers and farmers who were not young yet poorly educated to the Northwest Party School for learning. All units actively selected cadres to participate in the study of various theories and professional technologies. This was beneficial to the recovery of production and economic construction, and it prepared a pool of cadres to be allocated to the newly opened up areas. My husband Zhang Ke and I were directly cultivated at this time. Zhang Ke was transferred to Peking Renmin University in 1950 to study, and then went to university again to study science and technology. I took part in the study of Russian in the government organ. The Russian I learned was useful in the management of the original Russian design drawings and data for Soviet experts in the 22 national defense secret projects that the Soviet Union helped build in Shaanxi. The organization also sent me to the

In 1950, Peng Dehuai (first from the right) and Xi Zhongxun (fourth from right) attended the second meeting of the Northwest Military and Political Commission.

Northwest Party School to systematically study the Party history, philosophy, and political economics, which improved my ideological theory and understanding. At the beginning of my career, I was able to work in the revolutionary family of the Northwest Bureau for seven years to gain teaching and education from Secretary Xi and the other leaders, as well as the substantial help, solidarity, and friendship of my comrades, which laid the foundation for my growth and was a memorable experience in my life.

At the beginning of Liberation, because our work was not yet in place, many of the people did not know the Party's policies and understandably had doubts. This required mobilizing all aspects of the organization to do much work in the publicity, mobilization, and organization of the masses. Secretary Xi presided over and organized a series of large-scale meetings, including the Youth Conference of Northwest China (which I attended as a representative), the Northwest Literature and Art Conference, the Northwest Women's Conference, the Northwest Religious and Ethnic Affairs Conference, the United Front Work Conference, and the Party and government Work Conference, among others. The purpose of the meetings was to share information on the current situation and policies, to assign tasks and make requirements according to different fronts, to clarify ideas and understanding, and to unite the masses to further the work. When attending the meetings, Secretary Xi listened to the representatives' speeches attentively, took notes, met wide-ranging representatives, and listened to their views and feedback. The report Xi made at the conference was vivid, realistic, logical, and inspiring. People were enlightened and encouraged when they heard it, and they were clear about the situation, tasks, policies, and guidelines, as well as the practical methods and steps. The meeting helped every representative have a better understanding and greater confidence to complete the tasks.

Northwest China was a multi-ethnic area, with outstanding religious and ethnic issues, and it was essential to do a good job in the United Front. When a religious, ethnic, or United Front conference was held, the participants were adequately representatives in all respects, involving monks, Taoists, lamas, leaders of ethnic minorities, democratic scholars, key members of the former Kuomintang, and other United Front figures. Secretary Xi paid them great respect, treated them sincerely, and explained the Party policy patiently and carefully to them. His personality won the full trust of all, and participants always expressed their keen interest and desire to follow the leadership of and work with the Party. This played a great role in stabilizing the social situation and initiating various tasks. But some comrades did not see the importance of the United Front work. Seeing the past enemy become the guest today, being well treated with high standards of courtesy, they resented it. Some even complained that "revolution at a later stage is better than earlier, and counter-revolution is the best." Secretary Xi emphasized the importance of the United Front work several times at different meetings and organized all of us to study the Party's United Front work guidelines and policies to help us realize that the implementation of the Party's United Front policy could mobilize all positive factors, unite all the forces that could be united to build a big team, and complete our great task in the new historical period. The great work of Secretary Xi in this period fully reflected his work style and leadership, his open mind, honesty, and sincerity, his extensive contact with the masses, and his excellence in unity and mobilization of all positive factors.

Secretary Xi's United Front work was affirmed and praised by Chairman Mao. In the 1946 War of Liberation, according to Chairman Mao's instructions, Xi fought for the uprising of Hu Jingduo, deputy commander of the security forces in Northern Shaanxi of the Kuomintang in Yulin. Xi understood people well and knew how to motivate them. With meticulous hard work and strong personnel, Xi finally won Hu over. On October 13 that year, Hu Jingduo led more than 5,000 officers and soldiers of the new 11th Brigade of the 86th Division of the 22nd Corps of the Kuomintang and the 9th Regiment of the security guard to hold an uprising, and they later reorganized into the 6th Division of the Democratic Alliance Army. This large-scale uprising shocked the northwest and the entire country, disrupted the enemy's deployment, weakened the enemy's might, expanded the scope of the liberated areas, enabled the army in the border region to concentrate its main force against the enemy coming from the south, and created favorable conditions for the restoration of Yan'an, with its far-reaching influence. After the liberation of the five provinces in Northwest China, the bandits of Ma Bufang in Qinghai lured Xiang Qian, head of the Nganglha tribe, to revolt. How to deal with the rebellion of the Nganglha tribe was an issue studied many times by the Standing Committee of the Northwest Bureau, led by Secretary Xi. It was a huge challenge, as it involved a mix of ethnic and religious issues. Secretary Xi worked hard and finally decided to take the policy of political persuasion as the main principle, while making military preparations. After more than two years of constant negotiations and patient work, Xiang Qian was finally persuaded and came to trust the Communist Party. This not only helped stabilize Qinghai, but also had a great impact on the work in Gansu, Sichuan, Qinghai, and Tibet. In this regard, Chairman Mao praised Xi, saying, "Zhongxun, you were truly amazing. Zhuge Liang captured Meng Huo seven times. You were more powerful than Zhuge Liang."

In October 1950, Peng Dehuai went to North Korea to command the war, and Xi Zhongxun acted as the chairman of the Northwest Military and Political Commission to preside over the work of the Party, government, and army in Northwest China.

The United Front was one of the three "magic weapons" of the Party, and Secretary Xi's personal practice reflected its power, which was well-known at that time. Facts enlightened and educated our comrades, who have turned their negative emotions and complaints into positive action, and fully realized the importance of the United Front work in terms of both practice and theory.

After the founding of the new China, the leading teams of the government organs at all levels were equipped with democratic figures and non-Party comrades. This was not for show, but to get them to work with authority and responsibility. In this respect, Secretary Xi set an example for us with his personal practice, showing his great respect for the vice Chairmen of the Northwest Military and Political Commission, such as Zhang Zhizhong, Han Zhao'e, and Geshe Sherab Gyatso. When acting as the chairman of the Northwest Military and Political Commission, Secretary Xi supported, cared for them, listened to their opinions with an open mind, empowered them, created conditions for them to work boldly, and gave full play to their role. These celebrities had great influence. Under the influence and education of Secretary Xi, the comrades realized that it was everyone's responsibility, not merely the leaders' business, to do a good job in the United Front work. With the enhanced understanding and initiative in action, we Party members and cadres truly respected the non-Party democratic people who directly led us, strove to do our assigned jobs well, asked for instructions and made reports when we had problems, and actively supported the leaders' work.

Secretary Xi was frank, approachable, and humorous, naturally drawing people around him. In the winter vacation of 1950, Zhang Ke came back from Beijing. After the Spring Festival, we got married. On the third day after our wedding celebrations, Li Bingrong, deputy director of the Administrative Department, told Zhang Ke that Secretary Xi had a chartered plane to go to Beijing for a meeting and that Zhang could go with him. Zhang Ke was very happy to be on the same plane with the Secretary, and he promptly packed and boarded the plane with Comrade Li Jiafang, who was studying with him. It was a military aircraft, with seats on both sides of the cabin, and the passengers sat facing one another. Huo Weide, Vice Governor of Gansu Province, and his wife were also on board. They were subordinates of Secretary Xi, but they talked casually like old friends, and Secretary Xi laughed heartily from time to time. Seeing Zhang Ke and Comrade Li Jiafang feeling a little restrained and uncomfortable, Secretary Xi took the initiative to ask them about their studies and school life. They soon relaxed and expressed their gratitude for the leaders' care and the organization's training, saying they would study hard to live up to the leaders' expectations.

Since there was no recording device at that time, all important meetings, speeches, and instructions of the leaders were recorded by a stenographer. There were no written scripts of speeches then, some of which included outline while others didn't, and it required that the original words be recorded exactly to keep the authenticity of history. Shorthand work was both crucial and challenging. There were only a dozen people in the Northwest Bureau who took shorthand work, and it was common for us to take Secretary Xi's car to the meeting for records because of the nature of our work. Xi always talked casually to us about our work and life. The car that Secretary Xi took would stop to pick us up when we met on the road on rainy or snowy days. The young people who worked around Secretary Xi soon felt quite at ease, as he often motivated them with some humorous remarks or jokes. With no distance between him and them, the young people were encouraged and motivated to work.

Secretary Xi was devoted to the revolutionary cause, and he had no boundaries between work and leisure time. He often worked late at night, diligently and persistently. We knew that well. Doing shorthand work, we typically did minutes for meeting during the day and transcribed and sort them out at night. Some needed to be issued as important documents or instructions the following day, so we needed to finish the work on the same day of the meeting, which usually meant staying up late at night. Deep into night, we often saw the light in Secretary Xi's office on, and we knew that he was still working too. His spirit of selflessness always inspired us.

In order to enrich the cultural life of the organs, the Northwest Bureau Club organized dances every Saturday night. Everyone actively participated. The band was composed of music-loving comrades in the organ, and Zhang Ke was one of them. The dances were effective for bringing people together. When available, Secretary Xi and other leaders came to the parties to enjoy dancing with the masses. The leaders of other units came as well. Ma Xiwu, the president of the court, was a regular. Secretary Xi was active and straightforward, and he danced well. With no specific partner, he'd dance with any female comrade who could dance. They would chat and laugh, getting along very well, with no sense of hierarchy. We all knew that the Secretary came to dance not only for relaxation, but more importantly, as a way to get to know more about the people and their real life, so as to improve the work.

Secretary Xi was very compassionate and took good care of those who made contributions to the revolution and did good deeds, as well as the comrades and martyrs who sacrificed their lives for the revolution. In the early days of liberation, an old man named Li, who lived alone, was Secretary Xi's guest. Nobody knew what he had done, but only heard that he had done good things for the revolution. Later, Mr. Li got married, and he held the wedding ceremony in the guesthouse. He was also granted the title of deputy director of the guesthouse, and he was thus properly settled for his old age. The children of the martyr Huang Ziwen, who had made great contributions to the revolution, were in the rural area. They were taken to Xi'an when Secretary Xi learned about their situation. It was arranged for his son Huang Xiaoping to attend the Baoyu Primary School, and he grew up to become a teacher. Huang's daughter, Huang Jianzhen, was unable to go to school during the war era, so she went to the nearby primary school for studies in her teens. She cherished this rare opportunity to study, and she worked hard to catch up with other students. She eventually became a national cadre.

When he was transferred to the Publicity Department of the Central Committee of Beijing, Secretary Xi heard that Li Bingrong, deputy director of the administrative department of the Northwest Bureau (an old friend from the Liangdang uprising during the underground work) was seriously ill. Xi asked Li to go to the hospital in Beijing for examination and treatment. Li along with his secretrary, doctor, and civil servant, lived in Xi's house for more than a month, which really impressed me.

Secretary Xi always put the Party's interests first. Being a man of integrity, he held onto the principles, took the overall situation into consideration, sought truth from facts, corrected mistakes promptly, implemented the Party's policies steadily and accurately, opposed left-leaning tendencies, and launched rectification properly based on facts. All this was exceptionally educational to me.

In 1952, the movements against the "three evils" and the "five evils" were carried out with great momentum. Under the leadership of the production committee, the Northwest Bureau also launched the movement against the "three evils," which referred to corruption, waste, and bureaucracy. At the beginning of the movement, we studied documents to raise our awareness. We all thought it necessary to carry out the movement against the "three evils," which could once again sound the alarm for all of us to keep a clear mind and not make mistakes in a peaceful environment, which was of far-reaching significance. We all consciously carried out inspections, identified problems, plugged loopholes, and formulated systems. Zhang Ke worked as an accountant in the Northwest Bureau. Although he was transferred to other places in 1950, he was transferred back for isolation at this time. He began to be

Xi Zhongxun reporting to the cadres of Northwest Bureau, Xi'an City, and Shaanxi Province.

Xi Zhongxun at work.

persuaded and mobilized to expose others, and was then criticized and tortured. Zhang Ke always held onto the Party's principles and to seeking truth from facts instead of making up stories, and he was finally sent to the supervision department for investigation. He was detained in prison, based on mere suspicion, not facts. The day before the meeting, the Organization Department sent someone to talk me into mobilizing Zhang Ke to report and expose the problem. Otherwise, I would be ruined. My response was, "I believe that the organization will investigate the problems clearly, and I am willing to take any investigation and test of the organization." But three months later, no one asked about Zhang Ke. It was not a personal matter, but more about being responsible for the comrades and the Party's policies. I went to Secretary Xi to report this issue. After listening to my report, he immediately called Secretary General Wu Kaizhang and instructed him to "release Zhang Ke immediately, if there are no problems." The next day, the Secretariat sent someone to pick up Zhang Ke, and director Zhao Xinmin and the comrades locked up in the guesthouse also had their freedom restored. By seeking truth from facts, adhering to principles, and correcting mistakes fairly and decisively, Secretary Xi won the support of the public and his comrades. After that, when

Secretary Xi asked about Zhang Ke's situation one day, I said that his position as Section Chief and the corresponding salary were restored and the compensations made, and he was staying in the guesthouse for dispatch. Secretary Xi said sincerely, "Don't feel burdened. Work hard." Deeply moved by the Secretary's concern and love for his comrades, I was determined to work harder to live up to the Secretary's expectations.

The correction of false cases was a profound lesson to us. The comrades who were investigated did not lose the moral character of Communist Party members, and they adhered to the principles, sought truth from facts, withstood the test, and won high praise. This was exactly the result of years of teaching by Secretary Xi and the Northwest Bureau. Secretary Xi's noble personality was imprinted in people's hearts, and no one could erase it.

History is a mirror. Secretary Xi has left a precious spiritual treasure house for future generations, and he is an example we will always learn from. I will always keep him in my memory.

On April 4, 2009, Zhang Ke and his wife Zhang Yuying.

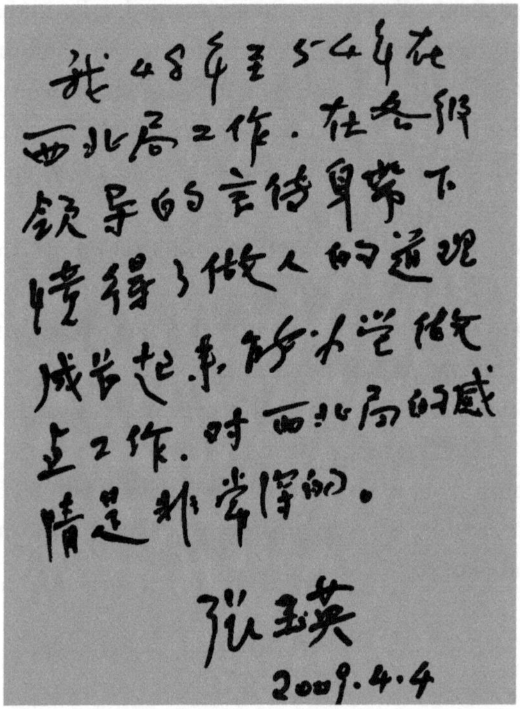

我48年至54年在
西北局工作。在各级
领导的言传身带下
懂得了做人的道理
成长起来，努力学做
好工作。对西北局的感
情是非常深的。

张玉英
2009.4.4

Comrade Zhang Yuying wrote an inscription for this book.

The Glory of the Northwest Bureau and My Soft Spot for Shaanxi

Ji Shilin

Born on December 1, 1929, Ji Shilin came from Duquan County, Hancheng. In 1947, he joined the revolution, working first as an administrative staff of the township government and as a primary school teacher, and then as the Party Branch Secretary of Duquan and Yuanzi Counties. In early 1949, he was transferred to serve as secretary of the Wangfeng district government and as the acting publicity member of the district. He served as secretary for Comrade Xie Juezai, where he was responsible for the sorting and compilation of works such as *Biography of Xie Juezai*, *Xie Juezai's Diary*, and *A Collection of Xie Juezai's Works*.

Editor's note: Although he worked for only two years in the Northwest Military and Political Commission, Ji Shilin was greatly impressed by Comrades Peng Dehuai and Xi Zhongxun, the main leaders of the Northwest Bureau. Talking about them today, he felt that everything was fresh in his memory, as if these things had happened just the day before.

The Establishment of the Northwest Military and Political Commission after Xi'an's Liberation

After the liberation of Xi'an, the Northwest Bureau was relocated there. I graduated from school in 1947, and worked for the township government beginning in February the following year. In 1949, I was selected to the Party School of the

Northwest Bureau of the Central Committee (later called the Party School of the Northwest Bureau of the Communist Party of China). At that time, the main task of the Party School of the Northwest Bureau was to train the cadres who were going to the south.

In March 1950, the Northwest Military and Political Commission was established, with Peng Dehuai serving as chairman. The cadres of the Commission were selected from the Northwest Party School, and I was sent to the Northwest Military and Political Commission in this way. At first, I was assigned to the Cadre Office of the Civil Affairs Department of the Northwest Military and Political Commission, and then transferred to the Office of the Personnel Section set by the Civil Affairs Department of the Northwest Military and Political Commission. At that time, the Minister of Civil Affairs was Wang Ziyi, who was also the Minister of the Personnel Department. The Cadre Office and the Personnel Section of Civil Affairs Ministry were mainly in charge of managing the cadres at or above the county level in the five provinces and counties in Northwest China and delivering the list of cadres.

In those days, the Northwest Bureau was located on Jianguo Road, while the Northwest Military and Political Commission was in the provincial government courtyard, also called the Xincheng courtyard. Peng Dehuai lived in the yellow building of the Xincheng courtyard and worked in the western part of the building, while Xi Zhongxun (then Secretary of the Northwest Bureau) worked in the Northwest Bureau on Jianguo Road. At that time, I would send the list of cadres to Xi Zhongxun and Peng Dehuai about once a week, and I met Xi Zhongxun once in a while. Later, I went more often and saw Xi more frequently. There were no automobiles in the streets back then, and not even a bicycle early on, so I had to walk to the Northwest Bureau.

Impressed by Xi Zhongxun

Wang Ziyi and Xi Zhongxun were together in Yan'an in their early years, so Wang often told me some information about Xi. In 1951, I was assigned to the Working Group on Land Reform, serving as leader for organizing and implementing various jobs concerning the reform. After the land reform (when the struggles against the "three evils" and the "five evils" had just ended), Wang Ziyi took me to Yan'an, specifically visiting the place where Xi Zhongxun had worked in Yan'an, to help me understand the situation.

The previous site of Guanzhong District in Malan.

The cave where Xi Zhongxun lived in Malan.

Mr. Ji Shilin (secretary of Xie Juezai) and the editor-in-chief of the book.

Wang Ziyi and Liu Zhidan came from the same county, and they were imprisoned with Liu Jingfan (Liu Zhidan's younger brother) and others during the leftist line movement. Chairman Mao sent someone to rescue them when the Red Army arrived in Yan'an. Then Wang Ziyi and Liu Zhidan worked with Xi Zhongxun in the revolution. During the Yan'an period, because Wang Ziyi and Liu Jingfan were both from Northern Shaanxi, they worked together frequently. Xi Zhongxun and Xie Juezai were leaders of the Northwest Bureau at that time, so they naturally became friends. Chairman Mao trusted Xi Zhongxun greatly, as Xi had originally guarded the South Gate (the base area at Malan at that time) and later transferred to the Suide local committee to serve as Secretary, then moved to guarding the North Gate and dealt with the Kuomintang. Xi Zhongxun was 30 years old at that time.

My first in-depth understanding of Xi Zhongxun came from the cadre meeting of the Northwest Military and Political Commission, where Xi Zhongxun and Peng Dehuai talked to the cadres of the Commission. Our first impression of Xi was that he was very courageous, determined, and straightforward about everything.

In 1952, I was transferred to Beijing and served as secretary to Comrade Xie Juezai in the Ministry of Internal Affairs of the Central People's government, and then as secretary of the Party group (appointed by the Central Organization Department). I then followed Mr. Xie to Shanghai to participate in the investigation and study of the first constitution drafting of the new regime in China. At that time, Xie was the Secretary and Minister of the Party group of the Ministry of Internal Affairs of the Central People's Government, and Wang Ziyi was the Deputy Secretary and Deputy General of the Party group. During that period, Xi Zhongxun was also in Beijing. I often went to see Secretary Xi with Wang, and I was very impressed when I met him. He talked to me in the Shaanxi dialect, saying that we were both from Shaanxi, and speaking in Shaanxi dialect rather than Mandarin made us feel closer and more relaxed. Xi always spoke to me in the Shaanxi dialect instead of Mandarin after he arrived in Beijing.

Memories of Mr. Xie's Northwest

In 1935, after the Red Army arrived in Northern Shaanxi, the Northwest Office of the central government was established. Xie Juezai served as the Minister of Internal Affairs, Secretary General, Minister of Justice, acting President of the Supreme People's Court, and finally as Chairman of the Audit Committee. During this period, he assisted and guided the improvement of grassroots political organizations in the Shaanxi-Gansu-Ningxia base area, implemented a universal, direct, equal, and anonymous election system, gave full play to the democratic rights of the people, and mobilized the initiative of the people, playing an important role in consolidating and developing the Shaanxi-Gansu-Ningxia revolutionary base.

That year, Mr. Xie met Wang Dingguo, who later became his wife. It was June, and the Number 1 and Number 4 Red Army Corps successfully met in Maogong. In Zhuokeji Town, both corps were preparing to cross the snow covered mountain. One day, Wang Dingguo and several comrades were chatting at the foot of the slopes. An old comrade walked over and said, "Young comrades, please do me a favor. We are going to cross the snow covered mountain. Please sew the two light clothes together and fill in the wool to make them into a wool coat." Wang Dingguo promised to send it back to him the next day. "My name is Xie Juezai. I live on the hillside and work in the cadres recuperation company of the Number 1 Red Army Corps," the old comrade said, introducing himself. The next day, when Wang Dingguo went to deliver the clothes, Mr. Xie greeted her from far away and took the wool coat. He said, "Thank you. You did a good job." When saying goodbye, he told her to prepare more chili to help her tolerate the cold weather.

During this time, Mr. Xie was the representative of the Lanzhou Eighth Route Army Office, and he later only remembered that the girl's surname was Wang, while Wang Dingguo remembered clearly that he was the most senior man in age in the Long March.

During the anti-Japanese war, Wang Dingguo and Xie Juezai got married when they worked together in the Lanzhou Eighth Route Army Office. From that time, from Lanzhou and Yan'an to Beijing, Wang Dingguo worked with Mr. Xie. In her mind, Mr. Xie, though more than thirty years older than her, was a comrade, a husband, and a mentor.

In 1939, as the Vice President of the Central Party School, Xie mobilized the workers to open up the wasteland and cultivate land, and he personally took part in the construction of the hall in an effort to overcome the economic difficulties they faced. When the hall was completed, Mao Zedong wrote on a large plaque the phrase, "Seeking truth from facts," for the hall. From then on, the famous saying "seeking truth from facts" spread across the anti-Japanese bases among the students of the Party school, and it was passed on from generation to generation as the ideological line and fine tradition of the CPC.

In May 1941, with the approval of the Central Committee of the CPC, the Northwest Work Committee of the CPC, and the Central Bureau of Shaanxi-Gansu-Ningxia border region were merged to establish the Northwest Bureau of the CPC Central Committee. Comrade Xie Juezai served as a member of the Standing Committee and Deputy Secretary of the Northwest Bureau, and also Secretary General of the border area government and the Secretary of the Party and League. Comrade Lin Boqu, then Vice Chairman of the border government, decided that the election laws of the Shaanxi-Gansu-Ningxia border area should be formulated under the leadership of Mr. Xie. In November 1941, Mr. Xie was elected Vice President of the Provincial Assembly at the second session of the Border Provincial Assembly.

In 1942, the Northwest Bureau of the Communist Party of China and the border government held a forum with non-Party members to discuss the government work and financial and economic issues. In order to gain insights into the opinions and suggestions of non-Party people, Lin Boqu, Party Secretary and chairman of the border government, and Jia Tuofu, Secretary General of the Northwest Bureau, organized the first symposium of non-Party members of the government of the Shaanxi-Gansu-Ningxia border area. In February 1943, Mao Zedong remarked on the report of the symposium that Xie Juezai and Jia Tuofu presented, saying that "in the future, it is advisable for the Northwest Bureau to convene a symposium every two months." Ren Bishi commented that "as for key policy subjects for the approval of the government to be implemented, opinions should be shared and exchanged prior to putting forward the proposal."

Mr. Xie worked for six years in the Northwest Working Committee of the CPC, the Central Bureau of the border area, the Northwest Bureau of the Central Committee, the border government, and the border area Provincial Assembly. He devoted his effort to the construction of the "triangular-organization" regime, and made the Shaanxi-Gansu-Ningxia border area a model for the construction of the "triangular-organization" regime in the anti-Japanese base areas and proposed to the Central Committee that the Provincial Assembly should be turned into the People's Congress, which was approved by the CPC Central Committee and Chairman Mao. Xie wrote to Mao Zedong and made suggestions on developing production and increasing the financial revenue of the border areas, and, according to Mao Zedong's proposal, Xie advanced a specific plan to improve the economy of the border areas. This period was the most difficult one in terms of the border's economic development.

With Peng Dehuai, Xi Zhongxun, and Chang Lifu

Apart from Peng Dehuai and Xi Zhongxun, Chang Lifu was the one whom I was most impressed with and worked most closely with in the Northwest Military and Political Commission. Chang Lifu, then Secretary General of the Northwest Bureau, was kind and approachable. Working with Peng Dehuai, Xi Zhongxun, and Chang Lifu, I felt like I was working in a family, in a friendly, casual way. I felt energetic at work, and I made no clear distinction between being on or off work. I worked from morning until night, often writing reports until midnight. I remember staying up all night writing reports when in the work group during the struggles against the "three evils" and the "five evils," as well as working for eighteen days without rest later in the land reform period. Even so, as long as I worked with them, I never found the tasks tiring or strenuous.

Peng Dehuai was straightforward and determined, and he always said what was on his mind. He was very polite and easy-going, frequently teasing and joking, and occasionally playing table tennis with Wang Ziyi and Chang Lifu in the Xincheng courtyard. It was fun and relaxing, and I never had any pressure working with him, as he didn't come across as a top leader.

My Soft Spot for Shaanxi

In 1982, Ma Wenrui (then Secretary of Shaanxi Provincial Party Committee and director of the Standing Committee of the People's Congress) asked Chang Lifu (then Secretary General of Shaanxi Provincial Committee) to transfer me from Beijing to Xi'an and send my Party files to the People's Congress of Shaanxi Province. That year, I was transferred to the Standing Committee of the Shaanxi Provincial People's Congress. I first worked in the editorial room of the general office, and then in the legal committee to participate in drafting and revising some national draft laws and local laws and regulations. I retired at the end of 1992.

I worked in the Northwest Bureau for more than thirty years. Recalling this glorious past, I will always bear in mind the passionate years imbued with great pain and the laughter mixed with tears.

Happy Time in the Northwest Bureau

Hao Shuhua

Hao Shuhua, a Beijing native, was assigned to the Party School of the Northwest Bureau in 1949. Her husband, Comrade Jiang Xibai, was the Secretary General and Acting President of the Northwest Bureau Party School, Standing Committee member of the Xi'an Municipal Committee of the CPC, Vice Mayor of Xi'an, and Secretary General of the municipal government.

Editor's note: In our interview, Comrade Hao Shuhua's laughter was her best comment on the days in the Northwest Bureau. We were greatly impressed and surprised by her joy in studying and working in the Northwest Bureau, as well as her nostalgia for those days. In the difficult times of extreme poverty, a young student went from Beijing to Northwest China, and her joy was quite an inspiration for us all.

By 2009, I had been in Xi'an for sixty years. My former residence, located at the corner of Dongsi, Chaoyang Gate, Beijing, has been demolished, and I have seven children, all near me in Xi'an, so now I have a deep attachment to Xi'an.

From Beijing to the Northwest

I remember that not long after I was admitted to the Renmin University of China (formerly the Revolutionary University), in order to celebrate the national liberation and establishment of the new China, North China University was founded. Later, I was assigned to North China University (where Wu Yuzhang served as President), where I studied social development history and political economics.

I think it was July 31, 1949, that North China University held a graduation ceremony, with 5,000 people attending. I remember clearly that Commander-in-Chief Zhu De said at the ceremony, "After graduation, most of you will be assigned to the south and the northwest. It is a very glorious task."

With the lack of talent in the Northwest Bureau, a group of students were selected from North China University to go to Xi'an. In this way, 1,800 students gathered together to form a northwest cadre team, singing "Go! Go! Go to the northwest, to the northwest. Go forward, for the people in the northwest are waiting." They went from Beijing to Tianjin, on to Dezhou, Shandong Province, and then to Yuci, Shanxi Province, or down the Fen River, to the south, or across Fenglingdu to the west, to Xi'an, and then to the Qinling Mountains, the Wei River Plain, the Hexi Corridor, the Helan Mountains, the Gobi Desert, and to every

June 1949, Xi Zhongxun's mobilization report at the general assembly for the battle to defend Xi'an.

The Bell Tower after the liberation of Xi'an.

point on the compass. Those students later supported countless towns in Shaanxi, Gansu, Ningxia, and Qinghai.

I came to Xi'an from Beijing in September 1949, where I was assigned to the Northwest Bureau. There were three teams at that time. I was only 19 when I arrived. I didn't even know what the northwest cadre team was. With the big team starting from Beijing, we came to Shaanxi Province through Shanxi Province. After passing Fenglingdu in Shanxi, we boarded the train. Shanxi was under Yan Xishan at that time, and he had the railway track built quite narrowly so that other trains could not enter, we had to go past Fenglingdu, then to Yuci, and then to Xi'an. At that time, I experienced the crossing of the Yellow River for the first time, when I couldn't even swim. I felt it was quite fun to sit on the boat. They were all wooden boats, with twenty people in each one. We weren't afraid at all. The trip took three months in total.

I remember that when I arrived in Xi'an, many students carried backpacks as they walked, covered with loess all over. There were more people climbing onto a few trucks. Everyone huddled together and rocked with the trucks on the bumpy road. We were excited when we neared the destination. In the end, we sang revolutionary songs with a loud voice.

Happy Life in Northwest China

Upon arriving in Xi'an, I was assigned to work in the library of the Northwest Bureau Party School, near the Little Wild Goose Tower. "The street is bumpy, the telephone is not working, and neither is the electric light." That was the scene in Xi'an when we arrived, without any exaggeration. The lights were dim. There was only one asphalt street, East Street, and the rest were cobbled roads. They were "the three typical things" the Northwest Bureau leaders told us about when we got to Xi'an.

The best store in Xi'an was the Xijing Department Store, which was on East Street. Another top hotel was the Northwest Hotel, also on East Street. Xi'an at that time was almost unimaginable compared with what it is today. If you go to Liuqing Memorial Hall to have a look at the pictures of Xi'an then, you'll see the appearance of West Street and North Street. Even so, our life was enjoyable, partly because of a sense of freshness, and partly because of the spirit of striving for a new China.

At that time, we got up every morning to study for an hour before starting to work, and we didn't feel that life was hard. The conditions were nothing like what they are today. The meals at the canteen were cooked on a big stove. The public bath house was open once a week, not every day, due to a lack of coal. But everyone enjoyed life, as we stayed together both at work and when we were off. We could go to the library to read or to the club in the Party School to play chess or carom, which kids today may not even know how to play. Back then, we often played Sifang cards as well, which was quite fun.

At that time, students in the Party School were mostly older, with fewer young or middle year students. Some teachers came from the Revolutionary University, and they mainly talked about the history of social development. Back then, colleagues were straightforward with each other and with their superiors, unlike what we see today. I was never at odds with anyone, and we were never calculating or manipulative. At that time, everyone was content and devoted to the construction of the new China.

Honestly speaking, even today, I am very nostalgic about my life at that time. Thinking back, I always feel peaceful. Everyone enjoyed the public life of working together. There was no gap between the director or the headmaster and the subordinates. Everyone was happy, as if there was nothing to trouble them. You see how quickly time flies. All this happened sixty years ago, but the memory of those days in the Northwest Bureau is as fresh as if it were yesterday.

Recalling Secretary Xi Zhongxun

When I was working in the Party School of the Northwest Bureau, Secretary Xi Zhongxun served as the President, and the other President was Gao Yangyun. At that time, the primary job of the Party School was to run study sessions for the training of the secretaries and county leaders from the five provinces and regions of Northwestern China, generally for three months. Secretary Xi Zhongxun would come to the school to attend the activities at the opening ceremony, graduation ceremony, and the anniversary of the founding day of the Party, so we met him frequently at that time.

Secretary Xi Zhongxun was very approachable. He came to the Party School without bringing special guards. He listened attentively to whatever we talked about. He often asked us if "the meals were good enough," showing concern about our daily lives. As we all came from out of town, he asked us if we were used to the local diet. We were straightforward, telling him that all the dishes were too spicy for us. It was true that many of the students couldn't get used to the food here, as the chili in Xi'an was really hot.

Leaders like Peng Dehuai and Wang Shitai often came to the Party School as well. They lived on Jianguo Road in Yongcun at that time. Now, the place is converted into the Provincial Committee's residential area. I found the veteran cadres like Peng Dehuai, Xi Zhongxun, and Wang Shitai very easy-going and casual. We felt quite at ease when going to their homes, partly because we were young and didn't know much about formalities. It's not as easy to meet a leader now, and we might feel a bit more awkward. After all, times are different, and it would be hard to say which is better. People like Premier Wen are like the leaders back then, approachable and easy-going, and the general public likes to talk directly and casually with them.

Secretary Xi Zhongxun was very practical and realistic, and he talked in a way we liked, because he didn't talk big or in a rigidly formal way. Instead, all he said was the plain, homely truth. At that time, Secretary Xi was quite busy, because the northwest was in a state of disorder, and the ethnic problems were particularly prominent. For example, there were troublemakers in the Hui ethnic street, and spies attacked the Little Wild Goose Tower Party School at night. However, the guard platoon in the Party School caught the spies, and the situation was better by around 1952.

Shortly after that, nearly a year later, the regional office was closed, and the Party School was transferred to the provincial management and turned into the Party

School of the Provincial Party Committee. Secretary Xi Zhongxun was transferred to other positions. We were not quite clear about the procedures of the handover, but it took a long time, three or four years. My husband Jiang Xibai worked in the Party School during the period of the Northwest Bureau, and he was transferred to the Provincial Party Committee after the relocation of the regional authority. He got along well with Secretary Xi Zhongxun and used to go to his home quite often.

Secretary Xi Zhongxun's Skillful Handling of the Qinghai Rebellion

Secretary Xi Zhongxun had his own way of settling ethnic problems. When he was in the Northwest Bureau, we all knew that he had done a lot of work in dealing with Xiang Qian's surrender in Qinghai. Although we only heard about it, we all thought that Secretary Xi Zhongxun was really strategic.

The situation in the northwest was more complicated back then. For economic, political, historical, religious, and other reasons, around the time of the founding of the new China, there were many rebellions, large and small, in Qinghai and Xinjiang, and bandits were rampant, which disturbed or destroyed the peace and stability of the northwestern region. Secretary Xi conducted many investigations and studies. At that time, his main approach to the ethnic contradictions was to win over the upper class and religious people of all ethnic groups, and then to mobilize them. And it could never be reversed. The effort made to secure Xiang Qian's surrender is an example of Secretary Xi's settling of various ethnic problems in Northwestern China.

Back then, Xiang Qian, Tan Chengxiang, commander of the 100th Division of Ma Bufang, Ma Chengxian, commander of the 14th Brigade of the Cavalry, and other counter revolutionary forces organized the second "anti-Communist corps to save the nation" and launched a rebellion. The attempt to win over Xiang Qian started from the end of 1949, and it was not until July 1952 that the work succeeded. In this process, Xi Zhongxun instructed the head of the Qinghai United Front Work Department, patriotic religious personages, and others to hold peace talks with Xiang Qian on as many as seventeen occasions.

The struggle was directly led by Secretary Xi Zhongxun, who pointed out to the leaders of Qinghai on multiple occasions that a proper solution to the Nganglha rebellion was of great importance not only to the settlement of the relationship between the Nganglha Tibetan compatriots, but also to our Party's foothold in other Tibetan areas and various ethnic minority areas in Qinghai to establish the people's regime for further work, impacting even the Gansu, Sichuan, and Kham Tibetan areas and Tibet. Xi instructed that we needed to adhere to the principle of giving priority to political struggle on the basis of full military preparations, being very cautious to adopt a policy of persistent persuasion and great tolerance toward Xiang Qian.

In response to some people's eagerness for military suppression, Secretary Xi Zhongxun telegraphed Secretary Zhang Zhongliang of the Qinghai Provincial Party Committee, clarifying that we should "never be belligerent and never launch military operations at will. Only when political attempts fail can we consider military suppression."

In August 1950, Xiang Qian agreed to surrender and came to Xining, expressing his deep regret to the government. However, upon returning to Nganglha, he broke his promise. In September 1951, after the eighth political attempt to win over Xiang Qian failed, many people were filled with righteous indignation. At the meeting of representatives of all ethnic groups and all walks of life in Qinghai Province, the representatives proposed that the government should send troops to Nganglha to suppress him.

At that time, Secretary Xi Zhongxun immediately called the leaders of Qinghai and instructed that it was politically advantageous for us to strive for a peaceful solution to the issue of Nganglha, that we should ask in detail the advice of Geshe Sherab Gyatso, the staff of the Panchen Lama, and other Tibetan people on how to win over Xiang Qian, and that we should sum up whether all the attempts we had made for persuasion were actually appropriate, so that we could do the work more efficiently. Back then, we were concerned about the impact of the issue on the broader Tibetan areas. If we failed to do a good job by means of military power, we would have more trouble when the rebels went to other regions. And even if we won the military battle, we would have greater problems, as it would exert a potential negative impact on the work of other Tibetan areas. If we did not do enough political work, we needed to be prepared both politically and militarily.

The anti-rebel battle was launched in May 1952. After three days into the battle, Xiang Qian was hiding in the Nanhujiagai Forest in Tongren County. Some said that it was impossible and of little value to win Xiang Qian over. Xi Zhongxun continued to call Zhang Zhongliang, Secretary of the Qinghai Provincial Party Committee, conveying that as long as we did a good job in the work of the Nganglha region and avoided making mistakes, there was a great possibility of winning over Xiang Qian, and that we should immediately send Han and Tibetan ethnic personnel whom Xiang Qian trusted to convince him that we would be responsible to the end if he surrendered, and that if Xiang Qian came back to express his intention, whether sincere or not, we should treat him honestly and cordially and move him with soft power.

Later, when meeting in Lanzhou in August 1952, feeling guilty, Xiang Qian clasped Secretary Xi Zhongxun's hand, bowed, and confessed his wrongdoings, offering his white hada to Secretary Xi. With tears in his eyes, he raised his glass to Secretary Xi as a token of gratitude.

With sincerity and kindness, Secretary Xi Zhongxun closely analyzed and studied the formation and existence of the social status, role, and influence of the upper class of ethnic minorities in their own regions, as well as the edification effect of political activities and attitudes and religious beliefs on their ideology and moral character under the political system of past dynasties. With his vision, open-mindedness, and compassion, Secretary Xi worked closely with the upper class of various ethnic minorities to allow them to feel that the Communist Party of China was truly the savior of their nation, thus successfully settling the ethnic issues in Qinghai. Later, his efforts were praised by Chairman Mao and became a widespread story.

Unforgettable Spare Time

When I was in the Northwest Bureau, I used to dance in my spare time. There was no other entertainment, and I didn't see many movies. The ideal place for dancing was the Xijing Guest House. At the corner of Jiefang Road, it was the best place for entertainment in Xi'an. Of course, it was the leaders of the Northwest Bureau and the city who went there. At that time, Wang Shitai of the Northwest Administrative Committee, his wife Wei Nai, Liu Qing, and his wife Ma Wei often went to dances.

Secretary Xi Zhongxun also often attended the dances on Saturday. Sometimes, he came to the Party school to dance. He spoke freely to us students. He didn't seem to be such a big leader then. When he came, more than a dozen of us were there, and we competed to dance with him. During one dance, he sometimes changed two or three partners, and he would dance with everyone. Secretary Xi Zhongxun danced very well. I also danced with him, doing a simple three-step or four-step dance. When I was dancing, he asked me, "How's your food? How's your study of social development history?" I had come to study social development history at that time. Secretary Xi lived in the Northwest Bureau then. Sometimes we went to his

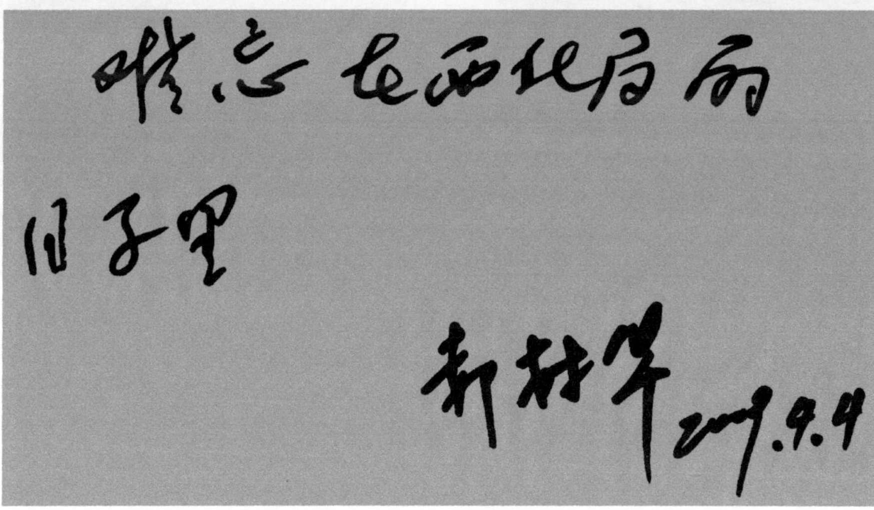

On April 4, 2009, Comrade Hao Shuhua wrote an inscription for this book.

house for leisure activities, which were all very casual. We often went to his house to eat. At that time, the Party School also had a culture and work room for drama rehearsal, and several comrades like Ge Ruiwu, Liu Guozhu, Wang Bingxin, Wen Chao, and Gao Bingcheng loved playing basketball.

In those days, the environment was hard, but the harmonious relationship between people made the hardship become happiness. The windows of the dance hall were often open in winter, because everyone wore cotton padded clothes when they danced. At the end of the dance, Yangko was often played until the dance ended.

Now, it has been more than half a century, but I yearn for those days when I recall them. That time in the Northwest Bureau was a happy time, and I have never forgotten it.

Missing the Days in the Northwest Bureau

Peng Shouren

Peng Shouren was born in Pucheng, Shaanxi Province in 1928. In 1949, he was assigned to work in the Northwest Bureau of the CPC Central Committee, transferring from Yan'an University. He worked first in the general affairs section and later in the administrative department of the general office of the Northwest Bureau. After the regional revocation in April 1954, he served as the Deputy Secretary of the Party Committee of the Northwest Architectural Design Institute.

Editor's note: Comrade Peng Shouren was the last veteran we interviewed in Xi'an. He was modest and approachable, which impressed us deeply. Recalling the days when he worked in the Northwest Bureau, the elderly fellow always stressed that it was a great honor to be in the Northwest Bureau, and he cherished those days very much, the feeling of which was very touching.

I went to Yaoshan Middle School in Pucheng County, Shaanxi Province. When I was about to graduate, I joined the revolution. At that time, there was the Hancheng branch of Yan'an University. After finishing middle school, I went to Yan'an University. When I graduated from university, I was assigned to the Northwest Bureau. Xi'an had just been liberated then. I went from Pucheng to Hancheng, and then from Hancheng to Xi'an. I remember entering the Northwest Bureau in September 1949. At that time, I was very young, just 21 years old, and I was very happy to work in the Northwest Bureau, because in my mind, it was a Party organ and a place that many young people yearned for.

Missing the Days in the Northwest Bureau

At first, I worked in the general affairs section of the Northwest Bureau, and later I was transferred to the administrative department of the general office to work as a secretary. Because we were engaged in specific work, we contacted many leaders. At that time, the secretary was Xi Zhongxun, the organization minister was Ma Wenrui, the publicity minister was Zhang Jiafu, and the secretary general was Wu Kaizhang. In the first year of the Northwest Bureau, I didn't see Secretary Xi very much. Later, because of the requirements of my work, I often met him. My first impression of Secretary Xi Zhongxun was that he was approachable.

At that time, we all respected these leaders of the Northwest Bureau, because they were revolutionaries of the older generation. When we went to deliver documents or handle the arrangements assigned by the leaders, their attitude was very calm, and they didn't have the air of a leader at all. So we young people were very relaxed and happy in the Northwest Bureau. At that time, the Northwest Bureau carried out some major activities, and we were mainly responsible for liaison work. For example, when the Northwest Bureau was going to open a standing committee, Secretary Xi Zhongxun needed to pick up some people for a meeting, and we were responsible for the work of picking them up and seeing them off. At that time, the most important meetings were held in the Xijing Guest House and the Zhiyuan Hotel, and later in the People's Mansion. Because of my work, I had a lot of contact with Chang Lifu, the Secretary General of the administrative committee at that time.

In addition to the specific operation of some affairs, we were also responsible for leading the preparations for the inspection, mainly the work contact before the inspection. At first, these jobs were in the Secretariat, and later they were assigned to the administrative office, so I had many opportunities to go out with the leaders. I remember that when Comrade Wang Lu went to work as a secretary in Xinjiang, I took the first stop and contacted him without any trouble, sent him to Xinjiang, and then came back by plane. It was my first flight.

The administrative department was also responsible for holding a memorial service after Comrade Cao Liru died in an accident. Comrade Cao Liru was on his way to Xinjiang to become president, but before that, he and Ma Wenrui went to Shangtong to visit. On his way back, he had an accident and was taken to the Guangren Hospital. Later, he died from serious injuries. The memorial service was arranged by the administrative department of the Northwest Bureau. And of course, I ran errands in preparation.

A group photo of the comrades in the Secretary's office in 1954, with Peng Shouren (back row, right).

When I was in the Northwest Bureau, my leisure time was relatively rich. The Northwest Bureau had a club. Sorkin and Wang Huayi were the backbone of the club, both of whom were from North China University. They were responsible for the entertainment activities of the Northwest Bureau, organizing us to watch movies and attend parties. Almost all the films were domestic, but there were also a small number of Soviet films. In addition, there were dances every week, which I attended. Secretary Xi Zhongxun and the others danced well. Sometimes they were in the club, sometimes in the auditorium of the municipal government, and sometimes in the Xijing Guest House, where Chiang Kai-shek was detained during the Xi'an Incident. At that time, the Northwest Bureau was full of people every weekend. Jia Tuofu and Li Qiming were all activists then.

Although I didn't work in the Northwest Bureau for a long time, I won't forget those days as long as I live. Looking back now, I miss the Northwest Bureau, especially the old leaders.

In 1952, Secretary of the Northwest Bureau Xi Zhongxun took a group photo with Jia Tuofu (right) in Xi'an.

Secretary Xi Zhongxun's Great Contributions to the Work of Land Reform

In 1950, near the end of the year, I went to Lantian County, Shaanxi Province, to participate in two phases of land reform, with each phase lasting three months. Land reform was basically the normal situation at that time, but there was also a deviation of expansion. In this process, Secretary Xi Zhongxun played a great role in rectifying the deviation.

The background of land reform was that since the winter of 1947, the Liberation Army was scoring more victories by the day, so the land reform movement was booming in all the liberated areas. During the movement, in the old Soviet region

On April 6, 2009, the editor in chief (left) was with Shao Jiyao (second from left) and Mr. and Mrs. Peng Shouren.

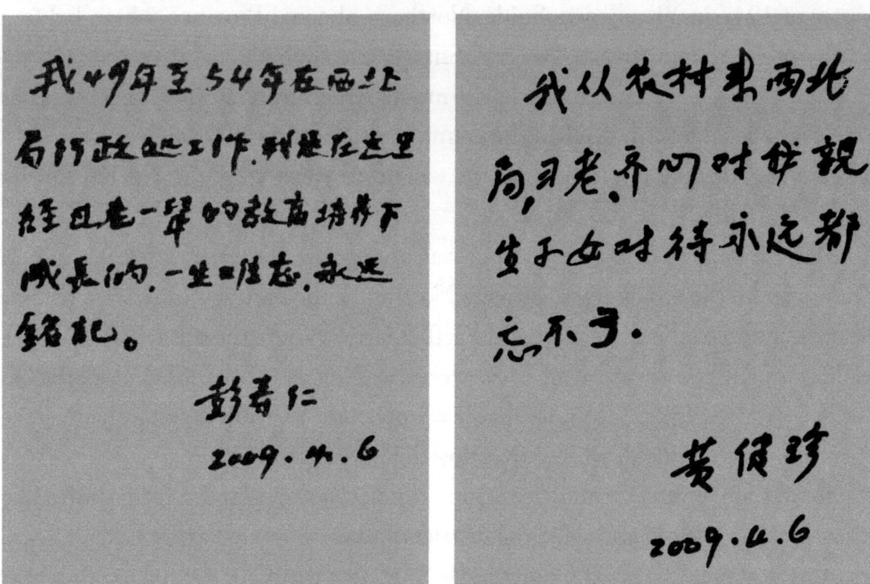

我49年至54年在西北局行政处工作，我是在这里经过老一辈的教育培养下成长的，一生难忘，永远铭记。

彭寿仁
2009.4.6

我从农村来西北局，习老、齐心对我亲生子女对待永远都忘不了。

黄健珍
2009.4.6

Comrade Peng Shouren and his wife Huang Jianzhen wrote an inscription for this book.

and the semi-old area from the anti-Japanese war, there was much extreme behavior, which was not very different from the new area. I heard at that time that in order to correct the deviation in the reform, Secretary Xi addressed letters to the Party Central Committee and Chairman Mao on three major issues, such as "land reform in the old liberated areas," "overcoming the leftist sentiment" in land reform, and "carrying out land reform in three different areas," and he put forward his own candid opposition to the leftist tendency.

In a letter to the Central Committee, Secretary Xi Zhongxun said that if we hoped to make the old district conform to the general situation, we would make mistakes. He cited many violations of policies in the Suide District of the Shaanxi, Gansu, and Ningxia border area. "This leftist mood is not originally from the masses, but has been brought by the cadres," he said to Mao Zedong, who said that he fully agreed to the opinions put forward by Comrade Xi at that time. He suggested that Xi closely guide the land reform work in various districts and counties in accordance with these opinions. It was necessary to make the land reform work in the border areas follow the right path and make fewer mistakes. It was also suggested that the old bases in Northern China should be observed.

Soon after that, Xi Zhongxun wrote another report on the issue of the Yihe Conference and sent it to Mao Zedong. The Yihe Conference was held in the winter of 1947 in Yihe Town, Suide, Northern Shaanxi Province, which led to a whirlwind in Shanxi, Gansu, Ningxia, Shanxi, and Suibian.

"The Yihe Conference had a leftist mood, which resulted in a far left bias as soon as the local reform reached the countryside," Secretary Xi said very seriously. "I think that if there is a leftist bias, we will destroy everything in less than half a month," he added.

Mao Zedong quickly gave his approval, saying, "I fully agree with Comrade Xi Zhongxun. In the old liberated areas of Northern and Central China, we must pay close attention to the correction of the leftist error. Where there is leftist error, the leading organs can correct it in a few weeks, as long as it is handled properly. Do not delay for too long. Also note that it is important to avoid making the mistake of coming to a standstill while correcting the leftist errors."

Soon, the Central Committee issued the decision on land reform drafted by Zhou Enlai in the old and semi-old districts and the liberated areas. Later, I heard that one day in early 1952, Comrade Bo Yibo went to Chairman Mao to report on his work. Chairman Mao was reading the report from Xi Zhongxun from Xi'an on the plenary meeting of the Northwest Bureau Committee of the CPC

Central Committee. The report mainly focused on land reform and United Front and ethnic work in Northwestern China. It was rich in content and brilliant in discussion. The report provided a blueprint for the central leadership in various work on the political reform of the Northwestern China, which had vast territory, numerous nationalities, and a complex society. Mao Zedong was very pleased. He asked Bo Yibo, "What do you say about Comrade Xi Zhongxun?" Bo replied, "He's young, but he's done a good job." In Yan'an, Bo Yibo heard Mao Zedong praise Xi Zhongxun, saying, "He's very capable in his work." From this, it is evident that Secretary Xi Zhongxun made a great contribution to the reform nationwide. In the work of the Northwest Bureau in the period of national economic restoration after the War of Liberation and the founding of the new China, Secretary Xi demonstrated the meaning of seeking truth from facts.

Accompanying the Leader to See a Doctor and Staying in Secretary Xi's House

I remember that in 1953, Secretary Xi had just transferred to Beijing. When Li Bingrong, director of the administrative department of the Northwest Bureau, became seriously ill but failed to be treated in Xi'an, the organization sent me, a doctor, and a colleague to accompany him to Beijing to see a doctor there. Because of the unfamiliar life in Beijing, the place that had been arranged for us to stay was far from the hospital, and it was very inconvenient to go back and forth. Learning this, Secretary Xi was determined to receive us in his home. During this period, we were carefully cared for by Secretary Xi and his wife, Comrade Qi Xin. We stayed for almost a month in total before we returned to Xi'an. Thinking of it now, I see that Secretary Xi was very concerned and caring for the cadres, and he and Comrade Qi Xin were very good to us. She had given birth to Jin Ping not long before, and she had two daughters, Qiaoqiao and An'an, who had been born in Northern Shaanxi and Xi'an. In this situation, Secretary Xi's family still took care of us, and we were very touched.

I worked in the Northwest Bureau from September 1949 to April 1954, then transferred to the Northwest Design Institute. I have been away from the Northwest Bureau for more than fifty years, but I feel I'm still there. I am very happy to hear that you are writing about the Northwest Bureau. I am glad to tell you about the events from that time. I hope this precious history can be preserved, as it will be instructive for future generations.

Accompanying Comrade Zhang Desheng in the Northwest Bureau

Wang Zhiqiang

Born in April 1931, Wang Zhiqiang was from Shenxian, Hebei Province. He joined the Communist Party of China in February 1947, and the People's Liberation Army of China in January 1948. From January 1948 to September 1949, he served as a guard member and platoon commander in the Third Battalion of the 22nd Regiment of the Fifth Independent Brigade, and as a guard member of the Gansu Provincial Committee and the Northwest Bureau from October 1949 to March 1953. From April 1953 to October 1965, he served as security officer, administrative secretary, driver, and personnel administrator of the Shaanxi Provincial Committee. From October 1955 to September 1991, he served as deputy chief of the administrative department and deputy department level coordinator and department level investigator in the Shaanxi Guest House. He left office in September 1991.

Editor's note: This manuscript was sent to us by Comrade Wang Zhiqiang, the author of this article, when he learned that we were compiling the book *In the Days of the Northwest Bureau*, in which he mainly recalls the details of his and Comrade Zhang Desheng's days in the Northwest Bureau.

During the War of Liberation, Comrade Zhang Desheng served as deputy director of the Northwest Field Corps, the Northwest Field Army, and the Political Department of the First Field Army of the People's Liberation Army of China. His tasks mainly focused on the local work.

When setting out to Xifu in 1948, Comrade Zhang Desheng followed Commander Peng Dehuai in action. The moment the troops arrived at the station, he set about looking for the comrades of the underground Party to gain some understanding of the local situation, make arrangement for the work, instruct the underground comrades to make use of the legitimate organizations of the Kuomintang as much as possible, and mobilize the masses to support our troops.

From the autumn of 1948 to the spring of 1949, our army launched the Chenghe Campaign, the Libei Campaign, the Yongfeng Campaign in Pucheng, and the Spring Attack, taking most parts of Weibei. During this period, Comrade Zhang Desheng personally presided over the mass meeting, went to the open field to publicize our Party's policies, and sometimes talked to the farmers individually.

After the liberation of Xi'an on May 20, 1949, Comrade Zhang Desheng stayed in the courtyard of the former provincial grain tax office of the Kuomintang in Xihuamen. Comrade Zhang directly led the working regiment of the army. Most of the cadres in the working regiment were locals transferred from the old districts who then worked as local leaders in the new districts.

In July 1949, after the Battle of Fumei, the main force of the First Field Army continued to march westward. In Pingliang, Comrade Sun Zuobin of the Political Department of the First Field Army often held activities with Zhang Desheng. When I arrived in Lanzhou, I learned that they were the main leaders of the newly established Gansu Provincial Party Committee, with Zhang serving as Secretary and Sun as Deputy Secretary. Zhang Desheng was also the first deputy director of the Lanzhou Military Control Commission. After the establishment of the Gansu Provincial People's Government, he served as the second vice chairman and political commissar of the Gansu military region. He had a great deal of work to do, and he worked very hard. He stayed in the office until two or three o'clock in the morning almost every day. One day, when he had just gone to bed, I saw the sign of the electric bell fall down, so I ran to his room and saw him sitting on the bed with his hands on his stomach. I immediately asked Comrade Meng Funan to come, and then went to get a doctor. When the doctor came, Zhang said he had a stomachache. After taking some medicine, he presided over the Provincial Party Committee meeting as usual the next day. He often went around doing investigations. He had been to the mountain areas in Longnan, the alpine nomadic areas in Gannan, the Gobi Desert in the Hexi Corridor, and the deserts at the junction of Gansu and Xinjiang. He went to the homes of Tibetan, Hui, and Mongolian herdsmen to ask about their lives. Once on a trip to Xiahe, Comrade

Xi Zhongxun (second from right) and Zhang Desheng (third from right) in Lishan, Xi'an.

Zhang Desheng and Ma Hongbin, third vice chairman of the Provincial People's Government were in the same car. Ma was of Hui ethnicity, and a general in the uprising. They sat in the car and discussed how to do well serving the Hui people in Linxia. When they got to Xiahe, Huang Zhengqing was waiting there. Huang was a Tibetan, also a general in the uprising. They went to the Labrang Temple together, where they held a forum with people from all walks of life concerning the work of the Tibetan people and in Tibetan areas.

In the first half of 1954, Comrade Zhang Desheng was transferred to serve as head of the United Front Work Department of the Northwest Bureau of the CPC Central Committee. In the second half of 1954, he took over from Pan Zili to serve as first Secretary of the Shaanxi Provincial Party Committee. When Comrade Zhang Desheng came to work in Shaanxi, it was the period in which work was being done for the socialist transformation of agriculture. He often told us that farmers had been private owners for thousands of years. Now, they voluntarily used their land, livestock, and farm tools to participate in agricultural production cooperatives. This was a great event, and it was the result of the long-term persistence of the Communist Party of China and Chairman Mao in educating the farmers. It was important to love and protect farmers' socialist enthusiasm and deal with various problems of agricultural cooperatives, especially economic problems. He went to the agricultural cooperatives many times to make specific investigations, called on cadres of districts and townships and leading cadres of prefectures and counties for discussion, and went back to the province to discuss with leading comrades of the relevant departments to formulate specific measures. Some of them issued documents, and some published newspapers. I didn't know much about those specific policies, but I was deeply impressed by Comrade Zhang Desheng's serious, conscientious style of implementing them.

Comrade Zhang Desheng was an honest man, both in what he said and did. In 1958, a director of an advanced agricultural cooperative went to Beijing for a meeting. Before he went to the meeting, Comrade Zhang Desheng told him that the yield of wheat per *mu* in our area had reached over a thousand *jin*, which was quite good. Upon arriving in Beijing, he said we should be realistic and not exaggerate or promise what we were unable to do. When the comrade arrived in Beijing, he failed to stand the pressure of "high-yield talks" at the meeting, and instead made big promises that were published in the newspaper. Comrade Zhang Desheng was extremely dissatisfied when he read it. When that comrade returned and went to the People's Mansion to see him, Zhang asked what had happened and warned repeatedly that what had been said couldn't be taken back, but we should never do that again.

Comrade Zhang Desheng respected the people on the front line of clothing production. When Comrade Zhao Mengtao, a textile worker, was hospitalized in the army hospital for treatment, Comrade Zheng went to the hospital one day to visit her. Holding Zhao Mengtao's hand, Zhang bent over and said softly, "You are a shining example for textile workers. I'm visiting you on behalf of the Provincial Party Committee and the provincial government to express our sincere greetings to you. All the comrades hope you will recover soon and return to the front line of production." At that time, Comrade Zhao Mengtao was quite seriously ill, but she sat up, clasped Comrade Zhang Desheng's hand tightly, and said tearfully that she was very thankful to the Party and Chairman Mao, and to the Provincial Party Committee and the provincial government for their concern. She added that she would work with the doctors in the treatment of the disease. On his way back, Comrade Zhang Desheng said that Comrade Zhao Mengtao was a worker of the new times, armed with Mao Zedong Thought and a noble communist spirit, and that everyone should learn from Comrade Zhao. Later, Comrade Zhang wrote a special article on this issue and published it in the *Shaanxi Daily*, calling on the people throughout the province to learn from Comrade Zhao Mengtao.

Comrade Zhang Desheng also cared about the surviving family members of the martyrs. Once he went to the township in Hanzhong, and in the company of the head of the United Front Department of the County Committee, he visited the widow of a martyr, who was unfortunately not at home, as she had gone to Chenggu. Comrade Zhang Desheng did not forget this matter when he arrived in Chenggu, and he went to visit her. Comrade Zhang told us that the husband of the woman was an important cadre of the Red Army. Her family was actually an underground organ of our Party. Most of the comrades who worked underground in Hanzhong, including him, had stayed in her home and been cared for and covered by her. Comrade Zhang Desheng told us that the victory of the revolution was brought about by countless martyrs at the cost of their lives. We who survived should not forget the martyrs, nor their relatives, but should help them arrange the production, life, and study of those who remained.

Comrade Zhang Desheng had a high sense of revolutionary alertness. On an afternoon in January 1955, when Comrade Zhang Desheng visited Comrade Yang Mingxuan, former vice chairman of the Northwest Administrative Committee, who was about to work in the Central Committee of the Democratic League, Comrade Duan Mingfa and I went along with him. When we arrived, Mr. Yang was receiving a visitor in the reception room. Seeing Comrade Zhang Desheng, Yang introduced the visitor as Li Wanming from Ankang. Duan Mingfa and I saw them chatting, and then we went out to talk with Comrade Wang Tianmin, the old guard of Mr. Yang. After a while, Li Wanming came out. He, dressed in an old army cotton suit, hobbled a little. Comrade Wang Tianmin told us that this man introduced him as the chief of staff and commander when he came. After a while, Comrade Zhang Desheng came out of the reception room. Upon returning to Yongcun, Zhang asked me to call Lanzhou and talk to Liao Hansheng, political commissar of the military region. I told Liao that Comrade Zhang Desheng said, "There is a man named Li Wanming, who claims to be the chief of staff of the 12th Army and commander of the 35th Division. He's going to Lanzhou to discuss important military affairs on the order of the Central Military Commission. In Xi'an, he introduced himself to vice chairman Yang Mingxuan and went for a visit. I just came back from Mr. Yang's place. Yang said he didn't know this person. Mr. Yang and I both found that there was a lot of inconsistency in what he said. We wonder if the military region will hold any important meetings soon." Liao replied that there were no such meetings planned, saying that Li could be a fraud. Comrade Zhang Desheng had formulated a rough idea in his mind, and he immediately invited several comrades to discuss the matter, then reported it to the public security department. After an investigation, a major political fraud was exposed. This was the sensational Li Wanming Case, known across the country in the 1950s. Lao She, a well-known playwright, wrote a play entitled *Looking to Chang'an in the West*, which criticized Li Wanming, the political liar, and uncovered the busy bureaucrats who lost their vigilance in the face of victory.

Comrade Zhang Desheng's honest style had a strong influence on me. When he first visited Gansu, some Tibetan leaders went to see him, and they often gave him some valuable ingredients for Chinese medicine, such as antlers and musk, and even some silver coins. He first announced the Party's policy and politely rejected the gifts, but when he was pressed to accept, he asked me and his driver Gao Zhicheng to send it to the administrative department of the general office for public use. A cadre from the Xi'an Glass Factory came to see Comrade Zhang Desheng, who was out on business. Upon leaving, the man left some local honey he had brought from his hometown. Comrade Zhang Desheng came back and criticized the civil servant who had accepted the honey and asked me to take it back to the man. In early 1963, life was still hard. Comrade Zhang Desheng, as Second Secretary of the Northwest Bureau of the CPC Central Committee and first Secretary of the Shaanxi Provincial Committee of the CPC, was given two bags of noodle flour by the administrative department of the general office of the Northwest Bureau as his portion, but he didn't keep it for himself. Instead, he handed it over to the canteen for public use. One year, a guest from Macao was supposed to be entertained at the office's expense. Comrade Zhang Desheng knew him when they were young, and thus invited him to have a typical local meal at home, which saved the public money.

Comrade Zhang Desheng was strict with the people around him and very concerned about them and their political maturity. I was not well educated, but with his arrangement, I studied in the provincial cultural cadre school for three years. After graduation, I was sent to the administrative department of the Provincial Party Committee to learn driving and car repairs for more than a year before I returned to serve as his administrative secretary.

In July 1964, Comrade Zhang Desheng was admitted to the Beijing Hospital for an examination, and the Central Health Care Bureau was responsible for organizing expert consultation. Director Fu Lianzhang and other experts agreed that he needed to have an exploratory laparotomy. As a result, Fu found there were tumors of various sizes in his belly. A walnut-sized section taken out for examination was identified as adenocarcinoma. There was a lot of fluid in his abdomen, so 200 ml was taken out, and cancer fighting drugs were used. His heart, lungs, liver, and gall bladder were closely examined. There was a 10 cm lump in the gall bladder, and two 10 cm lumps on both sides of the colon. The experts said it was in the late phase, and Zhang would live for at most two months. When I heard this, it was like I had suddenly been struck by a bolt of lightning. I was so sad that I couldn't stop crying. After his abdomen was closed, Comrade Zhang Desheng woke up and said, "Please tell me the truth and report to the Central Committee. I'm going back to Shaanxi. I can't spend time in a hospital bed. Please report to the Central Committee and ask them to send someone to take over my work."

At that time, Comrade Liu Lantao, the first Secretary of the Northwest Bureau of the CPC Central Committee, was having a meeting in Beijing. He reported Comrade Zhang Desheng's illness and request to the Central Committee. Secretary Liu Lantao came to the hospital to see Comrade Zhang Desheng. He said, "Chairman Mao, Chairman Liu, Comrade Zhou Enlai, and Comrade Deng Xiaoping are very concerned about your illness. Please take good care of yourself. The Central Committee has agreed to your request."

Two weeks after the operation, Comrade Zhang Desheng flew back to Xi'an and stayed in the Provincial People's Hospital. On the same day, he proposed that a meeting of the Standing Committee of the Provincial Party Committee be held, which was not done, due to the dissuasion of other comrades. After a few days' rest, he held two consecutive meetings in the conference room in the southern part of the provincial hospital. First, at the meeting of the Standing Committee of the Provincial Party Committee, he said, "In our team there are comrades from other places and comrades who have worked here for many years. Comrades from out of town have work experience from other places, and local comrades have local work experience. We need to learn from each other, draw upon each other's strong points, unite with each other, work together, and do a good job in Shaanxi." The medical staff cared for and respected him very much. Head Nurse Hong went and asked him to rest. He said, "Time is running out," so he talked for three and a half hours. The next day, a meeting of secretaries of the prefectural Party committee was held, and he spoke for another three hours. Later, Comrade Zhang moved to the First Affiliated Hospital of Xi'an Medical College for treatment, which lasted about twenty days. One day, he told the doctor he had stomachache, and it was unbearably painful. The doctors held a meeting to discuss matters, and they did one more surgery. His condition worsened each day until he could not eat anymore. He merely stayed in bed and relied on infusions and blood transfusions to sustain his life. During the Spring Festival in 1965, his family made six small dumplings for him. He just chewed a little, then spat them out. His wife, Comrade Wang Wen, came to him, and he said, "After my death, please donate my body for medical study, and it is unstoppable. Don't make any requests on the organization." He said this many times to all the relatives visiting him. When Comrade Zhang Desheng was seriously ill, many comrades wanted to visit him. I was afraid that it would affect his treatment, so I intended to politely reject the request. He said, "Please get them here. I don't have much time left." When Comrade Liu Guosheng came to see him, he took Comrade Liu's hand and said, "I'm sorry." Liu said, "It's not your fault."

During the period when Comrade Zhang Desheng was seriously ill, the medical staff worked hard to save his life, but it was all in vain. At 6:00 p.m. on March 4, 1965, the disease took his life. Shaanxi lost a good Secretary of the Provincial Party Committee, and I lost a good mentor. He said goodbye to us forever, but his revolutionary spirit remains alive in my heart.

Going to North Shaanxi with My Parents

WANG XIAOMIN

Wang Xiaomin, Zhang Desheng's daughter, was born in 1939 in the 115th Division of the Eighth Route Army, in Yunyang Town, Jingyang County, Shaanxi Province. In 1946, she was transferred from Yan'an with other family members of the staff of the Northwest Bureau of the Central Committee of the Communist Party of China, and then moved to Shanxi Province to the east of the Yellow River. She graduated from the Fourth Military Medical University in 1967 and worked for two years in Laos, helping on the front line of the war resisting US aggression. In 1989 and 1994, she worked first as deputy chief doctor, then as chief doctor. She retired in 2000 and was at the technical level 5 (deputy military level) of the civilian cadres of the army.

Editor's note: As a girl of only seven or eight years old, what was the Northwest Bureau like in Wang's eyes? What impression did the leaders she knew leave on her? In this article, Comrade Zhang Desheng's daughter, Wang Xiaomin, introduces us the days of the Northwest Bureau from a unique perspective.

When it comes to the Northwest Bureau, many old predecessors harbor great affection for it. As a child of seven or eight, I felt the same, and perhaps my affection was even greater.

My father, Zhang Desheng, from Yulin, Shaanxi Province participated in the revolution in the early years, and he traveled to Shaanxi, Gansu, Ningxia, and Qinghai provinces, where he engaged in the underground work of the Party and participated in the Long March in Northern Sichuan. He served as Secretary of

Xi Zhongxun with Ma Mingfang.

the Shaanxi Provincial Committee and the local committee of Guanzhong from 1941, and was Secretary General of the Northwest Bureau of the CPC Central Committee and head of the United Front Department from 1905. I was born in Yunyang Town, Jingyang County, Shaanxi Province, which was in the rear of the 115th Division of the Eighth Route Army. Since the age of three or four, I was traveling to and fro in Yan'an, Zhaojin, Malan, Yunyang, and other revolutionary bases with my father and mother, Wang Wen, who participated in the revolution in the 1930s. Sometimes in the daytime and sometimes at night, my parents sat on horseback, carrying me. After winter 1942, my mother was assigned by her superiors to study in the Second Party School of the Central Committee, and she stayed in Yan'an. I went to Yan'an Luoshanji Kindergarten, and I became pals with Xi Zhengning (Gongping, son of Xi Zhongxun), Ma Xiaowen (son of Ma Wenrui), and Wang Jiankai (son of Wang Feng), and we remained good friends when we grew up. I was always timid. I remember once when my mother went to pick me up from my kindergarten, one of the teachers said I could not speak. My mother was worried that I would be mute if I couldn't talk at the age of three. But when I got home, I started talking right away. During Chinese New Year, my parents took me to Chairman Mao's house to send New Year's greetings. I took the initiative to say hello to Uncle Xi and Aunt Qi Xin, and they were both fond of me. I still remember in the yard in front of the entrance of the Wangjiaping kiln,

Uncle Xi Zhongxun, Li Zhuoran, Ma Mingfang, and other comrades often chatted together after dinner. Sometimes they joked, and held each other up from the back and put them down to entertain us. Everyone laughed. The scene, the atmosphere of solidarity and friendship, and the revolutionary optimism remain fresh in my memory even after more than half a century.

I was almost seven years old when I went to the primary school near the new market in Yan'an. Sadly, I fell ill shortly afterwards, and when I went back to school after I had recovered, Hu Zongnan sent 34 brigades of about 250,000 soldiers to attack the Shaanxi-Gansu-Ningxia border area, and the Central Committee decided to evacuate Yan'an. My father, then Secretary General of the Northwest Bureau, was appointed Deputy Director of the Political Department of the Northwest Field Corps and sent to the front line. My mother (then a cadre of Northwest Bureau City Work Department, and she had a high fever in those days) and I were transferred with the Northwest Bureau and the Northwest Bureau family team. The children were placed in baskets on both sides of the camel's back, and the adults sat on the camel's back. After a few days of traveling, we arrived at a village and stopped at the wheat field. The adults went to the village for a meal. I accompanied my mother and some of the men to stay and look after the luggage (and many Northwest Bureau file boxes). Before long, an enemy plane suddenly came, shooting with its machine gun and bombing the area. At that critical moment, none of the camels ran around, and none reared. In the second round of bombing, several camels reared, and all of them reared when the third bombing came. I was tied in a pit and protected by one of the men. Mother stayed with the file boxes, which she counted as more important than her life. The bombing did not hurt us at all, and the documents remained intact.

For some reason, I didn't have a basket to sit in for the next few days. As a seven-year-old girl, I ran along with the adults. Once the team turned at a bend in the mountain path, and we couldn't see them, so we ran down the mountain, but we still couldn't find them. We then turned back and went up the mountain again. Looking ahead, we saw that the team had already reached the end of the bend of the mountain, so we rushed there immediately, and then we managed to catch up. On another occasion, when we were marching at night, we were separated from the troops. We did not know which road they had taken at several intersections. It was dark at night, and we could not ignite our torch, so we had to grope along the way. When there was no way to go, I saw a cigarette end that had not been put out. I immediately cried out, "Uncle, look!" We guessed that the team had taken this road and had not gotten far yet. We followed the road and soon caught up with the team. Another time, while climbing a very steep hillside, a woman in front of the line suddenly jumped off the camel and yelled, "There were enemies in the mountains." My mother and several women and men then discussed and concluded that the route we had taken was decided on by the Northwest Bureau, so there should be no problem and we should keep going into the mountains. Later, I heard that some of the family members who returned to the foot of the mountain were tricked by a spy and fell into the enemy's trap.

Later, the family members were basically scattered in Bao'an County (now Zhidan County) near the Northwest Bureau farm. My mother and I, and Aunt Chen Yin with her daughter, and Gougou (Yang Yanwu), Uncle Yang Zhengmin's daughter, stayed in Bailing Village near Antiaoling. Aunt Sun Ming and her three children and Uncle Li Zhuoran's wife and her son stayed in another village not far away. The two women dressed up as local women and wore their hair in a bun, but they were too fair-skinned to be taken as local farmers. My mother thought of finding a place to hide in the opposite mountains, in case the enemy attacked suddenly, so she took me down to the foot of the slope. It was beautiful in the valley, with clear spring water and verdant trees. We had planned to go up the opposite mountain, but failed to find the way. There were weeds, thorny shrubs, wild boars, and wolves in the mountains, so we did not dare to go up but had to go back.

Before long, it was said that the PLA troops were coming. We children cheered, and the adults rushed to share our joy. Xiaowen, Gougou, and I stood by the road and saw a huge military procession. For days, we watched soldiers carrying backpacks and guns and leading mules and horses loaded with weapons and cannons pass by. We saw the hope of victory, and we were too excited to sleep at night. A few days later, my mother and Aunt Chen Yin took us to the Northwest Bureau headquarters. On the way there, we encountered enemy planes firing. We hid by the side of the road and finally got to our destination. We were just in time for our meal. Lin Boqu served white rice to us children, and we wolfed it down without touching any of the dishes, as the rice was so delicious. This meal still remains fresh in my memory.

After the army's retreat from Yulin, according to the requirements of the Central Military Commission, the Northwest Field Army rested in the Suimi area. In order to ensure the safety of the rear organs and further disturb the enemy to force Hu Zongnan to make more mistakes in his command, General Peng ordered the Northwest Bureau of the Central Committee and the rear organs to move from Jiaxian to the east side of the Yellow River, taking some radio stations across the river and sending part of the troops to pretend to move. We went to

Songjiachuan, Wubao County, and we children went to school. Someone compiled a literacy textbook, but after a few days, the enemy planes suddenly attacked. The next afternoon, according to the party arrangement, all the family members got on several large boats. In my childhood memory, many people were busy at that time, but everyone got on the boat in an orderly manner. The animals loaded with boxes also got on the boat, and the boats went toward the opposite bank. When we reached the middle of the Yellow River, gunfire was heard everywhere in Chuankou, and the enemy planes flew low, throwing bombast at us and setting off a meter-high spray. (We later learned that the enemy mistook the Northwest Bureau and the rear organ family team for the main force of our army). The adults told us not to panic when the enemy came after us. As we spoke, the light on the opposite mountain was lit as a signal. Only when we arrived in Shanxi did we settle down temporarily. Soon, my mother and several women went to participate in the land reform, and we children gathered together to sleep on a big kang. Fuping was very naughty then, often ducking under the quilt to tickle our feet to make everyone get up and play with him.

Soon, some of us children were sent to the Baoyu Primary School to study at the foot of the mountain. Since then, Gong Ping, Xiaowen, and I become classmates. On April 21, 1948, the exciting news of Yan'an's restoration came. The students were very excited, and we rushed to spread the news that we could go home. Soon after, my father sent the driver Uncle Wu to take us back to Yan'an with a mule and a horse. (Because I was a little younger than the other children who were studying in the Northwest Bureau at that time, if I went back to Yan'an with my schoolmates, my father would be worried). After two days of hair-raising transfers, I returned to Yan'an on a bright, starry night, after being away for about four hundred days. I will never forget the pleasure I felt at seeing both sides of the mountain brightly lit.

There was another thing that impressed me greatly. In 1948, Uncle Xi Zhongxun went to the front line for a meeting. He was very good with kids, and he wanted to take me to see my father. My mother was worried about Uncle Xi's busy schedule during wartime and about me adding to his burden, so she didn't want to let me go. I really wanted to see my father, whom I hadn't seen for a year, so Uncle Xi insisted on taking me with him. I was very happy to go with him on the jeep. Uncle Xi talked to me all the way, asking me if I was happy when I could see my father soon. I was relaxed, no longer nervous or scared. When we went past Huanglong, where a battle just ended, we saw a red flag flying on the top of a hill and smelled smoke in the air. We soon arrived at the destination and met my father, whom I had missed day and night. At that time, he was the Deputy Director of the Political Department of the First Field Army. My father held me tightly, with tears in his eyes. In the evening, the military performing art troupe put on a performance. The first program was *Liu Hulan*, which was said to be performed by Liu Hulan's younger sister. The second was *The Battle on Wazi Street*. A real gun (without bullets) was used for the performance, and it was very loud. My father took me to the first row, and the sound was even louder. I was scared and rushed straight into his arms. He then had to take me out of the audience. Back at home, he criticized me severely, telling me that I should cherish the life that countless martyrs had given their lives for and that I should learn from them. The next day, I was brave enough to finish watching the show, and I was greatly educated. My father praised me, saying I was a good child. Just then, when a war journalist offered to take photos for me and my father, and he agreed. He squatted, putting his right arm around me. It was a precious moment captured in a photo to be forever treasured, as it was taken in a specific war environment when our army had launched a counterattack on all fronts before the dawn of the revolutionary victory.

Having returned to Yan'an from Shanxi, everything was settled, and I started my schooling in second grade at the Yan'an Number 1 Baoyu Primary School. My father continued to work in two roles, as head of the United Front Department of the Northwest Bureau and Deputy Director of the Political Department of the First Field Army. He remained in the frontline to preside over the local and political work of the Northwest Field Army in the Battles of Yichuan and Wazi Street. Then he participated in the command of the battles of Xifu, Chenghe, and Libei, and in the liberation of Xi'an. After the liberation of Xi'an, my father went westward with the army to liberate Lanzhou. On July 26, 1949, he was appointed Secretary of Gansu Provincial Committee of the CPC (with Sun Zuobin serving as Deputy Secretary). In 1954, he returned to the Northwest Bureau as the head of the United Front Department. In 1960, when the Northwest Bureau was reestablished, he was appointed Second Secretary of the Northwest Bureau. He worked hard in this post, fought to the very end for the cause he had long been dedicated to, and drew a perfect end to his revolutionary life.

In the war era, I was born in the Shaanxi-Gansu border area. In my childhood, I moved around with the Northwest Bureau in Shanxi and Shaanxi provinces. From the restoration of Yan'an to the liberation of Xi'an, nothing would have been possible without the Northwest Bureau. Our family and the Northwest Bureau had an unbreakable tie.

Deep Affection for the Xi Family

WANG QIUYING

Wang Qiuying, from Meixian, Baoji, worked in the Taibai Brewery. Her grandfather's family had strong ties with Xi Zhongxun, who was Special Commissioner of the Shaanxi-Gansu border region during the revolutionary war.

Editor's note: Wang Qiuying, an ordinary citizen in Meixian, Baoji, was still working in the local factory when we got to her place. She came back from the factory in a hurry when she heard that we had arrived. In her humble home, she told us about her family's long-time friendship with the Xi family.

Family Ties

My grandfather's mother, that is, my great grandmother, once saved Mr. Xi. From that time, our family forged an inseparable bond with the Xi family.

I heard all about it from my grandfather. Sometime around October 1933, underground intelligence passed the news that the enemy had sent a large force to besiege Zhaojin. At that time, Mr. Xi was a member of the special committee of the Shaanxi-Gansu border region and Secretary of the Military Commission. At that time, the special committee of the border region was located in Zhaojin, Yao County. Mr. Xi took the information from the underground network to Liu Zhidan and Gao Gang for consultation, and they immediately called a high-level military meeting to discuss how to hold over through the difficult period.

The final conclusion at the meeting was that we should not simply defend our territory and build up our government, but should also carry out guerrilla warfare,

In 1933, Xi Zhongxun participated in and presided over a joint meeting of the Shaanxi-Gansu Border Special Committee and the Red Army in Chenjiapo. Pictured is the former site of the Chenjiapo Conference.

expand the border areas, and expand our team. Because so many troops and cadres were crowded in this small area of a hundred *li*, it was difficult for the masses to survive. Further, if the enemy encircled them from all sides, it would be difficult to break through, so it was necessary to take one team out to expand our teams and the base areas, eliminate the enemy in guerrilla warfare, and rebuild the 26th Red Army. Finally, Mr. Xi suggested that Liu Zhidan be appointed deputy commander in chief and chief of staff, and that Wang Taiji lead the Red Army to the north. The border area was to be guarded by the special committee led by Mr. Xi, using a strategy described as "advancing and retreating according to the enemy's movement, and striking and pursuing the exhausted enemy when they're on the run" to handle the enemy.

Mr. Xi had made the decision to leave himself in the most dangerous place. Shortly after the meeting, the troops left Zhaojin and went north. Along the foot of Ziwuling Mountain, the team went past Malanchuan, Qiutou in Zhengning County, Jiuxian and Panke in Ningxian, traveling day and night. Along the way, the scenery was spectacular on those fine autumn days, and the mountain was covered in red leaves. However, no one was in the mood to enjoy the view. They all wanted to launch a surprise attack on the enemy at Heshui County. On October 10, Sun

Youren, head of the Kuomintang garrison at Xunyi County, received a telegram from Xi'an. The Kuomintang had learned that some Red Army troops were going north from Zhaojin, and they ordered the regiment to besiege Zhaojin and capture Xi Zhongxun, Zhang Xiushan, Wu Daifeng, Zhou Dongzhi, and others.

Sun Youren ordered the troops to attack Zhaojin on October 13, along with more than 1,000 people from the civilian troops of nine counties. When Mr. Xi received the news, he immediately went to discuss countermeasures with Zhang Xiushan, Wu Daifeng, and others. Finally, it was decided that Zhang Xiushan and others would lead the troops to break through the encirclement, and Mr. Xi would stay behind as backup. On October 15, the enemy was only 15 *li* away from Zhaojin, Xuejiazhai. The fire was raging, and the enemy launched a fierce attack. Our position was submerged in a sea of fire. Zhang Xiushan occupied the key spot, and he gave the enemy a severe beating, resulting in countless casualties on their side, but they kept regrouping, and the encirclement got smaller and smaller.

On October 16, the Red Army began to break through. After observing the terrain, Mr. Xi selected the breakthrough point at a cliff three *zhang* tall to the east of the stockade. The Red Army sent soldiers down the cliff with hemp ropes, then went three miles down the ditch and entered the dense forest. Finally, only Mr. Xi was left on the edge of the cliff, since he had insisted on putting himself in the rear. The enemy never expected the Red Army to break through in that spot. They went into the stockade, found no one there, and started to search all around. Mr. Xi stood at the cliff and looked at the mountains, tied the hemp rope to a small tree on the edge of the cliff, and then slipped off the cliff. Just then, a man from the Yao County civil corps came to the cliff and recognized Mr. Xi. He shouted, "Xi Zhongxun! Come and catch Xi Zhongxun!" He shot at Mr. Xi and hit his leg, injuring him. At the moment, Mr. Xi didn't feel the pain, but ran down the gully. When a group of enemy soldiers came to the edge of the cliff, Xi had already run into the forest. Suddenly, he tripped and fell. He felt the pain in his leg then, and realized he was injured. He heard the enemy on the cliff shout, "Go down and catch Xi Zhongxun!" Suddenly, someone lifted him from behind. He turned and found it was the chairman of the Revolutionary Committee, Zhou Dongzhi. Zhou pulled Mr. Xi up and put him on his back. Zhou was so strong that he ran five *li* on the mountain path with Xi on his back. When they came to a farmer's house, the family immediately helped Mr. Xi into the cave the minute they recognized him. Xuejiazhai was temporarily occupied by the enemy. That farmer's family was my great grandmother's.

Shortly after Mr. Xi came to my great grandmother's home, someone ran in, panicked, and said, "Chief, I heard that Chairman Zhou Dongzhi was killed by the enemy, along with Wang Mantang and Wang Wanliang."

"Oh dear!" Xi Zhongxun was extremely sad. He said tearfully, "Zhou Dongzhi is a good comrade. His application to join the Party is here with me. It hasn't yet been approved."

The man continued to tell Xi that "the enemy stayed in the village and seized villagers, torturing them and trying to extract information about Communist Party members or Red Army guerrilla team members. They started to burn, kill, and rob, and do all sorts of bad things. Even the cooking pots we left behind were smashed into pieces."

At this time, my grandfather came back and said, "Several Kuomintang civil corps in Qiangou are coming this way. They are shouting about searching the houses one by one."

"You should move now," my great grandmother told Mr. Xi. On hearing this, Xi immediately jumped off the kang and prepared to go into the forest behind the village.

After Xi went to hide, my great grandmother put his military uniform into the kang. Later, when the Kuomintang army got to the house, they hit one of her sons

In 1932, after the failure of Liangdang Mutiny, led by Xi Zhongxun, he hid in the Yaowang Cave outside the west gate of Changwu County. The cave pictured here is where Xi Zhongxun hid.

and broke three of his ribs, and another son was ill and bedridden, but she still didn't say a word about Mr. Xi. In this way, she saved him. When the KMT left, she did not dare to let Mr. Xi come home immediately, but instead hid him in a cave for months, secretly taking food to him at night. Xi was very kind. When they went to deliver his meals, they needed to use a password. Usually, my grandfather first made sure no one else was nearby, then he imitated the meow of a cat. Mr. Xi knew that was the signal that my grandpa was delivering the meal. When Xi gave a similar response, my grandfather would take the meal over. At that time, he often took steamed buns and egg soup to Mr. Xi, who gratefully told my grandfather many times, "Your life is hard enough, but you've given me all the buns and egg soup. I feel so bad about that."

In fact, it was not easy to hide him for three months. The KMT troops were constantly searching. Later, when Mr. Xi moved to my great grandmother's home to recover, he was particularly fond of the noodles my great grandmother cooked.

When Xi recovered, he enlisted my grandfather's younger brother, the youngest son in the army. My granduncle served in the cavalry regiment and was later killed on the battlefield, after which he was ratified as a martyr. When Mr. Xi later came to see my great grandmother, he told her that her son had followed him in the revolution and died with honor, and that now he would be her son and take her as his godmother.

Later, when Mr. Xi came to Shaanxi, he said he would come to see his godmother. The road was all rough dirt road. It happened to rain, and the car could not pass. He had to turn back half way to deal with other businesses. Later, Mr. Xi took my great grandmother to Beijing, planning to take care of her to the end, but she was not used to the life there and decided to come back.

Visiting the Xi Family in Beijing

My grandfather was a couple of years older than Mr. Xi, and he has passed away now. When he was alive, he went to Mr. Xi and asked him for a favor on behalf of a fellow villager. At that time, a man in the village had joined the army, but he didn't fight much in the later years of the war. As his family was poor and faced many difficulties, my grandfather asked Mr. Xi if the man could be categorized as a military family member so he could enjoy the state benefits. Mr. Xi coordinated matters and addressed the problem.

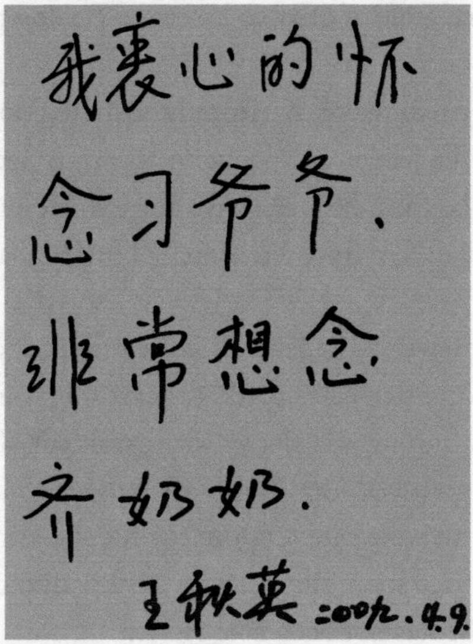
我衷心的怀
念习爷爷，
非常想念
齐奶奶。
王秋英 2009.4.9.

On April 9, 2009, Comrade Wang Qiuying wrote an inscription for this book.

When I was young, my grandfather took me to Mr. Xi's place. I only remember that in 1982 or 1983, I often heard Mr. Xi's name on TV, following that of Wan Li. It was during that time that my grandfather took me to visit him.

When we got to Mr. Xi's place in Beijing, he received us warmly. We were very happy to see him. At that time, he was working, so he asked the guards to buy tickets for us to visit places of interest. My grandfather and I stayed for twenty days, and we had a close bond with the Xi family.

In 1982, I was very young. Mr. Xi liked to eat fermented tofu. My grandfather sent it to him from time to time. Mr. Xi had a granddaughter named Nannan. When I was in my second year of junior high school, I went to Beijing. Mr. Xi asked me to accompany Nannan to school. I knew how to ride a bicycle, but I didn't dare to ride where it was crowded, nor did I dare to share a bike by taking a passenger.

In 1989, my grandfather passed away. When I went to Beijing on business, I visited Mr. Xi's place. Mr. Xi gave me a fan with the inscription that read, *For Wang Zhizhou's Granddaughter Shiying* (I used to be called Wang Shiying, because I was known to be practical). *Study and work hard and make more contributions to our country*. Mr. Xi didn't put his name on the fan. Instead, Granny Qi Xin did. In 1991, when I was at work, I wrote a letter to the couple. Granny Qi Xin invited me to go and stay for a couple of days, so I went to Beijing to stay at Mr. Xi's place for a while.

During the 2008 earthquake, Xi Jinping visited Baoji and went to Taibai County. At that time, the leader in Baoji who accompanied Xi Jinping to inspect the work happened to be from Meixian. At a meal, Xi Jinping asked him, "Where are you from?" He replied, "I'm from Meixian." Xi Jinping said, "Oh, I have a friend in Meixian."

Now, I work in a brewery. The leaders and workers at all levels say that I am practical. Granny Qi Xin often calls to ask if everything is fine. I reply, "It's all fine. We're all very well." Xi Jinping was elected vice president of the state last year, and I wrote a letter to congratulate him. Right after the earthquake, I called Granny Qi Xin to report that we were safe. On the phone, she said that she would come to Xi'an and visit my place soon. But because of her advanced age, it was not easy for her to come, and she has not been able to visit.

I am greatly pleased when I think of the days with Mr. Xi and Granny Qi Xin. Even as a major leader, Mr. Xi never put on airs. He treated us like his own children, with particularly close attention and care. I'll always remember Mr. Xi and Granny Qi Xin.

Part II

Years in Writing

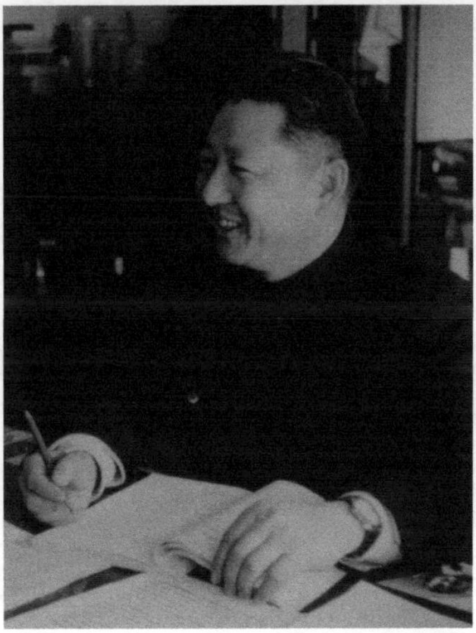

A Year in the Northwest Military and Political Commission: Commemorating Comrade Peng Dehuai's 90th Birthday[1]

CHANG LIFU AND JI YELI

Chang Lifu was born in May 1912 in Mizhi, Shaanxi Province. He joined the Communist Youth League of China in 1926, and he was transferred to the Communist Party of China in 1928. He once served as Secretary of the Mizhi County CPC Committee, Secretary of the North Shaanxi Special Committee of the Communist Youth League, and Deputy Director of the Grain Bureau of the Shaanxi-Gansu-Ningxia Border Region. After the founding of the new China, he served as Secretary General of the Northwest Military and Political Commission, Deputy Secretary General of the State Council, member of the Northwest Bureau of the CPC Central Committee, head of the United Front Department, member of the Standing Committee, secretary general and head of the United Front Department of the Shaanxi Provincial Party Committee, vice chairman of the Fourth CPPCC Shaanxi Provincial Committee, and vice chairman of the Fifth NPC Standing Committee.

Ji Yeli was born in February 1917 in Mizhi, Shaanxi Province, and was also called Ji Yegu. Ji joined the Communist Party of China in February 1937 and served as a member of the Standing Committee of the Central Party School, Deputy Director of the Political Department of the Party School, Deputy Director of the Finance Committee of the Northeast Bureau, Deputy Director of the General Office of the Northwest Military and Political Commission, and Director of the General Office of the Northwest Administrative Commission.

1. This article was originally published in *People's Daily* on October 27, 1988.

On March 16, 1947, Comrade Peng Dehuai was ordered to take command of the Northwest People's Liberation Army at the time of crisis, to fight against the invasion of the bandit army in the Shaanxi-Gansu-Ningxia border region, and to fight in the northwest battlefield for three years, which required arduous effort. On November 12, 1949, the PLA entered Xinjiang, and the liberation of Northwestern China was completed. General Peng triumphantly returned to Xi'an on December 25, where he served as the chairman of the Northwest Military and Political Commission. After disembarking from the plane, General Peng made a speech, calling on the entire army and all the people to live frugally and work hard to make the northwest take on a new look. His remarks had a profound impact on the army and the people in the northwest.

During General Peng's year of work in the Northwest Military and Political Commission, under the leadership of the Party and government at all levels, the people of all ethnic groups in the northwest united and worked hard, and they achieved great things on all fronts. With the cooperation of the masses, the People's Liberation Army eliminated more than 58,000 bandits and stabilized the social order. In order to reduce the burden on the people, the army launched a large-scale

Peng Dehuai leading the attack on Yichuan City.

production campaign, which opened up more than 1.6 million *mu* of wasteland for farming that year. Nearly 100,000 troops took part in the construction of the Tianbao and Tianlan Railway projects. In that year, 40% and 50% of the earthworks were completed, creating a miraculous feat. General Peng personally inspected the Qinghai-Tibet Highway, organized the military construction, specifically solved difficult problems in the construction, and ensured the smooth progress of the project. On the economic front, we implemented the central government's policy of unified leadership and management of the financial and economic work, steadily restored and developed production, and stabilized prices. Industry and commerce began to improve, and market transactions became more active. Coal, electric power, petroleum, and other energy industries all recovered and developed modestly. General Peng paid special attention to the recovery of the Yumen Oil Well, listened to Comrade Kang Shi'en's reports on several occasions, solved the problems in the recovery of production, and generally mobilized the masses to help themselves in production. General Peng pointed out that the Party, government, and army cadres and soldiers should save one or two grains a day to help the people in the disaster-hit areas and help many areas facing serious famine to tide themselves over. In rural areas, the policies of rent reduction and interest reduction, specified sower and reaper, free lending, and prosperity with production were implemented, which stabilized and improved the motivation of a vast number of farmers. The sown area of grain returned to pre-war levels, the grain in summer and autumn increased by 9.5% over the previous year, the area of cotton expanded beyond pre-war levels, and animal husbandry stabilized to its original level. Land reform was completed in 26 counties of old and semi-old districts, with a population of more than 1.7 million, the feudal system of exploitation was completely eliminated, and the people's democratic political power at all levels was established and improved. In the vast new areas, people's governments at and above the county level were first established from top to bottom. On the basis of mobilizing the masses to suppress bandits, fight hegemony, organize farmer associations, destroy the Baojia system, overthrow the landlord class's power, and establish the dominant force of farmers, the administrative power of the districts and townships was transformed from bottom to top. In the winter of 1950, land reform began in 51 counties in Shaanxi, Gansu, and Ningxia, involving a population of 7.6 million. Northwest China was a multi-ethnic region, and this sort of region began to implement regional autonomy. Nearly ten thousand ethnic minority cadres were trained within a year. A new relationship of unity, mutual assistance, support, and cooperation among all ethnic groups began to be established, which laid a good foundation for the construction

The founding meeting of the Northwest Army Political Committee in 1950, with Peng Dehuai (fourth left) serving as Chairman and Xi Zhongxun and Zhang Zhizhong as Vice Chairmen.

of a new northwest. In the short span of a year, General Peng put dedicated effort into these great achievements in the vast northwestern region.

General Peng paid special attention to the requirement that all cadres should establish the idea of serving the people wholeheartedly, carry forward the style of integrity, and oppose all adverse tendencies. After entering the city, some cadres began to feel overly proud of their achievements, and they grew content with what they had in hand, so that the phenomenon of extravagance and waste emerged, and a few people began to take the evil path of corruption. In response to this situation, General Peng promptly sounded the alarm. He first proposed that streamlining and efficiency should be taken as the principle for the establishment and staffing of government organs. It was important to guard against the establishment of excessive bureaucracy and increased staffing. The original plan of the Party and government system in the region was to cut off half of the 4,000 people. He then proposed that all government organs must strictly carry out a clean, simple, revolutionary work style when serving the people. It was important to strictly punish corruption, prohibit waste, and oppose bureaucracy that was separated from the masses. Every government staff was to take this article as a motto and faithfully implement it. He pointed out that extravagance and waste were in essence a resistance to the industrious, thrifty founding of the people, and self-centeredness was resistance to unified leadership, and he reminded that engaging in guerrilla habits was to resist the legal laws and regulations. All government staff was to unconditionally, resolutely, and thoroughly implement the central decision, direction, and policy and never allow a situation of "no order, no prohibitions, going one's own way, and an independent kingdom." If anyone dared to waste, corrupt, or violate the laws and regulations, they were to be severely punished by Party discipline and state law. Wrongdoings would not be tolerated, and there would be no mercy that would lead to damaging the interests of the people and undermining the reputation and prestige of the Party. Peng called on all organs to immediately launch a campaign against adverse tendencies, saying that each organ should conduct thorough inspection, and every staff member should regard the criticism and self-examination as both their right and their obligation. From March to May 1950, the Party, government, army, people's organs, and groups at the first level of the northwest region launched a general anti-adverse tendency movement. The local governments and provinces responded positively, and the phenomenon of extravagance, corruption, and violation of laws and disciplines was significantly reduced, and positive effect on educating cadres, improvement of work style, and promotion of work development was achieved.

General Peng was even stricter with himself. During his tenure as chairman of the Northwest Military and Political Commission, he lived in two rooms connected by a corridor on the east side of the conference room of the Xincheng Building. His office, reception, dining, and quarters were all combined in this facility. The leading comrades of the Northwest Bureau intended to give him a bigger house, but he resolutely rejected it. We planned to refit a toilet in the room, but he rejected that idea too. He was over 50 years old at the time, and his long, hard military life made him suffer from gastroenteropathy. During the time he was seriously ill, he could only take a little food, and the doctor prescribed water with protein powder and fruit juice. Even his wife, Comrade Pu Anxiu, can not make the decision on buying or not because General Peng would not take it. In the end, it was the Secretary General who bought the fruit juice and persuaded him to take it under the instruction of the doctor. At that time, the ration system had been implemented, and he often asked the director of general affairs to measure the meals so as not to exceed the standard. He wore a military uniform all year round, a thin one in summer and a cotton one in winter. He was like an ordinary soldier, and no one could tell that he was a commander and an extraordinary leader.

However, after the Lushan Meeting, some people said that "Peng Dehuai's frugal life is a false front." After this sort of unkind words came out, even Mr. Zhang Zhizhong disagreed. He said, "How could he disguise it throughout his whole life?"

Less than a year earlier in the Northwest Military and Political Commission, under the command of the Central Committee, General Peng led the Chinese Volunteer Army across the Yalu River and shouldered the arduous, glorious historical task of resisting US aggression, aiding Korea, and defending the motherland. During the war in North Korea, General Peng was still very concerned about the work in the northwest region. He often sent messages when he had a chance. His instructions and hopes played an encouraging, promoting role in leading the cadres and the work in Northwestern China.

Xi Zhongxun's Work in the Northwest Bureau[1]

Ma Wenrui

Ma Wenrui was born in November 1912 in Zizhou, Shaanxi Province. He joined the Communist Youth League of China in 1926, and became a member of the Communist Party of China in 1928. Before the founding of the new China, he served as Secretary of the Suide County Party Committee of the Communist Youth League, Secretary of the Anding County Party Committee of the Communist Party of China, member of the Special Committee of the Northern Shaanxi of the Communist Youth League, Secretary General of the Northern Shaanxi Provincial Party Committee of the Communist Party of China, Secretary of the Longdong Prefectural Party Committee, member of the Standing Committee of the Northwest Bureau of the CPC Central Committee, Director of the Organization Department, and in other roles and capacities. After the founding of the new China, he served as Deputy Secretary of the Northwest Bureau, Minister of Labor, First Secretary of the Shaanxi Provincial Party Committee, and Vice Chairman of the Sixth and Seventh CPPCC National Committee. He passed away in Beijing in 2004.

1. This article was originally published in *Xi Zhongxun's Revolutionary Career*, CPC History Press, China Literature and History Press, 2002.

In January 1948, a group photo in Yangjiagou, Mizhi, from left: Jia Tuofu, Gao Gang, Gao Changjiu, Gan Siqi, Shi Zhe, He Long, Lin Boqu, Ma Mingfang, Yang Mingxuan, Li Zhuoran, Li Jinglin, Xi Zhongxun, and Zhao Shoushan.

Comrade Zhongxun and I first met in the Shaanxi-Gansu border area base in the winter of 1934. At that time, he was Chairman of the Soviet Government of the Shaanxi-Gansu border region. I was sent by the Special Commission of Northern Shaanxi to carry out military movements. When I returned, I was ordered to stay in Nanliang. The next year, I served as Secretary of the Eastern Region Working Committee and Chairman of the Revolutionary Committee. In 1935, as a result of the mistaken elimination of the counterrevolution, Comrade Liu Zhidan and I were arrested and put in the same prison. Fortunately, when the Central Red Army and Chairman Mao arrived in Northern Shaanxi, we were released. After the beginning of the War Against Japanese Aggression, Xi Zhongxun served as Secretary of the Guanzhong Sub-committee, and I served as Secretary of the Longdong Prefectural Party Committee. We started to work together in the autumn of 1945, when Xi served as Secretary of the Northwest Bureau of the CPC Central Committee for several years.

Our work in the Northwest Bureau during those years can be divided into two periods, the period of the Third Civil Revolutionary War and that of the restoration of the national economy after the founding of the new China. Although the situation and tasks of the two periods were different, Comrade Xi Zhongxun attached great importance to the study of Marxism, Leninism, and Mao Zedong Thought, and he was good at proceeding from reality and combining the lines, principles, and policies of the Central Committee with the actual situation in Northwestern China. From its establishment to March 1948, the Northwest Bureau was constantly at the side of the Central Committee and Chairman Mao. In the defensive war, Mao Zedong, Zhou Enlai, and Ren Bishi insisted on moving

In 1937, Xi Zhongxun, then Secretary of the Local Party Committee of Guanzhong District.

to Northern Shaanxi to command the national military struggle, and they were concerned about the work of the northwestern region. Getting the instructions directly from the Central Committee and Chairman Mao was a very favorable condition for us.

When recalling the work of Comrade Xi Zhongxun and the Northwest Bureau, I can't help but remember Peng Dehuai's unique contribution to the overall work in his role as the first Secretary of the Bureau, where he served for a long period of time. On topics ranging from military to political activities, from economic construction to culture and education, and from principles and policies to working methods, he gave us countless tips and suggestions. On the ethnic issues of special significance in Northwest China and the issue of uniting non-Party personages, he patiently gave us corresponding instructions. He fully trusted and supported Comrade Xi Zhongxun, who also respected him. This was another very important reason why the Northwest Bureau did such a good job. In those years, He Long and Ma Mingfang gave great support to Comrade Xi Zhongxun in their work in the leading group of the Northwest Bureau, as well as Lin Boqu and Xie Juezai, who presided over the work of the border region government, and Jia Tuofu, Li Zhuoran, Zhang Jiafu, Zhang Desheng, Wang Feng, and Zhao Boping, who were in charge of the work in different aspects. Only by working closely together in unison, holding onto the Party principles and the spirit of taking the overall situation into consideration, and through selfless dedication, could we achieve the desired results in our work.

Chairman Mao asked the Shaanxi-Gansu-Ningxia border region to "be a role model for the entire nation," so as to "promote the democratization of the whole country," and the Northwest Bureau carried out the construction of the democratic regime accordingly

The CPC Central Committee and Chairman Mao attached great importance to the United Front Work of the Northwest Bureau and the government of the Shaanxi-Gansu-Ningxia border region. This mainly referred to strengthening the construction of the anti-Japanese democratic regime and consolidating and expanding the national United Front.

A group photo of the standing members of the Shaanxi-Gansu-Ningxia border region Council in 1949. Xi Zhongxun was acting speaker of the Shaanxi-Gansu border region (sixth from the right in the third row).

In 1950, a group photo of the chairman, vice chairman, and members of the Northwest Military and Political Commission. Peng Dehuai (third from right), Zhang Zhizhong (second from right), and Xi Zhongxun (fourth from right) in the front row.

There was a historical background behind Chairman Mao's decision to attach importance to the construction of political power in the border region. In order to oppose Chiang Kai-shek's "one party dictatorship," the Communist Party proposed that the War of Resistance Against Japan should be combined with democratic politics. Chairman Mao personally formulated the policy program for the Shaanxi-Gansu-Ningxia border region. In order to build the border region into a model democratic base, the "triangular-organization system" policy was also formulated, in which communists accounted for a third of the political power, non-Party leftist progressives for a third, and middle elements and other elements for another third.

Comrade Xi Zhongxun and I both participated in the border region's senate. He served successively as a member of the Standing Committee and Speaker. It was a new type of democracy. Communists were required to work closely with non-Party personages and discuss important matters with them. In Chairman Mao's words, the border region was a democratic anti-Japanese base area. It was necessary to "improve itself and help others" and "be a role model and example for the entire naiton" so as to "promote the democratization of the whole country." With the guideline of the Central Committee, we first tested the "triangular-organization system" in Suide, Longdong, and Fuxian, electing more than 30,000 senators at the township and county levels (including 29,460 senators at the township level and 2,624 senators at the county level). On this basis, we generally re-elected the township and county governments, and we elected 242 councilors (including 31 alternate members) from the border region. In November 1941, the second session of the Senate was held in the Shaanxi-Gansu-Ningxia border region, and the "triangular-organization system" was widely implemented. The honorable Mr. Li Dingming was elected as Vice Chairman of the government of the Shaanxi-Gansu-Ningxia border region, An Wenqin as Vice President of the Senate (and they both subsequently served for another term), Liu Di, He Liancheng, Huo Zile, Bi Guangdou, and others were elected as members of the government of the border region, and a large number of non-Party personages played a positive role in the construction of the regime in the border region.

Comrade Xi Zhongxun resolutely carried out the instructions of the Central Committee in the construction of the Senate and democratic regime, which ensured the effective implementation of the central policy. He set an example, in the way that he was always ready to unite others, help out, and work closely with

(from right) Peng Dehuai, Zhang Zhizhong, Jia Tuofu, and Xi Zhongxun at the meeting of the Northwest Military and Political Commission in 1950.

others. He was highly respected by non-Party members, with who he discussed issues in an equal, modest manner and made friends in an open, cooperative way.

In the fierce struggle of the War of Liberation, in order to support Peng Dehuai's command in the northwest battlefield, the Northwest Bureau vigorously strengthened the United Front work in the Kuomintang army. On the eve of our strategic counter attack against Chiang Kai-shek and Hu Zongnan, Hu Jingduo, deputy commander of the KMT's security forces in Northern Shaanxi, led the uprising and dealt a heavy blow to the enemy from behind. This was intrinsically linked to Comrade Xi Zhongxun's arduous work.

On January 19, 1950, the Northwest Military and Political Commission was established, with Peng Dehuai serving as Chairman and Xi Zhongxun and Zhang Zhizhong as Vice Chairmen. Our cooperation with the democratic personages took on a larger scale. Deciding whether to expand the United Front and cooperate with the democratic parties on a larger scale became a key issue in the construction of the democratic regime. The Northwest Bureau resolutely adopted the policy of upholding and expanding the United Front, and it recruited highly respected and representative democratic figures such as Zhang Fengao, Han Zhaoying, Deng Baoshan, Sun Weiru, and Tao Zhiyue to participate in the leadership work of the people's governments of various provinces and cities in Northwestern China. They all served as members of the Northwest Military and Political Commission, Vice Governors, and Governors. In all regions, cities, and counties, a large number of democratic personages were recruited to participate in the people's governments at all levels. At that time, we had friendly contact with the Panchen Lama before he entered Tibet. Some of these democratic personages were familiar with local conditions, while others had influence and connections with people of certain social strata.

Another major issue in the work of the Northwest United Front was how to strengthen national unity. Northwestern China was the most expansive region in China, with 3.39 million square kilometers of land. Of the five provinces (regions) under its jurisdiction, four were ethnic or multi-ethnic regions, with a total area of 3.39 million square kilometers. There were 15 ethnic minorities who believed in different religions. The feudal ruling class of the old society and the KMT reactionaries carried out the policy of oppression and massacre, leaving a deep ethnic gap. This situation meant that the work of the National United Front must play a key role in the cause of the people's revolution and liberation in Northwest China. Comrade Xi Zhongxun once said, "Ethnic issues are the reality of the northwestern region. If all the work in the northwest is divorced from ethnic issues, it is divorced from reality." This reflected our consensus at that time. As soon as the northwest was liberated in 1950, the Northwest Bureau formally discussed the more effective work in the principles and policies in ethnic areas and proposed taking in representatives of all ethnic groups. In all our work, we had to take into account ethnic characteristics, properly treat the religious beliefs of ethnic minorities, train a large number of ethnic minority cadres, and appropriately develop Party members. When Comrade Xi Zhongxun announced these policies on behalf of the Northwest Bureau, they were widely welcomed by all ethnic groups.

To promote the consolidation and development of the national united front, we opposed both Han chauvinism and local nationalism.

Having analyzed the leading ethnic minority figures, we started to publicize the Party's policies and appropriately placed in the organizations influential people like Ma Hongbin, Huang Zhengqing, Ma Fuchen, Geshe Sherab Gyatso, and other comrades in Northwest China and appointed comrades highly respected among the masses, such as Bao Erhan. They were appointed to engage in the leadership of the people's governments of each province as vice governors or governors. A large number of democratic ethnic people and religious communities were arranged in various regions and counties to meet them for sincere, friendly cooperation in order to quickly restore stability in the northwest. At this time, Comrade Xi Zhongxun, who was the United Front Minister, frequently contacted many democrats, discussed the situation and specific work, and established personal friendships with them.

The separatists among the ethnic minorities were also rampant at that time, but we adopted policies to help the masses restore production, build water conservancy, and develop trade. For example, we implemented a purchase policy in Qinghai that was conducive to the Tibetan, with 150 *jin* of wool, which was exchanged for one tea brick before the liberation, now being worth 15 pieces. The Tibetans there said happily, "Chairman Mao comes here, and our wool is now valuable." In the eyes of the masses, the good market and price for wool was the result of the Party's policy. We achieved great things in our aid to the Uyghur and Hui people, building water conservancy in Xinjiang and Ningxia with the support of the masses. We also assisted the development of national industry and commerce, such as Ma Fuchen power plant.

In addition, we respected the traditional culture and customs of the ethnic minority groups, which was welcomed by the masses. We vigorously restored the cultural and educational undertakings in minority areas, such as setting up schools, arranging for representatives of ethnic minority groups to visit the interior, and introducing excellent cultural and artistic works of ethnic minorities in various forms and through various opportunities, so that they recognized that we were serious about helping and respecting them, which made them feel the warmth of the extended family of the motherland.

As a result of the establishment of a broad national United Front and the adoption of the effective policies, the situation in the northwest soon stabilized, paving the way for the future work of land reform, bandits suppression and local despots opposition.

According to different historical conditions, the Northwest Bureau carried out land reform based on the local conditions and promptly spotted and remedied the left-leaning tendency, which was commended by the Party Central Committee and Chairman Mao

The land reform in Northwest China can be divided into the reform in the old areas of the Shaanxi-Gansu-Ningxia border region and that in the Northwest after liberation. The previous economy of the Shaanxi-Gansu-Ningxia border region was relatively backward. As a result of the protracted war and various natural disasters, cultivated land covered just 8.43 million *mu*, accounting for a little more than one fifth of the arable land area. In 1937, grain production was only 1.1 million *dan*. After the establishment of the Anti-Japanese National United Front, under the leadership of the Communist Party, the Shaanxi-Gansu-Ningxia border region reached a stage of relatively stable development. In order to mobilize the revolutionary enthusiasm of the masses and meet the needs of the anti-Japanese war effort, the Northwest Bureau, instructed by the Party Central Committee, put forward the slogan of "reducing rent and interest rates." By 1943, the movement of rent and interest reduction movement gradually intensified in the border areas. The movement reduced the exploitation of farmers by landlords, weakened the landlord economy, and transformed the class structure in the rural border areas, so that moderately affluent farmers became the main component of the rural areas. All this became an important issue in the later land reform of the Shaanxi-Gansu-Ningxia border region.

Historically, in the agrarian revolution, about half of the border areas were allocated land, while during the anti-Japanese war, due to the long-term policy of rent reduction and interest reduction, about half of the land occupied by the landlords had been transferred to the farmers. In the former category, the main problems were some land rights disputes and the individual landowner's illegal acquisitions of the land allocated to the farmers. In the latter, the most prominent problem was that the rent and interest reduction were not thorough. Based on this practical situation, the Northwest Bureau decided to settle the issue of land rights and consolidate the achievements of the land revolution in the areas where land had been allocated before. In areas where the land revolution was not yet implemented, on the basis of the masses, the Northwest Bureau carried out the struggle of rent reduction and tenancy protection, promoted production and development, and gradually took measures to achieve the goal of "each tiller having his own land." In order to soften the impact on the broader society, Comrade Xi Zhongxun went to Guanzhong in September 1946. Ma Mingfang and I went to Longdong to test the work of purchasing and distributing the excess land of the landowners. This was a new policy to address the land problem at that time. By the end of 1947, in more than 370 townships in the Shaanxi-Gansu-Ningxia border region that had not allocated land, after the acquisition of the landlord's land, more than 1.2 million *mu* of land were transferred to the farmers, but the policy was no longer implemented when the situation later changed.

It should be pointed out that the land reform in the Shaanxi-Gansu-Ningxia border region was successfully completed as a result of the timely remedy of the left-leaning tendency under the leadership of the central government. In the process of land reform, there was a left-leaning tendency in the Shaanxi-Gansu-Ningxia border region. The farmers with more property and a better livelihood were taken as the target of land reform, and the previous landowners who had become farmers became the subjects to be struggled against. This was mainly because of the influence of the idea of distributing all land without distinction and blindly following the experience of Jinsui and the Yihe Conference with their potential leftist tendencies.

In order to remedy the inertia that the cadres had developed in the prolonged stable environment, strengthen the concept of class struggle, and support the victory of the war, in November 1947, the Northwest Bureau held a cadre conference (the Yihe Conference) in Yihe, Suide. The meeting addressed these problems, but also developed left-leaning thought, which was not corrected until the December Meeting of the Central Committee held in Yangjiagou, Mizhi County, on December 28 that year. The comrades of the Northwest Bureau felt that the Central Committee had provided great guidance for us. Comrade Xi Zhongxun first discovered the problem, and he proposed many ideas and suggestions, all of which was appreciated by the Central Committee and Chairman Mao.

On January 4, 1948, Comrade Xi Zhongxun put forward in his report on the

In 1947, the Northwest Bureau of the Communist Party of China moved to Xuejiaqu, Yihe Town, Suide County. Pictured is the cave where Xi Zhongxun lived in Xuejiaqu.

land reform of the old liberated area in the Shaanxi-Gansu-Ningxia border region presented to the Northwest Bureau and the Central Committee that the basic situation of the new area established during the land revolution was different. The old area had more middle class farmers, and the number of poor and hired farmers with little or no land was no more than 20% of the total number of households. Most of the land of the previously wealthy landowners had been confiscated, and they had worked for at least seven years for their roles transformation.

Chairman Mao attached great importance to Comrade Xi Zhongxun's report. On January 9, Mao commented, "I fully agree to the opinions put forward by Comrade Xi Zhongxun. I hope that leaders can guide the land reform in various districts and counties in accordance with these opinions and make sure that the land reform in the border areas is carried out on the right track and with fewer mistakes. Attention should also be given to the old bases in Northern China." At the same time, Chairman Mao also advised that Xi Zhongxun, Ma Mingfang, and I, along with some other leading comrades, visit the counties.

According to Chairman Mao's instructions, Comrade Xi Zhongxun went to Suide, Ma Mingfang went to the branch affiliated to Yan'an, and I went to Sanbian, Longdong, and Guanzhong. Along the way, we publicized the policies of the Party

Central Committee, identified and addressed problems, and started to remedy the left-leaning tendencies in the land reform in the border areas.

On January 19, Comrade Xi Zhongxun sent another telegram to Chairman Mao on correcting the leftist tendencies in the land reform of the Shaanxi-Gansu-Ningxia border area, pointing out that due to the leftist tendencies at the Yihe Conference and the impact of Jinsui, when the land reform reached the rural areas, it led to extreme leftist tendencies, emphasizing the "route of poor and hired farmers" and opposing the "route of middle class farmers." It resulted in a small number of people who were not the real basic masses engaging in chaotic fighting, labeling, beating, and torturing people, confiscating property, and driving people out of the organization without reason. Although it was not a common phenomenon, it had a disturbing impact on the people and the rural areas were in somewhat chaos. In his telegram, Comrade Xi Zhongxun proposed nine measures to implement the spirit of the December Conference of the Central Committee and remedy the extreme leftist tendencies, primarily including: persisting in commending and protecting prosperity through hard labor; recognizing the newly transformed class components; not fearing the middle class farmers being in power; no longer conducting political struggle based on past events; adopting the policy of patient persuasion except to the "traitors" who went to the enemy's side; having a clear cut definition of "the bully" instead of issuing indiscriminate punishments; focusing on "adjustment" for land reform in the old area; and developing production and doing well in disaster relief work. The next day (January 20), Chairman Mao issued a directive stating that in the case of the same situations emerging in the old liberated areas in Northern and Central China, the leftist errors should be given close attention.

On February 8, Comrade Xi Zhongxun proposed four suggestions to the central government and Northwest Bureau. 1) At the current stage in the Shaanxi-Gansu-Ningxia border area, the middle-class farmers held most of the land. If the land was to be equally distributed, most or all of their land would be involved, so it was not suitable to make equal division. 2) In the old district, it was not appropriate to apply the poor farmers groups-oriented policy, because these groups there were quite mixed in composition. Their poverty may have been the result of barren or remote land, an increase in family population, financial difficulties, natural disasters, or a decline in living standard, or of simple laziness and idleness (indulgence in eating, drinking, gambling, or frequenting brothels). Once the poor farmers' groups were organized, they would definitely target the middle class farmers for gains, thus leading to leftist tendencies. 3) The rich landowners in the old district could not generally be driven out of the working team. In areas where the land allocation was properly made, those who were truly engaged in labor and became middle class farmers or new rich farmers should retain some or most of their property. 4) We needed to address the issue of the overly heavy burden on the middle class farmers. Otherwise, a trend of "overwhelming the middle class farmers and destroying the rural economy" would develop. These situations and the opinions on the land reform in the old district Comrade Xi Zhongxun expressed drew further attention from Chairman Mao and the Northwest Bureau.

When implementing the central government policy on the reform of the old and semi-old areas, we paid close attention to summarizing and sharing typical experiences, which was an important working method in the land reform. We summarized and drew upon the typical experience of the working group in Huangjiachuan Village, Yihe District, Suide County. They started from the actual situation of the old district and employed the method of re-distributing the land by balancing fertile and barren plots to meet the demands of poor and hired farmers and to consolidate unity with the middle class farmers for production and development. The Central Committee issued the Instruction on the Implementation of Land Reform in the Old and Semi-Old Districts on February 22, which confirmed the universal significance of Huangjiachuan's experience. On March 12, Chairman Mao transmitted Huangjiachuan's experience to the whole country, along with the typical experience in Pingshan County, Jinchaji District and in Guo County, Jinsui District, to remedy "the apparent anti-Marxist and anti-Leninist authoritarianism and tailism within the Party" with "vivid, specific experience."

According to statistics, in April 1948, after overcoming the leftist tendencies, the Shaanxi-Gansu-Ningxia border area saw great success in the land reform. In the areas that occupied half of the total population of the old area and the semi-old area (nearly 600,000 people), 900,000 *mu* of the land was redistributed, which eliminated the feudal land system of these areas, liberated productivity, developed the economic construction of the border areas, and mobilized the enthusiasm of the people in support of the War of Liberation. To sum up our experience, we noted that we took a zig-zagging route in the land reform in the old and semi-old districts. Before 1947, our policies and principles were based on the actual situation, with some creativity, which brought about the desired results. However, the leftist tendencies emerged in the spring of 1947, and it was not until the Yangjiagou Meeting that we got back on the right track. It was Comrade Xi Zhongxun and other leaders who spotted the leftist tendencies quickly and promptly remedied the deviation, minimizing the loss.

After the founding of the new China, we focused on two issues in the land reform of the northwest new area. The first was the vigorous education of the cadres so that they could grasp the general principles and policies of the land reform.

At the end of September 1949, the northwest was liberated. The issue of the land reform in Northwestern China was put on the agenda of the Northwest Bureau. It was to be the largest reform in the interests of the largest majority. In order to successfully accomplish this great task, the cadres needed to first grasp the general principles and policies of the land reform. The general line of the reform of the Party before 1950 was to "rely on poor farmers, unite the middle-class farmers, eliminate the feudal exploitation system systematically and judiciously, and develop agricultural production." In June 1950, the central government proposed the general line and policy of the land reform as "relying on poor and hired farmers, uniting middle class farmers, not interfering with the rich farmers to eliminate the feudal exploitation system systematically and independently, and developing agricultural production." The major shift here was in the non-interference with the rich farmers.

Politically, non-interference with the rich farmers aimed to better protect the middle class farmers and small landowners and isolate the landlord class. In the past, the revolutionary forces of the people had been relatively weak in the fierce battle against the anti-revolutionary forces. For one thing, the rich farmers tended to oppose the land reform and sided with the landlord class and Chiang Kai-shek. For another, the people's war required the farmers to send soldiers, offer grain for public use, and engage in compulsory work, which was a high price to pay in support of the war. The situation was different now. The basic task of the people throughout the country was to carry out economic construction. The political attitude of rich farmers had changed. Generally, they could remain neutral, and thus better protect middle class farmers and remove the concerns of farmers in development and production. It was therefore important to make this clear to thousands of groups working on land reform.

The second problem of the land reform in Northwestern China was that the land occupation was different from that in the Shaanxi-Gansu-Ningxia border area and other regions. Therefore, it was necessary to implement the policy and work based on the actual situation.

There were more than ten ethnic minorities living in the vast area of Northwestern China, some of which were engaged in animal husbandry, so that the land issue was different in nature from that in the farming areas of the Han. Although most of the Hui people mainly engaged in agriculture as the major industry, there was a complex relationship between the land and ethnic issues. Based on this specific

In December 1950, Xi Zhongxun inspected Qinghai Province. Pictured are Zhao Shoushan, the governor of Qinghai Province (middle) and Zhang Zhongliang, Secretary of the Provincial Party Committee of Qinghai Province (right).

situation, we decided that the land reform in Northwestern China should be carried out in two steps. First, it should be carried out in the farming areas where the Han nationality was concentrated, and then in the farming areas where ethnic minorities were concentrated, once the political and social conditions were ready. The second step aimed to steadily address the reform of the minority pastoral areas when the time was right, based on the actual local situation and the implementation of national policies.

Due to our prudent, steady implementation of the land reform policy, from the winter of 1951 to May 1952, the land reform was completed in 106 counties and eight cities in four provinces in Guannei, a large area with a population of 16 million. From the winter of 1952 to the spring of 1953, the land reform was completed in 62 counties in Xinjiang, covering a population of 4 million. By 1953, the land reform in Northwestern China had been completed.

From the winter of 1951 to the spring of the following year, the special achievement of the land reform in Northwestern China lay in the successful land reform in the areas with more ethnic minorities. About half of the areas in which the land reform was undertaken were those inhabited by ethnic minorities. We stipulated that "in carrying out land reform in these areas, we should take national unity as the foundation and the consciousness of the majority of the local people as the premise, with the local ethnic cadres participation in the work to fight against the landlords of their own ethnic groups mainly by the minority masses." At the same time, leaders of all ethnicities and sects were to be put on a list and properly protected in the land reform. For example, the protection of Ma Fuchen in Qinghai, Ma Juanqin in Gansu Province, and others ensured that the land reform in areas with many ethnic minorities could be carried out smoothly and steadily.

After the land reform, the farmers of all ethnic groups greatly improved their political awareness and production enthusiasm. A large number of farmers participated in production assistance groups, developed water conservancy, and increased fertilizer to enhance the yield. For example, Gansu Province basically completed the land reform in 1952, and by the end of 1954, the grain yield increased from 2.67 million tons to 3.17 million tons, and the fiscal revenue increased from 111 million yuan to more than 143 million yuan, which clearly demonstrated the achievements of the land reform and created conditions for the implementation of economic construction throughout the country. Another example was seen in Shaanxi Province's completion of the land reform in three phases, based on its own situation, which not only met the demands of the farmers with no or little land and developed production in combination with the land reform, but also collected a large number of guns and ammunition from the landlords, completely destroyed the feudal regime and its armed forces, and created the necessary conditions for stability.

In the unprecedented scale of the reform movement, it was inevitable that there were some rough or incomplete phenomena, but these were not the mainstream. Later, some people said that "the northwest land reform was incomplete" and "right leaning," which was a mistaken view.

It should be said that the victory of the land reform in Northern Shaanxi and the northwest, led by the Northwest Bureau, was a major event in the history of the revolution in the northwest. It firmly implemented the central policy and principle, which reflected Comrade Xi Zhongxun's concept of "starting from the actual situation" and "seeking truth from facts."

The effective struggle against bandits and despots in Northwestern China was the result of the correct policies and strategies we adopted in minority areas

During the People's Liberation War and the early period of liberation, the struggle against bandits and despots in Northwestern China was positive, steady, and effective. After the struggle, the bandits disappeared, the bullies were subdued, and the people were pleased.

After the liberation of the entire northwest, tens of thousands of bandits and secret agents scattered all over the country. They were agents of Chiang Kai-shek's reactionaries and imperialism in China. Relying on their armed forces, they occupied some remote places and continued to be enemies of the people. Eliminating them was an urgent task at that time.

There were mainly two types of bandits, political bandits, who were the remnants of the Kuomintang reactionaries, and hardened bandits, who practiced territorial separatist rule for the purpose of looting. Both were controlled and manipulated by secret agents, so their internal contradictions were very complicated.

In the summer of 1949, the Northwest Bureau held a meeting of the secretaries of the local Party Committee of the Guanzhong New Area. At the meeting, Comrade Xi Zhongxun delivered a report entitled "On the Work Direction of the Guanzhong New Area," which reviewed the task and strategy of suppressing bandits in Northwestern China. He pointed out that "suppressing bandits is a top priority, but we should combine pursuing the organized bandits and the general elimination of scattering bandits with defeating reactionary forces. Instead of fighting for a rout, we should wage a war of annihilation. We should make close investigation, full preparations, and a long-distance attack to surround the enemy for annihilation and pursue and arrest those who are defeated so that they will be wiped out."

In June 1950, after careful analysis and study of the bandit situation, the Northwest Bureau put forward the following seven policies and strategies to suppress bandits according to the guidelines of the central government.

1. We must resolutely eliminate bandits while taking appropriate steps and measures. We should concentrate our efforts on cracking down on bandit leaders and making their crimes known to the public. We should distinguish ordinary people from counter revolutionaries and resolutely protect the interests of the masses.

2. In the new areas, especially in minority areas, we should first guard against and then attack bandits. We should divide them before striking and do the work of persuasion before suppressing them. If necessary, we should combine suppression with pacification.
3. On the issue of eliminating secret agents, we should focus on leniency to win them over, divide and shake the enemy, and combine leniency with suppression.
4. As for Yiguandao, the reactionary secret society, we should carry out overall mass work, widely publicize and educate the masses, and strive for the masses to eliminate its influence. On this basis, we should be prepared to crack down on leaders of the society and contain secret agents, so as to fulfil the purpose of destroying the organization.
5. We should be good at distinguishing the nature of different problems. Some have been caused by bureaucracy in our work. For example, Guyuan County forcibly divided its administrative boundaries, which caused dissatisfaction among the masses. The county magistrate did not observe the people's situation, but insisted on his own opinions, which led to riots among the masses. This shouldn't be confused with the problem of bandit agents.
6. We should be more vigilant and promptly clear up the collusion between villains and bandits who have mingled in the revolutionary ranks.
7. In the fight against bandits, in order to isolate the enemy, we should take the initiative to unite all those who may cooperate with us, including landlords, imams, lamas, princes, and heads of a hundred and a thousand households. We should also win over the enemy agents who were separated from enemy organizations and are no longer against us.

According to these policies and strategies, from the establishment of the Northwest Military and Political Commission in January 1950 to the total liberation of the northwest, 60,000 or 70,000 bandits were eliminated. At the same time, it successfully dissolved the enemy's special forces, defeated the remnants of the Ma armies in Gansu and Qinghai provinces, and handled the Linxia and Pingliang Incidents.

Throughout the process of fighting against bandits, the Northwest Bureau and Comrade Xi Zhongxun paid special attention to the policies and strategies for bandits and rebels in minority areas.

At the beginning of summer in 1950, the relationship between the Hui and Han peoples in Pingliang, Haiyuan, Guyuan, Gaolan, and other places was tense. The bandits mainly took advantage of the historical estrangement between the

In 1950, Peng Dehuai and Xi Zhongxun took a group photo with ethnic minorities and religious figures. Second from the right, front row: Xi Zhongxun, Peng Dehuai, Zhang Zhizhong, Geshe Sherab Gyatso, Jia Tuofu.

Hui and Han nationalities and the weaknesses of our cadres in carrying out ethnic policies to stir up ethnic tensions and spread terror among the Hui people. As a result, 40,000 or 50,000 Hui people in Northwestern China fled to the Suixi area. The situation was very tense. In the face of this crisis, the Northwest Bureau first focused on easing ethnic contradictions and improving Hui-Han ethnic relations. Then, according to the instructions of the Central Committee: 1) we exposed the bandits and explained our Party's ethnic policies among the Hui and Han people; 2) we first suppressed the bandits in the Han area while in the Hui people's area, we temporarily focused on defense, combining political disintegration and appeasement; 3) after the Hui people understood our policy toward them, we eliminated the stubborn bandits; 4) we strictly distinguished the bandits and the people in our suppression efforts and strictly prohibited indiscriminate killing and torture; and 5) if reactionary societies in the area, such as Wujidao, Yiguandao, and Dadaohui, were solely Han people's organizations or only involved a few Hui people, they were declared illegal, and the Han bandits and special leaders who incited ethnic hatred and killing were publicly suppressed. In a word, by focusing on the core of ethnic issues, we solved the complicated contradictions one layer at a time, concentrated on attacking a small group of bandits, stabilized the revolutionary situation in the area, and won the fight against the bandits.

At the end of 1951, Xiang Qian, the feudal hereditary head of a thousand households in the Tibetan area of Nganglha, Qinghai, gathered more than 2,000 people for an armed rebellion. Comrade Xi Zhongxun made the political struggle his first priority, took the method of "capturing and releasing Meng Huo seven times," repeatedly publicized the Party's ethnic policy and the importance of national unity, and finally won him over to surrendering in support of the People's Liberation Army's work in eliminating bandits. Moreover, we still addressed him as "head of a thousand households," which had a very good impact on all the leaders in the Tibetan areas.

Around the time of the outbreak of the Korean War, the reactionary officers of the former Ma Bufang group, who were hiding in Qinghai, went all over the country in an attempt to use ethnic and religious issues to incite the masses to riots in Gansu, Qinghai, and Ningxia. Among them, Ma Liang and Ma Yuanxiang fled to the Tibetan inhabited areas in Gannan to cause disruptions. The Taiwan authorities of the Kuomintang appointed Ma Liang as "Commander of the 103rd Route of the Chinese Anti-Communist Army" and Ma Yuanxiang as "Commander of the 102nd Route." They airdropped secret agents in the region and gathered more than a thousand counter revolutionary forces. We organized a visiting delegation headed by Huang Zhengqing, a Tibetan democrat, to go deep into all parts of the Gannan Tibetan area, publicize the Party's policies among the leaders, religious figures, and the masses, persuade and unite with them, and alienate the Tibetan tribes from Ma Liang and Ma Yuanxiang. After doing well in the mass work, our army adopted an active military defense policy. By May 1953, the bandits of Ma Liang and Ma Yuanxiang were finally annihilated.

In the spring of 1951, the remnant forces of the rebels headed by Opsan Batyr in Xinjiang looted at the junction of Xinjiang, Gansu, and Qinghai provinces and destroyed national unity. The situation became quite serious. In addition, leftist practice emerged in Xinjiang's work, which made the problem more complicated and caused great concern for Chairman Mao and the Party Central Committee.

In July 1952, the Central Committee sent Xi Zhongxun and other comrades to Xinjiang to attend the second meeting of Xinjiang representatives of the Communist Party of China. They helped leaders of the branch bureaus and representatives from all over the country sum up their experiences, and they dealt appropriately with Opsan Batyr, who had incited people to revolt and loot. It was stipulated that the suppression of the counter revolution in pastoral areas should only be targeted at the leaders who were currently in action and at any ongoing revolts, along with tribal leaders who carried out armed rebellions. We were to do all we could to try political persuasion first and launch armed elimination only when all other efforts failed. In the pastoral areas, we were to first stabilize the social order, unite the upper class, and then mobilize the masses through the upper class. Building on the uniting of all the people in pastoral areas to develop animal husbandry production, we aimed to organize the herdsmen and the herd owners to negotiate with each other from top to bottom with our guidance, so as to conclude a voluntary, mutually beneficial agreement for reform. In an effort to protect and develop animal husbandry, we did not rashly encourage the herdsmen to abandon their work and switch to agriculture.

After this, we persisted in the policy of political struggle and military defense against the Opsan Batyr rebellion, especially in combination with suppressing bandits, resettling the displaced people, and helping out with addressing any obstacles to their livelihood. On this basis, we concentrated our efforts to crack down on the stubborn bandits and quickly quenched the Opsan Batyr rebellion.

In December 1952, under the leadership of the Central Committee, the Northwest Bureau properly solved the Xinjiang problem, the Xiji Incident in Pingliang, Gansu Province, the Amuquhu Incident, and the armed rebellion in Nganglha, Qinghai Province. In May 1953, we completely eliminated the Ma Liang

In July 1952, Xi Zhongxun's inspection of Xinjiang, with Bao Erhan (right) and Saifuddin Azizi (left).

and Ma Yuanxiang bandits, stabilized the political situation in the northwest, and fundamentally changed the social atmosphere. Gao Zicheng, a farmer in Wenxian, Gansu Province disguised himself as a beggar to scout the bandit's nest in order to capture the rebels. Qiu Yushan, a farmer in Kangxian, volunteered to walk for eight days and nights to capture Zhang Shouli, the chief of the secret agents. Of the 3,031 townships in Gansu Province, 3,186,000 people took part in the farmer associations, accounting for 38% of the total population, and 437,000 people joined the militia. The farmer's association and the militia became stronger, frightening and containing the bandits and despots.

Various means were used to prepare a large number of cadres for the liberation of Northwestern China

The Party building in Northwestern China was closely linked to the care and guidance of the Central Committee and Chairman Mao. In October 1935, the Party Central Committee and Chairman Mao led the Central Red Army to Northern Shaanxi. From then to March 1948, the Central Committee and Chairman Mao directly led the Shaanxi-Gansu-Ningxia border region for thirteen years. In order to win the anti-Japanese war, the Central Committee and Chairman Mao formulated a series of policies for the Northwest Bureau and the Shaanxi-Gansu-Ningxia border region, including a Party building policy. As a result, the Northwest Bureau had a unique advantage, in that it received constant guidance and help from the Central Committee as a result of being close to the committee. When the Central Committee discussed the work of the northwestern region, it often involved members of the Standing Committee of the Northwest Bureau. The Central Committee designated Comrade Ren Bishi to take charge of the work of the Northwest Bureau, and he attended some important meetings there. The Northwest Bureau was able to get timely guidance and help from the Central Committee in formulating important documents, and the Bureau occasionally put forward alternative measures to the instructions of the Central Committee, which gained recognition from the Central Committee, and which was of great significance to the Party building and development of the revolutionary cause in the Shaanxi-Gansu-Ningxia border region.

In fact, the border region had a population of only 1.5 million at that time. Ensuring the living needs of tens of thousands of soldiers, cadres, and students was a huge, arduous task, so it was important to consolidate the base areas where the

Central Committee was located. Following Chairman Mao's instruction, we pointed out that Party building should first focus on ideological and political construction and take ideological education and leadership as its priority. Party building was to be subject to the Party's general line. At that time, it was necessary to prioritize the complete victory of the anti-Japanese war, adhere to the general policy of "anti-Japanese war, unity, and democracy," consolidate and expand the Anti-Japanese National United Front, and resolutely build the border region into a model anti-Japanese democratic base. Secondly, another important task of Party building was the training of a large number of cadres to meet the needs of the border region and the entire country. To this end, we paid close attention to the education of cadres and put forth great effort to run the Party School in the Shaanxi-Gansu-Ningxia border region (later changed into the Party School of the Northwest Bureau of the Central Committee). Comrade Xi Zhongxun and I served as principals. We set up administrative and ethnic colleges, and trained a large number of administrative and ethnic cadres. We set up border agricultural, vocational, medical, writing, and other professional schools, and trained professional and technical personnel. In addition, normal schools and middle schools were set up in various districts, and a network of revolutionary education was initially formed. From 1937 to 1945, the Northwest Party School and its former District Party School trained more than 4,200 cadres for the northwest. There were 53 local cadre classes in all seven middle schools in the border region. By 1945, more than 3,000 cadres were transferred to enrich the cadre team in the border region, which provided a guarantee for the success of the work in the area. In addition, we strove to strengthen and give play to the fighting role of grassroots Party organizations. At that time, there were not many Party members in the border region, generally accounting for about 2% of the population, but they had strong fighting capacity with a leading role. According to the statistics on the eve of the Seventh National Congress of the Communist Party of China (CPC), at that time, the Yanshu Prefecture Party Committee had jurisdiction over ten County Party Committees, with 16,628 Party members. The Suide Prefecture Party Committee had jurisdiction over six County Party Committees, with 10,514 Party members. The Longdong Prefecture Party Committee had jurisdiction over six County Party Committees, with 5,051 Party members. The Guanzhong Prefecture Party Committee had jurisdiction over four County Party Committees and one Central District Party Committee, with 3,131 Party members. There were 4,021 Party members in the Sanbian region, and 2,850 Party members in border region organs, with a total of 42,195. As a result of the policy of building branches at the grassroots level, Party members played an exemplary leading role in reducing rent and interest, developing production, collecting grain and expanding troops, and maintaining social order and public security, who ensured the successful completion of these tasks. It was not until 1948, when the Northwest Bureau issued the instructions entitled "Attention to the Development of Party Members," in combination with the new army consolidation movement, that the number of Party members doubled to about 5% of the population. It can be seen that the combat effectiveness of grassroots Party organizations was not in the large number of Party members, but in their competence.

During the liberation war, the Party's organizational work was mainly to mobilize cadres to do a good job of pre-branch work and to organize the local Party to actively cooperate with the People's Liberation Army in destroying the reactionary rule of the Kuomintang. The local Party of Shaanxi, Gansu, and other provinces played an important role in mobilizing students to join the revolution and the PLA, organizing the masses to destroy the reactionary rule of the Kuomintang, and instigating uprisings by people's groups. Some places also organized guerrillas and guerrilla groups, such as the Xifu guerrillas and the Weibei guerrillas, which participated in the clamp down war and the fight against Hu Zongnan.

The most daunting task was to prepare a large number of cadres for the liberation of the northwest, which was the most overwhelming event in the region. There were only 23 counties in the Shaanxi-Gansu-Ningxia border area, and the quantity and competence of the cadres were limited. Meeting the needs of the cadres was a heavy, but glorious task. We vigorously trained cadres, expanded their sources, and accelerated their training and selection. According to statistics, about 10,000 cadres were successively transferred from the border area, and more than 2,000 cadres were transferred from Jinsui and Jinnan (at that time, the Shanxi Suiyuan branch was led by the Northwest Bureau). The local Party of Shaanxi and Gansu Provinces and the revolution in the three districts (Yili, Tacheng, and Ashan) in Xinjiang produced a group of cadres. Most of them worked hard, and soon worked with the people of the new area to create a new ground. Even so, we still felt we were not strong enough, we were understaffed, and our cadres were not sufficiently competent. Therefore, the Northwest Bureau adopted the following important policies and measures:

1. We sent comrades with high competence and prestige to serve as provincial leaders. For example, Shaanxi was led by Ma Mingfang and Zhang Bangying, Xi'an by Zhao Boping and Fang Zhongru, Xinjiang by Wang Zhen and Wang Enmao, Gansu by Zhang Desheng and Sun Zuobin, Qinghai by Zhang

Zhongliang and Zhao Shoushan, and Ningxia by Pan Zili and Zhu Min. They did not merely enjoy high prestige, but also held important positions in the army. They had experience and organizational ability. Upon working in their respective posts, they quickly organized a leading group and stabilized the situation in the local area.

2. We greatly improved the ideological level and working ability of on-the-job cadres, added deputy posts at various levels of organizations to play the veteran cadres' role of passing on experience, assisted and guided the young, and paid special attention to the nurturing of national cadres.
3. We actively nurtured and promoted young intellectual cadres. We expanded the Party school and established a revolutionary university to train the cadres while fighting. In order to strengthen the training of cadres, Comrade Xi Zhongxun and the Standing Committee members of the Northwest Bureau taught in these schools.
4. The local cadres were also a source for turning the army into a task force. We left some of the key cadres of the army in the vast newly liberated areas and helped them turn to do local political and administrative work. Many comrades who worked in the army became the leading cadres of the Party and government at all levels in Northwestern China.
5. We seriously strengthened Party Construction in the new area. In the various tasks carried out in the new area, especially in the land reform, we investigated and observed the training objects, actively and steadily developed Party members, and established grassroots organizations. According to statistics, there were 2,947 grassroots Party organizations in Shaanxi Province in 1949, which reached 6,797 in 1953, an increase of 1.28 times. In 1949, 64,861 people were members, and the number reached 114,590 in 1953, up 76%. The number of cadres also increased from 63,479 in 1949 to 121,964, nearly doubling. Due to the positive and stable policy, the northwest provinces basically realized the construction of Party branches in the countryside and townships in 1953, and the Party Committees in the districts and towns effectively led the social reform and economic construction in the early period of liberation.
6. The Northwest Bureau and Comrade Xi Zhongxun attached importance to properly handling the relationship between military cadres and cadres from the state controlled areas, between Han cadres and minority cadres, and between cadres within the Party and those outside the Party. We required local cadres to respect, cherish, and care for the army cadres, required the cadres from the old areas to care for the local cadres in the new liberated areas, Han cadres to

the minority cadres, Party cadres to those outside the Party, cadres with credit to those who had made mistakes, and so on, and required to unite on the basis of democratic centralism. We resolutely opposed the formation of cliques and small group activities. It was because of sticking to the principles by the Northwest Bureau and Comrade Xi Zhongxun that the cadres in the northwest made great contributions to the development of the Party's cause in the vast area and in various complex situations.

7. The Northwest Bureau of China held onto the tenet of serving the people, the mass line, and seeking truth from facts. Comrade Xi Zhongxun put forward a plain slogan, *Sitting on the people's side*. "We can't lord it over the people," he said. "If our cadres are seen as 'officials' or 'masters,' it will be horrible." He called on the Party cadres to go out of the "yamen" and into the rural areas to combine our work with uniting and educating the common people. It was only through the people that our tasks could be fulfilled in the fastest, most correct way. In the revolution, "new creations should be found among the common people."

In January 1950, the Northwest Military and Political Commission was established, marking the victory of the people's democratic regime in Northwestern China, which was established by all the people of the northwest under the leadership of the Communist Party of China. The victory was mainly attributed to the First Field Army of the People's Liberation Army under the command of Peng Dehuai and the Northwest Army under the command of He Long and Xi Zhongxun. At the same time, it was also the result of the determined implementation of the central line, policy, and principle by the Northwest Bureau, of the concerted effort in leading comrades of the Party and government of each province, and of the cadres at all levels relying on the masses and working together. On behalf of the Northwest Bureau, Comrade Xi Zhongxun called on all of us at that time to "continue to serve the people as usual" and "to be the loyal and diligent servants of the people of the northwest." After this, the ideological struggle against bureaucracy and authoritarianism was carried out in the Party and the cadre team.

We emphasized the regular training of cadres and their conscious learning and self-education. We required all the members to discipline themselves according to the eight standards of Party members, as put forward by Comrade Liu Shaoqi, to constantly improve themselves. Cadres at or above the county level were to study carefully and take the twelve books as "must read" items for cadres, as Chairman Mao required. Practice proved that this was an effective way to improve the consciousness of the cadres. It was under this strict requirement that many cadres in Northwestern China systematically studied Marxism, Leninism, and Mao Zedong Thought. Comrade Xi Zhongxun often said, "If the leading organs attach importance to and really do a good job in improving the ideological and political level of the cadres, we can say that 90% of our task would have been completed."

Some cadres took the excuse of having no time to read books. In fact, they did not see the significance of reading.

Recalling Comrade Xi Zhongxun's Revolutionary Career[1]

SUN ZUOBIN AND LÜ JIANREN

Born in 1908 in Xi'an, Shaanxi Province, Sun Zuobin joined the Communist Party of China in June 1929. From May 1928, he engaged in military movements in Yang Hucheng's unit, and after the founding of the new China, he served as Deputy Director of the United Front Work Department of the Northwest Bureau of the CPC Central Committee and Deputy Director of the Ethnic Affairs Committee of the Northwest Military and Political Commission. He died in Xi'an in 2002.

Born in 1908, Lü Jianren, was from Qianxian, Shaanxi Province. He joined the Communist Party of China in 1927. From May 1949 to November 1952, he was a member of the Shaanxi Provincial Party Committee, Secretary of the Baoji Prefectural Party Committee, and Political Commissar of the Military Division. From November 1952 to June 1978, he served as director and member of the Standing Committee of the United Front Work Department of the Xinjiang Branch of the Communist Party of China, vice chairman and second secretary of the Party Group of the First CPPCC of the Xinjiang Uyghur Autonomous Region, Secretary of the Secretariat of the Party Committee of the autonomous region, secretary of the supervisory committee, and executive secretary of the Party Committee. He died in Xi'an in 2002.

1. This article was written on October 15, 1992, from *Sun Zuobin*, edited by the Party History Research Office of Shaanxi Provincial Party Committee, Shaanxi People's Publishing House, 1997.

Comrade Xi Zhongxun is 80 years old this year. He is an excellent member of the Communist Party of China, trained in the revolutionary struggle in Northwestern China and a long tested communist fighter. He closely tied his whole life to the cause of the Party and the interests of the people, worked selflessly, and made outstanding contributions to the construction of the Party in the northwest, the establishment of the revolutionary base in the Shaanxi-Gansu border area, the development and growth of the United Front, and the liberation and socialist cause of the Chinese people.

Both of us and Comrade Xi Zhongxun were veteran comrades in Shaanxi who took part in the revolutionary work during the Great Revolution, and we are among the few still alive today. In the early 1930s, we met Xi when we were engaged in the military movement in the Yang Hucheng unit of the Northwest Army. After that, we fought side by side with him, working under his direct leadership, making frequent contact, and getting to know each other better. In the face of the political storm and unfair treatment, we cared for and cherished each other, and we maintained a deep revolutionary friendship in the long revolutionary years.

Xi Zhongxun and (from left) Sun Zuobin, Deng Baoshan, Li Furen, Jia Tuofu, Huo Weide, Zhang Jiafu, and Zhang Desheng in Lanzhou.

Xi Zhongxun and Lü Jianren.

I

Comrade Xi Zhongxun was infinitely loyal to the Party with a high degree of dedication to and steadfastness in the revolution. After the failure of the Liangdang and Jingyuan military movements in 1932, he went north to the Shaanxi-Gansu mountainous area. In response to Mao Zedong and Zhu De's call to develop revolutionary armed forces and establish revolutionary base areas in the south, he, along with Liu Zhidan and Xie Zichang, established the 26th Army of the Chinese Workers' and Farmers' Red Army and the Shaanxi-Gansu border revolutionary base areas, with Zhaojin as the center. At that time, the left-leaning opportunists slandered this, calling it the "Shaoshan doctrine" and the "bandit line," and they forced the 26th Red Army to go south to Weihua, where the KMT had strong ruling power, leading to serious losses for the revolutionary army. Comrade Xi Zhongxun firmly supported the correct line that Comrade Liu Zhidan held onto and opposed the left-leaning opportunist line. After the rapid restoration of the 26th Red Army, Xi established and developed the Shaanxi-Gansu border base and the Northern Shaanxi base. In the struggle against the enemy and against opportunism within the Party, he acquired experience, enhanced his abilities, and carried out a correct revolutionary line. However, Wang Ming's left-leaning opportunists slandered

Liu Zhidan, calling him a "white army officer" who "colluded with warlords," and saying Xi Zhongxun was the "secretary of the right front committee." In September 1935, during the misguided campaign of eliminating the anti-revolutionaries, they imprisoned a large number of cadres such as Liu Zhidan and Xi Zhongxun for fascist interrogations. During Xi Zhongxun's detention, someone secretly asked him if he could escape from danger. He hinted that he could help Xi Zhongxun escape, but Comrade Xi only replied resolutely, "Be loyal to the Party." This showed his nobility and revolutionary ideal, and that he adhered to the revolution and to the Party's correct line without being afraid of death, harboring no resentment for being wronged.

In October 1935, the central Red Army arrived in Northern Shaanxi after the Long March. Chairman Mao and the CPC Central Committee moved quickly to save the Shaanxi-Gansu base area and the northwest revolution. Comrade Xi Zhongxun was cared for and supported by Chairman Mao and the CPC Central Committee, and he held many important leading positions in the Party and

On February 5, 1935, the North Shaanxi Special Committee of the CPC and the Shaanxi-Gansu Border Special Committee held a joint meeting in Zichang County, Zhoujiajian, and decided to establish the Northwest Military Commission and the Working Committee of the CPC. Xi Zhongxun was elected as a member of the working committee. Pictured is the venue of the joint meeting.

government of the Shaanxi-Gansu-Ningxia border region. No matter what he did, he devoted all his effort and progressed bravely. He blazed the path and achieved great things. Chairman Mao wrote an inscription for Comrade Xi Zhongxun, which read, *Putting the interests of the Party first*.

In September 1936, Xi Zhongxun was appointed Secretary of the Guanzhong Special Committee and the Political Commissar of the Guanzhong guerrillas. Pictured is Xi Zhongxun's residence when the Party, government, and military organs of the Guanzhong Special Economic Zone were in Xinzheng County, Majiabao (now Xunyi, Shaanxi Province).

In September 1936, the Party Central Committee transferred Comrade Xi Zhongxun, who had participated in the Western Expedition, back to Bao'an and asked him to participate in the Central Committee Political Bureau meeting convened by Chairman Mao. At this meeting, we discussed winning over Zhang Xueliang's Northeast Army and Yang Hucheng's 17th Route Army and opposing the leftist closed-door tendency in the Party. After the meeting, Comrade Xi Zhongxun was transferred to the post of secretary of the Guanzhong Special Committee and Political Commissar of the guerrillas. At that time, the Soviet area in Guanzhong included Xinning, Xinzheng, Chishui, and Chunyao Counties and a part of Tong (Guan), Yao (Xian) and Yi (Jun), which was called "little Guanzhong." It was like a sharp sword inserted into the KMT ruled area, directly targeting Xi'an, the center of KMT rule in Northwestern China. As a result of the struggle and the need to carry out the work, Comrade Xi Zhongxun transferred the organs of the special committee in Guanzhong many times. Under the general policy of resisting Japan and saving the nation, Xi actively established various organizations, developed different forms of United Front relations around the base areas, made detailed investigation and analysis of each United Front object, faction, social group, and armed force, and established different degrees of United Front contacts according to different situations. We also had contacts with the KMT county government, security corps, and Baojia organizations. Underground Party members who worked in the enemy's local armed forces sent intelligence, guns, and ammunition to us. For example, Comrade Zhao Bojing, an underground member of the Communist Party of China who entered the Kuomintang county security corps, had frequent contact with Comrade Xi Zhongxun, delivering weapons and goods to the guerrillas. During the anti-Japanese war, the special committee developed the Guanzhong base area, formed regular local forces on the basis of guerrilla forces, established special regional political power, organized the Anti-Japanese National Salvation Association and other mass organizations, implemented the "triangular-organization system," executed the Party's United Front policy as an example, and constantly waged a "strategic, systematic, and sustained" struggle against the KMT diehards.

II

Comrade Xi Zhongxun had a profound understanding and flexible application of Marxism, Leninism, and Mao Zedong Thought. He always opposed dogmatism

Xi Zhongxun, then Secretary of the Northwest Bureau of the Communist Party of China and Political Commissar of the Shaanxi-Gansu-Ningxia Jinsui United Defense Force.

and opportunism, especially left-leaning opportunism. He was good at taking the Marxist stand, viewpoint, and method, combining it with reality, and creatively implementing the Party's line, principles, and policies.

During the Yan'an Rectification Movement in 1942, under the direct leadership of the Party Central Committee and Chairman Mao, a meeting of senior cadres of the Party, government, and army in the border region was held. The conference carried forward intra-Party democracy, carried out criticism and self-criticism, comprehensively studied the history and current situation of the border region, affirmed the correct line represented by Comrade Liu Zhidan, criticized some comrades' earlier mistakes in implementing the left-leaning opportunist line, and properly addressed a major problem in the history of the border region.

In October 1945, in order to adapt to the situation of opening up new liberated areas after the victory of the war against Japan, the CPC Central Committee and Chairman Mao appointed Xi Zhongxun as Secretary of the Northwest Bureau

On November 30, 1949, Xi Zhongxun was appointed Political Commissar of the military region after the merger of the First Field Army and the northwest military region with the approval of the Central Military Commission.

of the CPC to lead the work in the northwestern region. He agreed with Mao Zedong's view that Party building, the United Front, and armed struggle were the three "magic weapons" of the Communist Party of China to defeat the enemies of the Chinese revolution. Xi attached great importance to the study of Mao Zedong's theory and thought and used the three "magic weapons" to carry out his work. The Seventh National Congress of the Communist Party of China established Mao Zedong Thought as the guiding ideology of the entire Party. At this meeting, Comrade Xi Zhongxun was elected as an alternate member of the Seventh Central Committee. From that time, he more actively studied and publicized Mao Zedong Thought and resolutely implemented the lines, principles, and policies of the Seventh National Congress of the Communist Party of China. At the meetings held by the Northwest Bureau, he often talked about Mao Zedong Thought and the three "magic weapons," and, combined with practice, he shared his own experience, which was specific and vivid. In our contact with Comrade Xi Zhongxun, we benefited greatly from his understanding of Mao Zedong Thought. Xi often said that "any revolutionary theory should be combined with the actual local situation in a given time. The reason dogmatism is wrong is that it does not take into account the actual situation, but starts from books and applies theories mechanically." For this reason, Xi paid particular attention to investigation and research work. He often held symposiums on the work of the provinces and regions in Northwestern China, talked with various people, raised questions, asked about the situation, and sent staff to conduct onsite investigations, so as to understand and grasp the situation properly to give better guidance on the work. Under his guidance, the Gansu Provincial Working Committee compiled and printed "Survey of the Hui People in Gansu," "Survey of the Hui People in Qingshui," "General Situation of the Hui People's Issue," "Survey of the Fanshi (Tibetan) people in Gansu," "Survey of Ethnic Minorities in Xiahe County," "Survey of the Tibetan People's Life in the Southwestern Border Area of Gansu Province," and "Mongolian People," among other materials, and submitted them to the Northwest Bureau, which provided a reliable basis for the formulation of ethnic policies in the ethnic minority areas in the northwest.

Comrade Xi Zhongxun paid special attention to carrying out the Party's organizational line, treating and employing cadres properly in an effort to unite them. He believed that if the political line was wrong, the organizational line would also be wrong. If we engaged in left-leaning opportunism in politics, we would engage in sectarianism in organization. After he became Secretary of the Northwest Bureau, with the support of the Party Central Committee and Chairman Mao, he adjusted the working groups of the grassroots organizations of the Northwest Bureau, restored and established the Party's working committees in the Kuomintang ruled areas of the northwest provinces, and selected competent cadres who had experience in fighting against the enemy and were familiar with the situation to take charge of the work. Regardless of intimacy, he boldly appointed the cadres fit for the work that needed to be done. If the work failed to be done and no desired result was achieved, he would definitely make adjustment in the appointment. He not only gave the cadres space to work independently, but also offered specific guidance. In this way, a new situation of revolutionary struggle in Northwestern China soon emerged. Shaanxi successively established twelve local working committees, fifteen county working committees across counties and districts, and five guerrilla armed forces of different scales. Gansu established five prefecture-level working committees and seventeen county-level working committees, with each having its own armed forces, which laid a solid foundation for cooperating with the People's Liberation Army to liberate the northwest and win the people's war.

In February 1949, Comrade Xi Zhongxun was appointed Political Commissar of the northwest military region and third secretary of the Northwest Bureau (Peng Dehuai was the first secretary and He Long second secretary). He presided over the work of the Northwest Bureau and welcomed the liberation of the northwest. Under the command of Comrade Peng Dehuai, the First Field Army launched a spring counterattack and liberated Xi'an on May 20, 1949. In July, the Fumei Campaign was launched to annihilate more than 40,000 of the Hu bandit troops, completely smashing the joint counter offensive plan of the Hu and Ma bandit troops, and different parts of Shaanxi were liberated one after another. The army marched westward to fight in Lanzhou and wiped out the Ma bandit troops there. On August 26, Lanzhou was liberated. Ma Hongbin in Ningxia and Tao Zhiyue and Bao Erhan in Xinjiang launched uprisings. In this way, the people's liberation war in Northwestern China was largely completed in two and a half years. In November 1949, Comrade Peng Dehuai presided over the enlarged meeting of the Northwest Bureau of the CPC Central Committee in Lanzhou. The victory of the liberation of the northwest was summed up in the words, "The five provinces in the northwest have been basically liberated. After more than two years of great, arduous war, the northwest battlefield has largely completed its glorious historical task. This is due to the correct leadership of Mao Zedong and the Party Central Committee, the resolute implementation of the line and policies of the Party Central Committee by the Northwest Bureau and the first field Front Committee, the bravery and tenacity of all the commanders, fighters, and staff, the efforts from the rear to support the frontline work, the support of the people in the war zones and the liberated areas, and the cooperation of the troops in the liberated areas, especially the correct leadership of Comrade Mao Zedong, the wise leader of the Party, which was the decisive factor in winning the people's liberation war." Above conclusion was certainly correct.

III

Comrade Xi Zhongxun always attached great importance to the United Front work. When he was in the border region, he paid special attention to the United Front work of the Northeast Army, the Northwest Army, and other enemy forces around the border region that were marginalized by the Central Committee of the Kuomintang. He also worked to win over those local teams and gangs who did not resolutely oppose the revolution. His purpose was to win over as many allies as possible, dividing and isolating the enemy, so as to smoothly carry out the work in the base area. After Comrade Mao Zedong's *Communists* was published, his understanding became clearer, his consciousness improved, and he carried out the Party's principles and policies of the United Front more consciously.

After liberation, proceeding from the actual situation in Northwestern China, Xi Zhongxun proposed that we should attach importance to the United Front work in the newly liberated areas. In ethnic minority areas, the scope of unity should be wider and the policy more relaxed, including not only the democratic parties and non-Party patriots, but also the upper classes of ethnic minorities and religious circles. They united Zhang Feng'ao, Han Zhao'e, Sun Weiru, and Ma Pingfu in Shaanxi, Deng Baoshan, Jiang Yuntai, Huang Zhengqing, and Ma Fuchen in Gansu, Ma Hongbin in Ningxia, Geshe Sherab Gyatso in Qinghai, and Tao Zhiyue, Bao Erhan, and the revolutionary forces of three regions in Xinjiang. On January 10, 1950, at the founding meeting of the Shaanxi Provincial People's Government, Xi delivered a speech entitled "The United Front Policy of Persisting in Cooperation with Non-Party Members." He clearly advanced the idea that "the principle of realizing democratic cooperation between Communists and non-Party members is firm and will never change." This speech played a guiding role not only in Shaanxi, but also in the United Front work of the northwestern provinces at that time.

The main task of the northwest United Front was to do ethnic and religious work, which was an important direction for us in our fight against the enemy. When the Northwest Bureau was stationed in Xi'an, it analyzed the overall situation of the Northwest, noting that it was a vast land area of 3.39 million square kilometers with a small population of 23.5 million, while large pockets of ethnic minorities, including the Hui, Mongolian, Tibetan, Uyghur, and other ethnic groups. Ethnic minority areas accounted for most of the land area, which was rich in resources, but backward in economy and culture. The religious situation was complex: many ethnic groups are exclusively religion believers, and there were many religious factions, which determined the complexity and importance of the northwest ethnic United Front work. It was important and arduous work, especially in terms of policy. If we were careless and thoughtless, we would make mistakes. Therefore, Chairman Mao said that there was one fewer industry issue yet one more ethnic issue in Northwestern China. The Central Committee stressed that the policy of "prudent, steady progress" should be adopted. Everything concerning nationality, religion, the United Front, foreign affairs, and the struggle against the enemy was to be reported for instructions in advance and for summary afterwards.

At first, some comrades did not know enough about the importance of the work of the National United Front, so they despised it and thought that it was a dispensable thing, an excuse to "eat, drink, and entertain." Chairman Mao instructed, "All armed rebellions of a mass nature in ethnic minority areas shall be dealt with as ethnic issues… with political struggle as the main task and military suppression as the supplement. As long as they lay down their arms, we shall be lenient." It also pointed out that it was important to oppose Han chauvinism and local nationalism at the same time. "To really solve the problems of ethnic minorities, we need Communist cadres who have grown up in all ethnic groups." Comrade Xi Zhongxun resolutely carried out Chairman Mao's instructions, dealt with the Xiji Hui rebellion in Gansu Province, and won over Ma Zhenwu, the great imam. He dealt with the Amuquhu Incident and won over Huang Zhengqing. He coped with the Tibetan rebellion in Qinghai Province, captured and released Xiang Qian, and asked master Geshe Sherab Gyatso to cooperate. All this achieved good results.

Comrade Xi Zhongxun realized that the main concerns in the contradictions between ethnic issues at that time were at the upper echelons of the ethnic and religious groups. He proposed that the United Front work of striving for the upper strata of ethnic and religious groups should first be done well, and on this basis, the masses should be mobilized to carry out democratic reform. This was Comrade Xi's original idea of combining theory with practice and unifying principle with flexibility. In the "suppression of reactionaries" and the "land reform," he demanded that the list of leaders of all ethnic groups and sects be drawn up, and as long as they were close to us and supported the land reform, they were protected. We focused on cracking down on those who engaged in ongoing counter revolutionary activities. He proposed that the land of Lama Temple, mosque, Gongbei, and Daotang be preserved and claimed that in the pastoral areas, we would not publicize land reform, nor did we mention opposing the despots but protect animal husbandry. This strategic measure of maintaining a small part of feudalism in exchange for better conditions for mobilizing the masses and eliminating most of feudalism was in line with the actual situation at that time, which achieved remarkable results in practice, while creating the conditions for the implementation of regional ethnic autonomy.

Regional national autonomy was Chairman Mao's basic policy for using Marxism and Leninism to solve China's ethnic problems. It could not only realize the right of ethnic minorities to be masters of their own homes and enable them to develop and prosper according to the situation of the country and their own situation, but also enable all ethnic groups to jointly manage and develop their own areas on the basis of equal status and rights. Therefore, it was more conducive to the unity of the country and the unity of the various ethnic groups, and it was conducive to the common development and prosperity of all ethnic groups. On the basis of strengthening the National United Front and carrying out various democratic reforms, the Northwest Bureau carried out education campaign against Han chauvinism and local nationalism, opposed the ethnic separatist activities of "national self-determination," and resolutely cracked down on the religious rebellion instigated by the upper class of individual religions. When conditions were ripe, the ethnic townships, districts, counties, prefectures, and even autonomous regions would be established without compulsion. In this way, after the liberation of Northwestern China, the Xinjiang Uyghur Autonomous Region was established in 1955, followed by the Ningxia Hui Autonomous Region. The ethnic minorities in Northwestern China were fully integrated into the big family of the Chinese nation. The Han nationality and the ethnic minorities were united as one family and progressed together under the unified leadership of the Party and the state. Over the past forty years, the political level of all ethnic groups in Northwestern China has continuously improved, the economy and culture have prospered, and the people of all ethnic groups have enjoyed a stable, united, beautiful, and happy life. At present, they are marching forward along the path of building socialism with Chinese characteristics. Facts have proven that the establishment of self-governance in ethnic regions is a completely correct policy to solve China's ethnic problems. We firmly believe that all ethnic regional autonomous areas will unswervingly adhere to this plan and actively implement it in accordance with the regulations of ethnic regional autonomy.

Since the beginning of the new era, Comrade Xi Zhongxun has always been concerned about and attached importance to the work of the United Front. "Although the times and tasks are different, the three 'magic weapons' should not be lost," he said. He also proposed that the United Front should follow and serve the Party's basic line, fulfil socialist modernization, accomplish the great cause of the reunification of the motherland, oppose hegemonism, and safeguard world peace. He delivered many important speeches and articles on how to strengthen cooperation with non-Party personages and do a good job in ethnic and religious work under the new situation, which had important guiding significance for promoting the United Front work in the new period. Comrade Xi was a Party leader who had great ability and rich experience in United Front work.

IV

After the liberation, the Northwest Bureau and the Shaanxi Provincial Party Committee found that the land in the Guanzhong area was scattered and not concentrated, being small at both ends and large in the middle. Landlords accounted for less than 1% of the rural population, and plus wealthy farmers, about 6% in total, they occupied about 20% of the total land. Middle class farmers accounted for 40% to 50% of the rural population in household registration and occupied 50% to 60% of the land. Taking thirteen counties, one city, 102 districts, 775 townships, and 8,156 natural villages in Baoji District before the land reform in 1950 as an example, the survey showed that 807 households of landlords accounted for 0.27% in the entire province, with a population of 8,729, for 0.6%, 221,864.42 *mu* of land, for 3.18%, 27.7 *mu* per capita. A total of 4,711 households of rich farmers accounted for 1.6%, with a population of 58,596 accounting for 3.47%, and 491,973.78 *mu* land accounting for 7.06%, or 8.4 *mu* per capita. A total of 10,771 households of affluent middle class farmers accounted for 3.7%, with a population of 103,036 accounting for 5.8%, and 690,029.875 *mu* of land accounting for 9.89%, or 6.69 *mu* per capita. A total of 100,165 households of middle class farmers accounted for 34.12%, with a population of 673,432 accounting for 38.1%, and 3,001,136.4 *mu* of land accounting for 43%, or 4.45 *mu* per capita. A total of 152,592 households of poor farmers accounted for 52%, with a population of 800,515 accounting for 45.25%, and 2,350,192.6 *mu* of land accounting for 33.7%, or 2.93 *mu* per capita. A total of 19,775 households of hired farmers accounted for 6.73%, with a population of 102,792 accounting for 5.61%, and 157,970 *mu* of land accounting for 2.26%, or 1.53 *mu* per capita. This was basically consistent with the land data investigated by the Northwest Bureau, so the policies and measures formulated by the Northwest Bureau and the Shaanxi Provincial Party Committee in the land reform were based on reality and seeking truth from facts. For example, in the determination of class composition, it was emphasized that "we need to have evidence and think twice," and "those identified with a clear class composition are allowed to attend meetings and put forward different opinions." Further, "if there are difficulties or disputes over class composition, it should be suspended, studied further, and instructions requested from the higher authorities." In the review of the land reform, the Northwest Bureau clearly required that "those who can be designated as small land lessors… should not be categorized as landlords." It was emphasized that we should seriously deal with the issue of defining the composition and guard against the mistake of making wrong determinations. For example, Deng, a doctor in Pingtou Town of Baoji, was rich and powerful. His parents were categorized as landlords, but he was not. Hu Jingyi's family in Gongping County and Hao Jingsheng's family in Lintong County, which had made contributions to the revolution, were only categorized as landlords, but measures were taken to protect the individuals from suffering. Comrade Xi Zhongxun also made it clear that "when the mass movement is launched, it is like a canal of river water coming down. We must pay close attention to the breach of the embankment on both sides." Good leadership work was to be done "naturally." Thus, during the land reform, 33,165 households were categorized as landlords and rich farmers in Guanzhong, accounting for 2.35% of the total farming households at that time.

After more than 40,000 bandits were eliminated in the Battle of Fumei in the Baoji area, the remnant of the enemy fled to the southwest. When our 18th Corps followed the remnant to the south of the Qinling Mountains, our local troops and the armed forces of individual counties organized, according to the instructions of the Northwest Bureau, were instructed to thoroughly eliminate bandits, scattered soldiers, security teams, township guards, and other residual armed forces and confiscate all hidden guns. As a result, Qin Botan's security regiment and more than 400 bandits of "the loyal and righteous National Salvation Army" of secret agent Mei Shucheng were successively eliminated. Other eliminated security guards below the county level included Chen Goudan in Meixian County, Song Jiantang in Zuitou, Baoji, Wang Ruilin and Quan Shijun in Fufeng, Zhao Zijie in Longxian, and Li Zhengxi in Qianyang. We mobilized those who had contact with us, such as Han Zhaoxiong in Fufeng and Wu Yanchang in Meixian, to hand over their guns to the people's government, and the number reached as many as a few thousand. We immediately and resolutely eliminated individual rebels. In general, despots were more or less armed, and the elimination of local residual armed forces was closely linked to the fight against despots. The suppression of bandits, secret agents, and tyrants and the suppression of the backbone of the reactionary party, league, and other counter revolutionaries in the Guanzhong area were thorough, which was in line with the correct policies and requirements set by the central government.

With long-term contact and observation, we believed that the most prominent ideological style of Comrade Xi Zhongxun's revolutionary career was to proceed from reality and seek truth from facts. He was worthy of the nurture and trust of the Party and the people and the great cause he was dedicated to.

Attachment:

Mutual Trust and Friendship between Comrade Sun Zuobin and Comrade Xi Zhongxun

Sun Xiaobei

Sun Xiaobei is the daughter of Sun Zuobin, former Vice Minister of the United Front Department of the Northwest Bureau of the CPC Central Committee and Deputy Director of the Ethnic Affairs Committee of the Northwest Military and Political Commission.

My father, Sun Zuobin, was three years older than Uncle Xi Zhongxun. They met when they were working underground in Gansu Province in the early 1930s. In his later years, my father once said, "Comrade Xi Zhongxun is my teacher and good friend." We could see his respect for Uncle Xi.

From October 19, 1942, to January 14, 1943, the conference of senior cadres of the Shaanxi-Gansu-Ningxia border region was held in Yan'an for 88 days, and my father further increased his affinity for and understanding of Comrade Xi Zhongxun. After Chairman Mao's correction, the principle of "killing no one and capturing only a few" was proposed, so that the countercurrent of left-leaning opportunism and sectarianism was stopped.

In 1954, the Northwest Bureau was closed down, and there was some change in my father's work arrangement. Another candidate took over his original post, and my father was assigned to work in Qinghai. He was a bit frustrated and reluctant, wondering why he was sent to a place no one else went. Uncle Xi had a long talk with my father, saying, "Zuobin, Qinghai Province is a multi-ethnic area. You have the competence and experience in nationalities and religion… It's because other people don't want to go that you're assigned to go there. I'm sure your Party spirit will confirm that, too." Because of Uncle Xi Zhongxun's talk, my father happily went to his new post, where he served as Second Secretary and Governor of Qinghai Provincial Party Committee, working there for 25 years.

After the Third Plenary Session of the 11th CPC Central Committee, my parents returned to work in Shaanxi. My father was from Xi'an and my mother was from Yuling, and Uncle Xi was from Gongping. If they got together, it was like a Qin Opera Competition. Although they were comrades and brothers, they didn't get many opportunities to meet. But there were many other ways for them to get in touch, making phone calls and sending New Year cards. More often, they sent regards via other comrades. Lü Jianren, Liu Lizhen, and Li Lianbi all brought Uncle Xi's greetings to my father. Once a young stranger came, and when we asked what he wanted and whom he was looking for, he replied, "Mr. Xi asked me to visit Mr. Sun." It turned out to be the son of the singer Yun Enfeng. He visited Mr. Xi on behalf of his mother. When Mr. Xi heard that he was going to Xi'an, he asked him to visit Mr. Sun on his behalf and report back to him about my father. Apparently, my father was completely beside himself.

Hu Jun visited my father a couple of times a year. He was the grandson of General Hu Jingyi. My father, Hu Xizhong, and Mr. Xi were good friends during their school days. They had had a deep bond since childhood. At a class reunion of the Yan'an Baoyu Primary School, I thanked Hu Jun for his long-term care for and visits to my father. He said, "I knew Uncle Sun when I was little, in Yan'an. It's natural that I would go to visit him. Besides, I visited him on behalf of Uncle Xi Zhongxun many times. Whenever I met Uncle Xi Zhongxun, he always talked about your father. I think Uncle Xi's evaluation of your father was the highest of all. He often said that your father was loyal, honest, and frank with the Party and the comrades. Although he was wronged many times, he never retreated, and the more frustrated he was, the more brave he turned out to be."

One day in the late 1980s, Uncle Xi, who was in Xi'an at that time, hoped to meet with the five elders of Shaanxi, and he asked the Provincial Party Committee to make the arrangements. The five elders, Lü Jianren, Chang Lifu, Liu Haibin, Tan Weixu, and Sun Zuobin, finally met with Xi to have a good talk. They were full of enthusiasm and hope for the Party. They felt that a peaceful, prosperous era of China was just around the corner. At dinner, Uncle Xi invited my father to sit beside him.

General Secretary Hu Yaobang proposed that we dig into the Party history materials, especially those of the underground workers of the Party, and write about their history as early as possible while they were still alive. Sun Zuobin was listed as a living underground Party member to be written by the Party History Office of Shaanxi Province. Upon learning about this, Uncle Xi Zhongxun was glad to write a preface to the book *Sun Zuobin*. He wrote at the end of the preface that Sun Zuobin fought against leftism for the previous seventy years, since he joined the Party and revolution. Despite repeated difficulties, he remained tenacious and upright, and he always dared to tell the truth, instead of telling lies or riding with the tide. He should be viewed as a role model of seeking truth from facts and adhering to the truth.

Xi Zhongxun and the Hengshan Uprising[1]

LI FENGQUAN

Li Fengquan, a native of Weinan in Shaanxi Province, was born in 1930. He was a professor of Northwest University of Politics and Law, a consultant of the Party Construction Research Association, a member of the Shaanxi Veteran Professor Association, the Association of Senior Science and Education Workers, and the Research Association of Revolutionary History in the Shaanxi-Gansu-Ningxia border area. He engaged in teaching and research on Marxist theory, the history of the CPC, and the history of the Chinese revolution for many years. His works include *Biography of Hu Jingyi* and *The Uprising of Hengshan*. Xi Zhongxun, Qu Wu, and Ma Wenrui wrote the prefaces to his works.

The Hengshan uprising, also known as the Yuheng uprising, was a large-scale anti-Chiang armed uprising in the Kuomintang garrison in the Hengshan area of Yulin, Shaanxi Province in the early period of the liberation war. Under the guidance of Chairman Mao Zedong, the uprising was planned and organized by Comrade Xi Zhongxun. It held great significance in the history of the Chinese revolution led by the Communist Party of China and was an important part in Xi Zhongxun's revolutionary career.

In August 1945, after eight years of fierce fighting, the anti-Japanese war of the entire nation finally ended with a victory. While the people of the entire country celebrated their victory with singing and dancing and expected the two parties to continue to cooperate and work to establish a new, free, democratic country, the ruling group represented by Chiang Kai-shek actively prepared to

1. This article is selected from *Wide World*, Issue 4, 2009.

launch a comprehensive civil war and sought to eliminate the Communist Party of China and the people's army under CPC leadership. The Central Committee and Chairman Mao then set the political policy of "confrontation and fighting for every piece of land," took all possible measures to stop the outbreak of civil war, and required the whole Party to be more vigilant and resolutely crush Chiang Kai-shek's conspiracy.

Chairman Mao asked the Party and government leaders in all liberated areas to stress on the United Front work and the division and disintegration of the Kuomintang army while intensifying preparations for war. On October 25, the CPC Central Committee issued the instructions "Establishing the Work Department of the National Army," and decided to establish the National Army Work Department in the Central Military Commission, the central bureaus, and the central sub-bureaus to strengthen political publicity and to instigate a rebellion within the enemy camp against the KMT army.

At this time, Xi Zhongxun had just been transferred from the position of Deputy Minister of the Central Organization Department to the post of Secretary

In 1934, Xi Zhongxun was elected president of the Soviet government of the Shaanxi-Gansu border region. The picture shows the Temple of the Lord, which was the place where the Soviet government was located in the Shaanxi-Gansu border area.

of the Northwest Bureau of the CPC Central Committee and Political Committee of the Jinsui Defense Army in the Shaanxi-Gansu-Ningxia border area. After receiving instructions from the Party Central Committee and Mao Zedong, Xi immediately informed Secretary General Zhang Desheng to hold a meeting of cadres of the United Front Department of the Northwest Bureau, conveyed the central instructions, and made thorough arrangements for implementing the central instructions in the Shaanxi-Gansu-Ningxia border area.

The Shaanxi-Gansu-Ningxia border area was surrounded by Kuomintang troops at the time. To the south, there was the 200,000 soldier troop of Chiang's direct line, and Hu Zongnan and Ma Hongkui's cavalry divisions to the west. To the north, there was the command department of the Kuomintang's Jin-Shaan-Sui border area and its 22nd Corps and Baojiu Regiment, and to the east was the torrential Yellow River, which was opposite to the liberated area of Jinsui. At that time, there were 22 counties in the Shaanxi-Gansu-Ningxia border area, with a population of 1.5 million, and more than 20,000 troops. The gap in strength between the enemy and our army was evident, and the situation was extremely serious.

As one of the founders and leaders of the revolutionary base of the Shaanxi-Gansu-Ningxia border area, Xi Zhongxun knew the situation in the border area and its surrounding region very well. When analyzing the situation, he pointed out that the enemy was stronger in might and equipment, but we were a revolutionary team with the support of the people. In particular, with the direct command of the Party Central Committee and Chairman Mao, we could defeat the enemy. In order to ensure the victory of the war of self-defense, we had to mobilize the masses and prepare for war. In the meantime, we needed to strengthen the work of the United Front in accordance with the latest instructions from the Central Committee, especially the work of instigating rebellion within the enemy camp against KMT forces. Xi further explained in great detail how to carry out the United Front and instigation work in the KMT army. Judging from the surrounding areas, the north line was a weak part of the enemy, where the 22nd Troop and the Baojiu Regiment of the KMT were stationed, which were the "miscellaneous army" of the KMT and in conflict with Chiang Kai-shek and Hu Zongnan. There were also conflicts within the "miscellaneous army" with strong feudal consciousness as well. From Jing Yuexiu (the garrison envoy stationed in Northern Shaanxi after the 1911 Revolution and the founder of the 22nd Corps) to Zuo Xiezhong (the commander of the 22nd Corps), the army was run in a patriarchal rule, with strong hometown or family ties. During the anti-Japanese war, we had a good United

Front relationship with them. Now, we needed to keep this relationship, as far as possible, and break through their feudal consciousness, make use of their conflicts with Chiang Kai-shek and Hu Zongnan to further win them over, winning as many as we could, especially those with a patriotic mindset who would side with us and oppose Chiang Kai-shek, the civil war, and the pro-Chiang supporters and special agents in Yulin. If we could do well in this regard, it would be favorable to smashing the invasion of Chiang Kai-shek and Hu Zongnan.

After discussion, the United Front Department of the Northwest Bureau and the United Front Department of the Suide local committee were specifically responsible for the United Front work of the Yulin KMT army. The cadres and divisions in the Guanzhong District were selected as deputy directors of the United Front Department of the Suide local committee to assist and strengthen the activities of the national army of Yulin. After the meeting, Xi Zhongxun sent Cao Liru, Commissioner of the Yanzi District, and Liu Wenwei, Deputy Secretary of the Suide local committee, northward to Yulin to contact Hu Xizhong and gain some insight into the specific situation of the upper stratum of Yulin, especially the movement of Hu Jingtong, Vice Military Commander of the 22nd Corps and Security Commander of Northern Shaanxi Province, and Hu Jingduo, Vice Security Commander, so as to win them over and motivate them to hold an anti-Chiang uprising at the appropriate time.

Hu Jingtong and Hu Jingduo were the younger brothers of General Hu Jingyi, the famous patriotic general and the old democratic revolutionary, ranking fifth and sixth in the family, and thus addressed as "Hu Laowu (the fifth)" and "Hu Laoliu (the sixth)." Hu Xizhong was the son of Hu Jingyi, addressed as "Hu Dashao (the eldest son)." Hu Jingduo and Hu Xizhong were roughly of the same age. They were both from Fuping, Xi Zhongxun's hometown, and were classmates of Xi at the Licheng school. They participated in revolutionary activities together in their youth and had a strong friendship. Later, although they went to different places, they still kept in touch through letters. Hu Jingduo and Hu Xizhong had long been eager to join the revolutionary team in the border areas. Because of the need for revolutionary work, the Party organization had instructed them to continue to stay in the Kuomintang ruled area and Kuomintang forces, taking advantage of Hu Jingyi's influence to carry out the United Front work for the anti-Japanese war. Before the victory of the anti-Japanese war, they returned to Fuping, led more than 1,000 people from their subordinates and their hometown to the north to Yulin and Hengshan, and temporarily stayed under the command of General Deng Baoshan, the commander-in-chief of the Kuomintang Jin-Shan-Sui border area.

Hu Jingduo was appointed Deputy General Commander in charge of security in Northern Shaanxi, and Hu Xizhong was appointed as a consultant of the Jin-Shan-Sui commanding headquarter. They aimed to go to the Shaanxi-Gansu-Ningxia border area and participate in the revolution. When they arrived in Yuling and Hengshan, they contacted Xi Zhongxun secretly and hoped to get Xi's support and help. So Xi Zhongxun sent Cao Liru and Liu Wenwei to Yulin to meet Hu Xizhong, carrying Xi's personal letter.

Hu Xizhong reported to Cao Liru and Liu Wenwei the upper dynamics of the KMT in Yulin, saying that the 86th Division was the main force of the 22nd Corps. Xu Zhijia, the new chief of division, was a military secret agent and the main figure sent by Chiang Kai-shek to monitor Deng Baoshan and carry out anti-Communist activities. General Deng Baoshan was currently taking a wait-and-see approach to the dispute between the KMT and the Communist Party, and there was no sign of him going public in an anti-Chiang struggle. Hu Jingtong, Deng's uncle, followed Deng's orders, thus the conditions for instigating them to hold the uprising were not yet mature. Hu Jingduo, however, was different. He had already shown his firm anti-Chiang attitude, and he secretly contacted a group of progressive elements in his army, ready to go to the border area at any time. The conditions for Hu Jingduo to launch the uprising were thus mature. Xi Zhongxun was invited to send someone to Boluo Fort (the security headquarters in Northern Shaanxi) to contact Hu Jingduo.

Cao Liru and Liu Wenwei reported their understanding to Xi Zhongxun. Xi immediately decided to focus on Hu Jingduo to instigate the national army of the northern line, and he sent Shi Yuan to meet Hu Jingduo in Boluo Fort.

Shi Yuan and Hu Jingduo were old classmates and friends. When they met, they had a nice long talk, and soon reached an agreement. Hu Jingduo made clear that he was determined to follow the Communist Party and Comrade Xi Zhongxun in all his action, and he asked Comrade Xi Zhongxun to help him join the revolutionary team as soon as possible. Shi Yuan returned to Suide as soon as he completed his mission.

Xi Zhongxun went to Suide to hear a detailed report from Shi Yuan on his trip to Boluo Fort. Later, Xi convened a meeting of the Standing Committee of the Suide local committee to study on how to help with Hu Jingduo's uprising. Xi Zhongxun made a detailed analysis and explanation of the significance and preparation of Hu Jingduo's uprising at the meeting. He said that Chairman Mao attached great importance to our work on the northern line, with the aim of liberating Yuling and making more room for the self-defense war in the border area. Now our United Front work focused on Boluo Fort, which could provide a breakthrough for the instigation. Hu Jingduo was a reliable man with a relatively progressive mind. We aimed to continue to do the persuasive work and provide him with help to win him over when the time for uprising was ready. If it was done properly, we believed it would have a great impact and would help us thoroughly settle the northern line issue. Xi Zhongxun directed Shi Yuan to go to Boluo to discuss with Hu Jingduo the establishment of the Party organization in Hu's army as the core force of the uprising, and then to send a group of political and military cadres from the border area to his army to prepare for the uprising. Our policy was "to build the Party and the army, prepare for the growth in strength, remain unnoticed for a long time, and take action when the time is ripe," he said.

Throughout the summer of 1946, according to Xi Zhongxun's deployment, from Suide to Boluo, frequent covert activities were carried out around the Hu Jingduo uprising.

In May, Hu Jingduo joined the Communist Party of China, introduced by Xi Zhongxun and approved by the Central Committee of the Party. According to Hu Jingduo's request, the date on which he joined the Party was scheduled to be July 1.

Then, the Northwest Bureau of the CPC Central Committee discussed the list of potential candidates of the Party members proposed by Hu Jingduo, approved

The birthplace of the Hengshan uprising, Boluo Fort.

the joining of Comrade Li Zhenhua, Yao Shaowen, Zhang Yaxiong, Xu Xiuqi, Li Zhenying, Yang Hanshan, Wei Maochen, and others who joined the Party on August 1. At the same time, more than forty military and political cadres selected by the border Yanshu branch and Suide districts entered the security corps in Northern Shaanxi, such as Boluo and Shiwan, in various ways that were not easily perceived by the enemy. Underground Party members such as Zhang Yaxiong and Li Zhenying were arranged to join each company in a reasonable, proper manner, and they secretly did publicity and contact work.

At the end of June, Chiang Kai-shek launched a comprehensive civil war, attacking the liberated areas of the central plains, northeast, Northern China, Jinchaji, Jin-Ji-Lu-Yu, Jinsui, and other liberated areas led by the Communist Party of China. The situation around the Shaanxi-Gansu-Ningxia border area was very tense. Hu Zongnan intensified the mobilization of troops on the south line, pushed the vehicles of war to the border area gate, and ordered the troops of the northern line to attack the border area, in order to form a North-South attack against the border area. But at that time, Hu Zongnan had six divisions that were still far away from Henan and Southern Shaanxi, who could not reach the front line of the offensive border area for a while, so he was unable to quickly launch a large-scale attack on the Shaanxi-Gansu-Ningxia border area. When Xi Zhongxun reported to Mao Zedong about the situation of the border area and the United Front work among the enemy of the north line, Mao directed him to seize the opportunity to further strengthen the United Front work and at the same time, to organize the north line campaign by concentrating the troops and to resolve the north line issue by combining military and political methods, so as to concentrate on the attack of Hu Zongnan and gain more leeway for the border area's defensive war.

Xi Zhongxun had a clear understanding of Mao's important decision. On July 1, he convened a meeting of the Standing Committee of the Northwest Bureau in Huashibian, Yan'an, conveying the instructions of Chairman Mao Zedong, and focused on the issues of responding to the Hu Jingduo uprising and organizing the Northern Line campaign. At the meeting, we agreed with Comrade Xi that although the KMT army in the Yulin and Hengshan areas was weak in might, it was a serious threat to our rear area when it cooperated with Hu Zongnan. In particular, Shiwan, Gaozhen, and Wuzhen in Hengshan County were the outposts of the enemy 22nd Corps and the security headquarters in Northern Shaanxi, like knives inserted into our border area, and during wartime it would directly hinder our army's activities in Northern Shaanxi. Therefore, it was of great strategic significance to coordinate with the Hengshan uprising, organize the Northern Line

Xi Zhongxun, political committee member of Shaanxi-Gansu-Ningxia Joint Defense Army, and Commander He Long.

campaign, eliminate the direct threat of the National Army on the northern line, and create the conditions for the liberation of the entire Yulin and Hengshan areas. Our United Front work on the enemy forces of Yulin and Hengshan had achieved great success. The progressive forces led by Hu Jingduo had shown a firm attitude against Chiang and actively drawn closer to our Party. We had already made certain preparations in their troops. The conditions for organizing and launching an armed uprising were basically mature. In addition, we had made good preparations for the takeover work, and there was great potential for its success. However, the overall situation was that the enemy was stronger than us, and the situation in the Yulin and Hengshan areas was very complex. We needed to think more about the difficulties and problems that might be encountered in organizing and responding to the uprising, and the action plan needed to be very thorough. After discussion, the meeting proposed three action plans. First, with the support of the PLA, we would strive to win a victory in the Hengshan uprising, and then seize Yulin with the momentum gained from the victory, so as to settle completely the issue on the northern lines. Second, if, despite the victory in the uprising, effective attacks on Yulin were not likely to be organized, we would first liberate the area south of the Wuding River and remove the southwestern barrier of Yulin, and then attack Yulin when conditions permitted. Third, if anything unexpected occurred in the uprising, Hu Jingduo would immediately withdraw from the original defense and lead his backbone troops into the border area, and the border area would prepare to accept them.

The meeting also made two corresponding decisions. First, Wang Shitai, acting commander of the Jinsui Joint Defense Army in the Shaanxi-Gansu-Ningxia border area, and Zhang Zhongliang, deputy political committee member, were responsible for the preparation of the northern line campaign, and they would support and respond to the Hengshan uprising. Second, Fan Ming, Director of the United Front Department of the Northwest Bureau, was sent to Suide and prepared to go to Boluo to talk to Hu Jingduo on the specific plan for the uprising.

In late August, as a political member of the Shaanxi-Gansu-Ningxia Jinsui Joint Defense Army (Commander He Long went to the Jinsui liberation zone to command the war), Xi Zhongxun held meetings with military leaders such as Wang Shitai and Zhang Zhongliang. According to the spirit of the Huashibian Meeting, he discussed the deployment of the northern line campaign, established the Northern Line Battle Command Department, with Wang Shitai and Zhang Zhongliang as the chief and deputy commanders who were responsible for formulating the preparation plan and for the operations of the northern line battle.

After the meeting, Xi presented a written report on the principles and plans of the northern line campaign to Chairman Mao Zedong of the CPC Central Committee. Mao Zedong approved on September 2, saying, "Act upon the principles set out here."

After the plan for the northern line campaign was approved by Mao Zedong, Xi Zhongxun immediately went to Suide to check on the preparations before the war, and he assigned Fan Ming to take his letter to Boluo to meet Hu Jingduo, convey the instructions of the Central Committee of the Party and the Northwest Bureau, and discuss the specific plan for the armed uprising face to face.

Just after the Mid-autumn Festival, Hu Jingduo received Fan Ming at home, who had been sent by Xi Zhongxun disguised as a teacher of the Licheng Middle School. They had never met, but they immediately hit it off, and soon began talking business. Fan Ming conveyed to Hu Jingduo the analysis of the current situation, the basic principles of the Party, and the decision and basic plan of the Northwest Bureau for launching the Hengshan uprising. When he said that Chiang Kai-shek had launched a civil war with the support of American imperialism and that the Chinese revolution would experience some difficulties, Hu Jingduo firmly responded, "We should take part in the revolution when the Party and revolution are still in difficulty, and never be part of Chiang Kai-shek's team. If we only participated in the revolution in a favorable revolutionary situation or when we had no other options, what would be the point?" Hu Jingduo clearly expressed his firm determination to launch the uprising and fully agreed to the Northwest Bureau's policy and plan for it.

On the third day of the talks, they discussed in detail specific issues about the uprising, including the date and place of the uprising, the list of cadres serving as its leaders, the response of the PLA to the various departments of the uprising, the name of the rebel forces, the slogan, the control and treatment of the reactionaries, the content of "the cable" after the uprising, and the specific methods for the contact between the two sides, among other things. On the basis of common understanding, a detailed plan for the implementation of the uprising was jointly formulated.

With the pressing challenges of time, Fan Ming immediately returned to the border area. Hearing the report on Fan Ming's trip to Boluo, Xi Zhongxun took Fan to Zaoyuan and reported to Chairman Mao. Chairman Mao listened to their reports and looked at the layout plan of the Yulin and Hengshan enemy sent by the combat section of the Joint Defense Force Command, and then said to Xi Zhongxun and Wang Shitai, "It's time to start the uprising." He ordered the Joint Defense Command to concentrate the forces of six regiments and do well in response to the uprising.

When the specific plan of the uprising had been drawn up, Hu Jingduo immediately informed the backbone leaders in his troops to step up the preparation before the uprising and strictly keep it secret. However, the KMT agents and Hu Jingtong's messengers did not sleep. They were always alert to catching all suspicious signs, especially when, under the guise of organizing army cadres' session, Hu Jingduo trained the backbone of the uprising. This aroused their suspicion, and they reported it to Yulin headquarters. Hu Jingtong immediately called Hu Jingduo to Yulin for inquiry. Hu Jingduo realized that it was a dangerous signal that, if not well handled, it would have an adverse effect on the armed uprising that had been planned for so long and was about to be put into effect. After careful consideration and meticulous arrangement, he decided to go to Yulin regardless of the threat to his personal safety, and he met Hu Jingtong, his elder brother, and the vice military commander of the 22nd Corps and security commander of Northern Shaanxi. Hu Jingtong asked him severely, "What on earth were you doing in Boluo? Were you trying to ruin my decades of hard work in Northern Shaanxi? Did the people you took with you have hidden motives? What exactly were you thinking when you ran the training sessions for officials?" Composed and determined, Hu Jingduo defended himself with explanations that he was "straightening up the military outlook, boosting morale, and eliminating various bad elements," thus removing any doubts that his brother had. Because the scheduled date of the uprising was approaching, Hu Jingduo cleverly got free from the entanglement of Xu Zhijia, the chief spy, and fled from Yulin back to Boluo.

Xi Zhongxun watched Yulin and Hengshan closely. On the third day of Hu Jingduo's return from Yulin (October 5), Xi convened a meeting of leaders of the northern line battle headquarters, including Wang Shitai, Zhang Zhongliang, and Xu Liqing, to respond to Hu Jingduo's uprising and take liberating the area south of the Wuding River as the basic point. He ordered all the PLA departments under the jurisdiction to enter a battle state immediately, and he organized 3,000 militia members to cooperate in the operation.

On October 11, when the KMT forces occupied Zhangjiakou, the capital of the liberated area of Jinchaji, Chiang Kai-shek immediately ordered the convening of the "National Congress" he had arranged and ordered Hu Zongnan to actively prepare to raid Yan'an. He threatened to eliminate the Communist Party within three months, and he generally put on an arrogant air.

On October 13, the northern line campaign (also known as the Yuheng Campaign) was launched under the command of Wang Shitai and Zhang Zhongliang. In the early morning, the battle started from the Wuzhen and Zhenchuan Forts between Yulin and Hengshan. The new 4th Brigade chief, Zhang Xianyue, led the main force to launch an attack on Wuzhen. Luo Yuanfa, commander of the brigade in Yanshu District, led the troop to attack the Zhenchuan Fort, annihilated one regiment and two battalions of the enemy at one stroke, and continued to push northward all the way to the South Gate of Yulin, which kept the enemy in Yulin from taking the initiative. At the same time, Zhang Zhongliang led the new 4th Brigade, Suide Police Brigade, and the new 11th Brigade to surround Hengshan County, which put the KMT garrison's Wang Yongqing cavalry regiment in a dilemma.

The PLA military operations on the east and west sides created a favorable condition for the Hu Jingduo uprising. Under Hu's command, the security headquarters in Northern Shaanxi and its subordinate departments simultaneously launched armed uprisings in the Boluo, Shiwan, and Gaozhen areas in Hengshan County.

In Boluo, Hu Jingduo gathered all the main figures of the reactionaries under house arrest on the night of the 12th, under the guise of a meeting held at headquarters. On the morning of the 13th, he personally went outside the city to meet the reception troops led by Fan Ming into the city, and then called a general meeting of all officers and soldiers and officially announced the uprising. Hu Jingduo delivered an inspiring speech at the general assembly, declaring, "It is unpopular for Chiang Kai-shek and Hu Zongnan to launch the anti-Communist civil war, and we should not serve as their gunpowder. We are the men of the Shaanxi, and our blood should be sprinkled on the battlefield for justice. Yulin is not our world yet, though it is good. We should go north to Yulin and south to Xi'an to drive away Hu Zongnan and put the red flag on the bell tower in the center of the provincial city. We are now the Northwest Democratic Joint Army, and the PLA is our friend. We had a common purpose to overthrow Chiang Kai-shek and the Nanjing government, and to liberate China." In this way, without a single shot, the Boluo Uprising declared a victory. A cavalry company in the 11th Brigade of the enemy troops stationed near the Boluo joined the uprising under the leadership of Company Chief Yang Hansan.

In Shiwan, Zhang Yaxiong, deputy chief of the Baojiu regiment, Fan Zhiying, director of military logistics, Xu Xiuqi, commander of the machine gun crops, and others opened the gate on the morning of the 13th and welcomed the reception troops led by Gao Langting, deputy political commissar of the Suide army, arrested all the reactionaries who tried to resist, and surrounded the regiment of Baojiu, forcing Zhang Ziya, the head of the regiment, to surrender. That afternoon, all the officers and soldiers gathered on the playground to announce the success of the uprising. Shiwan, the most important military town closest to the Shaanxi-Gansu-Ningxia border area, declared liberation.

In Gaozhen, Qin Yuewen, deputy head of the Baojiu regiment, and Wu Fengde, leader of the Baojiu regiment, announced the uprising to all the officers and soldiers on Hu Jingduo's order. When Gao Langting and Zhang Yaxiong came from Shiwan to aid, Gaozhen had already raised the flag of the uprising.

In Hengshan County, under the influence of the Boluo uprising, the besieged Wang Yongqing cavalry regiment was persuaded by Hu Jingduo and joined the uprising. Thus far, the Hengshan uprising had won a complete victory as planned. Under the leadership of General Hu Jingduo, the officers and men of the Baojiu Regiment of the Yulin security headquarters of the Kuomintang and the new 11th Brigade of the 86th Division of the 22nd Corps, with a total of more than 5,000 people, embarked on the revolutionary road under the leadership of Hu Jingduo.

After the victory of the Hengshan uprising, the troops and the PLA jointly launched the Xiangshui Campaign, destroying ten companies of Yulin reinforcements and one battalion of the garrison in Xiangshui and bringing a successful end to the north line campaign. The direct result of the victory of the northern line campaign and the Hengshan uprising was that 120,000 people and a large area of land in Northern Shaanxi were liberated, the 6th Cavalry Division of the Northwest Democratic Alliance Army was created, and the Yuheng Special Zone under the leadership of the Communist Party was established. As a result, KMT forces on the northern line of the border region lost 25 solid strongholds and 40 military units, which expanded and strengthened the PLA's northern line positions, creating favorable conditions for the CPC Central Committee to move to Northern Shaanxi, command the national war of liberation, and topple the attacks of Chiang Kai-shek and Hu Zongnan.

After reorganization and training, the troops from the uprising were transferred to Yan'an in mid-December on order from Chairman Mao Zedong. Wherever they went, they were warmly welcomed by people from all walks of life in the border region. What was most unforgettable for Hu Jingduo and the other officers and soldiers of the uprising was the day of December 24. On that day, Mao Zedong, Liu Shaoqi, Zhou Enlai, Zhu De, Ren Bishi, Peng Dehuai, Xi Zhongxun, Deng

Xiangshui Fort, which was attacked by Shaanxi-Gansu-Ningxia Jinsui United Defense Forces during the Hengshan Uprising.

Yingchao, Kang Keqing, Wang Shitai, and other comrades of the CPC Central Committee and the Central Military Commission cordially received Hu Jingduo and other leading cadres from the uprising troops. Mao Zedong clasped Hu Jingduo's hand and said, "Comrade Jingduo, you got off Deng Baoshan's ship and got on Xi Zhongxun's ship when the enemy was strong and we were weak. You have chosen the right path. Your revolutionary action has pointed out a bright path for the old army in the northwest."

The Hengshan uprising was of great historical significance because it took place on the northern front of the Shaanxi-Gansu-Ningxia border region, where the CPC Central Committee was located. It took place in the Kuomintang troops that directly surrounded the Shaanxi-Gansu-Ningxia border region, and it occurred at a historical moment when the enemy was strong and we were weak, when the enemy attacked and we defended, and when the enemy was very arrogant. Against this historical background, the Hengshan uprising had a significant political and military impact, and "pointed out a bright path" not only for the old army in the northwest, but also for all patriots. As Commander-in-Chief Zhu De said, General Hu Jingduo's uprising in Hengshan and countless other similar events "formed a trend." This trend "became one of the important factors for the people to defeat the reactionaries in the war of self-defense and bring about the independence, peace, and democracy of the country.

On Xi Zhongxun's Revolutionary Achievements[1]

FAN MING

Fan Ming was from Lintong, Shaanxi Province. He joined the Communist Party of China in 1938. During the anti-Japanese war, he was sent to the 38th Army of the 17th Route Army of the National Revolutionary Army as a member and secretary of the CPC Working Committee, leader of the 38th Army's instruction team, and commander of the company directly under the search company to engage in United Front work. During the War of Liberation, he served as Director of the United Front Department of the Northwest Bureau of the CPC Central Committee and Director of the Political Department of the 6th Cavalry Division. In 1949, he served as Secretary General of the political department and Director of the Liaison Department of the First Field Army. He took part in the battle of Yan'an and the Battles of Qinghuabian, Yangmahe, Panlong, Shajiadian, Yichuan, Libei, Fumei, and Lanzhou. After the founding of the new China, he served as commander and political commissar of the Tibetan troops of the northwest People's Liberation Army, deputy secretary of the CPC Tibet Working Committee, and deputy political commissar of the Tibet Military Region.

1. This article was originally published in *Xi Zhongxun's Revolutionary Career*, CPC History Press and China Literature and History Press, 2002.

My acquaintance with Comrade Xi Zhongxun was not through organizational or working relations, but because of an accidental opportunity. At that time, I was working underground in the 38th Army of Yang Hucheng's troops. Externally, I was the leader of the instruction team (actually a branch of the Anti-Japanese University). Internally, I was a member of the Working Committee of the 38th Army of the Communist Party of China, the organization minister, and the United Front minister. In September 1942, I returned to Yan'an, following Chairman Mao's order to report work. When I passed Malan, where the Shaanxi provincial committee and Guanzhong district committee were located, I visited my elder brother Hao Boxiong, who worked in the Department of Culture and Education in the Guanzhong Military University after he graduated from the Anti-Japanese Military and Political University. I learned that his superior commissioner was Xi Zhongxun, the former president of the Soviet in the Shaanxi-Gansu border area. Introduced by my brother, I met Xi Zhongxun. As fellow villagers, we went along well. I asked them questions freely. The bold, unrestrained temperament of people in Guanzhong and their approachable style made us friends from the start. From then on, I established a close relationship with Comrade Xi Zhongxun.

I

In April 1944, I returned to Yan'an to report to Chairman Mao, and then went to the Second Party School of the Central Committee to study. In August 1945, the War of Resistance Against Japanese Aggression was won, and I was assigned to work in the Northwest Bureau, serving as the United Front Director of the United Front Department. In December, I was sent to Malan, Guanzhong to carry out the dispatch work of the five provinces in Northwest China, completed 108 locales in white district distribution points, and returned to the Northwest Bureau of Yan'an. At this time, Gao Gang, the former secretary of the Northwest Bureau, led a large number of cadres to the northeast, and Xi Zhongxun took office as Secretary of the Northwest Bureau. After I reported these points to Minister Zhang Desheng, he asked me to go with him to report to Secretary Xi Zhongxun.

Comrade Xi Zhongxun clasped my hand and said joyfully, "We have finally come to work together." He listened to my report and said, "Good. This is a new achievement in the completion of Chairman Mao's new strategic deployment." He asked me to write a detailed outline for submission to Chairman Mao. Liu Geng, who was the head of the United Front Department of the Northwest Bureau, told me that Comrade Xi Zhongxun was democratic in his working style, approachable, and open to various views, and he made proper decisions in line with the actual situation.

Having taken his post, Xi Zhongxun first strengthened the United Front work of the northern line of the Shaanxi-Gansu-Ningxia border area and completed the task of instigating the uprising of Hu Jingduo, deputy commander of the security headquarters of Northern Shaanxi of the Kuomintang (the Hengshan uprising).

In June 1946, Chiang Kai-shek tore up the truce agreement, and the KMT army attacked the liberated area on all fronts. First, the south line troops surrounding the Shaanxi-Gansu-Ningxia border area were constantly increased, and apart from that, he ordered Deng Baoshan's troops in Yulin to prepare to go southward. Ma Bufang and Ma Hongkui of Qinghai and Ningxia were ready to go eastward, trying to occupy the Shaanxi-Gansu-Ningxia border area with one stroke. The Central Committee of the Party actively led the military and people in the border areas to step up preparations for the war, and they proposed "protecting the border areas and safeguarding Yan'an." At the meeting for strengthening preparations held by the Central Committee, Chairman Mao told Xi Zhongxun that to safeguard Yan'an and protect the border areas, the United Front work on the northern line must be strengthened and the KMT army uprising in the Yulin area should be conducted, so as to grant more time to the preparation for safeguarding Yan'an.

At the enlarged meeting of the Standing Committee of the Northwest Bureau, Xi Zhongxun conveyed the important instructions from Chairman Mao, and he decided to send me as a representative to the Suide local committee to carry out the United Front work in the Yulin area and work to persuade Hu Jingduo, deputy security commander of Northern Shaanxi Province of the Hengshan Boluo Fort, to hold the uprising. Xi Zhongxun said that Hu Jingduo was his classmate in the Licheng Middle School (private middle school of the Hu family). They had a strong tie with each other, and Hu held progressive ideas as well. Previously, Shi Yuan, the Deputy Minister of the United Front Department of the Suide local committee, also a classmate of Hu Jingduo, was sent to join forces in Yulin as the staff of the Eighth Route Army. He tried to win Hu over for the first uprising to liberate the area south of the Wuding River, especially the Shiwan area, which was embedded in the border area, to alleviate our army's concern about the northern line and gain some leeway for our force's operation. Xi Zhongxun told me that this was a very important task and encouraged me to bravely take the task. He asked me if there was any support or assistance I needed. I told him that I needed nothing but a secret letter of introduction, written by him. He said he hoped that

I could make full use of my specialized knowledge in this field and accomplish this strategic, important, and glorious task. I said I might not make a military pledge, but I would do all I could to overcome difficulties and strive to accomplish the task entrusted to me by the Party. Xi Zhongxun called me to his room and wrote an introduction letter on white silk, and he asked me to sew it into my soft vest. In early July 1946, I first went to the Suide local committee with the letter from Xi Zhongxun to Hu Jingduo. With the help of local Party secretary Bai Zhimin, Commissioner Yang Heting, Commander Wu Daifeng, United Front Minister Liu Wenwei, and Deputy Minister Shi Yuan, I conducted a thorough investigation and study on Yulin. In particular, I made a detailed analysis of Hu Jingduo's ideological and political preferences, family background, social relations, and personal hobbies. Then I made a detailed arrangement, with the help of his special relationship with Xi Zhongxun and the special social relationship between my family and the Hu family (through Hao Longguang, my uncle, the former chief of Hu Jingyi's 10th company, who was killed in the battle against Chen Shufan and Lu Jianzhang, the deputy of the Northern Warlords in Shaanxi Province, and had his memorial stone tablet in Meiyuan Town in Fuping). I then disguised myself as a teacher from the Licheng Middle School and went to meet Hu Jingduo.

On the Mid-autumn Festival, on the 15th day of the eighth lunar month, 1946, I was accompanied by Comrade Shi Yuan as I entered the Shiwan area from Zizhou County via Zhoujiaqi and made my way to the border area. I went alone into the Shiwan area when we got to the junction of the border area and Shiwan, which was enemy occupied territory. I first contacted Xu Xiuqi, a company chief of Hu's army, to explain my intention.

The next morning, Xu sent a sergeant to escort me on horseback. After two days of walking in the desert, we safely reached the town of Boluo and directly entered the headquarters of Hu Jingduo. I first met Hu's secretary Zhang Chun, who reported to Hu that I had arrived. Hu then sent his guard Xiao Jiashou to see me. Xiao took me into Hu's private room. I gave Xi's secret letter to him and introduced myself. After some small talk, I explained my aim of urging him to rise. He jumped off the kang with great joy and clasped my hand tightly. He said excitedly, "Xi and I were classmates and good friends. I've long been determined to launch an uprising. I'm lucky and very grateful that you've come now. It is truly like divine help. Absolutely."

In the early morning, with a meticulous watch, Hu Jingduo and I sat on the upper floor of the South Gate of the Boluo Town, mapping out the trend of the revolution, discussing in detail the political and military deployment of the uprising, and there and then, we reached ten agreements on the uprising program, which involved several parts. After the uprising, Hu's troops would be reorganized as the 6th Division of the Cavalry of the Northwest Democratic Coalition Army, with Hu as the chief of the division. Hu would be accepted as a Communist Party member, with his membership starting from July 1 that year. He also proposed that he make appropriate arrangements and grant awards to the active personnel Zhang Yaxiong, Yang Hansan, Xu Xiuqi, Yao Shaowen, Fan Zhiying, and Li Zhenhua, the chief of staff who still visited his relatives in Guanzhong, and appoint Zhang Yaxiong, the chief of Shiwan, as the head of the first regiment, and Yang Hansan as the head of the cavalry corps. Hu Jingduo and other cadres were progressive in ideology and made great contributions in the uprising. They were to be approved for Party membership, which would commence on the date of the uprising. It was decided that the uprising would be held on the Kuomintang Double Tenth Day (October 10).

I brought the plan for the uprising back to Yan'an and made a detailed report to Comrade Xi Zhongxun. He decided that I would lead more than fifty cadres assigned by the Yan'an and Suide local committees and a strengthening company of the new 4th Brigade to set out at the Shuigou border southwest of Xiangshui (originally scheduled to rise on October 10, but rescheduled to October 13 because of rising water levels in the Wuding River), and we would arrive at Nantutai about 500 meters outside the South Gate of the Boluo before dawn as planned, and set up the deployment of our troops. We were to make contact using the agreed code and cooperate with Hu Jingduo to lead the uprising.

After the uprising, the central government ordered Hu Jingduo to be the 6th Division of the Cavalry Division, and I was the director of the Political Department and secretary of the Party Committee. In late November, the central committee ordered the 6th Division to Yan'an for training.

On December 24, Chairman Mao met with the officers and assistants above the battalion level of the 6th Cavalry Division at the headquarters of the Jinsui Joint Defense Army in the Shaanxi-Gansu-Ningxia border area. Xi Zhongxun made an introduction to Chairman Mao. When introducing me, Chairman Mao clasped my hand smilingly, "Comrade Hao Keyong, you have emerged again." Before I could reply, Comrade Xi Zhongxun made quick correction, saying "This is Comrade Fan Ming." Chairman Mao replied, "I know. Hao Keyong was his original name in the 38th Army. You didn't know?"

When he had praised and welcomed the officers of the uprising, Chairman Mao said, "The Kuomintang is a big Party, and its army is a large army. The KMT ship

In 1946, Xi Zhongxun organized and planned the Hengshan Hu Jingduo Uprising. Pictured is the Hengshan Uprising Monument.

is large, but it is a ship that is going to sink. Many insightful people have observed this. Everyone wants to withdraw from a ship that is going to sink and find a new way for themselves. This is the Communist Party's boat. Although the ship is small now, it is a growing ship which is very strong, not as some say, a thief's ship, but a strong iron state ship. Things are moving from zero to a humble beginning, and then on to maturity, and from failure to victory. Although we are in a difficult period, judging from the overall situation, I believe we will overthrow Chiang Kai-shek in three years and liberate China."

II

Whether in the work of the local or the Central Committee, Comrade Xi Zhongxun devoted great effort to the United Front and the national and religious work of the Party. He poured great effort into mastering and implementing the Party's policies creatively, and he properly resolved the difficult problems in the actual work and successfully completed all major tasks, achieving remarkable things. Over the past few decades, especially in the early days of liberation, the following things impressed me most.

Proper handling of the rebellion in Xiahe (Labrang) via the people of the upper class United Front. Huang Zhengqing was the leader and security commander of Labrang in the Tibetan area of Gannan. One of his younger brothers, Huang Zhengguang, was Jamyang Zhepa, the fifth living Buddha of the Gannan Labrang Monastery, one of the six temples of Tibetan Buddhism, and he was named Tampe Gyaltsen. Another brother, Huang Zhengming, was Jikmé Tsultrim Namgyalwa, a living Buddha in Amchok, Labrang Monastery. His son, Huang Wenyuan, was the husband of Tashi Tsering, the Qinwang, or Mongol Queen of Sogpo (Henan). The Huang family was conferred the title "Yao Xi" because of Jamyang Zhepa, and because Huang Zhengqing's daughter-in-law was the Queen of Sogpo, or Henan Province. The family held great military, political, and religious power in the Labrang area, with great influence in Amdo, Qinghai, and even Tibet. As early as the period of the great revolution, the Party sent Xuan Xiafu, who had done political work in the Feng Yuxiang army, to conduct the national United Front work in the southern part of Gansu. Xuan stayed in Huang Zhengqing's place and became a close friend to Huang. Xuan Xiafu taught Huang Zhengqing and Jamyang Zhepa, the living Buddha, both spoken and written Chinese. More importantly, Xuan Xiafu publicized and conveyed the Communist Party's principle of national equality and national unity between the Han and Tibetan peoples, laying a foundation for their ideological progress.

Before the liberation of Lanzhou, Huang Zhengqing lived in the Amuquhu grassland, more than 100 kilometers away from Xiahe. In order to win Huang Zhengqing over, the Northwest Bureau directed Wang Zhen and Wang Enmao to send a message to him, and asked me to send Jia Zhipu, who had contact with Xuan Xiafu and Huang Zhengqing, to carry the announcement from the People's Liberation Army of China (The 8 Articles) and a large number of publicity materials to be posted and distributed along the way, publicizing the Party's national and religious policies. Jia Zhipu and Huang Lizhong, the former head of the security troop of Huang Zhengqing, and the chief of the Labrang Temple went deep into the Tibetan grassland on the border between Sichuan and Gansu. After working in different areas, they managed to persuade Huang Zhengqing to go back to Labrang, Xiahe County and lead the uprising on September 20, 1949. General Peng immediately ordered that Huang Zhengqing's residence in Lanzhou be vacated, and he sent Jia Zhipu and Huang Lizhong to pick up Huang

Zhengqing and his wife, Tsering Lhamo, and take them to Lanzhou to be received by the communication section of the First Field Army. General Peng and Huang Zhengqing had a cordial conversation and made proper arrangements. Later, Xi Zhongxun also met Huang. On New Year's Day in 1950, Huang Zhengqing attended the People's Congress with people from all walks of life in Gansu Province and was elected a member of the People's Government of Gansu Province. In all this work, Huang Zhengqing and I got along well, chatted frequently, and became close friends over the years.

In February 1950, the Linxia local committee made the mistake of leaning too far left. It agitated Wu Zhengang, subject of the Queen of Sogpo and a newly converted Communist Party member, to fight against the Queen. And it also stimulated to fight against the living Buddha of Amchok in the Labrang Temple (the younger brother of Huang Zhengqing) as if fighting against semi-landowners in the interior. A major leader of Amuquhu, the territory of Amchok was assassinated. All these led to a rebellion in Amuquhu, and the housekeeper of the Queen of Sogpo assassinated Wu Zhengang. The rebels also threatened to conquer the Xiahe County Public Security Bureau, and the situation grew even tenser. The Northwest Bureau and Gansu Provincial Committee sent me there as plenipotentiary with a strengthening company to deal with the incident. I proposed to Zhang Desheng, Secretary of the Gansu Provincial Party Committee, that in order to solve the ethnic problems, we must go through the ethnic leaders. In other words, to settle the Xiahe Incident, we needed to go through Huang Zhengqing. Otherwise, even if we had a troop stronger than a company, it would not work. Zhang Desheng agreed and asked Huang Zhengqing to help me deal with the incident.

When we came to Xiahe, Huang Xiang, the head of Xiahe County (Tibetan head of one of Huang Zhengqing's former troops), was considered to be the leftist head of the upper class Tibetan people at that time, and with the erroneous support of the left-leaning policy, they fought against the Huang Zhengqing group (including the Labrang Monastery). They organized demonstrations in the daytime and shot at us at night, demanding the surrender of the perpetrators who killed Wu Zhengang. In order to protect Huang's family and the monastery, the Amuquhu local cavalry was dispatched to surround Xiahe. It was a critical, tense moment, and both sides were ready to fight. I did the corresponding work concerning the temple and Amchok through Huang Zhengqing, and the work concerning the left-leaning group through Huang Xiang. We managed first to ease the crisis of vengeance and killing, and then through rational, favorable, systematic struggle and arduous, patient mediation, the incident finally came to a peaceful, smooth resolution. The decision was to detain the three men who killed Wu Zhengang (the chief of Yaoxi of Huang Zhengqing and the heads of the Queen of Sogpo) in Lanzhou and hand them over to the provincial high court for sentencing (they were released in 1951). After the incident was settled, I wrote A Comprehensive Report on the Xiahe (Labrang) Issue to the Gansu Provincial Committee in April 1950. Secretary Zhang Desheng reported to Northwest Bureau immediately after he read it. Upon reading the report, Secretary Xi Zhongxun commented it was a good one, in that it combined theory and practice to settle ethnic issues in accordance with Chairman Mao's national policy for the first time, and he directed that the report be published in the full text in the 54th issue of *Northwest Party Communication of Northwest Bureau* in 1950, with the title "Work at Xiahe: Comrade Fan Ming's Work Report."

Persuasion and tolerance in Handling Ma Liang, the leader of the Hui bandits. In the winter of 1950, the Kuomintang enemies in Taiwan took advantage of American aerial planes to send new weapons and appoint Ma Liang as the commander-in-chief of the "bandit suppression" in the northwest, ordering him to carry out a counter offensive rebellion, rob houses, and intimidate the Tibetan people in the area. At that time, there were more than 1,000 armed bandits under Ma Liang, and they looked fierce. At the same time, Taiwan also sent an appointment and a seal for appointing Huang Zhengqing as the commander in chief of the guard. Ma Liang's bandits secretly colluded with Huang Wenyuan, Huang Zhengqing's son, asking him to transfer the appointment seal and letter to Huang Zhengqing to require him to escape to Gannan and start the rebellion. After receiving these documents, Huang Zhengqing reported this serious situation to me late one night and asked that Huang Wenyuan and these documents to be handed over to the military area. He was going to personally lead the Tibetan armed forces to cooperate with the PLA in the suppression of Ma's bandits. I first applauded his patriotic spirit and impartiality in dealing with his family members, but I advised him not to rush into action, but instead to stabilize Huang Wenyuan and hand in the documents secretly, and then consult the northwest military region and the Gansu Provincial Committee. Unfortunately, the proposal that Huang Zhengqing lead his troops and cavalry regiment to cooperate in the campaign was not adopted. Instead, a cavalry regiment was sent by the Gansu military region to go deep into the Gannan Tibetan area. Due to the unfamiliar terrain and unknown situation, and because of the lack of help from the Tibetan people, the suppression went nowhere after more than a month, and there appeared a steadily decreasing number of soldiers and horses and a diminishing supply of grain. As a result, they had to withdraw and recover their strength. The Gansu provincial committee discussed this issue, and they thought it necessary to turn to the top Tibetan leaders and the Tibetan line to settle the problem and discard their suspicion of Huang Zhengqing. I was asked to mobilize Huang Zhengqing to serve as commander of the Gannan bandit suppression.

Huang Zhengqing returned to Xiahe County and made the appeal to his troops. Within three days, he formed a Tibetan bandit suppression group of about 3,000 people. In cooperation with our cavalry regiment, Huang Zhengqing headed to the vast grassland in Northern Sichuan of Gannan to conduct a second encirclement and suppression of the bandits of Ma Liang. As the leader of the Labrang Temple and as Yaoxi on the mother's side of Jamyang Zhepa, head of the Labrang Monastery, Huang Zhengqing issued a notice of the joint suppression of the Ma bandits to the leaders of all temples in the Tibetan areas in Northern Sichuan and Gannan. Where the bandit suppression forces went, they would receive the great welcome of cheers and thundering applause from the leaders and the armed masses of the Tibetans who rode horses and fired guns. And the local Tibetan even sent out a competent cavalry to carry out the campaign with the army. Huang Zhengqing employed carpet-sweeping tactics and kept attacking day and night, which made Ma's bandits run without a moment's break. Meanwhile, the policy of preferential treatment for prisoners was carefully implemented. After less than a month, all the rebels and Ma Liang, the leader of the bandits, were captured. The Northwest Bureau reported Huang Zhengqing's achievements to the Central Committee, and Huang was awarded the rank of major general by the Central Military Commission in 1955.

After Ma Liang, the bandit leader, was brought to Lanzhou, some people advocated killing him and reporting it to the Northwest Bureau. According to Chairman Mao's policy of tolerance of the rebel leader, Xi Zhongxun gave instructions not to suppress but to do persuasion work. The leaders of the Hui nationality in Lanzhou came out to bail Ma out and arranged for him to work in the National Affairs Committee. Ma Liang changed for good, and he sent people to persuade other gangsters who were hiding in Gannan to surrender, which played a positive role in stabilizing the situation in the region. Similarly, in the case of Ma Teng'ai, a member of the upper class of the Hui people in Lanzhou, Xi Zhongxun disapproved of killing but later arranged for him to take the post of CPPCC member and other positions, which had a great impact on the Hui people.

Effectively implementing the Party's policy of freedom in religious belief and first approval of the enthronement of Tibetan Buddhism in the Jamyang Zhepa incarnation. The head of the Gannan Labrang Temple, one of the six major temples of the Tibetan Buddhism, Dge-lugs-pa, was Jamyang Zhepa. The fifth Lobsang Jamyang Yeshe Tenpai Gyaltsen (i.e., Huang Zhengqing's younger brother Huang Zhengguang) passed away on April 14, 1947, liberated before the selection of reincarnated children could be completed. In 1950, Huang Zhengqing proposed to select the reincarnated spiritual child according to the Tibetan Buddhism procedure as the sixth Jamyang, which was officially approved by Xi Zhongxun, Secretary of the Northwest Bureau. Under the guidance of Comrade Xi Zhongxun, Huang Zhengqing first convened the living Buddha monks and representatives of the temple of the Labrang Monastery and invited the living Buddha Tuken of the Youning Temple in Qinghai to attend the meeting to decide the direction of the reincarnation of the living Buddha, which could not be found. In February 1951, they prayed for the Panchen Lama to make a prediction to decide on the candidate. After the Panchen Lama's visit to the Labrang Monastery on October 19, the Secretary General of the Conference Hall of Panchen Khenpo announced that "according to the Master Panchen Lama, the fifth Jamyang was born in the upper part of Gangcha County, Qinghai Province. His father's name is Gonbo Tseten Duolahai, and his mother Sonam Drolma. His Buddha name is Gönbo Cêdän." Then the Labrang Temple sent people to Gangcha, Qinghai to invite the Buddha, and on March 6, 1952, the enthronement ceremony of the sixth living Buddha Jamyang was held in the Labrang Temple. Wang Feng, Director of the National Affairs Committee of the Northwest Bureau, Huang Zhengqing, member of the Northwest Military and Political Commission, and Xu Guozhen, Commander of the Gansu Military Region, attended the enthronement ceremony and conveyed their congratulations on behalf of the Northwest Military and Political Commission and the Gansu Provincial People's Government. This was Jamyang Lobsang Jumie, Tudang Chökyi Nyima, President of the Gansu Buddhist Association, and it was the first time the Panchen Lama decided on the reincarnation of the living Buddha under the leadership of the Communist Party after the founding of the People's Republic of China.

A special trip to Xining to see off the Panchen Lama and give important instructions to the work in Tibet on behalf of Chairman Mao. On December 15, 1951, the Panchen Lama left the Khenpo Monastery to go to Xining for saying goodbye to the leading comrades of the Party, government, and army and the people of all ethnic groups in Qinghai Province. At this time, Xi Zhongxun, Secretary of the Northwest Bureau

In April 1951, Xi Zhongxun met Panchen Erdeni, Choekyi Gyaltsen in Xi'an before he attended the peaceful liberation negotiations in Beijing.

of the CPC Central Committee and Vice Chairman of the Northwest Military and Political Commission, made a special trip to Xining to celebrate the return of the Panchen Lama to Tibet on behalf of Chairman Mao, the Central People's government, and the Northwest Military and Political Commission. Secretary Xi visited the Panchen Lama, giving him 30,000 silver yuan and double checking the preparations for his return to Tibet. He delivered a lecture to the officials of the Panchen Lama. Secretary Xi encouraged them to love the motherland, support the Communist Party, and earnestly act upon the agreement for the peaceful liberation of Tibet. He hoped that they and officials of Kashag would develop mutual understanding and work together to build a prosperous new Tibet.

On December 16, more than 1,000 people from all ethnic groups and all walks of life in Qinghai Province held a grand farewell gathering in Xining. At the gathering, Xi Zhongxun delivered a congratulatory speech on behalf of Chairman Mao, the Central People's Government, and the Northwest Military and Political Commission. "Mr. Panchen Erdeni, like the Dalai Lama, has an excellent reputation among the Tibetan people," he said. "He has been away from Tibet for 28 years, and the Tibetan people have always kept him in mind. You will be warmly welcomed by the Tibetan people upon your return to Tibet at this time. This is the inevitable result of the agreement reached by the Central People's government for the peaceful liberation of Tibet, and another reason for great joy after the peaceful liberation. This shows that under the correct leadership of Chairman Mao and the Central People's government, the Dalai Lama and Panchen Erdeni have started to work together, and the people of Tibet have been united. From now on, all the peoples of our motherland will be united closely." Then, the Panchen Lama expressed his sincere thanks to Chairman Mao, the Central People's Government, the Northwest Military and Political Commission, and the Qinghai Provincial Party and Political Army for the concern they had shown since the liberation, and for the warm farewell gathering. After returning to Tibet, he expressed his determination to work closely with the Dalai Lama to fully realize the peaceful liberation of Tibet under the leadership of Chairman Mao, the Communist Party of China, and the Central People's Government's agreement. At this solemn farewell gathering, the Panchen Lama talked about his feelings and thoughts, saying, "We have been in exile in the interior for nearly thirty years. Without the correct leadership of the Communist Party of China and Chairman Mao, without the sincere help of all our Chinese brothers and the various peoples, the peaceful liberation of Tibet would not be possible, and it would be impossible for us to return to Tibet. Therefore, we must say that the Communist Party of China and Chairman Mao are the great saviors of the Tibetan people and our great benefactors. Only by following the Communist Party and Chairman Mao and being closely united with the brothers and various peoples of the motherland can our Tibetan nation be liberated completely. There is no other way." The leaders of the Party and the political forces in Qinghai Province, Zhang Zhongliang, Zhao Shoushan, Liao Hansheng, Geshe Sherab Gyatso, and Huang Zhengqing, member of the Northwest Military and Political Commission, attended the farewell gathering. They all gave gracious speeches at the gathering, and representatives from all walks of life and the children in Xining city offered banners and flowers to the Panchen Lama, and they conveyed congratulatory messages to the Dalai Lama in a united, friendly atmosphere.

On December 18, Secretary Xi Zhongxun summoned Ya Hanzhang, the assistant representative of the Northwest Military and Political Commission stationed in the Panchen Xingyuan, who was scheduled to escort the Panchen Lama to Tibet, and Liang Xuanxian, Deputy Secretary General of the Party to the Panchen Khenpo Conference Hall, and issued the Instructions on the Panchen Work and Anti-Imperialist Patriotic United Front in Accordance with Chairman Mao's instruction on Tibet. The main points of the instruction were as follows:

1. In doing work in Tibet, we should adopt the policy of "steady progress and prudence," rather than being rash in action. "Steady progress" does not mean no advancing, but thinking broader and deeper about whether we should do it or not, and what the consequences will be if we do. In doing so, we will make steady, sure progress thus consolidate what has been done. This is the very policy that helps to manage Tibet in success. In Tibet, some things are better done later than in a hurry, so we should not fear being slow. If it is right, we will not have to take a detour.
2. Good job must be accomplished in Tibet regarding the United Front work now, and it should take us as the main body. First, we should do a good job of building unity between the Dalai and Panchen Lamas, then the unity between the ethnic groups, the upper and lower levels of religious circles, the Dalai Lama and the common people, and finally farmers and herdsmen, forming a unified front of patriotic anti-imperialism. The basis for Tibet to engage in a United Front is the love for the motherland and anti-imperialism. The United Front is to carry out the anti-imperialist struggle and consolidate and expand the United Front in the struggle. It is too early to fight feudalism in Tibet. We should first strive for the Dalai Lama and the Panchen Lama to come to the anti-imperialist United Front. This should be made clear among cadres in the ideology. Otherwise, there will occur problems (such as disrespect for customs, excessive eagerness to reform, and an unwillingness to approach feudal forces).
3. We should investigate and get familiar with various situations in Tibet (politics, military, economy, culture, religion, customs, history, etc.). We should form an environment for learning. If we fail to understand the big picture, we will not find the right approach. At present, we should not overdo in the division of labor in Tibet. Every comrade should understand the overall or multiple situations. We keep mentioning "extracting the essence from the raw." The raw in this case is the very foundation of the essence that can't be ignored.
4. In the beginning, we should not rush to send working groups and cadres to create sects or factions. Instead, we should hold more representative meetings, symposiums, and sociable sodalities to allow the upper level members of all regions to come to the stage of explaining policies and establishing bonds. After the establishment of the Military and Political Commission, we should organize people in all sectors to go to different places to visit, investigate, form relief teams, and form medical teams. When the work is done, those people will come back. We should adopt frequent bottom-up and top-down approaches.

5. We should offer more assistance and support to the Panchen group and share with them our ideas and solutions. The Panchen group, oppressed in Tibet, counts on us for support, who will work with us for a long time. We should help them make progress in our cooperation. Today, they are united with us on the big picture, which is good enough. We should not be too demanding in areas in which they are underdeveloped. Provided that we are on the same side on the big picture, minor differences are acceptable. Sharing the same goal while recognizing small differences is the core of the United Front. We should fight on key issues, while being more tolerant on small things. This is the principle and flexibility of a Communist.
6. Cadres from the northwest should be united with those from the southwest. There should be no separation between comrades. They should be especially close and united. The Tibetan comrades who went to Tibet with the Panchen Lama should also work to be united with the Tibetan people when arriving in Shigatse and be modest instead of being proud, so as to avoid leaving a bad impression among the Tibetan people.

After escorting the Panchen Lama to Lhasa in May 1952, Comrade Ya Hanzhang immediately conveyed Xi Zhongxun's instructions to the Tibet Working Committee. The Committee believed that Secretary Xi's instructions on the work of the United Front in Tibet were based on the actual situation in Tibet and that Xi made a dialectical exposition in theory, principles, policies, and leadership, which was crucial for Tibet to manage its anti-imperialist work, the patriotic united front, and the unity between the Tibetan and the Han peoples, among the Tibetan people, as well as the cadres. The instructions were thus immediately forwarded to all the sub-working committees for their close study and discussion in combination with the local reality as well as their resolute implementation.

Practice has proved that the Instructions on the Panchen Work and the Anti-Imperialist Patriotic United Front issued by Comrade Xi Zhongxun to Ya Hanzhang and Liang Xuanxian has played a positive role in managing Tibet well and developing the unity between the Dalai Lama and the Panchen Lama. Both in the past and in the present, they were correct and in line with the actual situation.

Mao Zedong's Praise for Xi Zhongxun[1]

Tang Luo

Tang Luo, formerly known as Tian Shuji, used the pseudonyms Tian Leng and Dong Fanghong. Born in 1925, he was from Yan'an, Shaanxi Province. He studied in the Shaanxi-Gansu-Ningxia Border Region Middle School in 1938 and in the Department of Administration at Yan'an University in 1945. He was formerly the editor of a literary journal (supplement), a war correspondent, a reporter from the First Field of the Xinhua News Agency and the Korean front line, a special reporter from the Northwest Branch of Xinhua News Agency, a leader of the political, legal, cultural, and educational interview group, the first deputy editor-in-chief of *Yanhe*, and a professional writer of Xi'an Writers' Association.

A Leader of the Masses Coming from the Masses

In 1945, after the victory in the anti-Japanese war, Gao Gang, former Secretary of the Northwest Bureau of the CPC Central Committee, following orders from the CPC Central Committee and Chairman Mao, left Yan'an for the northeast to open up the liberated area there. When selecting the secretary of the Northwest Bureau, Mao Zedong said, "We should choose a young person to be secretary of the Northwest Bureau. He is Comrade Xi Zhongxun. He is a leader for the masses and a leader of the masses, coming from the masses."

That year, at age 33, Xi Zhongxun worked as Vice Minister of the Organization Department of the CPC Central Committee.

1. This is an abridged version of an article originally published in the 11th issue of *The History of Chinese People* in 1999.

Mao Zedong's comments on Xi Zhongxun came from his impression ten years earlier. In 1935, Mao led the Central Red Army on the Long March to the Northern Shaanxi base. On the walls and trees of several villages, he saw the long-standing Notice of the Soviet Government on the Shaanxi-Gansu Border, which was signed by President Xi Zhongxun. Later, when he met Xi Zhongxun in Wayaobao among the comrades released from the detention by the left-leaning party, Mao was surprised that Xi was "so young." At that time, Xi Zhongxun was 23 years old.

On July 1, 1951, on the occasion of the 30th anniversary of the birth of the Communist Party of China, Xi Zhongxun wrote an article entitled "Following Mao Zedong to Victory." "Following Mao Zedong" was Xi Zhongxun's lifelong motto.

Fully Accomplished

In recent years, when Xi Zhongxun's relatives went to pay New Year's greetings to Bo Yibo, Bo recalled Mao Zedong's praise of Xi Zhongxun, calling him "perfect." That was in early 1952, when Xi Zhongxun was Secretary of the Northwest Bureau and Vice Chairman of the Northwest Military and Political Commission.

One day, Bo Yibo went to Mao Zedong's office. Mao was reading the report "About the Plenary Meeting of the Northwest Bureau Committee of the CPC Central Committee," sent by Xi Zhongxun from Xi'an. The report was rich in content, involving the land reform, United Front, and ethnic work in Northwestern China, and it included inspiring illustrations. The report provided a blueprint for the central government to lead the political reform in Northwestern China, which had a vast territory full of different nationalities, and had a complex society. Mao Zedong was very pleased about the report and asked Bo Yibo, "Could you tell me how you see Comrade Xi Zhongxun?"

"Young and promising," Bo Yibo said. When in Yan'an, Bo Yibo heard Mao Zedong praise Xi Zhongxun, saying, "He is fully accomplished."

Xi Zhongxun's keen observation was widely acknowledged, especially of the leftist phenomenon. In the winter of 1947, the People's Liberation Army was victorious, and a vigorous land reform movement rose in each liberated area. During the movement, no distinction was made between the old areas in the Soviet period, the semi-old areas in the anti-Japanese war, and the new area, which led to some excessive actions. Within the span of a month, from January 4 to February 8, 1948, Xi Zhongxun sent three telegrams to the Party Central Committee and

Xi Zhongxun in the office of Qinzheng Hall in Zhongnanhai.

Chairman Mao on such major issues as "the land reform in the old liberated areas," "guarding against the left-leaning tendency in the land reform," and "launching the land reform according to the three different types of areas" and directly advocated opposing the left-leaning sentiment.

In a letter to the Central Committee on January 4, Xi Zhongxun pointed out that "if the land reform of the old district were carried out in general concept, mistakes in principle would be inevitable. The idea that landlords and rich farmers account for about 8% of the rural population in China is not applicable in the old areas, which must be altered." Otherwise, he said, "serious mistakes would be unavoidable." He pointed out earnestly that "in launching mass movements in the old areas, we should firmly oppose the leftist formalism of the petty bourgeoisie."

On January 9, Mao Zedong made a prompt approval that he "fully agreed to the opinions put forward by Comrade Xi Zhongxun. It is hoped that the land reform work in each district and county should be guided closely according to these opinions, so as to ensure the land reform in the border areas remains on the right track and fewer mistakes are made. The old bases in Northern China should also stay alert."

In his telegram, Xi Zhongxun made a scientific analysis of the class situation in the old district from the Marxist point of view, noting, "In the old district, the rural poor and hired farmers are few. Among them, some are poor due to accidental disasters, others are transitioning from being landowners or rich farmers but have not well transformed yet, and still others are poor as a result of their laziness and idle lifestyles... To ask them to lead the land reform is to give the reins to bad people, frightening the cadres of the district and township so much they will escape and commit suicide... The good masses are among the middle class farmers and a small part of poor farmers."

Mao Zedong immediately stated on January 29 that he "fully agreed to Comrade Xi Zhongxun's opinions. If we encounter the same situation in the old liberated areas of Northern and Central China, we should pay close attention to the correction of the leftist errors. Where there is a left-leaning error, the leading organ should be able to correct it; properly handled, it would take within weeks rather than over a prolonged period. At the same time, we should guard against the view of mistaking the correction of left-leaning tendencies as inaction."

Soon, the Central Committee issued to the liberated areas *The Decision on the Land Reform in the Old and Semi-old Areas*, drafted by Zhou Enlai.

Xi Zhongxun once told his secretary Tian Fang that before Wang Zhen, commander of the south branch of the Eighth Route Army, went south in 1944, Comrade Mao had spoken to Xi, saying that we could not be confined to the border area of Shaanxi, Gansu, and Ningxia, and that for the liberation of the entire country, he would advise Xi to go south with Wang Zhen. But after a few days, Mao again spoke to Xi, saying that on second thought, he believed it better for Xi to stay in Northern Shaanxi and work with him to build and consolidate the Shaanxi-Gansu-Ningxia border area, as it was an urgent task.

Zhuge Liang Captured Meng Huo Seven Times, but You're Even Better than Him

Li Ruihuan, chairman of the National Political Consultative Conference, once told a comrade, "The speeches and works of Comrade Li Weihan and Xi Zhongxun on the work of the National United Front are the 'magic weapons' of the United Front work today."

In July 1952, on orders from Mao Zedong, Xi Zhongxun went to Xinjiang and properly settled an ethnic dispute there, stabilized the political situation, and helped all ethnic groups restore their harmonious ties.

The northwestern region was vast, with a total of 3.39 million square kilometers. There were more than ten ethnic groups, including the Han, Hui, Tibet, Uyghur, and Mongolian groups, with a total of 23.5 million people. Its political situation was complex, and its economy underdeveloped. Xi Zhongxun proposed that all work should be carried out on the basis of national unity by adopting the principle of "steady progress and prudence."

"Work to win over the upper class of all nationalities and religious people, and then to motivate them, rather than reverse the work order." This was the formula Xi Zhongxun followed to settle the ethnic contradictions at that time. The success in winning over Xiang Qian, the twelfth generation head of a thousand households of the Ngangha tribe in Qinghai Province, was one of the models in Xi Zhongxun's settlement of many ethnic problems in the northwest. Later, when he met Xi Zhongxun, Mao Zedong said, "Zhongxun, you are truly resourceful. Zhuge Liang captured Meng Huo seven times, but you're even better than him."

In combination with Tan Chengxiang, chief of the 100th division of Ma Bufang, and Ma Chengxian, head of the 14th Cavalry Brigade, Xiang Qian organized the Second Corps of the so-called Anti-Communist Salvation Army and launched a rebellion. The work of winning Xiang Qian over to return from the Nahujiagai Forest lasted 31 months, from December 1949 to the afternoon of July 11, 1952. From September 1950 to April 1952, more than fifty people, including Zhou Renshan, head of the United Front Ministry of Qinghai Provincial Committee of the CPC, Geshe Sherab Gyatso, Tibetan Buddhist master, Tibetan tribal leaders, and living Buddhas in temples, went to Ngangha and conducted peace talks with Xiang Qian more than seventeen times. It was complicated, challenging work, fraught with numerous dramatic turns. Xi Zhongxun directly led the fight, exhibiting his "accomplished" wisdom and competence.

With great foresight, Xi pointed out to Qinghai leaders multiple times that proper settlement of the rebellion in Ngangha was not only crucial for the unity of the Tibetan community in the area, but also to enable the Party to stand firm in other Tibetan areas and ethnic minority regions in Qinghai, to establish the people's power, and to carry out various types of work. It also had a significant impact on Gansu, Sichuan, Kham Tibet, and Tibet. Xi said that it was important to adhere to the principle of taking political struggle as the major tool on the basis of full military preparation, and to be prudent, using peaceful means first and being particularly tolerant with Xiang Qian, by means of constant persuasion.

In response to some people's eagerness to launch military suppression, Xi Zhongxun told Zhang Zhongliang, Secretary of the Qinghai Provincial Party Committee, via cable that "we should not employ military operations without authorization. Only when political efforts have failed should we consider military operations and suppression."

In August 1950, Xiang Qian traveled to Xining to express his repentance to the government and surrender, but he broke his promise when he returned to Nganglha. In September 1951, after the eighth political effort to win over Xiang Qian failed, the public was indignant. At the meeting of representatives of all ethnic groups in Qinghai Province, the representatives proposed that the government should send soldiers to launch the suppression.

Xi Zhongxun immediately sent a telegram to discourage the move, pointing out that striving for a peaceful solution to the Nganglha issue would be to the Party's political advantage, and that we should patiently consult such Tibetan people as Geshe Sherab Gyatso and the Panchen Lama on how to win over the Nganglha head of a thousand households. He added that we should review our past work to see if we had acted appropriately in winning him over, so that we could do a better job in the future. What we were really concerned with, he said, was the impact on the vast Tibetan area. If we failed to do proper work, we wouldn't be able to guarantee a military victory, not to mention the trouble caused by the exile. Even if we won a military victory, there would be many negative effects on other Tibetan areas, which would increase the challenges for the future work. If we had not yet made sufficient political efforts (and military preparations), we might as well postpone the military campaign.

After the suppression of the rebels on May 1, 1952, Xiang Qian hid in the Nanhujiagai Forest in Tongren County. Some thought it both unnecessary and meaningless to win Xiang Qian over. However, Xi Zhongxun, Secretary of the Provincial Party Committee, said to Zhang Zhongliang that it was highly possible to strive for the return of Xiang Qian, if things were done well in Nganglha and no serious mistake was made. Instead, we should send both Han and Tibetan personnel that Xiang Qian trusted as early as possible to express our desire, with the promise that he would be taken care of if he worked with the government. He added that we should treat Xiang Qian with earnest sincerity if he came back to make some attempts.

On August 11, 1952, in Lanzhou, Xiang Qian clasped Xi Zhongxun's hand in regret and guilt and gave his white hada to Xi as a confession of his guilt. With tears of joy in his eyes, he made a toast to Xi to express his gratitude.

This was how Xi Zhongxun treated others with earnest sincerity and patient tolerance. From the perspective of historical materialism, he analyzed and studied the formation and existence of the social status, social role, and social influence of the leading ethnic minorities in their own ethnic areas, the influence of the political activities and attitudes, and the religious beliefs on their ideological consciousness, spirit, and morality under the political systems of previous dynasties. Xi followed the broad vision and honesty of the Communist Party and worked with great compassion and patience along with the top ethnic minority people who ultimately recognized the sincerity and friendship of the Communist Party of China.

Huang Zhengqing, the Tibetan leader in Gannan, was a close friend of Xi Zhongxun. When Xi was ill, Huang traveled a long distance to visit him. Through the course of their long-term friendship built up over a decade-long cooperation, what impressed and moved Huang Zhengqing most was Xi Zhongxun's unswerving trust in him.

In the spring of 1953, Ma Liang, the former KMT county councilor in Linxia, Gansu Province, gathered the remnants of the KMT army and the bandits in the Tibetan area along the border of Gansu and Sichuan. Under the guidance and assistance of the Kuomintang, he continued to fight against the people, and he behaved very arrogantly.

Meanwhile, the Taiwan KMT special affairs agency attempted to use official titles and material rewards to mobilize Huang Zhengqing, who was already a member of the Northwest Military and Political Commission, to separate from the government, so that Ma Liang could start a rebellion in the Gannan area.

In order to resolutely and thoroughly eliminate Ma Liang's anti-revolutionary armed forces, the 11th Division of the People's Liberation Army and several cavalry regiments joined the campaign. Huang Zhengqing was appointed deputy commander-in-chief of the bandits suppression operation. (Commander Zhang Dazhi, Political Commissar Huang Weisong, and Deputy Commanders Zhu Shengda and Xu Guozhen were also appointed.)

When Huang Zhengqing was leaving Xi'an to join the front line of the bandit suppression effort, Xi Zhongxun went to see him off. Xi gave the Boker pistol that he had kept for years to Huang Zhengqing, saying, "Take it for protection." Huang took the pistol and was moved into tears. When he was under suspicion by the Taiwan Kuomintang, Huang was extremely touched by the Communist Party leaders' great trust in him.

After Huang Zhengqing took his seat, Xi Zhongxun said with great concern, "The organization believes you can finish the task of suppressing the bandits. You should work boldly and exert your influence. We have been working together for years, and I have come to know you very well and believe in you. You can come to us any time in the future. No matter what others have said, you should not worry about it." Xi Zhongxun told Huang Zhengqing frankly about the situation, based on information obtained by the relevant parties. The Kuomintang in Taiwan was looking for Huang everywhere and had sent planes over Gannan to air drop him an appointment paper, a stamp, and a radio, which were all in Ma Liang's hands. Xi continued, "When you get to Gannan, if someone sends you the appointment paper, the stamp, and the radio, you need not be afraid. After taking them, you can hand them in."

On the third day of Huang Zhengqing's arrival at Xiahe, Gannan, Ma Liang sent the letter of appointment signed by Chiang Kai-shek appointing him as Guard Commander, along with the stamp. He immediately handed everything to Zhu Xiafu to forward to the Northwest Military and Political Commission.

(This material was provided by Tian Fang, former secretary of Xi Zhongxun, Fan Xinmin, Zhang Zhigong, and Cao Zhenzhong)

Secretary Xi's Persistance in Seeking Truth from Facts[1]

An Zhiwen

An Zhiwen was born in March 1919 in Zizhou, Shaanxi Province. He joined the Communist Youth League of China in 1936. He studied at the Yan'an Anti-Japanese University in 1937 and joined the Communist Party of China that same year. He worked as an inspector of the CPC Shaanxi-Gansu-Ningxia Border Region Committee, Secretary General of the Suide Prefectural Committee, Secretary of the Northwest Bureau of the CPC Central Committee, Director of the Democratic Movement Ministry of the Nenjiang Provincial Party Committee, Deputy Director of the Policy Research Office of the Northeast Bureau of the CPC Central Committee, Deputy Director of the Industry Ministry of the Northeast Administrative Committee, Deputy Director of the National Construction Commission, Deputy Director of the National Planning Commission, Minister of the Sixth Machinery Industry Ministry, and Deputy Director of the National System Reform Commission.

From late 1990, Xi Zhongxun stayed in Shenzhen as he recuperated. I visited him there many times. Every time, as he had always been in the past, he was open-minded and optimistic, always thinking about the major events of the Party and the state, and hoping that Deng Xiaoping's reform, opening up, and modernization drive would achieve tremendously. In July 1993, I went to Shenzhen again to talk with him. On my departure, he said to me affectionately, "Looking

1. This article was originally published in *Xi Zhongxun's Revolutionary Career*, CPC History Press and China Literature and History Press, 2002.

Xi Zhongxun (third from right), Secretary of the Local Party Committee in Guanzhong District, with his comrades.

back on the history of our Party, all our major mistakes were mainly due to the influence and interference of the leftist ideology. This lesson should be borne in mind." On hearing this, I was deeply moved and my mind remained stirred up for a long time after.

I worked with Xi in early 1943. At that time, he was transferred from the Guanzhong district of the Shaanxi-Gansu-Ningxia border region to the Suide district to serve as Secretary of the Prefectural Party Committee. I was Secretary General of the Prefectural Party Committee. In less than two years, I had gained a profound understanding of his approachable working style, his care for his comrades, his efforts to connect with the masses, and his commitment to seeking truth from facts, which have remained in my mind until today.

At that time, the Suide area was a strategic channel for Yan'an to connect with the anti-Japanese bases in Northern and Central China. When the Rectification Movement began in 1943, some comrades from various base areas returned to Yan'an to study the Rectification Movement or make preparations for the Seventh Congress of the CPC. The branch school of the Anti-Japanese University was also transferred from the front to Suide. Xu Xiangqian served as the president, and the military cadres who came back from the front remained at the university to study.

Xi Zhongxun came to Suide just after the senior cadres' meeting of the Northwest Bureau, and the Central Committee emphasized unified leadership. He was the Secretary of the Prefectural Party Committee and concurrently served as the Political Commissar of the Garrison District. After the Anti-Japanese University moved to Suide, Xu Xiangqian served as Commander of the Garrison District. At that time, the historical Rectification Movement was gradually unfolding. According to the decision of the Party Central Committee, not only was a school for young cadres set up in Suide, but a large number of cadres were also transferred from central organs and schools to Suide to carry out investigation and research and participate in practical work. For example, Feng Wenbin, the head of the Central Youth Commission, went to Mizhi to serve as Secretary of the County Party Committee, Han Tianshi went to Jiaxian to serve as Secretary of the County Party Committee, and the writer Liu Qing went to experience life in rural areas, where he worked as secretary. After these comrades arrived in Suide, Comrade Xi Zhongxun kept in close contact with them.

Upon arriving in Suide, Comrade Xi Zhongxun emphasized that rectification and production should be carried out in the same way. Cadres of government organs should not only produce ample food and clothing with their own hands, but also go deep into the countryside to promote mass production. He personally led Song Yangchu, Secretary of the Suide County Party Committee, and us to Haojiaqiao Village for investigation. It was found that Liu Yuhou, a farmer in the village, had been working hard all along to make his family's life reach the level of middle class farmers, and he had led all the villagers to work hard, making Haojiaqiao a model village at that time. Learning this, Comrade Xi Zhongxun, suggested that the local Party Committee and the special office issue a notice, calling on the farmers across the region to learn from Liu Yuhou, who was also elected by the local people. Another famer, Wu Manyou who had a labor competition later with Liu Yuhou, also became a labor hero in the Shaanxi-Gansu-Ningxia border region.

Given that many cadres were transferred from the Central Committee and the base areas to Suide at that time, Comrade Xi Zhongxun emphasized that in the rectification study, we should properly handle the relationship between local cadres and military cadres, local cadres and cadres from other areas, and worker-farmer cadres and intellectual cadres, so that they could learn from and help each other and build bonds with the local people to overcome the temporary difficulties caused by the provocation and blockade of the KMT diehards in the border region.

During this period, with the progression of the Rectification Movement, work in all areas in Suide was vigorous, which was closely connected to the leadership of Comrade Xi Zhongxun. Admittedly, there were twists and turns during the Rectification Movement. Due to historical reasons, Suide was a region of serious opposition between the Red and the White during the period of the Soviet movement. From 1937 to 1940, the regime was again in the hands of KMT diehards. In 1940, when the first anti-Communist climax was defeated and the Kuomintang diehard Commissioner He Shaonan fled, we managed to establish a democratic regime. Accordingly, the Kuomintang had a certain impact on the education community and in society in general. When the rectification movement reached the stage of examining cadres, in an attempt to properly deal with those historical issues, the Prefectural Party Committee decided to report to the Northwest Bureau and the Central Committee of the Communist Party of China. At that time, Kang Sheng, the head of the Ministry of Social Affairs of the CPC Central Committee, was at the meeting. Hearing the report, Kang Sheng criticized that the Suide leaders did not pay enough attention to the enemy's dynamics and stressed the need to oppose the KMT's "red flag policy," believing that the Communist Party in some places was actually the KMT's "red flag Party," "red outside and white inside," and so on. He instructed Suide to carry out the movement of "rescuing the wrongdoers" as Yan'an had done. Under the influence of Kang Sheng's extreme leftist thought, there was the error of expanding the movement of eliminating reactionaries in a short period in the Suide Normal School, the Mizhi Middle School, and society at large. Aware of this situation, Comrade Xi Zhongxun took decisive measures to carry out remedy screening, apologized to those comrades who had been unfairly accused, restored their reputation, and took the initiative to assume the responsibility for leadership, so that those comrades who had been wronged could go back to work and study.

In 1944, when the Suide cadre examination movement ended, according to the instructions of the Party Central Committee, in order to sum up the historical lessons, a senior cadre study group was set up in the Suide area, headed by Xu Xiangqian and Xi Zhongxun and with the participation of Li Jingquan, He Changgong, Wang Shangrong, Bai Zhimin, and other comrades in charge of the Anti-Japanese University, the Prefectural Party Committee, the Special Office, and the garrison area. The study group was to summarize the historical lessons of the struggles in the two routes by studying the left-leaning line adopted after the failure of the Great Revolution, especially the error of Wang Ming's line. In the study, we read the historical document entitled "The Struggle in the Two Lines," compiled and printed by the Central Committee. At the group meeting, Comrades

Xi Zhongxun as secretary of the CPC Suide Prefectural Committee.

Xu Xiangqian, He Changgong, Xi Zhongxun, and others explained the influence and harm of the leftist line on the Soviet areas, which greatly educated us younger comrades. In particular, Xi Zhongxun focused on Liu Zhidan, Xie Zichang, and other comrades' experience of intense struggle in the process of establishing the Shaanxi-Gansu Border Soviet Area and the Northern Shaanxi Soviet Area. At that time, Xi Zhongxun was the chairman of the Soviet government on the Shaanxi-Gansu border. It was through the lessons of many failures that they learned to establish the Shaanxi-Gansu revolutionary base in the middle of Qiaoshan, with Nanliang as the center. Comrade Xi Zhongxun said humbly that they were only plain materialists and only saw the importance of establishing base areas in practice. However, the executors of the leftist line thought that they were the "Shaoshan school," following the "right-leaning escape line." The leftists even arrested Liu Zhidan, Xi Zhongxun, and other comrades, calling them "counter revolutionaries," in 1935. It was not until Chairman Mao and the Party Central Committee arrived in Northern Shaanxi that they were released and resumed their work. When talking about his past experiences, Comrade Xi Zhongxun focused on summing up the lessons of history, instead of his personal gains and losses. This kind of broad mindedness greatly enlightened the comrades who participated in the study.

Looking back on Comrade Xi Zhongxun's experiences, we found that before the national liberation, he had achieved brilliantly in the establishment of the Soviet region along the Shaanxi-Gansu border, in the construction of the Shaanxi-Gansu-Ningxia border area, and in the struggle for the liberation of the northwest. After the liberation of the country, he went to the Central Committee to assist Premier Zhou in the administration of the work of the State Council, carried out the basic line of the Party, and made important contributions to the Party and the people. At any time, he could adhere to the ideological principle of emphasizing practice, connecting with the masses, and seeking truth from facts. He was not overly proud of success or discouraged in the face of failure. He treated his comrades with enthusiasm and a broad mind, and he was strictly self-disciplined yet always generous to others. This noble sentiment and moral character greatly inspired those working with him in different periods and won him the respect and gratitude of all.

Years of Trust and Friendship[1]

Hu Jingtong

Born in 1910, Hu Jingtong was a native of Fuping, Shaanxi Province. He served as Deputy Military Commander of the 22nd Corps and Commander of the 86th Division of the Kuomintang government before his uprising in Suiyuan in 1949. After the founding of the new China, he served as a senior advisor of the Northwest Military Command, Vice Chairman of the Fourth to Sixth CPPCC of Shaanxi Province, member of the fifth and sixth Central Standing Committee of the Revolutionary Committee of the Chinese Kuomintang, the Fourth and Fifth Vice Chairman of Shaanxi Province, and a member of the Sixth CPPCC.

Xi Zhongxun and I were both from Fuping County, Shaanxi Province. As I was older, I was several grades ahead of him when I studied at the Fuping Licheng School. When I graduated, I joined the army in the summer of 1924, so I did not know much about his childhood. Later, I heard from some old comrades that he was a revolutionary worker who achieved remarkable things in the struggle of the Party leadership in the creation of the Weibei Soviet region, because he was dissatisfied with the corruption of the Beiyang government that gave power to foreign countries to bully and oppress our own people. This made Xi determined to save the country and the people. As far as I know, the establishment of the Party organization at the Licheng School happened relatively early on in the area north of the Weihe River in Shaanxi Province. Comrade Xi Zhongxun was one of the early participants.

1. This article was originally published in *Xi Zhongxun's Revolutionary Career*, CPC History Press and China Literature and History Press, 2002.

I left Shaanxi in 1928 to study abroad and returned in 1932. To continue my studies, I often traveled to Nanjing and Beiping, so I didn't know much about Comrade Xi Zhongxun's activities. By 1935, I had joined the army of Jing Yuexiu, the leader of the Yulin local army. Comrade Xi Zhongxun worked in the Shaanxi-Gansu Soviet region at that time, and I learned from military intelligence that he had become one of the important leaders of the Soviet region along the Shaanxi-Gansu border (chairman of the Soviet government of the border of Shaanxi and Gansu). My contact with him was after the July 7 Incident. At that time, the KMT and the Communist Party cooperated for the second time, and all the people rose to fight against Japan. The Yulin area was adjacent to the Shaanxi-Gansu-Ningxia border area, and the contact between the two sides was frequent. I also resumed contact with my acquaintances who were working in the border area. People in my hometown of Fuping who had been afraid to contact their fellow villagers and classmates in the Red district changed their ideas at this time. Because "there was a leader from Fuping in the Red zone," many young people flocked to Comrade Xi Zhongxun to sign up for the revolution. When Comrade Xi was transferred to work in Suide, I was serving as commander of the Sixth Calvary Division of the 22nd KMT Corps and later appointed as Deputy Chief of the Corps and Commander of the Security Section in Northern Shaanxi Province. We were able to keep regular contact in Yulin, Hengshan, and Sanbian. The staff we sent included teachers and classmates from the Licheng School. They all came back to say that Comrade Xi Zhongxun was as enthusiastic and sincere as he had always been. The people in the border areas and those inside and outside the Party who I had contact with all praised him highly. In particular, when it came to the land reform, they all agreed that the land reform in the areas under the leadership of Comrade Xi Zhongxun was carried out in accordance with the policies of the Party Central Committee. They also said that when they were correcting the deviations in some local land reforms, the CPC Central Committee and Chairman Mao adopted some suggestions from Comrade Xi Zhongxun. At the same time, both the people we sent to the border area for business and those sent by Yan'an to handle affairs in Yulin, commented that the employment of people by the Communist Party and Chairman Mao was not based on regional division, as was publicized, but rather, involved people from all parts of the country, regardless of where they were from. For example, though he was young and not a Long March cadre, Comrade Xi Zhongxun gained great trust and responsibility from the Party Central Committee, and he was very capable. It made me think a lot. Taking the internal situation of the Kuomintang army at that time as an example, if you were a local force, no matter your military training and discipline were good or not, and you had any military achievements or not, you would definitely suffer discrimination and exclusion. It was clearly a case of making appointments based on relationships. Judging from this, we local forces, the so-called "miscellaneous army," sincerely admire the Communist Party for its selfless and its proper cadre line.

After the War of Liberation, Commander He Long and Comrade Xi Zhongxun were very concerned about my political future. Special recruiters Cao Liru, Liu Wenwei, and Tian Ziheng, director of our office in Suide, came to Yulin and said to me, "Commander He and Comrade Xi would like you to follow General Gao Shuxun's example and lead an uprising." I replied, "As Commander-in-Chief Deng Baoshan worked for my brother Hu Jingyi for a lifetime, I should also give him my lifelong service. He is now in Chongqing, and I must listen to him." In this way, I bluntly rejected their deep concern and care for me. I later realized that if a man who had been in the exploitative class for years with a certain status and influence intended to be transformed into the people's camp, without the timely help and instruction of the Communist Party, it would hardly be possible, if it depended only on his own long-term self-improvement.

In October 1946, under the direct guidance and leadership of Comrade Xi Zhongxun, my brother Hu Jingduo led the sixth division of the Kuomintang cavalry and the security forces I supervised to launch an uprising in Boluo Fort, Hengshan County. I was then dismissed and investigated by the Nanjing authorities for being "ineffective in supervision." Comrade Xi Zhongxun was very concerned about my safety. He sent some powerful colleagues who were with Hu Jingduo in the uprising back to Yulin to be my assistants as I went to the people's camp. He also sent back Wu Zhizhen, a classmate from the Licheng School, whom both he and I trusted, to convey to me a secret letter written on a piece of silk and sewed in a quilt. After Liberation, Comrade Xi Zhongxun told me what was written in the letter. It said, "If you agree to come to the border area, please send someone to see me secretly, and I will send troops for support." Unfortunately, when they came back to Yulin, they did not dare to deliver the message to me because of the supervision of the secret agents all around, and they didn't tell me that they had burnt the covert letter on the way. Fortunately, the Party had a policy of equal participation in the revolution, regardless of the sequence, so that everyone had the opportunity to contribute to the construction of the new China. After two battles, the 22nd Corps of Yulin lost Fugu, Shenmu, and Hengshan. Over ten entire army camps were destroyed, and only Yulin was preserved as an isolated city. The KMT government not only failed to provide sufficient supplies, but also suspected many people who guarded the city.

They believed that those people were either "communists" or "frustrated soldiers" who would have issues when given the chance. Therefore, in the early summer of 1948, under the guise of meeting the guards of Yulin City, the Nanjing authorities sent me there with Commander-in-Chief Deng Baoshan and Commander Zuo Shiyun. On the surface, I remained in Nanjing for training, but actually, they were afraid something unfavorable to them might happen if I went back to Yulin. In early 1949, as acting president, Li Zongren held peace talks with the Communist Party in Beijing. I was recommended by Xu Yongchang (Minister of Defense) and Zhang Yaoming (Commander of the Nanjing Garrison) and was re-appointed as vice military commander of the 22nd Corps and commander of the 86th Division. I then went back to my original troop. I flew to Shaanxi, traveled past Gansu and Ningxia, and arrived in Baotou City, Suiyuan. At that time, General Dong Qiwu, who presided over the military administration of Suiyuan, and many other key members had forged a friendship with me in the era of the national army or fought side by side with me in the anti-Japanese war. They were planning an uprising, according to the instructions of Fu Zuoyi and Deng Baoshan. They knew that I had followed Fu and Deng for years, so they welcomed me to Suiyuan and asked me to unite the 22nd Corps in Suiyuan and prepare to join the people's camp with them.

At that time, Xi'an had been liberated. General He and Comrade Xi decided to send Wang Bomou, the chief of new recruits of the 22nd Corps in the Xi'an uprising, to bring the letter written by my old friend, Shi Zijing, for persuading me to launch the uprising early. They also asked Wang Bomou to take another letter to Comrade Gao Kelin, the head of the Suiyuan Military District, asking Gao to give assistance in the uprising of my troops. Because Wang Bomou was delayed by a car breakdown a couple of times on the way, my troops, under instructions from Generals Fu and Deng, had followed General Dong Qiwu and announced the uprising on September 19, 1949. Although Wang Bomou did not arrive before the uprising, I would never forget the two leaders He and Xi's great care for my political future. My troops were reorganized as PLA troops, setting off from Suiyuan and going past Ningxia to Qingyang, Gansu Province. In the summer of 1950, I was asked to attend a meeting of the Northwest Military and Political Commission in Xi'an, and I met with a number of leading comrades in the First Field Army. Comrade Xi Zhongxun urged me to get ready for a speech at the general assembly, so as not to be in a rush, since it was the first time I was attending the meeting. He knew that I had many long-time friends in the Party, but I had little knowledge of Marxism, Leninism, Mao Zedong Thought, and the current Party lines, policies, and principles. He asked for my consent, then arranged for me to leave the army and serve as a senior counsellor of the Northwest Military Command. He also gave me *A Must-Read for Cadres* to help me focus on learning and improving myself. After that, Comrade Xi Zhongxun was transferred to the Central Committee office. Whether I went to Beijing or he came back to the northwest, he always asked to meet me, showing concern about my work arrangements, study, and transformation. I suffered from the Cultural Revolution and other movements, as many people did. Although I felt anxious and pained, I could always manage to go through it, which was closely linked to the care and help given by Comrade Xi Zhongxun during my study and transformation.

Comrade Xi Zhongxun was open-minded, courageous, honest, and approachable. He was a man of principles and flexibility, so that people outside the Party let down their guard, willing to approach him, talk to him, and ask him for advice and solutions at any time. Comrade Xi did not make any differentiation when dealing with people inside or outside the Party. At first, I thought his concern for me may be out of the personal relations of fellow townspeople and classmates. Later, in my talks about Comrade Xi Zhongxun with those who had frequent contact with him, such as Zhang Zhizhong, Fu Zouyi, Deng Baoshan, Zhang Xiru, Dong Qiwu, Yang Mingxuan, Sun Weiru, Qu Wu, Tang Shengming, and other leading comrades, I felt that he was concerned about them as well. At the same time, he paid great attention to the work of the United Front, for the sake of the reunification of the motherland. This was evident in an incident Xu Junwen had shared with me. Xu Zhijia, previously a senior commander of the 22nd Corps of the Kuomintang army in Yulin, was transferred to the Zhenhai Fortress in Fujian Province to serve as commander-in-chief in 1949. When he left the Mainland for Taiwan, his son Xu Junwen, who studied in Shanghai, was not able to go with him, and he later suffered because of his family ties during the Cultural Revolution. Having learned that Comrade Xi Zhongxun had served as the political commissar of the Suide Police Reserve District in Northern Shaanxi Province and must have known his father's situation in Yulin, Xu Junwen wrote to Xi to appeal for the rectification of his case. Upon receiving the letter, Xi transferred it to the central United Front Department. Xu Junwen's case was soon settled, and the relevant policies were implemented. His parents, brothers, and sisters in Taiwan and the United States were delighted to hear the news. Xu Junwen applied for two visits to Taiwan to meet his relatives from Zhejiang. After the talks, he made clear the facts of the construction in the Mainland and the policies for overseas Chinese and Taiwanese. Then I clearly understood the idea that "if one is unhappy, all around him are unhappy," and I saw that the implementation of the policy concerning even one individual would have a great impact on the cause of the peaceful reunification of the motherland. Sometimes, when I talked to those who had met Comrade Xi Zhongxun only once, they all agreed that he was a dedicated follower of the Party, Chairman Mao, and Zhou Enlai and a model practitioner of the United Front policy. Comrade Xi Zhongxun remained concerned about me even during his recuperation. In the winter of 1992, when I went to Shenzhen City, Guangdong Province to see him, he said to me, "Mr. Hu, you are still healthy. Don't be lazy with your studies. Listen to the news on the radio. Read and understand the general political principles of the Party Central Committee in the newspaper. Study the reports and speeches of the leading comrades of the CPC Central Committee and Comrade Deng Xiaoping's socialist theory with Chinese characteristics. Otherwise, you won't know what our country is doing now. The most regrettable thing in one's life is to be abandoned by the times and disconnected from reality." What he said gave me the strength to continue learning, which was also a way to stay young and happy throughout one's life. For me, an idealist preoccupied with the idea of a hero-making an era, it would be extremely hard to join the people's camp, accept the materialist idea of the times making a hero, and enjoy life in the new society. It would have been impossible for this transformation to occur without the great care and close instruction of Comrade Xi Zhongxun, a mentor and a friend, let alone obtaining the position I hold today and the respectful treatment the Party and the people have endowed to me.

Profound Friendship of Bo and Zhong[1]

Xi Zhongxun and Zhao Boping in the Northwest Bureau

Qi Xin

Born in 1926, Qi Xin was a native of Gaoyang, Hebei Province. She was the former Vice Director of the Advisory Commission of the Central Committee of the CPC, and wife of Xi Zhongxun, Vice Chairman of the National People's Congress. On March 18, 1939, she was sent to the Anti-Japanese University (then in the anti-Japanese base of the Taihang Mountains, Southeastern Shanxi) to study. After graduation, she was assigned to the women's cadre team of the Changzhi Cadre School to work as an instructor, and then returned to the Maintenance Office of the First Branch of the Anti-Japanese University to serve as a secretary in the General Affairs Office. After the merger of the university, she worked as a secretary in the General Affairs Department and the Health Department of the university. In the winter of 1940, she was approved to study in Yan'an. In the spring of 1941, she went to the Central Party School for study and was sent back to Longdong in the autumn for the Party School's food collection work. The next spring, she returned to Yan'an and was sent to the Secondary School Section of Yan'an University to study. In the spring of 1943, she went to Suishi, joined the Party on August 14, 1943, and became a Communist Party member. Later, she studied in the Marxism and Leninism College and remained in the Central Party School.

1. This article was compiled by the author of this book based on Qi Xin's "Identifying the Strong Grass in the Fierce Wind and the Evergreen Tree in the Severe Frost: In Memory of Comrade Zhao Boping." Qi Xin's original text was published in the *Shaanxi Daily* on July 14, 2012. The title was added by the editor of this volume.

Born in 1902, Zhao Boping, a native of Lantian County, Shaanxi Province, was eleven years older than Xi Zhongxun. In the spring of 1932, after launching the Liangdang Mutiny, Xi Zhongxun went to the Zhaojin base area to meet Liu Zhidan and Xie Zichang. At the end of the year, dispatched by the organization, Xi returned to the Weibei region for revolutionary activities. During this period, Comrade Xi Zhongxun, who was then Secretary of the Communist Youth League of the Sanyuan Central County Committee, had frequent contact with Comrade Zhao Boping, then Secretary of the CPC of the Sanyuan Central County Committee, and they formed a deep revolutionary friendship in that tough environment. Half a century later, Xi Zhongxun still clearly recalled the talks he and Zhao Boping had on the wall of Sanyuan County.

Focusing on Agriculture, Rural Areas, and Farmers

After the liberation of Xi'an on May 20, 1949, Zhao Boping served as the first Secretary of the Xi'an Municipal Party Committee, member of the Standing Committee of the Northwest Bureau of the CPC Central Committee, Second Secretary of Shaanxi Provincial Party Committee, and Governor of Shaanxi Province. Under the leadership of the Party Central Committee and the Northwest Bureau, together with Fang Zhongru and other comrades, he did a great deal of hard work for the smooth takeover of Xi'an, including the restoration of people's normal life, the modification of the urban outlook, the suppression of reactionaries, the stabilization of the social order, the campaign against the "three evils" and the "five evils," and the socialist transformation. After taking the leading position as governor, Zhao achieved tremendously in promoting industrial and agricultural production, building water conservancy works, developing culture, education, and health, strengthening the construction of the Party and people's political power, and improving the people's lives.

During his work in the Northwest Bureau, Zhao Boping was in charge of rural work for a long period and was very concerned about agriculture and farmers. The Shaanxi Agricultural Development Program was formulated under his direct leadership. He was very familiar with the geographical conditions of Guanzhong and Northern and Southern Shaanxi, and he was concerned about mass production, mass life, mass emotions, and mass interests. He attached great importance to the development of market trade. He not only asked cadres at all levels to conduct detailed research, but also made many in-depth market investigations on his own.

Later, in the early 1960s, Zhao Boping advocated liberalizing and invigorating the free market instead of closing or banning market trade. He said, "If you open the market, it will prosper. If not, it will die. The result of this shutdown would be turning the near market into the far one, the open market into the underground one, and low prices into high prices, which would be unfavorable to both producers and consumers." During the three year period of difficulty, due to the leftist influence, the issue of contracting production to households was debated in Shaanxi for a long time and across a broad range. It moved back and forth numerous times, shifting between implementation and rectification. As a result, the enthusiasm of the masses was seriously dampened, and production was not improved. Zhao Boping was aware of the situation, and he dared to tell the truth. He said frankly, "It went too far and inappropriately to take contracted production to the households as the struggle between two routes."

In July 1962, during the Fourth Enlarged Meeting of the Third Shaanxi Provincial Committee of the Communist Party of China, Zhao suggested that "the contracted production to the households was not the revival of something old, but the beginning of something new, which may be the creation of Chinese farmers." He stressed that the socialist direction in rural areas should be adhered to, but the practice should be diversified rather than single-tracked. For example, contracted production to households or groups, the expansion of private plots, and the reduction of the evaluated areas were all adaptable to local conditions and in line with the wishes of the farmers. However, Zhao Boping's original ideas were not valued or promoted at that time, but were instead unfairly criticized.

Artistic Achievements

Zhao Boping also made great achievements on the literary front. From the 1930s to the early 1960s, he participated in and led major activities in Shaanxi's literary and art circles. As early as the 1930s and 1940s, he wrote modern Qin opera scripts such as *New Examination, Deception, Catching Traitors, Qi Banxian,* and *Special School.* From different perspectives, he effectively publicized the political proposition of "resistance over surrender, unity over division, and progress over retrogression" put forward by the Party Central Committee, and he exposed Kuomintang reactionaries' passive resistance against Japan and their active opposition to the Communist Party and the people. In 1942, in order to cooperate with the Rectification Movement in Yan'an, Zhao Boping adapted three plays, namely *National Spirit, Shi Dakai,* and *Three Drops of Blood*, which became huge sensations in Yan'an after their performances in the central auditorium of the border region. After watching the performance, Mao Zedong, Zhu De, Lin Boqu, Xie Juezai, and other leading comrades praised Zhao for his adaptation of the three plays.

When Zhao Boping was Minister of the Publicity Department of the Northwest Bureau, Zhao Shouyi was the Vice Minister and Director of Literature and Art, who founded the Shaanxi Drama School. Zhao Boping was directly involved in the reform and creation of Shaanxi opera, which was strongly supported by Xi Zhongxun. The two ministers worked together and organized local Shaanxi opera performances in Beijing many times. The performances caused a sensation in the capital and became a grand event in the process of Shaanxi's cultural construction. In the 1950s and 1960s, when Zhao Boping was the main leader of the Provincial and Municipal Party Committees, despite his busy work, he still put great effort into the reform and development of local drama.

In the spring of 1956, he presided over a forum on drama reform, which offered a penetrating exposition on the inheritance and reform of Shaanxi opera, especially Qin opera, from the perspective of theory and practice. In terms of performing arts, in view of the phenomenon of unrefined production and discarding historical heritage, he required strict training in the basic skills of "singing, speaking, acting, and moving," to make the performance representative, distinctive, typical, and appealing with the presentation of various professional techniques. His speech inspired, encouraged, and promoted the implementation of the "double hundred" policy and the prosperity of Shaanxi drama at that time. It can be said that during the period of the Northwest Bureau, Zhao Boping made special contributions to the rescue of traditional excellent operas such as Xianbanqiang, Agongqiang, and Tongzhou Bangzi. Tongzhou Bangzi, inactive for nearly forty years and on the verge of extinction, was the origin of a variety of Bangzi operas. Zhao Boping directly organized a team to preserve the old artists, make adaptions of the old scripts, and recruit new actors for new programs. In the end, he founded a drama school with local characteristics, which gave this ancient drama new life.

Xi Zhongxun also loved the art of drama, especially many local operas. In the early days of liberation, when the Party and the government took over the Xi'an Yisu Society, Zhao Boping invited Xi Zhongxun to attend the conference. The moment Xi Zhongxun stepped into the hall and saw the banner that read, *Celebrating the Party and the Government on Taking Over the Yisu Society* hanging on the stage, he told Comrade Zhao Boping that it should be called "managing" instead of "taking over," as taking over was for the organizations left behind by the

KMT, but for progressive literary and art groups such as the Yisu Society, it should be "managing," meaning continuing with the practice. Zhao Boping agreed and immediately had the banner changed.

Protecting the Ancient City Wall

Zhao Boping also contributed to the protection of the Ming Dynasty city wall in Xi'an. In 1958, during the Great Leap Forward, some comrades saw the city wall of Xi'an as a feudal relic and advocated its demolition. Zhao wrote to the State Council in support of its preservation. With the support of Xi Zhongxun and the approval of the State Council, the Xi'an city wall was listed as one of the first key cultural relics under state protection in China. In the early 1980s, after comprehensive renovation and overall management of the walls, rivers, forests, buildings, and roads, it became the best preserved tourist attraction in China.

The Strong Bond between Bo and Zhong

Xi Zhongxun admired Comrade Zhao Boping for his fearless, selfless character, his persistence in truth, his tolerance and fortitude, and his open-mindedness. Xi commented that Comrade Zhao was firm and clear-cut in the face of both right and wrong. His outstanding characteristics were "embracing challenges with courage, crises with bravery, danger with composure, and unfair treatment with tolerance." In the late 1950s, faced with the left-leaning trend, he did not say anything against his integrity or do anything against his conscience, nor did he follow the tide or the crowd. In September 1962, at the Tenth Plenary Session of the Eighth Central Committee of the CPC, according to the fabricated charges Kang Sheng made, Xi Zhongxun and others were wrongly accused of using the novel *Liu Zhidan* to oppose the Party, and Zhao Boping remained silent. When urged to take a stand, he said seriously, "No comment. Xi Zhongxun is a good comrade." He was then unfairly treated.

In 1975, both Xi Zhongxun and Zhao Boping were released from years of imprisonment and were sent separately to Luoyang, Henan Province, and Sha City, Hubei Province. They concerned and inquired about each other. Shortly after arriving in Sha City, Zhao Boping asked his grandson to go to Beijing to inquire about Xi Zhongxun. He wasn't reassured until his grandson met Xi Zhongxun in

Luoyang and reported back to him on the specific situation. This was enough to suggest the brotherly revolutionary friendship between Xi Zhongxun and Comrade Zhao Boping, which was like sunshine in winter. It was an unforgettable memory. In March 1988, Xi Zhongxun called Comrade Zhao Boping his mentor and friend in front of many old leaders and comrades. He also combined the characters "Bo" and "Zhong" in their names and said, "In Bo and Zhong, you are Bo, and I am Zhong. You are my elder brother." The media later reported the meeting between Xi Zhongxun and Comrade Zhao Boping. Xi Zhongxun not only expressed his deep revolutionary friendship with Zhao Boping, but also displayed the noble character of Comrade Zhao Boping to the people.

The deep friendship and comradeship between Xi Zhongxun and Zhao Boping remained constant throughout their lives. Even later, when Xi Zhongxun worked as Secretary of the Northwest Bureau of the CPC Central Committee and the Party and as state leader, becoming a superior of Zhao Boping, Xi respected Mr. Zhao as he always had, always addressing him as "elder brother" and "mentor and friend."

Jia Tuofu in the Northwest Bureau[1]

Qi Xin and Zhou Weiren

Zhou Weiren, formerly Jia Hongsheng, was born in Yan'an in September 1933. He was a native of Shenmu County, Shaanxi Province, and the son of Jia Tuofu, the former Deputy Director of the National Planning Commission. Zhou joined the army in 1962 and the Communist Party of China in 1965. He was a council member of the China Disabled People's Welfare Foundation and Deputy Secretary General and Director of Internal Affairs of the Foundation. He is now president of the Fellowship Association of the 26th Corps of the Red Army of Workers and Farmers of China.

Jia Tuofu was known for his extraordinary competence at work and his leadership among the old comrades from the bases in Shaanxi and Gansu. In the most difficult period of the anti-Japanese war, the Central Committee assigned him to do economic work. Due to his hard work and excellent investigation and research, he soon became an expert in this field and was highly appreciated by Mao Zedong, Zhang Wentian, and Chen Yun. Xi Zhongxun once recalled that in 1942, Chairman Mao delivered a report on economic and financial issues at the high-level cadre meeting of the Shaanxi-Gansu-Ningxia border region, and many of the materials were provided by Comrade Jia Tuofu.

1. This article is based on Qi Xin's article "Lifelong Dedication to the Party: Commemorating the Centenary of Comrade Jia Tuofu's Birth" and Zhou Weiren's *The Biography of Jia Tuofu*. Qi Xin's original text was published in the *Shaanxi Daily* on November 24, 2012, and Zhou Weiren's *The Biography of Jia Tuofu* was published by the History of the Communist Party of China Press in 1993. The title was added by the editor.

Picking up Quickly and Applying Appropriately

The Northwest Financial Office, established in 1942, was an institution that coordinated the financial work of the entire Shaanxi-Gansu-Ningxia border area. In October 1945, Comrade Chen Yun went to Northeastern China, and Jia Tuofu took the post of Director of Northwest Finance and Economics Office. Under the leadership of the Central Committee of the Communist Party and the Northwest Bureau, he firmly implemented the policy of "developing the economy and ensuring the supply," studied and applied Comrade Chen Yun's guiding ideology to financial work, and carried out financial and trade struggles against the KMT ruled areas on the basis of developing production in the border areas, so that the

In 1947, Jia Tuofu, the Director of the Northwest Finance and Economics Office, transferred to Northern Shaanxi Province.

military supplies for civilian use in the border areas were basically guaranteed, the border currency and prices were basically stable, and the balance of income and expenditure was maintained. It made remarkable contributions to the victory over the KMT's economic blockade and military attack in Northwestern Shanxi and the Shaanxi-Gansu-Ningxia border area, and to the victory of the liberation war in the northwest.

In March 1947, the Northwest Finance and Economics Office evacuated Yan'an with the Northwest Bureau and transferred to Northern Shaanxi. In May 1948, it moved back to Yan'an and was housed in Wangjiaping. During this period, Jia Tuofu and Xi Zhongxun got along very well and worked closely together. They also participated in the Xiaohe and Yangjiagou Meetings held by the CPC Central Committee. Both meetings were important ones held at critical moments in the people's liberation war, especially the Yangjiagou Meeting in December 1947 when Comrade Xi Zhongxun, on behalf of the Northwest Bureau, made a speech to the Central Committee on the left-leaning tendency in the local land reform at that time, such as cruel struggles against landlords and damage to the interests of middle-class farmers. Mao Zedong listened to Xi Zhongxun's opinions and put them into the conference documents drafted by Ren Bishi. The opinions Comrade Xi Zhongxun put forward on behalf of the Northwest Bureau also won Jia Tuofu's support.

Due to Hu Zongnan's disruption and the ten months of cruel fighting on the internal lines, the economy of the Shaanxi-Gansu-Ningxia border region was seriously damaged. Under the leadership of the Party Central Committee and the Northwest Bureau, by the end of 1948, the economy of the border region had been greatly restored, and most of the people hit by the disaster were rescued. After the liberation of the whole northwest, industrial and agricultural production in the region was rapidly restored and developed, and the people's lives were significantly improved.

Taking on the Mission at the Critical Moment

On April 21, 1948, when Yan'an was restored and the holy land of the revolution was returned from the hands of Chiang Kai-shek and Hu Zongnan to the embrace of the Communist Party and the people, the PLA in the northwest battlefield reached the stage of a comprehensive counterattack. Taking over the work of the KMT ruled area, especially the preparation for takeover of Xi'an, was part of the agenda of the Northwest Bureau of the CPC Central Committee. On February 9, 1949, Jia Tuofu reported to the Northwest Bureau *The Preliminary Plan for Taking over Xi'an*, which was approved by the Bureau. The plan included eight aspects: a) information collection and investigation of Xi'an, b) policy research and preparation for taking over Xi'an, c) organization and preparation of the Xi'an Military Control Commission, d) preparation for taking over the Xi'an cadres, e) preparation and training of garrison troops, f) training of cadres entering the city, g) necessary preparation for supply, and h) other technical issues. On February 28, the Standing Committee of the Northwest Bureau decided to set up a sixteen member Preparatory Committee for taking over Xi'an, with Jia Tuofu serving as its director. In April, the takeover groups were formally established and the cadre allocation work was completed. On May 12, *Discipline and Precautions for Entering the City* was issued. On May 18, Jia Tuofu was officially appointed Mayor and Secretary of the Xi'an Municipal Party Committee. On May 20, the principal and deputy directors of the Military Control Commission and members of the Public Housing Management Committee were appointed. On May 20, the PLA's vanguard troops attacked Xi'an, and the personnel of the Military Control Commission entered on May 23 and officially opened its office on May 24. At the same time, the notice *Guanzi Number 1* was issued to announce the formal establishment of the Commission, along with the appointments of Director He Long and Deputy Directors Jia Tuofu, Zhao Shoushan, and Gan Siqi.

By this point, the takeover of Xi'an was in full swing. As a member of the Standing Committee of the Northwest Bureau, member of the Northwest Military and Political Commission, Deputy Director of the Northwest Finance Commission (with Peng Dehuai serving as Director), and the first Deputy Director of the Xi'an Military Management Commission, Secretary of the Xi'an Municipal Party Committee, and Mayor of Xi'an, Jia Tuofu immediately went into the core leadership and directed the takeover of the city. At that time, he was just 37 years old. In February 1949, at the Joint Meeting of Permanent Members of the Shaanxi-Gansu-Ningxia Border Region Senate, Government Members, and Representatives of the Jinsui Administrative Office, the Northwest Finance and Economics Office was reorganized into the Northwest Finance and Economics Branch, with He Long appointed as director, Jia Tuofu as deputy director, and Xi Zhongxun, Liu Jingfan, and ten other members serving concurrently as members. That June, the Northwest Finance and Economics Branch moved to Xi'an.

The most important thing for Jia Tuofu after he entered Xi'an was to quickly stabilize the social order and resume various forms of production according to

Members of the newly formed Xi'an Municipal Committee of the Communist Party of China after the liberation of Xi'an.

the instructions of the Party Central Committee. They drew upon Chen Yun's experience in taking over Shenyang, which specifically involved "each based on its own system, from top to bottom, keeping intact and taking over before work division," so that the takeover work was smoothly fulfilled. Since Director He Long focused on cooperating with Liu and Deng's troops to march into the southwest and the other two deputy directors, Zhao Shoushan and Gan Siqi, were both working in the former general office, the work of the Xi'an Military Control Commission was basically conducted by Jia Tuofu. He was also responsible for the establishment of the leading organs of the Party and government in Xi'an and the important tasks of financial and economic work in Northwestern China. In the secretariat, including Jia Tuofu, Secretary General Chang Lifu, and Deputy Secretary General Yang Xiaochu, there were only just over ten people. The staff were very capable and flexible at work. Chang Lifu recalled that he and Jia Tuofu often wrote documents at night, usually Chang sleeping for a while while Jia writing first, then swapping roles at three or four o'clock in the morning. After dawn, they took the manuscript to issue the report or sent it to the Northwest Bureau for revision. They were never tired, yet always full of pride and joy.

Curbing Prices Three Times

Two months after the smooth takeover of Xi'an, Jia Tuofu pointed out to the Northwest Bureau, Peng Dehuai, He Long, Xi Zhongxun, and other leading comrades that the focus of Xi'an's work in the next stage "should be shifted to the full recovery and development of public and private production, and at the same time, refugees, vagrants, and the unemployed should be organized to hunt for jobs or evacuate to the countryside in a planned, systematic way, so as to increase production and reduce consumption for further stabilizing the social order and the people's livelihood… We need to focus on the central tasks of production and employment, ensuring that they move hand in hand rather than in isolation."

He believed that "this is an economic and social issue with the most extensive and fundamental nature. It is an inevitable phenomenon of a consumer city in the early days of liberation. Other major urban issues, such as public security and finance, are closely tied to this one. The basic way to address the issue is active production and employment, rather than passive relief and maintenance." He boldly put forward that "in order to facilitate centralized leadership, after summing up the work of military control, the Military Control Commission should transfer the various production undertakings and administrative businesses needed to the leaders of various competent departments in a planned, systematic manner, so as to put the work on the right track and push it forward swiftly." Accordingly, a series of work principles, measures, and policy suggestions were put forward to strengthen management, develop production, improve business, end the takeover work, and reinforce the management system.

In March 1950, Jia Tuofu conscientiously organized the inventory of warehouses and made strict calculations. At the same time, he carefully determined staffing and consumption, and he practiced a strict economy. According to the requirements of the central government, except for local surcharges, he handed over all public grain, taxes, and materials to the central government for unified dispatch and use. He established and implemented a unified national revenue and expenditure management system and other powerful measures, which quickly curbed the soaring prices caused by long-term inflation and stabilized finances and living costs.

After entering the city, the new regime immediately faced the challenge of fighting against various currency systems and the circulation of silver, copper, and speculative activities. Jia Tuofu immediately led the government and financial institutions to fight against the sale and use of silver and copper currency. He banned trade with silver and copper currency and raised the exchange rate of

In 1952, Jia Tuofu was transferred to work in the Central Committee, and the leaders of the Party and government in the northwest went to Huashan to see him off. Front row from left: Yang Mingxuan, Jia Tuofu, Xi Zhongxun, Zhang Jiafu, Zhang Zhizhong, and Hong Xihou (wife of Zhang Zhizhong).

silver by 58%. He ordered the utilities organs to reject silver coins, instead taking only Renminbi. Under the premise of abolishing a few unreasonable exorbitant taxes, the tax authorities immediately levied taxes according to the original tax system and tax rate and checked and banned silver currency dealers in the market. The judicial authorities were not allowed to accept any case involving silver debt disputes, and they actively publicized the maintenance of the RMB and the disuse of silver currency. At the same time, the state-owned trading companies actively arranged goods, sold commodities, and curbed prices. This series of measures soon came into effect, which brought silver currency into the black market, completely banned copper currency, stabilized prices, and expanded the RMB market.

After a short time, the KMT troops at bay still attempt to put up a desperate fight, and they returned to Xianyang and Xi'an. The bandits strengthened their destruction and publicity, which led to hesitation in people's minds. The silver currency in the black market soared more than three times, which once again caused a sharp rise in the living cost. Many shops refused to take RMB, and many others closed down. The struggle over silver currency became more complicated for political and military reasons. Jia Tuofu worked with other government departments to crack down on the counter revolutionary activities of bandits and agents and actively expanded the publicity work by taking advantage of the arrival of the army in Northern China and the news of victory on the front line. At the same time, the trade companies increased the amount of goods and materials they had arranged for, sold them to the market, levied a profit-making income tax for the first half of the year, and announced a 50% discount on public grain. The banks actively carried out the business of exchange, deposit, and loans, and they sold silver on the black market at a low price, so as to defeat the black market by using black market means, thus subduing the second fluctuation.

In the third month of the new regime, silver currency again stirred up trouble, and prices rose again. However, due to the favorable political and military situation, a series of measures continued to take effect, and there was no big fluctuation. The struggle against silver currency was essentially a struggle to stop inflation and stabilize prices, which was the primary task of the takeover work in the economic field. After several months of hard work, prices in the northwest region were basically stable by the beginning of summer in 1950.

At the second meeting of the Xi'an Military and Political Commission on July 10, 1950, Jia Tuofu recalled as follows: in late February 1950, the average prices of sixty kinds of commodities in Xi'an increased by 243% compared with those at the end of December 1949, and those of fourteen kinds of commodities increased by 381%. However, after March, the situation changed. The average prices of the same sixty commodities fell by 30% compared with the last ten days of February, of which fourteen commodities fell by 38%. In April, they fell by 52% compared with the last ten days of February, and the prices of the same fourteen commodities fell by 62%. By the beginning of May, it had stabilized the prices, curbed inflation for more than ten years in a row, and solved the problems that the Kuomintang had not been able to solve for over ten years.

Attaching Importance to the Working Class

From the period in Xi'an to 1952, Jia Tuofu did a great deal of work and made outstanding contributions to the recovery, stability, and development of the financial front in Northwestern China. During the period of leading the financial and economic work in Northwestern China, Jia Tuofu attached great importance to the leading role of the working class and gave full play to the enthusiasm of the workers. There were 500,000 workers in the northwest, and Jia Tuofu was elected Chairman of the Northwest Federation of Trade Unions. In order to further mobilize the masses of workers, under the leadership of the Party and the government, he and the comrades of the Federation of Trade Unions resolutely abolished the feudal system of bullying workers and the system of searches that insulted workers, banned reactionary sectarians, and first selected industrial workers (from railways, oil mines, textile mills, KMT logistics Quartermaster factories, etc.) to conduct self-management and self-education. Special attention was to be paid to mastering policies to prevent workers from putting forward overly high demands that they would be unable to do after they were mobilized. At the same time, the correct implementation of the principle of giving consideration to both public and private affairs and the interests of both labor and capitalists coordinated the complex labor relations, stabilized the workforce, improved the awareness of workers, and promoted the recovery and development of the economy. Du Yanqing, Vice Chairman of the Northwest Federation of Trade Unions at that time, recalled that "when Comrade Tuofu got to Xi'an, he was very busy. The Northwest Federation of Trade Unions was his part-time work, but he attached great importance to the work of the trade unions. He set aside time to listen to important reports. He directly deployed important work, without considering it as an extra burden. I remember in 1950, Jia Tuofu directly presided over the conference on popularizing the successful experience of the Number 53 factory." The struggles led by Jia Tuofu played a great role in the economic stability, recovery, and development of Xi'an and the entire northwest region, all of which have become valuable experiences in the work involving urban takeovers.

In 1952, the Northwest Bureau of the CPC Central Committee was closed, and both Xi Zhongxun and Jia Tuofu were transferred to work in Beijing. Xi Zhongxun worked in the Publicity Department of the CPC Central Committee and the State Council, while Jia Tuofu was engaged in industrial and financial work. Xi Zhongxun spoke highly of Jia Tuofu's competence on several occasions. He said that Mao Zedong's important article "On Ten Relations" absorbed many of Jia Tuofu's opinions.

At the beginning of the ten-year turmoil, the Gang of Four fabricated many charges to frame up Jia Tuofu. After being cruelly persecuted, he passed away on May 7, 1967. At the time of his death, Comrade Jia Tuofu was not yet 55 years old. What is worth learning is his lifelong dedication to the Party and the people, his humility, prudence, approachability, and close ties with the masses, as well as his scientific attitude in adhering to principles and seeking truth from facts.

Missing Huang Zhi[1]

MA WENRUI, CHANG LIFU, LI LI'AN, LI ZHIWEN, AND JI YELI

Li Li'an, or Zibing, formerly known as Liangsheng, was born in July 1920 in Wutai, Shanxi Province. He joined the Communist Party of China in October 1935 and the vanguard of Chinese national liberation the next year. He served as Director of the Department of Work on the Enemy and Director of the Organization Department, both in the Second Hebei-Shanxi Prefectural Committee of the CPC, and as Secretary of the Jingjing County Party Committee of the CPC, Deputy Secretary of the Liangyun Prefectural Committee of the CPC in Southern Shaanxi, Director of the Organization Department of the CPC Central Committee, Secretary of the Heilongjiang Provincial Party Committee, First Secretary of the Harbin Municipal Party Committee, and Secretary of the Heilongjiang Party Committee.

Li Zhiwen was born in September 1918, and was a native of Qingzhou, Shandong Province. He joined the revolutionary work in November 1937 and the Communist Party of China in March 1938. He served as the Cadre Section Chief of the Pingsui Railway Bureau, member of the Fourth Prefectural Party Committee of the Communist Party of China in West Manchuria and Director of the Publicity Department, First Secretary of the Qiqihar Municipal Party Committee, member of the Northeast Bureau of the CPC Central Committee and Director of the Organization Department, member of the Standing Committee of the Liaoning Provincial Party Committee, member of the Standing Committee of the Shandong Provincial Party Committee, and First Secretary of the Qingdao Municipal Party Committee. He was the representative of the 8th, 10th, 11th, and 12th National Congresses of the CPC.

1. This article was originally published on the second page of the *Shaanxi Daily* on January 3, 1994.

It has been a year since Comrade Huang Zhi passed away. We worked with him for a long time and miss him greatly. We all felt it a great loss and paid our respects for his dedication to the cause of the Party, his meticulous professionalism, his prudent and rigorous writing style, and his decency and integrity.

I

The persistent pursuit of communism was the essential feature of Comrade Huang Zhi's personality and revolutionary character. As a student, Comrade Huang Zhi was a passionate youth who tirelessly pursued the truth of Marxism and Leninism. He had loved reading since he was a child. In 1931, when studying in the senior high school of Zhongshan University in Guangzhou, he secretly circulated among his comrades the works of Marx and Lenin and left-wing literature and art books and periodicals from Shanghai, especially the works of Lu Xun. After the September 18 Incident, the anti-Japanese war broke out across the country. In November, Comrade Huang Zhi initiated the Anti-Japanese Drama Club of Zhongshan University to carry out anti-Japanese, anti-imperialist, and anti-feudal publicity among students, workers, and citizens in Guangzhou, using drama as a weapon. The next year, he joined the Guangzhou Branch of the Left-wing Dramatist League at Zhongshan University as one of the leaders of the branch. In May 1934, the left-wing alliance was destroyed by the enemy. Comrade Huang Zhi was wanted, so he transferred to Kowloon, Hong Kong. Under the guise of a Zhirenyong Primary School teacher, he continued to engage in revolutionary publicity activities. In July, he joined the Communist Youth League. In 1935, introduced by the Party organization, he went to Shanghai to participate in the work of Shanghai Intelligence Group of GRU. He collected information from newspapers and magazines every day, translated it into Japanese and English, and handed it to his superior organization. Soon after, the organization was destroyed by the enemy, so he was forced to go to Beijing to hide for a while, but he soon returned to Shanghai to continue the work he had been assigned by the Party. Despite all these twists and turns, Comrade Huang Zhi did not lose confidence in the revolution, but endured the trials in the struggle and nurtured a more determined revolutionary enthusiasm and willpower.

In September 1936, according to the arrangement of the Party organization, Comrade Huang Zhi traveled a long way and overcame multiple difficulties to leave Shanghai for Bao'an, where the Party Central Committee was located, and began a new revolutionary career. He worked first in the Publicity Department of the

Central Committee, then as the Director of the Anti-Japanese War Drama Club. Later, entrusted by the organization, he went to the Suide police garrison area. Under the direct leadership of Comrade Wang Zhen, he founded the newspaper *Anti-Japanese War* against He Shaonan, Kuomintang reactionary Commissioner, and the *Suide Daily*, where he served as the editor-in-chief. During this period, Comrade Huang Zhi focused mainly on writing editorials. He often stayed up all night to write important editorials. His comments were clear-cut, sharp, persuasive, and effective. As a result of adhering to the correct policy of running newspapers and stressing on struggle strategies, *Anti-Japanese War* fully exposed the silver case, the opium case, and the extortion case of He Shaonan and his gangs, which was a heavy blow to the Kuomintang reactionaries who specialized in stirring up conflicts. It also gave full play to the role of the close coordination between the Party newspaper and the armed struggle.

After liberation, Comrade Huang Zhi worked in the Northwest Bureau of the CPC Central Committee, the Organization Department of the CPC Central Committee, the Ministry of Finance and Trade of the CPC Central Committee, the Northeast Bureau of the CPC Central Committee, and the Shenyang Municipal Committee of the CPC. During the Cultural Revolution, he was persecuted and sent to the countryside for labor. No matter whether it was during the war or during a period of peace, in good times or adversity, and despite the changes in his position, he was magnanimous, open-minded and unswervingly committed to the Party's belief and to safeguarding the Party's interests, manifesting inspiring uprightness and the extraordinary bearing of a Communist Party member in all that he did.

In 1979, the Central Committee accepted Comrade Ma Wenrui's suggestion, and Comrade Huang Zhi was transferred from the Shenyang Municipal Party Committee to serve as Standing Committee and Publicity Minister of the Shaanxi Provincial Party Committee. He worked day and night in spite of his physical weakness. In restoring the Party's ideological line of seeking truth from facts, organizing and carrying out the discussion on the standards of productive forces, promoting the Party's ideological and theoretical construction, and paying close attention to the rectification of the news team, he did much fruitful organizational and leadership work, which was acknowledged by the leaders of the Provincial Party Committee such as Wen Rui and the Publicity Department of the Central Committee. In particular, in view of the issues in the ideological theory and news team construction at that time, he repeatedly emphasized that the Party's interests were above everything, that publicity and ideological workers must unconditionally keep in line with the Party Central Committee in politics, that publicity workers, theoretical workers, and journalists must play the role of the Party's mouthpiece and serve as a link connecting the masses with their creative work, and that the whole publicity and ideological work team should maintain a high degree of purity. At the same time, he organized human resources to formulate corresponding documents through investigation and research, which was very courageous and far-sighted at that time. In 1982, Comrade Huang Zhi served as a consultant to the Provincial Party Committee and a member of the Standing Committee of the Provincial Advisory Committee. With a strong sense of political responsibility and mission, he constantly put forward work suggestions to the Provincial Party Committee on major issues. Even when he was seriously ill, he continued to participate in the organizational activities, with others' assistance. He learned about the publicity and ideological front work after Comrade Deng Xiaoping's Southern Tour and the implementation of the spirit of the report of the Fourteenth National Congress of the Communist Party of China. He asked for information about the situation in the Soviet Union and Eastern Europe, expressed his views without hesitation, and encouraged the cadres, especially the young cadres, to strengthen their studies and improve their understanding of complex situations so as to keep a clear political mind.

II

Most of Comrade Huang Zhi's life's work was in writing. The nature of his work made him develop a rigorous, realistic, hardworking, and meticulous style of work and writing. When he wrote and revised articles, we were impressed by his good command of materials, clear views, logical summary, good grasp of ideology, theory, and policy, and fluent style. He was proficient in the elaboration and refinement of words. Comrade Huang Zhi was opposed to writing that was full of empty talk, stereotypes, and falsehoods. He shared a story about when he was working for the *New China Daily*, he proofread Chairman Mao's "On the Long-term War." In the process of typesetting, late one night he suddenly received a letter from Chairman Mao, telling him how to revise a specific line on a page of the manuscript and saying that he should carefully review it. This touched him, which became the ideological basis of his writing style. During his nine years of working in the Northwest Bureau, he wrote many high-level documents for Comrade Xi Zhongxun and the Northwest Bureau, according to the intention of the leaders. For example, many of the important documents issued in the name of Comrade Xi Zhongxun or the Northwest Bureau, including telegrams and reports to the Party Central Committee and Chairman Mao, were drafted by Comrade Huang Zhi. During the working period of the Finance Committee of the Northeast Bureau, the important documents issued by the Finance Committee of the Northeast Bureau or drafted by the Finance Committee on behalf of the Northeast Bureau were generally checked by Comrade Huang Zhi. When he worked in the Ministry of Finance and Trade of the CPC Central Committee, the Ministry held a national meeting and special meetings every year. As a member of the Ministry and Secretary General, he drafted most of the reports to the Party Central Committee. In 1959, he wrote an article on behalf of Comrade Ma Mingfang on the integration of production, supply, and marketing. Comrade Mingfang was very happy with it and later published it in the magazine *Red Flag*. The article played a positive role in guiding the work of finance and trade at that time.

Comrade Huang Zhi's style of writing was simple and precise. When he dealt with the documents issued by the leading organs, he carefully deliberated and revised them based on the principles and policies of the central government and a large number of research materials, closely tying them to the actual situation. When drafting the documents, he would first think over and carefully consider the intentions of the superiors and leaders, then go through the materials day and night, talk to comrades who knew more about it, and collect materials from all sides. With the first draft, he would check for possible errors in the theme, viewpoint, paragraph organization, logic, and diction. He was meticulous about every word and punctuation mark. Sometimes he would make a careful inquiry into some unclear words. In November 1954, Comrade Ma Mingfang made a report at the National Working Conference of Rural Grassroots Organizations held by the Organization Department of the Central Committee of the Communist Party of China. The report lasted quite a long time, during which there were many interruptions, and we didn't hear everything clearly. After the meeting, Comrade Huang Zhi was responsible for sorting out the notes. He spent half a month pondering the notes on Ma Mingfang's speech and carefully deliberating on them. On the premise of retaining the original words and meaning, he sorted them out into a file. Everyone thought that the materials were well compiled. After reporting them to the Central Committee, Comrade Liu Shaoqi only corrected one line, then disseminated it to the entire country. On another occasion, immediately after the work report of the Ministry of Finance and Trade was submitted to the Central Committee, Comrade Huang Zhi asked the staff to retrieve it. We thought there was a big mistake in the report, but he only revised one word. It was a trivial matter, but we were all impressed by his meticulous and serious style.

Writing can be tiring, but Comrade Huang Zhi was truly devoted and industrious in his work. When he worked in the Northwest Bureau, because the situation at that time was different from the actual situation in the northwestern region, he had to work on one manuscript after another because time was very tight. In order to complete the task, he worked overtime and stayed up all night. At that time, he worked late in his office almost every night. His enthusiasm and efficiency were widely acknowledged by his comrades. Because of his overwork, his hemorrhoids became so serious that had to be treated with surgery. But he knew that the workload was heavy and he had no time to be hospitalized. After the surgery, he didn't have a good rest, but instead stayed in the office to write manuscripts. A few days later, he had a good deal of bleeding, soaking his pants and chair cushions, and blood filled his office spittoon, too. On the way to the Northwest Army General Hospital, he was in a coma. When he got to the hospital, he still remained unconscious. In a daze, he said to himself, "The report is finished." When his body temperature returned to normal, he was still very weak. He failed to follow the doctor's advice and early discharged from the hospital, resuming back to work. For years, he devoted his time and effort to writing manuscripts, but he did not publish articles in his own name. This spirit and moral character were truly admirable.

At the same time, Comrade Huang Zhi paid great attention to the nurturing of young people. He encouraged young people to closely study the works of Chairman Mao Zedong, Marxism, and Leninism, be familiar with the Party's line, principles, and policies, be good at managing the overall situation, and learn to think critically. Moreover, he encouraged them to often go deep into the grassroots units, conduct investigation and research, grasp the actual situation, and proceed from reality in everything. They were asked to be good at thinking and studying issues and develop a diligent, rigorous, and realistic ideological work style. He encouraged young people to learn to be "head-shaking" cadres. They should ask more questions about the underlying reasons, try to understand the central government's documents and the spirit of the leaders' instructions, and implement them in combination with the actual situation. Meanwhile, they should "say no" more often about their own works, and constantly refine and improve them. In the autumn of 1950, a young comrade working in the Research Office of the Northwest Bureau summarized an investigation report on the Caijiapo Cotton Mill's implementation of the enterprise democratic reform movement and promotion of enterprise democratic management. Huang Zhi read it carefully a couple of times and considered it as a valuable report of universal significance. However, the investigation report failed to grasp the "core" of democratic management and was "not good enough." Therefore, under his direct organization, he set up a working group led by the Research Office of the Northwest Bureau, involved by the participation of relevant government departments and mass organizations, to re-investigate the factory. Based on the raw materials, they formed an investigation report on strengthening the democratic management of enterprises. Huang Zhi seriously revised the investigation materials and reported them to the Central Committee. The central government attached great importance to this survey report, which had an important guiding significance for strengthening democratic management of enterprises in Northwestern China. Today, some of those young people have taken up leading positions in the Party and government, and some have become prestigious professors, scholars, and journalists. Every time they recall Comrade Huang Zhi's teaching, they feel that they have benefited a great deal.

III

The report, documents, and articles written by Comrade Huang Zhi were highly praised by leaders and colleagues for their content and quality. One important reason was that he paid close attention to investigation and research. Comrade Ma Mingfang once praised him for writing "fine works out of slow work." In fact, this "slow work" derived from Comrade Huang Zhi's building the argument on meticulous investigation and research, so that the "fine works" that resulted would stand the test of time.

When working in the Northwest Bureau, Huang Zhi often led the team to investigate and study. Sometimes, when it was hard for him to get out of the office, he would listen to the comrades who went to the countryside and the factory to report, study, and analyze the situation with them, or find a county Party Secretary, factory Party Committee Secretary and factory Director who were on the frontline to grasp the situation in detail and discuss policy issues with them. When he was transferred to the Central Ministry of Finance and Trade, he continued to adhere to the work style of investigation and research. At that time, the Central Ministry of Finance and Trade was newly established, and most cadres were not familiar with the work, so they must make clear provisions on their scope of responsibility and the guidelines and tasks for a certain period of time in the future. In order to give the newly established Ministry of Finance and Trade a practical rule and to make them understand the actual situation of finance and trade, the ministry organized four or five working groups to investigate the work in different provinces and cities. Huang Zhi personally took a working group to a county in Shanxi Province for field investigation. The investigation was very detailed, involving financial and trade grassroots organizations, cadres, work achievements, problems, and experience. The investigation and research coexisted for a more in-depth study. By the end of the day, the cadres who participated in the survey reported that it was equal to attending a training course, which improved their understanding of the financial and trade work and increased their confidence in doing well in the field. In early 1959, he led a group of comrades to Qichun County, Hubei Province to investigate the new situation and problems in the financial and trade work after the Great Leap Forward. At that time, due to the overheating of growth, there were much blindness, boasting, and policy violations in financial and trade work. Huang went deep into the grassroots level, approached the masses, listened to opinions with an open mind, studied and discussed with the comrades there, and reported the actual situation clearly and truthfully. In the work briefs prepared by the Ministry of Finance and Trade under his supervision, the Party Committee and the leading comrades of the provincial and municipal committees would be promptly informed of the actual situation and problems in their work. After working with the Finance Committee of the Northeast Bureau, Huang Zhi still regarded the investigation and research as his priority. That was a period of temporary difficulties. It was important to arrange people's lives, improve market supply, and adjust financial and trade work. In particular, many problems in business during the Great Leap Forward needed to be comprehensively rectified. It was necessary to investigate and study closely, summarize experience and lessons, and formulate targeted measures. Huang Zhi was directly involved in the investigation and research: in addition to the in-depth investigation at the grassroots level, he also presided over and held a symposium of relevant personnel in Liaoning Province and Shenyang City multiple times, listened to the report on the actual situation, and had discussions, unified our thoughts and understanding, and drafted the commercial work regulations on the basis of clarifying the situation, and brought about the desired results. As a leading cadre, no matter in Xi'an or in Beijing and Shenyang, Huang Zhi often led his comrades to the grassroots level. In the market, he checked the stall, dug into the possible problems in each step about vegetables, grains, and oil supplies, and prepared for the decision making. In the practice of investigation and research, he emphasized working methods such as "being a head-shaking cadre," "practicing with sharp vision," "learning to dissect problems like sparrows," and "settling problems in a forward-looking way," which are still completely correct and applicable today.

IV

Comrade Huang Zhi was strict with himself, honest, upright, humble, and cautious, working selflessly for the public interest without caring about personal gains and losses or taking advantage of his authority. He often said that a Communist Party member had the duty to wholeheartedly serve and work for the people and had no right to ask the Party or the people for fame and fortune or to exercise one's privilege. Otherwise, many revolutionary martyrs would have sacrificed their lives for nothing. This was the basic principle he held onto and acted upon throughout his life. During his work at the Central Ministry of Finance and Trade, his 80-year-old father became so seriously ill that he was hospitalized. In order not to affect his work and add a burden to the organization, he hired someone to take care of his father, despite his financial difficulty, and he often took the bus to the hospital to see his father on Sundays and holidays. When his father passed away, he was accompanying Comrade Yao Yilin (then Vice Minister of the Central Ministry of Finance and Trade) to conduct investigation and research in various provinces and cities in the south. Hearing the news, he immediately called the general office of the Ministry of Finance and Trade and asked the authorities to handle the funeral on the behalf of him, while he devoted himself to his work. What's more, he was strict with his family members and often told his children to be self-sufficient and rely on their own abilities and skills to "get ahead." At the end of 1960, he was transferred to the Finance Committee of the Northeast Bureau to work. He arranged for his oldest and second sons to study and accommodate in a middle school in Beijing on their own, and then took his wife and other children who were in primary school and kindergarten to Shenyang. When he was transferred to Shaanxi in 1979, only his wife went with him. Now, his children are doing well in their respective posts in different parts of the country. When he was seriously ill last year, he insisted that they should not come to Xi'an to visit him. He was worried that they would be distracted and their work disrupted.

He was a person of conscientiously doing practical work for the people, learning humbly from the people, and always keeping the closest relationship with the people. In 1960, China was in a difficult period for three years. In order to grasp the grassroots situation, he directly led the cadres of the Finance Committee of the Northeast Bureau to the factories, rural areas, institutions, and schools, specifically made arrangements for the masses, organized production, and helped the masses overcome difficulties and tide them over. During his work, he often went to the grassroots units to check the supply of vegetables, grain, and oil that were so closely related to the people's livelihood so that he promptly identified and solved problems. On New Year's Eve, he went every year with the officials to the catering service department near the railway station to send dumplings to the passengers so that they could enjoy a happy, peaceful New Year's Eve thousands of miles away from home. In December 1969, Comrade Huang Zhi was assigned to join the Mengjia production team of the Chaoyang Commune in Xiuyan, Liaoning Province, as a May 7 soldier. There, he humbly learned from the masses of farmers and soon mastered a set of skills such as sowing, management, and collection and established a strong bond with the local farmers. Later, when the authorities mistakenly announced that Huang should "labor under supervision" and criticized him, many farmers comforted him, saying, "Mr. Huang, people like you are unlikely to be capitalists or reactionaries. Chairman Mao's policy has been distorted and the practice will be short-lived, like the rabbit's tail." In October 1972, Comrade Huang Zhi said goodbye to the farmers he had worked and stayed with for so long and returned to a leading position. Thirteen years later (1985), he went back to the production team that he had stayed with to gain insight into the production and living conditions of the farmers. When he saw that the lives of the masses had improved greatly, he was very pleased. He was always emotional when recalling this unusual part of his history. This emotion was sincere and consistent. Comrade Huang Zhi had great respect for Ms. Zhang, the housemaid who had worked for him since 1950. He often said that she was also part of the revolutionary work, and without her hard work, nothing would work well. Zhang's family was in Chang'an County, Shaanxi Province. Her daughter wished to go to Beijing to visit her every summer or winter vacation. On learning this, Comrade Huang Zhi told Zhang to ask her daughter to come, saying that he would pay for her transportation and food expenses in Beijing. It was only when her daughter graduated from university and had her own children that Zhang, who had worked at Comrade Huang Zhi's home for fifteen years, returned to her hometown, feeling reluctant to part with the Huang family.

Comrade Huang Zhi stood up to various challenges courageously, worked selflessly, and always maintained the fine tradition and style of our Party and army. In 1947, the Kuomintang reactionaries concentrated 34 brigades and 250,000 soldiers to invade the Shaanxi-Gansu-Ningxia border region, where the Party Central Committee was located. At that time, he was suffering from hemorrhoids. The medical facilities in mountainous areas were very poor, which could not offer adequate medical care. Even taking a few tablets of SD and SG had to be approved by the leaders. For lack of proper treatment, Huang's health deteriorated, leading to rectal prolapse and bleeding. Even faced up with this circumstance, he resolutely followed Comrade Xi Zhongxun to work in the front headquarters of the Northwest Field Army. The changes and progress of the war situation required the former general positions to be transferred frequently. Every time he moved, he endured the piercing pain, to stand on the stirrups to march forward. As soon as he arrived at the station, the very first thing he did was to push the prolapsed rectum back into place, and then he went immediately about his intense work. After the liberation of the entire country, Comrade Huang Zhi took up the leading post. His status changed, but the spirit of hard work and selfless dedication did not change a bit. In today's tide of Reform and Opening Up, to strengthen Party building and fight against corruption, we should vigorously embrace and carry forward the excellent character and exemplary deeds of veteran Communist Party members such as Comrade Huang Zhi and educate the younger generation and other comrades with his Party spirit, work style, and noble character. This is exactly why we miss Comrade Huang Zhi.

Attachments:

In Memory of Comrade Huang Zhi

Zhang Xiaochen

To take the revolution as home
And a simple rifle as the best weapon
With footprints spanning China, along with his writing
These decision making articles benefit the nation
Selfless endeavors for the good of all
Honest, upright, and trustworthy
Striving for truth all his life
Pure, with nobility and integrity

November 1993

Mourning Huang Zhi

Feng Yuanshuo

With the departure of Comrade Huang Zhi, I lost another old leader and comrade. I would like to offer this humble poem as a tribute to him.

White like the snow in the north
Bright like the moon in Jiangnan
A life of integrity and honesty
Worthy to meet Marx and Lenin

December 1992

Mourning for Chang Lifu, a Leader and Mentor[1]

JI YELI AND WANG BOHUI

Born in 1925, Wang Bohui was a native of Kelan, Shanxi Province. He started working in April 1940 and joined the Communist Party of China in January 1947. He served as secretary and section chief of the security office of the Shaanxi-Gansu-Ningxia border region and the local government. After the founding of the new China, he served as Deputy Director of the General Office Secretariat of the Northwest Military and Political Commission, Deputy Director of the Secretariat of the State Council, Secretary of the Xianyang County Party Committee, Deputy Director of the Agricultural Office of the Shaanxi Provincial People's Committee, President of the Xianyang Party School, Deputy Director of the Ministry of Agriculture and Industry, Deputy Director of the Provincial Agricultural Committee, President of the Provincial Party School, and standing member of the Sixth Shaanxi Provincial Committee of the CPPCC.

When Comrade Chang Lifu passed away, we grieved deeply as we had worked under his leadership for a long time. All his life, he did much work for the Party and the people, made great contributions, and set an example for us. He is always in our minds even today.

1. This article is an abridged version of the one originally published in the *Shaanxi Daily* on February 22, 2006.

Outstanding Representative of Secretarial Work

Comrade Chang Lifu had long been engaged in the leadership work of the Secretary Department, and had done a very good job in giving full play to the role of the department in political assistance, contact, coordination, and connection. He was able to assist the main leaders in organizing various important meetings and promoting important overall work.

As early as 1948, in order to strengthen the unified leadership of the Party Central Committee and overcome the state of undisciplined anarchy and the ideological style of empiricism, the Party Central Committee issued the *Instructions on the Establishment of the Reporting System*. Comrade Chang Lifu took it as an important task of the whole secretarial work and consciously carried it out. After the founding of the new China, he presided over the drafting of the *Provisions on the Work Report System of the Departments Under the State Council* and *Provisions of the State Council on the Work Report System of the People's Committees of All Provinces, Autonomous Regions, and Municipalities Directly Under the Central Government*. At the plenary session of the State Council where the two regulations were discussed and adopted, Premier Zhou Enlai asked the premiers and vice premiers to contact several provinces according to their respective responsibilities, in order to strengthen direct contact between the top and the bottom, and establish a system of direct contact between the Secretary General, Deputy Secretary General of the State Council and chief leading comrades of various provinces. All this played a positive role in the State Council's timely understanding of the situation and promotion of the relevant work.

Comrade Chang Lifu was shrewd and skillful in dealing with government affairs and thoughtful and meticulous in handling them, and he was a good leader of the Secretary Department, equipped with multiple talents. He often said that the Secretary and the Secretary General were the staff assistants of the Party and government leaders. We participated not only in government affairs, but also in management affairs. We were literate and military, as a link between what was preceding and what was upcoming. It was certain that we would play the "supporting role," which was by no means a small thing. We must make vertical and horizontal connections and manage internal and external communications, functioning like a coordinating and mediating force. We had to take care of everything in detail and manage it properly. In both government and administrative affairs, he did an outstanding job, always working appropriately with his meticulous consideration.

Setting an example with his words and deeds, he fostered a number of good cadres in secretarial work and organ affairs management.

Leaders Good at United Front Work

One of the most important aspects in which Comrade Chang Lifu was a good political assistant to the leaders was that he took the initiative to do the United Front work within the organs very well. To strengthen the work, the Northwest Military and Political Commission set up a United Front Working Committee, and he was put in charge.

He closely linked the United Front work with the improvement of the political, ideological, and leadership level of the leading Party cadres in the organs. He emphasized that only by enhancing the pure organizational leadership to the level of political and ideological leadership and constantly strengthening the ideological and political work could the United Front and other work of the organs be done well. At work, he set an example and took the initiative. He treated others cordially and equally, whether Zhang Zhizhong, famous democrat and vice chairman of the Northwest Military and Political Commission, or the leaders at all levels and the democratic personages among the old civil servants. In study, he paid close attention to improving their ideological and political awareness. At work, he did all he could to help them and respect their authority. In daily life, he offered them meticulous arrangements and care. When there were issues with their thought and work, he talked to them individually and resolved conflicts in an honest way, so as to attain mutual understanding, mutual trust, and unity. With Comrade Chang Lifu's unremitting efforts, the General Office of the Northwest Military and Political Commission became a model unit of the United Front work, playing an exemplary and leading role.

Comrade Chang Lifu worked in every detail to manage the work concerning the representative non-Party members. He highly respected vice president Zhang Zhizhong and made proper arrangements for the documents he needed to read, the official documents he needed to give instructions on, and the government affairs he needed to be involved in. Chang once accompanied Zhang Zhizhong to Gansu, Ningxia, and Qinghai to inspect the production and disaster relief work for a month and a half. He settled each problem identified in the inspection and took good care of Zhang. Zhang was greatly impressed by the work style of the cadres of the Communist Party represented by Comrade Chang Lifu. Tan Weixu, Deputy

Secretary General of the Northwest Military and Political Commission and the Executive Committee, was primarily in charge of the democratic revolution in Shaanxi Province. Comrade Chang Lifu worked with him for five years, and they became close comrades and friends. After the beginning of Reform and Opening Up, Tan Weixu became chairman of the CPPCC Shaanxi Provincial Committee and member of the Standing Committee of the CPPCC National Committee. He applied multiple times to join the Communist Party of China and asked Chang Lifu to be his introducer. Tan finally fulfilled his long-time wish.

In 1961, Comrade Chang served as the head of the United Front Department of the Northwest Bureau of the CPC Central Committee. Although he was seriously disturbed by the leftist thinking, he did his best to properly implement the Party's ethnic policy, emphasizing the restoration and development of production in pastoral areas, taking the initiative to improve relations with the upper classes of ethnic minorities and strengthening the training of ethnic minority cadres.

The Spirit of Seeking Truth from Facts

Comrade Chang Lifu never engaged in empty talk or exaggeration, let alone speaking falsely. He was engaged in writing all his life, but he never wrote anything empty or exaggerated. In all previous political movements, he was able to stay level-headed. Instead of talking big, interrogating, and "extorting confessions," he was able to find out the truth of a problem through meticulous in-depth investigation and research. He made no unjust or false cases. In that era when class struggle was the mainstream, along with numerous other movements, it was very difficult to do so.

He dared to speak up on major issues and supported the implementation of the household contract system in rural areas. In the 1960s, in support of the "three red flags" of the general line, the Great Leap Forward, and the people's commune movement, most of the serious difficulties in the national economy were attributed to severe natural disasters. According to the actual situation observed in his investigation in the Gaoxigou Brigade of Mizhi County, Comrade Chang Lifu pointed out at an enlarged meeting of the Provincial Party Committee that the farmers believed that the serious difficulties in the national economy resulted partly from natural disasters, but mostly from man-made disasters, which clearly revealed the great harm caused by serious mistakes such as the "three red flags."

In the autumn of 1961, Chang Lifu led the working group to the Yulin area for investigation. At that time, there was a dispute about whether a donkey should be distributed to each individual household. On the basis of fully understanding the facts and listening to the opinions of all parties, Chang Lifu agreed with the working group and Dingbian County Party Committee that a donkey should be distributed to each household, which effectively promoted the great development of agriculture and animal husbandry in Dingbian County and its neighboring areas. After the beginning of Reform and Opening Up, Chang was very concerned about the development of the rural household contract system, and he directly conducted an investigation and worked closely with the Ministry of Agriculture and Industry of the Provincial Party Committee in this area.

Honesty and Integrity

Comrade Chang Lifu often said that compared with those comrades who had gone through the Long March, those who had fought courageous fights, especially the revolutionary martyrs, we were really walking on a smooth path, or even a shortcut. What was there to be dissatisfied with, and what was worth showing off in our work? He never cared about his personal position or benefits, and he gave his best to do the work assigned by the organization under all circumstances. He was hardworking, thrifty, honest, and self-disciplined. He did not accept any gifts or invitations for meals. He was pure with great integrity. In 1982, Kim II-Sung, General Secretary of the Central Committee of the Korean Workers' Party and President of the Democratic People's Republic of Korea, visited Xi'an and gave Chang Lifu two bottles of Korean ginseng wine as a gift. Chang immediately handed them over to the General Office of the Provincial People's Congress and reserved them in the warehouse for fourteen years. He detested bribery and corruption and argued firmly that "fighting against unhealthy tendencies should not exclude one's families or friends. We should take the revolutionary tradition as an example, and be ready to take complaints and curses."

A Communist with the Yan'an Spirit and Style[1]

In Memory of Comrade Cao Liru

Xi Zhongxun, Ma Wenrui, Zhang Xiushan, Yuan Renyuan, Zhang Bangying, and Zhang Dazhi

Born on October 15, 1913, Xi Zhongxun was a native of Fuping County, Shaanxi Province. He passed away in Beijing on May 24, 2002 at the age of 89. In May 1926, he joined the Youth League of the Communist Party of China and became a member of the CPC in 1928. After the victory of the anti-Japanese war, he served as Secretary of the Northwest Bureau of the CPC Central Committee, political member of the Shaanxi-Gansu-Ningxia Jinsui Joint Defense Army, Political Member of the Shaanxi-Gansu-Ningxia Field Group Army and Vice Political Member of the Northwest Field Army. After the founding of the new China, he served as a member of the Central People's Government, a member of the People's Revolutionary Military Commission of China, Second Secretary of the Northwest Bureau of the CPC Central Committee, Vice Chairman and Acting Chairman of the Northwest Military and Political Commission, Vice Chairman of the Northwest Administrative Committee and the First Field Army, and Political Member of the Northwest Military Region. He oversaw the overall work of the northwest Party, government, and army for many years. He was Secretary of the Secretariat of the 11th Central Committee of the Communist Party of China, a member of the 12th Political Bureau and Secretary of the Secretariat of the 12th CPC Central Committee, and Vice Chairman of the Standing Committee of the Fifth and Seventh National People's Congress.

Born in July 1911, Zhang Xiushan was a native of Shenmu, Shaanxi Province. In the autumn of 1929, he joined the Communist Party of China and became one of

1. This extract was taken from *Cao Liru*, Shaanxi People's Publishing House, 1996.

the founders of the Northwest Red Army, the Northwest Revolutionary Base, and the Northeast Revolutionary Base. From January 1943 to June 1944, he was Deputy Director of the Organization Department of the Northwest Bureau of the CPC Central Committee. From March to May 1943, he was the President of the Northwest Party School. He was later the Director of the Education Department of the Party School of the CPC Central Committee, Secretary of the Songjiang Provincial Committee of the CPC, Secretary of the Liaoning Provincial Committee of the CPC, political member and Secretary of the Party Committee of the Liaoning military region, standing member and Secretary General of the Northeast Bureau of the CPC Central Committee, Second Deputy Secretary of the Northeast Bureau of the CPC Central Committee, and Deputy Director of the State Council Agricultural Commission.

Born in May 1898, Yuan Renyuan was a native of Cili, Hunan Province. From November 1940 to September 1942, he served as Director of the Political Department of the 389th Brigade of the Number 10 Division of the Eighth Route Army, and member of the Military and Political Committee of the 359th Brigade in April 1941. At the end of 1940, he join the troops to cultivate waste land for farming in Nanniwan, setting up a model in the large-scale production movement of the Shaanxi-Gansu-Ningxia border area. He later worked as Secretary of the Jilin Municipal Committee of the CPC, Vice Chairman of the Hunan Provincial Government, Deputy Minister of the Ministry of Internal Affairs, and member of the Standing Committee of the Fifth National People's Congress.

Born in 1911, Zhang Dazhi was a native of Jiaxian, Shaanxi Province and one of the founders of the base area in Northern Shaanxi. He served as the Minister of Public Security of the Northwest Military and Political Commission, Commander and Commissar of Political Committee of the Northwest Public Security Force, Commander of the Lanzhou Military Region, Artillery Commander of the People's Liberation Army, member of the Military Commission of the Central Committee of the Communist Party of China, and member of the National Defense Committee. He was awarded the rank of Lieutenant General in 1955.

In the winter of 1949, when Comrade Cao Liru was ordered to assist Comrade Wang Zhen in Xinjiang, an unexpected disaster took his life. The news shocked the cadres and people in Northwestern China. Many regretted the loss of this dedicated communist soldier and excellent leading cadre of the Party. Whenever we recalled the hard years we spent with him, the memories flooded through our minds.

Comrade Cao Liru and Comrade Liu Zhidan had been friends since they studied in the same primary school. When studying in the Yulin Middle School in Northern Shaanxi Province, Cao was influenced by Wei Yechou and Li Zizhou, the founders of the Communist Party organization in Northwest China, and he accepted revolutionary thought. He helped Wei Yechou to copy and organize the translation work of the basic principles of political economics, and he learned many revolutionary principles from Wei. He, along with Liu Zhidan and other students, publicized new ideas and the new culture, led the student movement, which was stigmatized as one of "the eight culprits" by the reactionary warlords.

During the first revolutionary war in China, Cao Liru gave up writing and joined the army. He first studied in the radio workshop of the Second Corps of the national army, then served as a lieutenant secretary in the artillery camp under Yang Hucheng and joined the Communist Party of China at the end of 1926. The Party organization sent him to work in the 10th Corps of the national army under Yang Hucheng, serving as acting Director of the Political Department of the Army and Director of the Political Division of the Second Division. He went out of Tongguan with the Yang troops and made great contributions to the cooperation between the Kuomintang and the Communist Party during the Northern Expedition.

After the April 12 anti-revolutionary coup, General Yang Hucheng was forced to go abroad. Sun Weiru acted as commander of the 10th Corps, and Chiang Kai-Shek sent his people to stay in the 10th Corps to supervise the "purge of the party." At this critical juncture, Comrade Cao Liru was composed in the face of danger and fought against the reactionaries in an intelligent and courageous manner. As the Special Envoy of the 10th Corps at that time, he convinced Sun Weiru to protect a group of Communist Party members. After the August 7 CPC Congress, he served as Secretary General of the Special Committee of the Northern Anhui Province and was entrusted with transportation duties for the Central Committee of the Party on many occasions, transporting people to Henan and Shaanxi Provinces to pass on documents and instructions. In order to implement the spirit of the August 7 Conference, he left the army, went deep into the countryside, armed workers and farmers, and resisted the suppression of the Kuomintang. On April 9, 1928, the riot in Northern Anhui was launched. Comrade Cao Liru also served as Commander of the Red Guard, leading the workers and farmers to fight bravely. When the Democratic Government of Workers and Farmers in Northern Anhui was established, Comrade Cao Liru served as Secretary General. In the arduous revolutionary struggle years, his selfless, fearless spirit and witty, brave deeds were most admirable.

After the failure of the riot in Northern Anhui Province, Comrade Cao Liru returned to his hometown of Bao'an County in Northern Shaanxi. Under the leadership of Comrade Liu Zhidan, he did a good deal of work to conduct the armed struggle along the Shaanxi-Gansu border. With some efforts, he and Comrade Liu Zhidan served as the General and Deputy General of the Civil Corps of Bao'an County and commanded the local armed forces. In spring 1931, Comrade Cao Liru was arrested and imprisoned in the Yulin KMT prison for the leaking of secret messages concerning a weapons purchase. The enemy threatened, seduced, and tortured him in an attempt to force him to surrender. Comrade Cao Liru was steadfast and unyielding, manifesting the lofty moral character of a Communist Party member. Having been rescued by the Party organization on medical parole, he returned to his hometown. During his recuperation, he continued to work hard and entered the enemy camp in person to persuade the People's League to surrender, ultimately eliminating the White area and expanding the Red zone.

After the Long March of the Central Red Army arrived in Northern Shaanxi, Comrade Cao Liru served as Secretary General of the Shaanxi-Gansu Provincial Committee and Military Minister of the Shaanxi-Gansu Working Committee. During the Western March of the main force of the Red Army, he followed the instructions of Vice President Zhou Enlai and led the guerrilla forces and independent battalions to maintain the guerrilla war in Luohechuan and eliminate a large number of enemies. After the peaceful settlement of the Xi'an Incident, he was appointed as Secretary of the Zhidan County Party Committee to precisely carry out the Party's instructions, helping the county to achieve remarkable things in various areas of work, and he wrote articles and shared his experiences in the *New China Daily* on multiple occasions.

During the anti-Japanese war, Comrade Cao Liru served as Secretary General of the Shaanxi-Gansu-Ningxia border region government, Deputy Director of the Department of Finance, Deputy Commissioner of the Suide Special Office, Commissioner of the Yanzhi Special Office, and Commissioner of Northern and Western Shaanxi. He conscientiously carried out the instructions of the Party Central Committee and Chairman Mao. Under the leadership of Comrade Lin Boqu, chairman of the Shaanxi-Gansu-Ningxia border region government, he organized the War of Resistance Against Japanese Aggression and various production activities, united the parties and troops on our side with a variety of anti-Japanese and patriotic social forces, and made important contributions to building the border region into a model anti-Japanese base. Comrade Lin Boqu once said, "The remarkable achievements in the economic construction of the border region are due to hard-working cadres like Comrade Cao Liru."

During the War of Liberation, Comrade Cao Liru served as Deputy Secretary General of the Northwest Bureau of the CPC Central Committee, Vice Minister of the Urban Engineering Ministry, Director of Yulin Military Management Commission, Director of the Northern Shaanxi Administrative Office, and others. In March 1947, Chiang Kai-shek and Hu Zongnan's troops invaded the Shaanxi-Gansu-Ningxia border region, and the Party Central Committee and Chairman Mao moved to Northern Shaanxi in response. Comrade Cao Liru and Wang Weizhou were ordered to organize the border region organs to withdraw safely from Yan'an according to the unified deployment of the Central Committee, accomplishing a successful transfer. After our army restored Yan'an, at the meeting of secretaries of the Yan'an Prefectural Party Committee, according to the instructions of the Northwest Bureau of the CPC Central Committee, Comrade Cao put forward the tasks and requirements for urban work in the northwestern region and made preparations for the liberation of the northwest. In October 1949, Xinjiang was peacefully liberated, and the Northwest Bureau of the CPC Central Committee sent Comrade Cao Liru to take up an important position in Xinjiang. Unfortunately, on December 8, he was killed in an accident in Baqiao, Xi'an at the age of 48.

Comrade Cao Liru was an excellent member of the Communist Party of China and a loyal communist fighter. He was loyal to the Party, generous, and resolute, never concerned about personal fame and fortune, and never giving in to difficulties. Whenever he received tasks assigned by the Party, no matter how difficult the conditions were or how complicated the environment was, he always did his best to accomplish them. He was good at connecting with the masses and relying on them to work together, so that the places where he worked developed a new look and a new atmosphere. In particular, when he was Secretary General of the Government of the Shaanxi-Gansu-Ningxia border region, Comrade Lin Boqu often went out to work. Comrade Cao Liru organized different groups and looked deep into the actual situation. Based on the local conditions at that time, he dealt with various major issues flexibly and put all the work in its proper place. His shrewd, efficient, and humble work style greatly impressed the cadres and the masses. Later, the Party sent Comrade Cao Liru to the new Suide Special Office to serve as Deputy Commissioner. At that time, the enemy situation there was complex and the task was arduous. Under the direct leadership of Comrade Wang Zhen, Comrade Cao Liru relied heavily on the masses, reduced rent and interest rates in the rural areas, implemented the "triangular organization systems" in the anti-Japanese democratic regime, united open-minded people, and thus won support of people from all walks of life and made an important contribution to the stability and unity of the new area.

Comrade Cao Liru was an excellent leading cadre who grew up during the long-term practical struggle. He was familiar with the situation in Shaanxi and Gansu, understood the popular customs, and had a wealth of practical experience. He tirelessly studied Marxist and Leninist works and Comrade Mao Zedong's instructions, and constantly improved his theoretical competence. He went deep in practice, conducted investigation and study, pooled the wisdom of the masses, and put forward new methods based on the analysis and study of new situations. His comrades said that he was capable, resourceful, and flexible in dealing with problems. On January 7, 1939, in the face of the military encirclement and economic blockade by the Kuomintang reactionaries, the Party Central Committee held a production mobilization meeting in Yan'an. Comrade Mao Zedong issued a call for the people to be self-reliant to overcome difficulties. As the Secretary General of the Shaanxi-Gansu-Ningxia border region government, Comrade Cao Liru was responsible for the work of the production committee. He conscientiously carried out the instructions of the Party Central Committee and Chairman Mao, and quickly transferred one third of the cadres of the border region government organs to Mashichuan to set up farms. He took the lead in labor, went into the fields, arranged farm work, asked the veteran farmers for guidance, invited scientific workers to give lectures, and summed up the labor experience with vivid proverbs, all of which has won the popular praise among the folks. Later, he wrote an article entitled "To the Production Committees of All Organs in Yan'an," which put forward eight policy and guiding principles, including taking self-sufficiency as the standard, paying attention to the fertility of the land, planting crops according to the soil quality, sowing on time, emphasizing cultivation methods, raising and using cattle, accurately calculating the number of *mu*, and allowing private cultivation of small plots of land. His pragmatic, hard-working spirit not only won the recognition and praise of the leaders and the masses, but also played a positive role in driving the rapid, healthy development of the production movement of the organs at that time.

Being far sighted and ambitious, Comrade Cao Liru took the overall situation into consideration to precisely implement the Party's Anti-Japanese National United Front Policy. He was good at winning over all the people he could and uniting all the forces he could. He established friendships with open-minded citizens in the border region, such as Li Dingming, An Wenqin, Huo Zile, Liu Jiesan, and Huo Zhusan, and he had friendly contact with the progressive people of the Mongolian upper class. In accordance with the instructions of the Party Central Committee and the Northwest Bureau, he went to Yulin three times to do United Front work, and each time he successfully completed the task. He made friends with Deng Baoshan and Zuo Xiezhong. He was ordered to go to Guyuan, Gansu Province to invite Du Bincheng to the border region to participate in government and political affairs. Cao was experienced, courageous, and resourceful, and he highlighted struggle strategies. In May 1949, under the victorious march and powerful attack of the Chinese People's Liberation Army, as the plenipotentiary representative of the northwest military region, Cao led a delegation to negotiate with the representatives of the 22nd Corps of the Kuomintang. He analyzed the situation, affirmed justice, publicized the policies of our Party and army, pointed out the way out for the 22nd Corps, adhered to the position on issues of principle, which convinced and moved the KMT generals. When the delegation reached Yulin, the KMT secret service was rampant, and it threatened to kill Cao Liru. However, Comrade Cao Liru stepped forward, led the delegation to the city that night, went out in public, contacted people from all walks of life, carried out publicity activities, inspired the progressive forces, attacked the morale of the enemy spies, and soon reached an agreement through negotiations. As a result, Yulin, an important town in northern Shaanxi, returned to the hands of the people.

Comrade Cao Liru always maintained a fine style of hard work and selfless dedication to the public. He was in charge of economic work for many years, and he never wasted a penny. In those tough years, the food department took care of the rice for the leading cadres every month, but he never went to take it. He had strict requirements for his wife and children, who took advantage of no privilege. When there was nutritious food, he always had it sent to the leading comrades of the Central Committee, the sick, and the injured. The fine style of Comrade Cao not only allowed him to make outstanding contributions to the Party and the people throughout his short life, but also moved and influenced many young people to fight bravely for the cause of the revolution.

Today, the people of all ethnic groups in China are carrying out the four modernizations wholeheartedly. In order to express our respect and gratitude for Comrade Cao Liru, we must learn from and carry forward his revolutionary spirit, his practical, hard-working style of serving the people wholeheartedly, earnestly implement the spirit of the Third Plenary Session of the 12th Central Committee of the CPC, make great efforts to do well in economic Reform and Opening Up to the outside world, contribute to the revitalization of China, and further create a new situation of socialist modernization.

A Transient and Splendid Life[1]

Review of Comrade Cao Liru's Work in the Northwest Bureau

Comrade Cao Liru was a Communist Party member during the great revolution, and he made great contributions to the cause of the liberation of the Chinese people in the long-term revolutionary struggle. In the early days after the founding of the new China, he was killed at an early age in a car accident on his way to Xinjiang, where he was meant to take up a new post. People today will always remember this communist soldier who devoted his life to the cause of the liberation of the Chinese people.

Cao Liru, also called Hanhan or Chongben, was born January 28, 1902, into a farmer's family in Diaoping Village, Danba Town, Bao'an County (today's Zhidan County), Shaanxi Province. In 1946, he was transferred to serve as Deputy Secretary General of the Northwest Bureau of the CPC Central Committee. On February 16 (the 15th day of the first month of the lunar calendar), on behalf of the people of six townships in Chuankou District, Yan'an County, Comrade Cao Liru presented a plaque engraved with the words *Savior of the People* to Mao Zedong to express the love and respect the people of the border area had for the leader. On February 19, Cao went to Bayao Fort on a special journey to attend a ceremony recognizing the completion of the Zichang Mausoleum and a public memorial ceremony honoring the martyr Xie Zichang. In April, Cao started to work as a member of the Preparatory Committee of the Revolutionary History Museum of the Shaanxi-Gansu-Ningxia border region.

1. This article was compiled by the editor based on the book *Cao Liru*, published by Shaanxi People's Publishing House in September 1996.

In March 1947, Chiang Kai-shek and Hu Zongnan gathered 250,000 soldiers to invade the Shaanxi-Gansu-Ningxia border area. The Party Central Committee and Mao Zedong made the wise decision to temporarily abandon Yan'an, employ the mushroom tactic to confine the enemy forces to Northern Shaanxi, and eliminate them there.

At this critical moment, Xi Zhongxun, Jia Tuofu, and Ma Wenrui, members of the Standing Committee of Northwest Bureau, were ordered to work on the front line (though in August, Ma Wenrui returned to the rear office). Comrade Cao Liru, as Deputy Secretary General, and Ma Mingfang, as Deputy Secretary, remained in the organ. Comrade Cao Liru held an emergency meeting of the border government in a cave in Hougou at the new Yan'an market and quickly conveyed and implemented the decision and deployment of the Central Committee. He introduced the enemy situation in Longdong to Xie Huaide and sent him to assist Zhang Zhongliang in the work at Longdong. Comrade Cao Liru maintained his composure as he arranged the work and directed the withdrawal of the border organs in an orderly way, greatly encouraging the people through his good conducts.

Mao Zedong, Zhou Enlai, and Ren Bishi led the central organs and the PLA headquarters to fight in Northern Shaanxi, commanding the PLA to fight bravely against the Kuomintang troops on battlefields across the country, winning one victory after another. According to the central deployment, in order to protect the Party Central Committee and contain the enemy forces, Lin Boqu, Ma Mingfang, Cao Liru, and Wang Weizhou led the Northwest Bureau, the border region government, the organs of the Shaanxi-Gansu-Ningxia-Jinsui Joint Defense Headquarters, the mass groups, and family members to withdraw from Yan'an on the morning of March 18 and move northward along another route. This transfer team was code named the Fifth Regiment, or the Second Column. Cao Liru came later. Lin Boqu was ordered to cross the Yellow River and go to Shanxi. Yang Mingxuan, the leader of the Northwest Democratic League, who returned to Northern Shaanxi from the Kuomintang-ruled area, followed the Second Column.

At that time, the enemy aerial bombed us, and on land, they closely pursued our troops. In the face of these urgent, harsh conditions, Comrade Cao Liru promptly contacted the Party Central Committee and the Northwest Field Army by radio, reported the situation, and received orders. In order to fight against the enemy and preserve our army, Comrade Cao Liru organized the organ guerrillas and appointed Yang Jingren as captain. During the march, Li Wanchun and Zhang Zhenbang were sent to take on the task of guarding. Cao always took the lead, marched

Cao Liru.

ahead, promptly sent soldiers to scout, and grasped the enemy's situation. When encountering the enemy's pursuit, he quickly rushed to the back of the team to make quick decisions and cover the shift. When stationed in Zichang County, the troop was attacked by enemy planes constantly. Comrade Cao Liru immediately ordered all the people to move to the nearby Wanfo Cave. The enemy planes circled outside the cave, with bombs exploding everywhere, but the people in the cave were all safe. When the enemy attacked Qingyangcha, Jingbian County, Comrade Cao Liru directed the security team to shoot with machine guns from different spots to confuse the enemy thereby covering the safe retreat of the troops.

On the afternoon of May 14, 1947, 50,000 soldiers and civilians of the Shaanxi-Gansu-Ningxia border region held a victory celebration in Zhenwu Cave, Ansai. After the meeting, Vice President Zhou Enlai made a special visit to the Second Column and discussed with Cao Liru and Wang Weizhou the transition to warfare and the work of supporting the front line. Vice President Zhou made a report on the situation to the cadres, which greatly encouraged them. According to Zhou Enlai's instructions, Cao Liru and Yang Jingren drafted a document on the policy of United Front and urban work. Comrade Cao Liru sent it to the front line. After being signed by the major leaders of the Northwest Bureau of the CPC Central Committee, the document was widely sent to all parts of the border region, promoting the underground work and the work of disintegrating the enemy in the KMT ruled areas.

In 1947, a group photo of the comrades of the Party, government, and army from the Shaanxi-Gansu border area. From left on the front row: Lin Boqu, He Long, Zhao Shoushan, Xi Zhongxun, Zhang Bangying, and Cao Liru. From left on the back row: Wang Weizhou, Jia Tuofu, Yang Mingxuan, Ma Wenrui, Yao Jingchen, Chang Lifu, and others.

When news came that the three victories in the Battles of Panlong, Qinghua, and Yangmahe had destroyed more than 20,000 enemy soldiers, Comrade Cao Liru instructed the telegraph operator to send a clear code telegram to the KMT garrison in Yulin and broadcast the ballad written by Fan Changjiang, "Barbarians are useless, and the Yanyu road is blocked. Panlong is lost, followed by Suide, and the march has ended in vain. Six thousand officers and men were taken prisoners, and seven and a half brigades showed themselves cowards. Deng Baoshan is dangling in the air in Yulin." Comrade Cao Liru used this ballad to publicize the victory of the PLA and shake the morale of the enemy.

In the days when he moved to Northern Shaanxi, Comrade Cao Liru was very concerned about the life and safety of the central leadership. When the central column was stationed at Qingyangcha, Cao sent Fang Suozhu, a cadre of the administrative department, to deliver some dried vegetables to the Central Committee. Upon learning that the CPC Central Committee and Mao Zedong had come to Yangjiagou, Mizhi County, Comrade Cao Liru sent comrades of the transportation team to drive several mules and send a batch of grain and vegetables to the central column. In order to do a good job of supporting the frontline, Cao organized the counties in the border region to set up frontline support brigades to transport food and ammunition, the sick, and the wounded, and he spared no effort in supporting the northwest liberation battlefield. He personally cooked and bottled the honey collected from the rural areas, sealed the bottles, and sent a specially appointed person to deliver it to the leading comrades of the Central Committee. He often went to see Comrade Guan Xiangying, who was ill, and to aid in his treatment, he often sent him nutritious food. When Wang Zhen was ill, Cao made a special trip to find buckwheat flour from Zhidan County and sent it to him to aid his recovery.

Comrade Cao Liru was enthusiastic about women's and children's work and helped a good deal of practical work in this field. He was awarded the title of Model Women's and Children's Worker by the Central Women's Federation. He was concerned about the guards and soldiers, and he always wrote to the local governments to help solve problems in their families. In winter, he would give a brazier to the soldiers, while he himself endured the cold. He was strict with himself and his children, and he did not allow them have special treatment in the canteen of the organ, nor to enjoy any privilege. To take care of the leading cadres, the grain department stipulated that 8 *jin* of rice should be supplied to each cadre every month, but Cao never asked his guard to collect it. Once, the guard took back 3 *jin* of rice without telling him and cooked porridge for him. He severely criticized the guard and said, "Later, you'd better not worry about my meals. I will eat whatever the canteen provides." He took the lead in planting vegetables, tilling the land, watering, weeding, fertilizing, and doing various farm work. The tomatoes and pumpkins he planted were big and bright. Once they were picked, they were all sent to the canteen to improve everyone's diet. In response to the call for mass production, Cao worked overtime to spin, and he won the first prize in the border spinning competition. He was full of revolutionary passion, his moral character won him the trust and love of the people, and his style of hard work influenced every comrade.

In order to avoid the enemy, the Northwest Bureau temporarily crossed the Yellow River and was stationed in Nankequ, Linxian, Shanxi Province. At that time, the red dates were ripe and the autumn harvest was ready. Comrade Cao Liru promptly publicized the mass discipline, "No eating of the people's red dates, and no touching of the people's crops. Pay for anything you take." Two months later, the Northwest Bureau moved back to Xuejiaqu, Yihe, Suide. Comrade Cao Liru participated in the preparation of the Yihe Meeting of the Northwest Bureau. At the meeting, he conveyed the spirit of the central land reform meeting and made a decision on thoroughly completing the land reform and carrying out the Party consolidation work. After the meeting, government officials were organized to carry out land reform pilot projects in the rural areas.

On the way to battle in Northern Shaanxi, Comrade Cao Liru always shared the burdens of the cadres and soldiers. When marching, he would not ride his horse, but would give it to the comrades to carry their luggage. Like his comrades, he often ate black beans, which would cause diarrhea, and no medicine was available. He sent people to the KMT ruled area to purchase food, cloth, and cigarettes to improve the people's lives. He worked hard, marching or having meetings in the daytime, while reading documents and drafting reports at night under a kerosene lamp, so that his nostrils were often blackened.

Comrade Cao Liru attached great importance to the Party's classified work with a strong sense of confidentiality. He put forward the principle of "proficient in business and strict in confidentiality," and he strictly required the personnel of the organs to follow it. He reviewed important telegrams and documents word by word and corrected the mistakes quickly to ensure smooth, accurate contact between the Northwest Bureau and the Party Central Committee as well as the headquarters of the Northwest Field Army. When he knew that it was not clear on which pack animal the list of underground workers in the ruling area of the northwest Kuomintang was put, he immediately sent people to look for it, and he did not let up until it was found and stored properly.

Comrade Cao Liru always thought about others rather than himself on the way to Northern Shaanxi. He directed the General Affairs Section, saying, "You should find ways to take care of Comrade Ma Mingfang and Comrade Yang Mingxuan, like making some delicious meals for them." When General Zhao Shoushan came to the border area, Comrade Cao Liru sent special personnel to receive him, making him feel the warmth of the people in the Shaanxi-Gansu-Ningxia border area. When Zhou Zhixuan died of lung disease, and even when a groom died of a heart attack, Comrade Cao Liru personally chose the burial spots, arranged the funerals, and conveyed the Party's concern to the revolutionary team, helping the revolutionary team become stronger and more united.

On April 21, 1948, Yan'an was restored to the people's hands. The Northwest Bureau of the CPC Central Committee began working in Wangjiaping. Comrade Cao Liru organized cadres and guards of the organs to clear mines and clean doors and windows, so as to resume office work promptly and organize production, support the frontline, and various restoration works.

Comrade Cao Liru worked conscientiously and meticulously, and he knew the situation in the border area very well. He had detailed summary notes on food production, support for the front line, disasters and bandits, the land reform, and security work against agents in each district. For some important meetings, he sometimes did the records himself and paid attention to collecting information on policies and regulations during the War of Liberation, classifying and analyzing the experiences and practices of other liberated areas, and providing decision-making basis and reference experience for the implementation of the instructions of the Party Central Committee and Chairman Mao Zedong.

Comrade Cao Liru also served as Deputy Minister of the Urban Engineering Department of the Northwest Bureau. He understood the Party's policy of fighting against the enemy, and he tried to collect the enemy and social situation, and he summarized the urban work experience and lessons. At the meeting of the secretaries of the local committees held in August 1948, he proposed on behalf of the Northwest Bureau that the policy of urban work was to "unite and launch all anti-Chiang and anti-Hu forces so that they can cooperate closely with the field army to liberate the vast areas of the northwest... Based on this situation, the local working committees should select cities that our army will first occupy and siege in the future, and we should work extremely hard." After the meeting, the Northwest Bureau issued the *Instructions on the Policies of Handling Enemy Personnel in the Restored Areas and New Areas* and the *Decision on the Secret Urban Work in the Enemy Areas*, which promoted the development of urban work in Northwestern China and effectively supported the liberation of the northwest region.

On May 5, 1949, the Northern Shaanxi Provincial Bureau was established, with Comrade Cao Liru serving as Director. He required that the executive branch "strive to improve the competence of the cadres and the ideological style and implement the mass line, so as to complete all tasks." To improve the working system and the efficiency of the work of the organs, Comrade Cao Liru organized and formulated the *Temporary Rules for the Work of the Northern Shaanxi Provincial Bureau*, which detailed procedures and regulations such as the documentation, meeting, reporting system, archives, political report, statistics, and office system, and he made efforts to ensure both top-down and bottom-up communication, complete the tasks of production and support the frontline, and promote the progression of the liberation war.

On January 31, 1949, Peiping was liberated peacefully. At this time, the three major battles of Liaoshen, Huaihai, and Pingjin wiped out 1.54 million enemies. On April 23, the People's Liberation Army liberated Nanjing. On April 24, the

PLA conquered Taiyuan. The Northwest Field Army was approaching Xi'an, and the 22nd Corps and the 86th Division of the Kuomintang, which were hiding in Yulin City, were isolated and hesitant. The Northwest Bureau and the Northwest Military Region reviewed the situation and put forward the policy of "striving for the peaceful liberation of Yulin to influence other major cities in Northwestern China" and sent people to make contact. Seeing the irreversible trend, the Kuomintang 22nd Corps sent Zhang Zhiyin, chief of staff, to Yan'an for negotiations.

On May 4, the Yulin peace talks delegation arrived in Yan'an and arrangements were made for them to lodge in the communication office of the border government. The next day, Xi Zhongxun, Secretary of the Northwest Bureau, received the delegate. On May 10, the Northwest Military Region delegation, with Comrade Zhang Jingwu and Cao Liru as the chief and vice chairman and Li Qiming, Zhu Xiafu, and Luo Ming as members, officially began the negotiations with the delegation of the Yulin 22nd Corps for peace talk. On behalf of the Northwest Military Region, Comrade Cao Liru said, "We communists do not oppress people. You are most welcome here. Let's sit down and have a detailed discussion." During the negotiation, there were two central issues. One was that Yulin had only one division in actual force, but it required reorganization into a corps, which we clearly rejected. Secondly, after the reorganization, the KMT asked the PLA to send fewer divisions, regiments, and battalion cadres, yet we insisted on sending more. The Yulin side changed stands frequently in the negotiations. The military chief Zuo Xiezhong stopped the negotiations with an emergency cable, and intended to lead the troops to Suiyuan in the north. The head of the delegation, Gao Lingyun, sent an urgent cable, saying, "I will never leave." When Zhang Zhiyin was at a loss about what to do next, Zuo Xiezhong called to say that "the negotiation will continue," but insisted on the change of negotiation venue to Yulin City.

On May 20, 1949, Comrade Cao Liru was appointed Plenipotentiary of the Northwest Military Region of the Chinese People's Liberation Army and Secretary of the Yulin Front Temporary Working Committee of the Communist Party of China. Together with Zhu Xiafu, Luo Ming, Zhang Hanwu, Tian Ziheng, Shi Dakang, Dong Ying, and the 22nd Corps negotiation delegation, he went north to Yulin to continue the peace talks. On May 22, upon arriving at Zhenchuan Fort, Comrade Cao Liru delivered the instructions of the Northwest Bureau and the Northwest Military Region on the peaceful liberation of Yulin at the regional headquarters of the Yulin army. Comrade Cao Liru said, "You are besieging outside, attacking the absconders hard, and making it difficult for them to escape, so that we have strength inside. We strive for peaceful liberation, but we will not give up our preparations for liberation through battle." Comrade Cao Liru also read the telegram about the Northwest Bureau's report on the Second Police Brigade's crossing of the Yellow River to the west to fight in Yulin. He also organized people to study many specific issues concerning the peaceful liberation of Yulin and asked for the formulation of implementation plans.

At that time, Kuomintang spy activities in Yulin City were rampant, the reactionary forces were arrogant, and reactionary slogans appeared on the streets. It was said that "the city is dangerous, and we should not enter it." Comrade Cao Liru said after analysis that "if we don't go to the city, it will increase the difficulty in our negotiations. After going to the city, we can do more work on dividing the enemy." At 9 o'clock that night, Comrade Cao Liru led the northwest military region negotiation delegation to enter Yulin City and stayed in the guest house of the 22nd Corps. In the early morning on the next day, a black note was found abusing the delegation, such as the so-called "people's representatives from all walks of life in Northern Shaanxi" also went to protest the liberation of Yulin, which raised the so-called leftist issues in the land reform of the border areas, such as "sweeping out the door" and "torturing the landlords," and interfered with our army's liberation of Yulin. Comrade Cao Liru sternly refuted the other Party's slander and pointed out that "the liberation of Yulin is a major event of the people and cannot be decided by the will of a few."

On the night of May 24, Commander Zuo Xiezhong accompanied the delegation to the Zhongshan Hall in Lianhuachi to watch a Qin opera performance. On the way back, walking to the Department of the 22nd Corps, they were suddenly attacked by a mob. The mob threw stones at Comrade Cao Liru, who said, "Leave them alone. The enemy can't escape the people's law." Upon coming back, Cao worked late into the night. He said, "We must work and act boldly. We should do what we're supposed to in the proper way. We should not let the enemy interfere with our work, but we should be vigilant." The members of the delegation not only showed up in public, but also went to the streets and alleys to extensively contact the masses from all walks of life, creating momentum and urging the negotiation process.

On May 25, Zhang Dazhi led the Second Police Brigade and the Yulin army's divisional troops to the city of Yulin. Our army not only had an advantage in quality, but also in quantity. On May 27, the two sides held formal negotiations. The focus of the dispute was determining who would be the division and regiment commanders after the reorganization of the 22nd Corps. The two sides drew up the Yulin Partial Peace Agreement. On the same day, Comrade Cao Liru sent a letter signed by himself and Zhu Xiafu through the underground intelligence station, which read, "Wu (Daifeng) and Liu (Changliang), the negotiation has reached an agreement as planned. We hope to speed up the preparations for taking over the city today. We are safe and sound and will return soon."

On May 28, the CPC Yulin Front Line Provisional Working Committee held an enlarged meeting in Sanchawan, outside Yulin. Comrade Cao Liru presided over the meeting and reported the content of the *Yulin Partial Peace Negotiation Agreement*. He stressed that "we should have a high degree of vigilance and a strict defense, and we must enter the city in a fighting posture to prevent unexpected events." He asked us to "strictly abide by the three major disciplines and the rules for entering the city, never violate the Party's urban, industrial, and commercial policy, and strictly prohibit individuals from taking gifts." The meeting determined that a grand ceremony would be held for the PLA to enter the city on June 1. It determined the order of the troops, the disposition of the infantry, and the light and heavy weapons. At the same time, it called for the progressive forces of the 22nd Corps to control the key spots such as the North Gate and the Bell Tower.

On May 29, the two sides reached a formal agreement through negotiation. Cao Liru and Zuo Xiezhong signed the *Yulin Partial Peace Negotiation Agreement*. Comrade Cao Liru immediately telegraphed He Long and Xi Zhongxun the contents of the agreement and transferred it to the Northwest Bureau of the CPC Central Committee.

June 1 was the Dragon Boat Festival, and it was sunny in the old city of China's northern wilderness. At about 10 o'clock, the frontline infantry, cavalry, and artillery units of the Chinese People's Liberation Army in Yulin, holding up huge portraits of Chairman Mao and Commander-in-Chief Zhu, were fully armed. Led by Cao Liru, Zhang Dazhi, Wu Daifeng, and Zhu Xiafu, they entered the South Gate from the airport in three columns. Under the leadership of Chief of Staff Zhang Zhiyin, the officers and men of the army headquarters and division headquarters of the 22nd Corps of the former Kuomintang went out of the city to welcome them. As soon as the PLA showed up, twelve guns thundered a salute in unison, and 23 representatives from the masses presented gifts to the leading comrades of the PLA and Yulin military divisions. Along the way, they were welcomed by 30,000 people. In the five-*li* long street, slogans, military music, singing, and cheering were clearly heard. The city was decorated brightly, with nine boiled water stations set up and four citizen drum bands playing welcome songs. The people sang and danced to celebrate the peaceful liberation of Yulin City.

On June 2, the Yulin Military Control Committee of the Northwest China

In the summer of 1949, a group photo of Xi Zhongxun (front right), He Long (front middle), and Li Jingquan (front left) in Xi'an.

People's Liberation Army was established, with Comrade Cao Liru as Director and Wu Daifeng, Zhu Xiafu, and Zhang Boxue as Deputy Directors. Military Control Committee issued Notice Number 1 on "implementing military control," Notice Number 2 on "RMB issued by the People's Bank of China as the standard currency," and Notice Number 3, which announced the cancellation of the pseudo court and the establishment of Yulin District and the People's Court of Yulin City. At the same time, the committee issued Order Number 1, which announced eight requirements that all organs and troops must strictly abide by. Comrade Cao Liru took the lead in carrying out the notice and order of the Military Control

Commission, and he set an example by strictly following the rules. When the Party Committee held an expanded meeting at Lianhuachi, Cao learned that a guard had picked a lotus leaf from the pond, and he immediately ordered that the soldier be isolated for three days. He informed the troops and organs of the meeting of this decision, and he was praised by the people.

Comrade Cao Liru attached great importance to publicity work. After the establishment of the *Yulin Daily*, he carefully read every issue, gave guidance on the key points for publicity, and promptly corrected mistakes. One day after breakfast, he asked a correspondent to send the newspaper he had read to the newspaper office. The four pages were full of his comments and notes, as well as marks on the wrong characters and reversed words. This conscientious, responsible, meticulous, down-to-earth work style greatly moved the comrades of the newspaper office, who determined to work together to run the paper well.

After Yulin's liberation, the first problems encountered were social security, such as rampant bandits, spy damage, shooting, and theft cases. On June 3, Comrade Cao Liru presided over the meeting of the temporary working committee and decided to take decisive measures to suppress the bandits and eliminate the secret agents, putting Zhang Hanwu in charge. When Zhang reported to Comrade Cao Liru on the plan of action, Cao directed the troops to send out a company to assist in the search and arrest operation. On June 4, the troops raided the bandit's nest and arrested more than 20 bandits and secret agents. On June 15, another attack was launched to arrest eight bandits and secret agents. The two actions deflated the enemy's morale, restored social order, and put production and commerce on the right track.

The second problem after Yulin's liberation was food and finance. At that time, there were 70,000 people in Yulin City, and the food supply failed to meet the demand. If the grains were transported from the old area with the cattle and the donkeys, it would be "distant water that could not quench the present thirst." On hearing that the Military Control Committee did not have the money to buy the grain transported by camels from Ningxia, Comrade Cao Liru couldn't sleep well for days. He added the word "expedite" on the telegraphs he signed requiring grains. On hearing that some small units refused to provide funds even when they had reserves, Comrade Cao Liru said to Zhang Hanwu, "I will back you up in what you do. As long as it is beneficial to the revolution, don't be afraid to be tough." With the effort of the Military Control Commission and governments at all levels, the local financial resources were tapped and local trade was developed, and the food problem was finally settled. On hearing that 40,000 *jin* of grain was bought at one time, Comrade Cao Liru was as excited as if he had won a battle on the battlefield, and he turned into "an old youth" in a flash.

The third problem was the frequent harassment of the bandits running outside the city. On June 11, the Independent Division I and the Yulin Branch army dispatched troops to Ikh Juu in Inner Mongolia, exterminated more than 2,000 armed bandits, destroyed their contact points, quelled the bandits, and created a good environment for the reorganization of the 22nd Corps.

The fourth issue was the reorganization of the 86th Division of the 22nd Corps. For this purpose, a committee for reorganization was established. After investigation and research, Cao Liru, Zhang Dazhi, and Zhu Xiafu discussed matters frequently and sent three telegrams on June 16, 24, and 27, to report the ideological and emotional situation of the officers and soldiers, and the arrangements for sending relevant cadres to the Northwest Bureau and Northwest Military Region. They arranged former Kuomintang officers and soldiers in accordance with the Party's policies. Zuo Xiezhong was transferred to serve as Deputy Commander of the Shaanxi Military Region, and the 86th Division was reassigned as the Independent Division II of the Northwest Military Region, with Gao Lingyun as the Division Commander and Huang Luobin as the Political Commissar. After the reorganization, the Independent Division II, under the leadership of the 64th Corps of the 19th Legion, was ordered to enter Ningxia. When Gao Lingyun, the Division Commander, worried that he could not complete the task, Comrade Cao Liru patiently encouraged him, "the Independent Division I is a veteran army that participated in the liberation of Taiyuan, and to join Division I in the march, camp, and fight would be conducive to consolidating Division II. The liberation war is close to the end, which provides an excellent opportunity for Division II to make some contributions." Before his departure, Comrade Cao Liru presented his saddle to Gao Lingyun. Inspired and encouraged by Comrade Cao, Gao took the troops westward even when he was ill.

The fifth issue was how to ease the war trauma and restore industrial and agricultural production as soon as possible. On June 4, Comrade Cao Liru called on the representatives of the underground Party members and those in industry, agriculture, commerce, education, and women's work to discuss urgent issues such as resuming production and ensuring supply. Within a week, shops and schools re-opened, and urban and rural trade began to recover. The Yulin Trading Company supplied food, cloth, oil, and daily necessities at a fair price, and the public spoke highly of it. When the Yuxi River flooded, broke through the river bank and submerged the farmland, Comrade Cao Liru went out in the rain to check the situation and had the breach blocked to reduce losses. Then he immediately organized production activities for self-rescue to tide the people over through the disaster. Afterwards, the government allocated funds to build the Yuxi Aqueduct with a length of 50m and a width of 1m, and to build a drainage tunnel at Xiaoximen to eliminate potential flood hazards and ensure the water for irrigation of 650 *mu* of land, and the plentiful cabbage supply met the demand for vegetables in the urban area.

According to the characteristics and tradition of the Yulin Handicraft Industry, Comrade Cao Liru proposed the establishment of a wool textile mill, leather tannery, and carpet factory. "Raw materials are made from local sources, which can increase income and employment," he said. His proposal was gradually implemented. More than forty years later, the products of the Yulin Wool Textile Mill and other factories became the flagship products in Northern Shaanxi and entered the international market. Comrade Cao Liru also proposed that the Yulin mule and horse trade fairs be resumed. The "border guests" of Mongolian people came with thousands of mules, horses, and cattle to exchange for the knives, scissors, wooden wares, hardware, general goods, and carpets they needed, which boosted trade exchanges between the Mongolian and Han nationalities and the restoration and development of Yulin's industry and commerce.

On June 14, Zuo Xiezhong, the former commander of the 22nd Kuomintang Corps, along with the officers of the corps, divisions, and regiments jointly sent a telegram to Chairman Mao Zedong and Commander-in-Chief Zhu De, stating that they would "firmly support the propositions of the Communist Party of China and follow the leadership of the Central Committee of the Communist Party of China, Chairman Mao, Commander Zhu, and the Northwest Military Region of the People's Liberation Army. In accordance with the principles of democracy, they will be reorganized into the PLA in the designated area to be separated from the dark forces and move toward a bright future of serving the people."

On July 11, Chairman Mao and Commander Zhu replied in a telegram to General Zuo Xiezhong and all the officers and soldiers of the 22nd Corps of the Kuomintang that "it is inspiring to have learned from your telegram that General Zuo and other officers with your troops would like to accept the peace resolution, allowing those in your army and the people of Yulin to celebrate the liberation. We hope that you will work hard to unite the troops, strengthen their training, improve the relationship between the officers and the soldiers as well as the military and the civilian people, and strive for the great mission of joining in the northwest liberation war." The reply from Mao Zedong and Zhu De greatly encouraged the military and civilians in this key town in the Chinese wilderness and accelerated its reorganization and economic recovery.

On June 18, the Celebration Conference of Yulin's Peaceful Liberation was held in a Yulin playground. Comrade Cao Liru pointed out in his speech at the assembly that "the liberation of Yulin is not only a joy for the Yulin people, but also for all the people of Northern Shaanxi." He also explained in detail the eight important tasks during the military administration, calling on all to "be united and build a new Yulin."

On July 5, at the conference of 800 workers from fifteen industries, Comrade Cao Liru publicized the Party's policy on industry and commerce as well as the position and the role of the working class as the master, and he encouraged the recovery and development of Yulin's industry and commerce.

On September 9, at the Yulin Party Cadres' Conference, Cao demanded that we should not be proud and let down our guard, nor should we hold the idea of "having no worries" and "having all conflicts settled." Instead, we should be vigilant, completing all tasks and consolidating the new area. Under the leadership of the Party and with the support of the people and the PLA, Comrade Cao Liru managed a great amount of work in a systematic way, swiftly and properly accomplishing the tasks of peace negotiations, takeovers and reorganization, and restoring production. This famous city in China's wilderness area was thriving, the people were living and working in peace and contentment, and the military and civilians were alike celebrating their prosperity together.

In mid-September 1949, Comrade Cao Liru was ordered to return to Yan'an. At that time, the central task of Northern Shaanxi was to heal war trauma, recover and develop production, and organize forces to support the front line. The Northern Shaanxi Provincial Bureau of China led the people of Northern Shaanxi to increase the sowing of winter wheat, the picking of mountain products, and the opening up of wasteland to develop agricultural production. Land certificates were issued in combination with the yield in the rural areas, and the People's Congress at the township level was re-elected. Cao also organized 30,000 migrant workers in the old district to support the front line, formed stretcher teams to transport large quantities of food and materials to the front, completed the task of recruiting new soldiers, and effectively supported the liberation of the northwest.

At that time, when the Northwest Bureau and the border region government moved to Xi'an, they needed to dispatch a large number of cadres to support the liberation of the northwest and take over power there. The cadres had some hesitation and misunderstanding about the transfer in their work. The administrative office promptly organized cadres to study articles such as "On the Communist Attitude Toward Labor" and patiently did persuasive talks to help those who left feel pleased and those who stayed feel at ease.

On October 1, the People's Republic of China was founded. On October 3, people from all walks of life held a celebration in Yan'an and sent a salutatory telegram to the Party Central Committee and Chairman Mao. On October 26, Chairman Mao replied to the people of Yan'an and the Shaanxi-Gansu-Ningxia border region, "Comrades of Yan'an and the Shaanxi-Gansu-Ningxia border region, I am very pleased and grateful to receive your congratulatory telegram. From 1936 to 1948, Yan'an and the Shaanxi-Gansu-Ningxia border region were once the seat of the CPC Central Committee and the general rear guard of the Chinese people's liberation struggle. The people of Yan'an and the Shaanxi-Gansu-Ningxia border region have made contributions to the people of the entire country. I hope for the continued unity of the people of Yan'an and the Shaanxi-Gansu-Ningxia border region, rapid recovery from war trauma, and the development of economic and cultural construction. I also hope that all revolutionary workers throughout the country will always maintain the style of hard work that they have practiced in Yan'an and the Shaanxi-Gansu-Ningxia border region over the past ten years."

Comrade Cao Liru immediately organized the cadres of the administrative office in Northern Shaanxi to carefully study Mao Zedong's reply to the telegram, sent cadres to the countryside for publicity, simultaneously carried out investigation and research, drew up the construction outline of Northern Shaanxi, put forward plans to resume the development of production, and discussed and finalized the amendment at the meeting of the Secretary of the County Party Committee. Under the leadership of Comrade Cao Liru, the Northern Shaanxi administrative office paid close attention to grain production in the valley, gully, and tableland, closed the gully with saplings, ran veterinary study groups to improve the survival rate of lambs and encourage pig rearing and cattle feeding, focused on the construction of roads from counties to Yan'an, resumed classes at schools, and launched a large-scale campaign to heal war wounds and resume production.

At the beginning of December 1949, Comrade Cao Liru was ordered to leave his post for Xinjiang to serve as the First Vice Chairman of the Xinjiang Provincial Government. The Northwest Bureau sent a special car to Yan'an to pick up Comrade Cao Liru and take him to Xi'an, from which he would transfer to Xinjiang by plane.

Comrade Cao Liru quickly handed over his work. At the farewell party, he said earnestly, "I hope all cadres can study the work of economic construction, improve the level of cultural theory, and make Northern Shaanxi a better place."

On December 1, Comrade Cao Liru wrote a letter to the leaders of the Party Committee and the Administrative Office of Northern Shaanxi, saying, "I am determined to do a good job in Xinjiang. I hope you will write letters to guide and criticize me. Northern Shaanxi and Yan'an had a glorious history in the past, and we should do a good job in the future."

On December 3, Comrade Cao Liru sent a letter to the Party Committee of Northern Shaanxi, saying, "My answer (referring to the study of political theory) is generally drafted. Please allow me to take it to Xi'an and hand it to the Publicity Department of the Northwest Bureau."

On December 5, Comrade Cao Liru went past Luochuan. In a letter he sent to the Administrative Office in Northern Shaanxi, he said, "Those anarchists who ignore rules and discipline on expenditure should be strictly criticized. They should not be accommodated, and we don't need to be afraid of offending them."

Comrade Cao Liru also wrote letters to Cui Huanjiu and He Mingtang in Yulin, encouraging them to "read more revolutionary books and stick to the stand of the masses." He wrote to Cui Yi of Zhidan County, encouraging him to "work hard for the education undertaking of Zhidan County." All these letters represented Comrade Cao Liru's high sense of responsibility for the revolutionary work, and all the encouraging lines expressed his sincere care for and friendship with his comrades.

No one expected that only three days later, on December 8, Comrade Cao Liru would be killed at the age of 48, after he was seriously injured in a car accident on his way to his new post.

On December 16, 2,000 people in Yan'an, and another 10,000 in Yulin on December 17, held memorials for Comrade Cao Liru. On December 22, 2,000 people from the Party, government, and military organs of the Shaanxi-Gansu-Ningxia border region and Xi'an held a grand memorial for Comrade Cao Liru. The Party Central Committee, the Government Affairs Council, the Northwest Bureau, the border region government, the First Field Army, and the provincial and municipal organs in Northwestern China all sent mourning wreaths. Lin Boqu, Xie Juezai, Peng Dehuai, He Long, Wang Zhen, and Xu Liqing sent telegrams of condolence to express their grief for their long-time comrade.

At the memorial meeting, Xi Zhongxun, Secretary of the Northwest Bureau of the CPC Central Committee, spoke highly of Cao Liru. Xi said, "Comrade Cao

Liru was killed in an accident. The Party lost an excellent Party member, the people of Northwest China lost a loyal attendant, and we lost a close comrade in arms… Comrade Cao has worked industriously for twenty years. He never bargained with the Party or bowed to difficulties. When he received the tasks the Party assigned, he was determined to accomplish them regardless of his own circumstances, and he worked based on the actual situation. This was his excellent, consolidated Party spirit. He dared to carry out strict criticism and self-criticism on himself and his comrades, and he had an admirable learning mindset." In an elegiac couplet, Comrade Wang Zhen wrote, "Dear comrade Cao Liru, you've served the people whole-heartedly, with boundless loyalty and dedication, setting a role model for all. We pledge to carry on your unfinished cause to the end."

After the memorial, Cao Liru, an outstanding communist soldier and member of the Communist Party of China, was buried on the Xiaoyanta Welfare Farm in the southern suburb of Xi'an, and later moved to the Nanjiao Cemetery of Martyrs.

Sun Zuobin in the Northwest Bureau[1]

Sun Xiaodong

From July 1947 to December 1952, my father served as Deputy Secretary of the Gansu Provincial Committee of the CPC, Minister of United Front Department of the Provincial Committee, and Secretary of the Discipline Inspection Committee of the Provincial Party Committee. The new Gansu Province, which had just been liberated, was ready to develop. The epoch-making victory allowed my father to return to where he had fought arduously underground. From August 1937 to June 1939, my father served as Secretary of the Gansu Working Committee of the CPC. Together with the Eighth Route Army Office in Lanzhou, he achieved remarkably in the mass anti-Japanese and national salvation movement to restore and develop the Party organization in the Kuomintang ruled area of Gansu Province. The Eighth Route Army Office (the Eighth Office) mainly engaged in legal struggle, while the working committee mainly engaged in covert struggle.

Those working in the Eighth Office included Xie Juezai, Wu Xiuquan, Peng Jialun, and others, while the working committee included Sun Zuobin, Liu Jie, Liu Rixiu, Dou Zhi'an, Lin Keyi, Zheng Chongyuan, and Wu Hongbin. As a representative of the CPC Central Committee and Mao Zedong, Mr. Xie often participated in the work committee meetings and guidance work. During this period, the Gansu Working Committee completed all the tasks assigned by the Party through close cooperation with the Eighth Office under the leadership of the CPC Central Committee and the specific help of Mr. Xie. Over the previous three years, a large number of people had become Communist Party members, and

1. This article was compiled by Sun Xiaodong based on the book *Sun Zuobin*, published by Shaanxi People's Publishing House in December 2008.

Sun Zuobin in Lanzhou in 1938.

a large number of magazines were published to publicize the anti-Japanese struggle, greatly strengthening Party members' education. In short, over the previous three years, the Gansu Working Committee had successfully motivated the people to engage in the anti-Japanese and national salvation movement in Gansu and strengthened the Party organization team.

Secretary Zhang Desheng, my father, and other people went to Gansu in 1949, and the first things they focused on were building a good Party and a good government, setting up a good example, and leading the people forward. On the day after Lanzhou's liberation, my father convened a meeting of underground Party members, fully affirmed that the local Party organizations and Party members had made immortal achievements for the cause of the Gansu people's liberation, and encouraged all Party members to achieve new things in the construction of Gansu. My father assisted the Provincial Party Committee and the provincial government, mainly focusing on the Party and government construction at all levels of the province, prefecture, and county, selecting 7,605 leading cadres at all levels, and training nearly 3,000 ethnic minority cadres, which prepared the conditions for economic construction.

In the construction of the Party in minority areas, my father stressed that based on the characteristics of the ethnic minority communities, we should not be overly strict. Any progressive individual who was willing to follow the Communist Party and acknowledged the Party Constitution could be accepted as a Party member. We should not take giving up religious belief as a condition for joining the Party, as religion was a complex issue of historical mass belief and would not go away with the elimination of the feudal system. Religious beliefs would exist for a long time before the adequate economic and cultural development of ethnic minority groups and the enhancement of people's awareness came about. The religious beliefs of the minority Party members would be settled gradually when they had been educated for a prolonged period after joining the Party, on the basis of the improvement of their Marxism and political consciousness. Practice has proven that my father's view was right, and it was affirmed by Xi Zhongxun, the Northwest Bureau, and the Central Committee of the Party.

Land Reform

Gansu Province basically completed the land reform from September 1951 to June 1952. About 2,000 townships abolished the feudal land ownership system and realized the land ownership system of farmers cultivating their own fields. The whole province distributed 12.27 million *mu* of land to its farmers.

In the land reform, my father directly participated in the pilot land reform in the Linxia area. For years, more people in the Party feared the right than the left, believing that the left was better than the right, and that "it is no big deal to slightly beat the landlords and the rich farmers when the masses are better-off." And my father pointed out that "this view seems understandable, but as cadres of the land reform, we shouldn't confine our vision to that of the farmers. Instead, we should avoid falling and deviating from the right track. When motivating and empowering the masses, we should put the power in the right hands for handling affairs according to policy, rather than in the wrong hands that might violate policy." This clear-cut view sounded a timely alarm to the cadres, so cases of coercing or beating people during the land reform in the Linxia area were rare.

In the meantime, they mobilized the masses based on the characteristics of different customs and religious beliefs of ethnic minority groups according to Xi Zhongxun's instructions, which involved "doing a good job in the United Front work of the upper class ethnic groups and religious people, and then mobilizing the masses, which cannot be reversed," because the ethnic minority communities regarded the upper class religious people of their nationalities as their own representatives and holy people. To win over the higher levels for the land reform was to ensure a smooth land reform among the masses.

When confiscating the property of the landlords, it was important to refrain from taking their religious instruments or devices. When distributing the rewards of the campaign, the houses of the Hui landlords were reallocated to the Hui people to avoid disputes among the ethnic groups. My father kept pointing out that "the disrespect for their ideological beliefs and customs is disrespect for their nation, which will certainly hurt the ethnic feelings and hinder the freedom of their religious belief. It's not only a national issue, but a political one as well."

My father criticized some left-leaning people for being overly simplistic. They confused religious beliefs with feudal systems, trying to eliminate religious beliefs along with the feudal system. This blind anti-religious sentiment was a manifestation of political ignorance. At the time when these problems were emerging, my father promptly made resolute corrections, and thus prevented major deviations.

When the land reform was reviewed, it was proposed by Zhang Desheng and my father and approved by the Northwest Bureau, then clearly announced that the land of mosques, Qubbah mosques, private abbeys, and Lama temples should remain intact and the land that had been confiscated should be returned or compensated for. In this way, the misunderstanding was removed and national unity was consolidated.

Lessons Drawn from the Counter-Insurgency

From November 1948 to May 1952, armed rebellion occurred in Linxia, Xiji in Pingliang, and Gaolan of Hui inhabited area in Gansu Province, and Amuquhu of the Tibetan area. Among them, the most serious cases affected four to five counties, with 200,000 to 300,000 people being coerced and victimized. At that time, my father was Deputy Secretary of the Provincial Party Committee and head of the United Front Department in charge of the United Front work of nationalities and religions. He assisted the Provincial Party Committee in presiding over and dealing with these incidents. He visited the rebel areas many times, conducted in-depth investigations, managed to win over the upper class members, educated the masses, and strengthened national unity.

Since all the rebellions took place in ethnic minority areas, they were handled with great care, regardless of whether they were big or small. All the dealings were made only after the Provincial Party Committee consulted the Northwest Bureau and the Central Committee for approval. Only when the political struggle was ineffective or it was impossible to do the persuasion but military pressure did we carry out military suppression. After the military suppression, it was important to continue with the political struggle. At that time, my father summed up this policy as "persuasion before fight, fight amidst persuasion, and more persuasion after the fight." Political struggle was the main instrument, supplemented by military suppression, with the two working in complementary coordination.

After the Xiji Rebellion, with policy publicity and persuasion, some of the bandits surrendered, and the vast majority of those who had been cheated went home to resume production. However, Ma Guoyuan, the bandit leader, and his followers did not surrender, which caused many uncertainties and much hesitation. Given this, my father and Ma Zhenwu, Ma Zhongwu, Ma Jiwu, and other religious elites agreed that Ma Zhenwu, as the leader of the religion, would issue a statement to Ma Guoyuan that "rebellion is betrayal to religious belief," and that whoever did not break away from the rebellion would be separated from the ties to the two worlds, which aimed to dissuade the people from going astray. In particular, after Xi Zhongxun explained to my father and Ma Zhenwu the policy of "surrender over death" to the upper class of the insurgency, i.e., "focusing on the present instead of the past. Even if someone was fighting against us with a gun yesterday, he will be accepted today, provided he puts down his arms." Then my father and Ma Zhenwu promptly went into Xijitan alone and used the Party's leniency policy to recruit Ma Guoyuan. As a consequence, the Xiji rebellion began to subside, and tens of thousands of people returned to normal life.

When summing up his experiences in quelling several rebellions, my father said, "Rebellions are generally related to the upper class of the nation, so they should not be dealt with as ordinary bandits or counter revolutionary rebellions, but as ethnic issues. When necessary, we need to solve these problems through influential people." For example, the Xiji Incident in the Hui area and the Amuquhu Incident in the Tibetan area were all peacefully resolved after Ma Zhenwu and Huang Zhengqing, the representatives of the upper levels of the Hui and Tibetans, had done much persuasion in the form of a "consolation group" and other means. The most important thing was to stick to constant persuasion for the local upper level of ethnic people, implement a particularly lenient policy, and try to unite all those who could strive for unity. The settlement of those issues was closely linked to Comrade

Xi Zhongxun's correct guidance. Comrade Xi saw that the main contradiction in ethnic issues at that time was between the ethnic and religious upper classes. He proposed that the United Front work of winning over the ethnic upper class and religious personages should first be done well, and on this basis, the masses should be mobilized to carry out democratic reform. This was Comrade Xi Zhongxun's original idea of combining theory with practice and unifying principle with flexibility. In the "anti-insurgency" and "land reform," he asked for a list of leaders of all ethnic groups and sects, saying that as long as they came to us and supported the land reform, they would definitely be protected. We focused on cracking down on those who engaged in current counter revolutionary activities, proposed that the land of mosques, Qubbah mosques, private abbeys, and Lama temples should remain intact, that no publicity on land reform would be conducted in pastoral areas, nor would publicity on the fight against the despot be done, and animal husbandry be protected. This strategy of preserving a small part of feudalism in exchange for better conditions for mobilizing the masses and eliminating most of feudalism was in line with the actual situation at that time, and it achieved remarkable results in practice and created conditions for the implementation of regional national autonomy.

Governing Qinghai and Bearing Humiliation

From January 1953 to June 1954, my father served as Deputy Director of the United Front Department of the Northwest Bureau of the CPC Central Committee and First Deputy Director of the Northwest Ethnic Affairs Committee. From July 1954 to March 1958, he was transferred to work as Second Secretary and Governor of Qinghai Provincial Party Committee and was a representative of the Eighth National Congress of the Communist Party of China. Under the unified leadership of the Provincial Party Committee and the Provincial People's Committee, he creatively carried out the Party's National United Front policy, worked hard to complete the First Five-Year Plan for the development of the national economy and the socialist transformation of agriculture in Qinghai, and made proper decisions with the desired results.

As soon as my father arrived, he took the implementation of the Party's ethnic policy and the resolution of ethnic conflicts and disputes as an important task. In December 1954, when he conveyed the spirit of the National People's Congress at the First National People's Congress in Qinghai, he explained at length the policy of strengthening national unity and equality in the first Constitution of China in combination with the reality of ethnic issues in Qinghai. He said, "Unity entails strength and happiness. Any policy that goes against national unity and equality is not conducive to the people of various ethnic groups."

Every time he went to a region or unit, he asked the Party members and cadres to study the Party's ethnic policies, love the people of all ethnic groups, respect the status of the people of all ethnic groups, and establish a sense of honor and mission to serve the ethnic minorities. When he went to religious monasteries and areas inhabited by ethnic groups, he always patiently publicized the Party's ethnic policy and the policy of freedom of religious belief to the religious elites, asking them to live in harmony based on equality and unity in the ethnic family.

My father was the first Governor to visit Yushu, Hainan, and Guoluo after the founding of the new China. He held various symposiums attended by cadres, religious representatives, and democrats in the three areas more than ten times, and he publicized the Party's ethnic and religious policies, answered their questions, and removed their misunderstandings and doubts.

In discussing how to carry out socialist transformation in the minority pastoral areas, my father stressed that starting from the principle of being conducive to national unity, peaceful transformation, development of production, and improvement of the people's lives, we should adopt a prudent and moderate approach, adhere to the policy of no division or fighting, no division of class, mutual benefit of farmers and herdsmen, support the development of production of poor herdsmen, and carry out joint consultation from top to bottom. He believed that "the main contradiction in ethnic areas is ethnic contradiction including class contradiction." Under the historical conditions at that time, he boldly put forward this proposition, which not only showed that he had done in-depth research on ethnic issues, but also that he had political courage.

From 1957 to 1958, a nationwide Rectification Movement against the right was carried out. At that time, due to the popularity of leftist thought in the Party, and the fact that the main leading people of the Qinghai Provincial Party Committee could not take advice and criticism but viewed many exploratory opinions and well intentioned criticisms as "anti-Party and anti-socialism" and a "rampant attack on the Party." As a consequence, a group of comrades who spoke frankly and dared to remonstrate were wrongly accused of being "the right."

On March 8, 1958, the Fifth Session of the Second Provincial Party Committee decided to expel Sun Zuobin and remove all his posts both inside and outside the Party. He was classified as an extreme rightist who was demoted to the post of Director of Qinghai Provincial Library. He carried that label for twenty years.

In that special period, Uncle Xi Zhongxun was unable to protect my father politically. However, when discussing the welfare of my father after he was classified as a rightist, Uncle Xi explained that "Sun Zuobin is an old comrade, who has many children. We need to treat him as a senior cadre." In this way, my father's administrative level was maintained at level 13.

When he was hard hit in politics and very depressed, his real friends and fellow comrades did not forget him. In 1958, Uncle Xi Zhongxun, then Secretary General of the State Council, flew from Beijing to Xining and asked my father to meet him in a Xining hotel. When they met, they clasped hands and exchanged greetings. My father asked, "Brother Xi, are you coming to the west for inspection?" Xi Zhongxun replied, "I'm here to see you, brother. You are in trouble! Take care of yourself. How are your children, wife, and parents?" My father was moved to tears by Xi's heartfelt greeting. After that, they had a long talk. When asked about my father's age, my father replied that he was 49. Uncle Xi said that there were opportunities, till things could always be sorted out. He encouraged my father not to be pessimistic, but to keep fit. At this meeting, my father was deeply touched. Uncle Xi Zhongxun's kindness and sincerity brought warmth and encouragement to my father, which was beyond description.

Sun Xiaodong, son of Sun Zuobin, talking with the editor-in-chief of this book.

In addition, Yang Mingxuan, Deng Baoshan, Gao Kelin, Yang Ziwei, Geshe Sherab Gyatso, and some of my father's previous subordinates quietly came to the library to visit him. The concern of these veteran comrades and fellow comrades greatly comforted my father in his time of adversity. In later days, my father spoke of these past events to us children many times, which was of great significance to our education about proper human behavior.

My father was nearly blind in his old age. On May 24, 2002, Uncle Xi died of illness. When he heard the news, my father was filled with grief and tears. He kept choking and murmuring, "How did that happen? He's a few years younger than me!" Like-minded, fraternal confidants could no longer meet each other or get together and talk at home. The loss my father felt was beyond expression. Suffering from the pain of illness and the death of Uncle Xi, my father remained quiet, having no appetite, and his health declined. On August 1 that year, my father came to the end of his life, and he followed his comrades in arms with deep affection. Looking back on the friendship between the veteran people and their determination to be dedicated to the country and the people despite their own difficult lives, their strict self-discipline, generous mind, and integrity and the spirit of daring to take on responsibilities were truly touching. It was good to remember and learn from them, and it is sure to benefit us throughout our lives.

Part III

Great Exploits

Peng Dehuai's Conception and Practice of Developing and Constructing the Northwest in the Early Days of the People's Republic of China[1]

Qi Ruoxiong

After the founding of the new China, as the first Secretary of the Northwest Bureau of the CPC Central Committee and Chairman of the Northwest Military and Political Commission, Peng Dehuai put forward a series of ideas on how to develop and build the northwest, and he conducted many explorations on the topic. This article discusses major issues in Peng's conception and practice of developing and constructing Northwestern China.

Based on investigation and research, we should make an overall plan to develop the economy and give different tasks to different regions

Northwestern China was a vast land with many nationalities and rich in resources, forming the favorable conditions for development and construction. However, due to historical reasons, it was very poor, and its economic development lagged far behind that of other parts of the country. In addition, there were huge differences in the natural conditions, population distribution, and economic conditions among Shaanxi, Gansu, Ningxia, Qinghai, and Xinjiang. For example, Qinghai, located

1. This is a revised version of an article originally published in *The Study of the History of the Communist Party of China*, Issue 1, 1999.

on a plateau, primarily developed animal husbandry, while Xinjiang, which was largely covered by the Gobi Desert, developed partly based on farming and partly based on animal husbandry, though both areas were rich in mineral resources. Gansu and Ningxia were mainly agricultural areas with poor natural conditions. Only in Shaanxi Province was agriculture dominant, the natural conditions better, and the degree of economic development relatively high. In terms of population distribution, Qinghai and Xinjiang were vast and sparsely populated, while Shaanxi, Gansu, and Ningxia had a relatively large population. In addition, some areas of Xinjiang, Qinghai, Ningxia, and Gansu were also inhabited by ethnic minority groups.

In the face of the complex situation in the northwest, Peng Dehuai thought that the development and construction of the region must first rely on in-depth investigation and study. He not only asked the leaders of the northwestern provinces to conduct close investigation and study, but he himself set an example. When he was in charge of the northwest, Peng Dehuai took the time to study a large number of local chronicles, historical materials, and Zuo Zongtang's collected works about the five provinces in the northwest. Meanwhile, he asked around and discussed with those familiar with the local situation to gain an understanding of the history and current situation in the northwest. He maintained this working style during the war, going to the frontline on his own. He made two special visits to Xinjiang in 1949 and 1950, and he constantly reminded the cadres that they should go to the field and the frontline of production, instead of sitting in an office and giving orders to guide production.

Based on a large number of investigations and studies, Peng Dehuai put forward at the Fifth Session of the Central People's Government Committee that "the current work plan of Northwestern China is to give different tasks to different regions based on the local situations."[2] Xi Zhongxun also pointed out in this telegram that "there should be an overall (i.e., five provinces together) planning for all the work, especially economic construction, so as to make production, transportation, and marketing better planned. Comrade Jia Tuofu should immediately hand over his tasks as Mayor of Xi'an and from the Military Control Commission and devote all his energy to the planning of the economic construction of the northwest. After the end of the war, the financial expenditure of the northwest must be within the limits of its income, and the bank issue (currency) should be used to develop production

2. *People's Daily* (January 7, 1950).

Marshal Peng Dehuai.

as much as possible."[3] On November 15, 1949, Peng Dehuai made a special report to Chairman Mao on the preliminary arrangements for economic construction in the northwestern region in 1950. In August and September 1950, he convened the Standing Committee of the Northwest Bureau of the CPC Central Committee to study and formulate the draft of the three-year economic construction plan for the northwestern region. At the meeting, Peng Dehuai proposed clear, specific views on the distribution of industrial and mining enterprises, the manufacturing of agricultural machinery, the exploration of oil and non-ferrous metals, and other aspects, claiming that the plan was not complete, but merely an outline which needed to be gradually enriched. However, the overall goal should be set and sent to the five provinces and one city (Xi'an) in Northwestern China to solicit opinions.[4]

In economic construction, it was important to pay attention to investigation and research, carry out comprehensive planning, and give different tasks to different regions. This was Peng Dehuai's important exposition on the development and construction of the northwest more than forty years ago. Even today, it should be a basic principle that the five northwestern provinces and regions, and even Marshal Peng Dehuai, follow for the entire country's economic development and construction.

3. *Biography of Peng Dehuai* (Contemporary China Press, 1993), p. 388.
4. *Biography of Peng Dehuai* (Contemporary China Press, 1993), p. 391.

Training minority cadres and improving their competence are of utmost importance for the development of Northwestern China

With the liberation of the northwestern provinces, the focus of the Party's work in the northwest began to shift to economic construction. Regarding how best to conduct the development and construction of Northwestern China, Peng Dehuai brought forward the issue of cadres, especially the cultivation of minority cadres and the improvement of their quality, which was the most important proposition for the development of Northwestern China.

Peng Dehuai attached great importance to the nurturing of ethnic minority cadres. In January 1950, at the Fifth Session of the Central People's Government Committee, he pointed out that the northwest was a multi-ethnic area. It was important to adhere to the policy of ethnic equality and vigorously train cadres of various ethnic minority groups.[5] On February 3, the first executive meeting of the Northwest Military and Political Commission, presided over by Peng Dehuai, passed a resolution establishing a college for nationalities in Lanzhou to train ethnic minority cadres in a planned way and submitted it to the State Council for approval. At the same time, the northwestern provinces were required to hold schools and training classes for minority cadres. In view of some Han cadres' misconception that "it is backward for ethnic minorities to believe in religion and not to eat pork, so it is difficult to develop Party members among them," Peng Dehuai criticized and educated them, saying that communists as materialists advocated atheism, but we should also have specific analysis of the specific situation. We must see that some customs and habits of ethnic minority peoples were formed under long-term social and historical conditions. While absorbing advanced elements from ethnic minority communities to join the Party, it was important to proceed from the specific local conditions, mainly according to their consciousness and their performance in the past revolutionary struggle and current practical work. It wasn't enough to see whether they believed in religion or ate pork. It was as counter-revolutionary for Chiang Kai-shek to eat pork as it was for Ma Bufang abstain from eating pork.[6]

With Peng Dehuai's efforts, nearly 10,000 ethnic minority cadres were trained in Northwestern China within one year, with remarkable achievements. Peng Dehuai also expressed opinions on how to improve the quality of cadres to meet

5. *Historical Events of the Communist Party of China in Xinjiang* (Xinjiang People's Publishing House, 1993), pp. 21–22.
6. *Biography of Peng Dehuai* (Contemporary China Press, 1993), p. 394.

the needs of the development and construction of the northwest. In January 1950, he pointed out at the first meeting of the Northwest Military and Political Commission that "governments at all levels should pay adequate attention to workers' education, social education, and the education of ethnic minorities. In order to adapt to various necessary social reforms and construction undertakings, a large number of in-service cadres and technical cadres should be trained in turn in a planned way."[7] In August and September, he emphasized at the Standing Committee of the Northwest Bureau of the CPC Central Committee that a group of new cadres engaged in economic construction should be trained as soon as possible.[8] After Peng Dehuai left the northwest for the Korean battlefield, he was still very concerned about the progress of this incident. In his letter to Xi Zhongxun on December 12, 1951, he suggested that "after the completion of the land reform in Shaanxi this winter and next spring, we'd better consult with Comrade Ma Mingfang to dispatch a group of cadres with literacy and experience for short-term training and turn to industry to meet the needs of national large-scale economic construction in 1953."[9] Cultivating and improving the quality of minority cadres was still an important task for the northwestern provinces.

The PLA should become one of the major forces in building a new Northwest

On December 5, 1949, the Chinese People's Revolutionary Military Commission issued an order calling on the PLA to undertake part of its production tasks in addition to continuing to fight and serve, so as to work with the people of the entire country to overcome the difficulties resulting from the prolonged war and strengthen the economic construction of the new democracy.

To combine this instruction with the development and construction of the northwest, Peng Dehuai proposed that the PLA should become one of the key forces in the construction of the new northwest. "It's a big issue for so many troops to be supported by the state. We should engage in production," he said. "In peacetime, the PLA should inherit the tradition of arduous struggle, become the main force in production and construction, and become one of the major forces in

7. *Intra-Party Communication of the Northwest Bureau,* no. 91.

8. *Biography of Peng Dehuai* (Contemporary China Press, 1993), p. 391.

9. Archive No. 1–1, Volume 1/3, Xinjiang Uyghur Autonomous Region Archives Collection.

building a new northwest."[10] Under the leadership of Peng Dehuai, the Northwest Military Region issued an instruction on December 27, 1949, demanding that the vast majority of the northwest army actively participate in production and construction, "to be brave, resolute, active, and responsible, as if at war, and act as a pioneer in the development of the northwest."[11] Peng Dehuai also called on the local garrison to settle down and take root in the border areas, working with other ethnic groups to build the northwest well. In January 1950, Peng Dehuai pointed out at the first session of the Northwest Military and Political Commission, "Now all the five northwestern provinces have been liberated, who are carrying out winter training, suppressing bandits, doing local work, and actively preparing for production. According to the different conditions of different regions, we should prepare to reclaim wastelands, build water conservancy projects, railways, and highways, and prohibit commercial activity. In accordance with Chairman Mao's instructions on the army's participation in production and construction, the results of which should be considered both public and private. Forty percent of the production bonus should go to the individual producer, while the remaining should go to the production unit and the state. More than 100,000 soldiers stationed in Xinjiang will participate in the production, preparing to open up 600,000 *mu* of wasteland. If the grain yield per *mu* is calculated by five *dou*, 300,000 *dou* of grain can be obtained. If the cotton yield per *mu* is calculated by 20 *jin*, 50,000 *mu* of cultivated cotton can yield more than 1 million *jin* of cotton. It is estimated that more than 400,000 people in the army will participate in production in Shaanxi, Gansu, Ningxia, and Qinghai provinces. This production army has a high degree of political consciousness and previous production experience, and I believe that they will accomplish the production tasks as resolutely and bravely, as if in battle."[12]

After the spring of 1950, the PLA officers and soldiers carried out a mass production movement with great enthusiasm in the northwestern provinces and achieved remarkably. According to incomplete statistics, in the previous year, more than 1.6 million *mu* of wasteland was cultivated, 19 water conservancy projects were built, more than 1.7 million *mu* of arable land was irrigated, 168,000 cattle, sheep, and pigs were raised, and numerous coal mines, gold mines, paper mills, and woodworking plants were set up. Nearly 100,000 officers and men participated in the construction of the Tianbao and Tianlan Railways, and more than 3 million cubic meters of earth and stone works were completed in the Tianbao section alone.

10. *Biography of Peng Dehuai* (Contemporary China Press, 1993), p. 391.
11. *Biography of Peng Dehuai* (Contemporary China Press, 1993), p. 392.
12. *Xinjiang Daily* (February 1, 1950).

These facts suggested that the PLA was an important force in the development and construction of the northwest.

For a certain period of time, the economic construction should focus on agriculture and animal husbandry

There were good natural conditions for the development of agriculture and animal husbandry in Northwestern China. Agriculture and animal husbandry accounted for a large proportion of the local economy. According to statistics, before the founding of the new China, agriculture accounted for 75% of the economy in the northwest, animal husbandry for more than 20%, and modern industry and handicraft industry for less than 5%. However, due to historical and other reasons, Northwestern China was poor in infrastructure and production conditions for agriculture and animal husbandry and highly vulnerable to natural disasters, and its production was quite unstable. Many places were "relying on nature for grain." In particular, in the autumn of 1949, many places in Northwestern China suffered from disasters, and more than 500,000 people faced difficulties. The vast new areas were plundered and squeezed by the long-time KMT reactionary rule, resulting in a widespread spring famine. In the meantime, after the liberation of the five provinces in Northwestern China, a large number of KMT military and political personnel were reassigned to positions of political power at all levels. As a result, the number of military and political personnel reached more than one million, accounting for about 4.5% of the total population. The contradiction between supply and demand of food and other necessities was acute, which was fully illustrated by the situation in Xinjiang at that time. On January 2, 1950, Peng Dehuai pointed out in his telegram to Chairman Mao that "the food shortage in Xinjiang is one of the serious problems this year… Dihua District in Northern Xinjiang alone has more than 100,000 soldiers, and the food shortage is very serious. Dihua has only 5,000 *dan* of grain, and it needs 150,000 *dan* of grain from January to September. That's a gap of 145,000 *dan*."[13]

Given this situation, Peng Dehuai advocated that the economic construction in Northwestern China should be based on agriculture and animal husbandry for a certain period of time. In January 1950, at the first meeting of the Northwest

13. The Central Government Telegram Volume (Volume 8) of the General Office of the Regional Party Committee in 1950, collected in the Archives of Xinjiang Uyghur Autonomous Region.

Military and Political Commission, he pointed out that for a certain period of time, the economic construction of the northwest region should focus on agriculture and animal husbandry. In agriculture, it was necessary to boost farmers' enthusiasm for production, improve seeds and farming methods, restore and develop water conservancy works, stress on the protection and cultivation of forests and grasslands, and prevent and control disasters, so as to complete the tasks assigned by the Central People's Government in 1950, i.e., increasing the output of coarse grain by 330 million *jin* and lint by 120,000 *dan*. Livestock production in Gansu, Ningxia, Qinghai, and Xinjiang should not be lower than it had been in 1949.

Under the leadership of Peng Dehuai and with the effort of the people's governments at all levels and all the people in the northwest, by the end of 1950, agriculture and animal husbandry in the northwest had made great progress, with 100 million *mu* of grain sown in summer and autumn, close to the prewar level. More than 2 million *mu* of land was reclaimed and 3.7 million *mu* of water conservancy irrigation area was restored. Animal husbandry maintained its original level that year, which gradually recovered. The recovery and development of agriculture and animal husbandry provided sufficient material guarantees for the development of Northwestern China.

Improving transportation is a prerequisite for economic development

At the beginning of the founding of the new China, the backward traffic conditions seriously restricted the development and construction of Northwestern China. Peng Dehuai had a very clear understanding of the importance of transportation in the development and construction of the northwest, and he put forward the conclusion that vigorously improving transportation was a prerequisite for economic development.

On December 29, 1949, he pointed out regretfully that "Xinjiang is a vast region with underdeveloped transportation. It is difficult not only to get help from the interior, but also to transport grain more than 2,000 *li* from Southern Xinjiang, where there is more grain, to Northern Xinjiang, where there is a food shortage. It costs more than ten *dan* of military expenses to transport one *dan* of grain to Xinjiang."[14] In order to improve the traffic conditions in Northwest China, Peng

14. Permanent Volume 16 of the General Office of Xinjiang Branch Bureau in 1949, collected in Archives of Xinjiang Uyghur Autonomous Region.

Dehuai advocated the seizing of the railway as a key point, emphasizing that the construction of the railway was the most important thing for the development of the regional economy.[15] On November 15, 1949, in his report to Chairman Mao, Peng Dehuai demanded that in addition to building the Tianbao (Tianshui-Baoji) Railway, the Tianlan (Tianshui-Lanzhou) Railway should also be built with the help of the Ministry of Railways of the Central People's Government. Peng also called Chairman Mao and the Central Committee to inquire if we could "work with the Soviet Union to build railways from Tacheng or Ili to Dihua and Hami?"[16] Peng Dehuai's suggestions were approved by Chairman Mao and the Party Central Committee. With the support of the central government, Peng mobilized nearly 100,000 soldiers to participate in the construction of the Tianbao and Tianlan Railways. After the completion of the plan, he strove to extend the railways to the northwest and finally reach Xinjiang. In the process of construction, Peng Dehuai often directly checked the progress, went to relevant leaders to study with them, and resolved each difficulty and problem in construction to ensure the smooth progress of the project. Vice Minister Lü Zhengcao and Soviet experts were invited to inspect the progress and quality of the project and exchange views on the northwestern transportation construction plan. With Peng Dehuai's efforts, by the end of 1950, the original railways in Northwestern China had been rapidly restored and opened to traffic. The Tianbao and Tianlan Railways not only started to operate smoothly but also completed 40% and 50% of the total earthwork projects that year.

In addition to the railway, Peng Dehuai was also committed to the development of Northwest Airlines. At that time, it was very difficult for the newly established New China to develop aviation on its own. Given this, Peng suggested to Chairman Mao and the Central Committee on December 29, 1949, that "the northwest region is vast in territory and underdeveloped in transportation, which greatly affects the progression of the guidance work. Therefore, it is necessary to negotiate with the Soviet Union to extend the civil aviation agreements with Almaty, Dihua, and Hami to Lanzhou, Xi'an, and Beijing." Chairman Mao and the central government adopted this proposal. After negotiation between the two governments, the Agreement on the Establishment of the Sino-Soviet Civil Aviation Joint Stock Company was formally signed on March 27, 1950.

---

15. *Biography of Peng Dehuai* (Contemporary China Press, 1993), p. 389.
16. The Central Telegram Volume (Long-term Volume 8) of the General Office of the Regional Party Committee in 1950, collected in the Archives of Xinjiang Uyghur Autonomous Region.

Peng Dehuai also attached great importance to highway construction. In January 1950, he made timely arrangements to repair the main roads damaged by the enemy. That April and May, he took pains to set foot on the snow-covered Qinghai-Tibet Plateau, personally surveyed and determined the route for building the Qinghai-Tibet Highway, and organized human and material resources mainly from the army to go to the construction site. Peng Dehuai remained concerned about the traffic construction in Northwestern China after he left the post, and he particularly shared the experience of North Korea for reference.

Today, although the traffic situation in the Northwest has greatly improved, there is a considerable gap compared with other parts of the country, which restricts the economic development of the northwest. It can be seen that Peng Dehuai's assertion that vigorously improving transportation was a prerequisite for the development of the regional economy more than forty years ago remains highly valuable today when we are to continue to build the northwest.

We should actively introduce foreign capital and technology and develop foreign trade to accelerate the development of the northwest

Determining how to develop and build the northwest more quickly was an issue Peng Dehuai often thought about when he was in charge of the region. Through investigation and study, he proposed that in addition to self-reliance and arduous struggle, it was important to actively introduce foreign capital and technology and carry out foreign trade to accelerate the development of the northwest.

The rich mineral resources in Northwestern China remained hidden underground and the new China could not immediately invest a large sum of money into its development due to its limited financial resources. Given these above situation, inspired by the fact that the Kuomintang government had sent Zhang Zhizhong to negotiate with the Soviet government on the joint development of mineral resources in Xinjiang, Peng Dehuai thought that foreign capital and technology could be introduced to develop the mineral resources in Northwestern China by means of Sino-foreign joint ventures. On December 29, 1949, he suggested to the Central Government that "we should carry out local economic cooperation between Xinjiang and the Soviet Union, so as to gradually develop Xinjiang's resources. In the past, during Zhang Zhizhong's time, he negotiated with the Soviet side on the Sino-Soviet Joint Oil Company and Rare Metal and Non-Ferrous Metal Company, which resulted into the formulation of a draft agreement. It would be better for these two companies to be established promptly through negotiations."[17] After careful study, the central government reported this to Chairman Mao, who was visiting the Soviet Union, and gave consent to the report. Then the representatives of the two governments signed the Agreement on the Establishment of Sino-Soviet Union Non-Ferrous and Rare Metals Joint Stock Company in Xinjiang and the Agreement on the Establishment of Sino-Soviet Union Oil Joint Stock Company in Xinjiang after negotiations in Moscow on March 27, 1950.

In order to promote the economic development of the northwest, Peng Dehuai also spared no effort in advocating the development of foreign trade in the northwest. On December 29, 1949, he suggested to Chairman Mao and the Central Committee that Xinjiang should make use of its geographical advantages to conduct foreign trade, i.e., "Xinjiang and the Soviet Union should set up official trade, so that Xinjiang can exchange local products for necessary supplies from the Soviet Union."[18] On January 2, 1950, Peng called Chairman Mao and asked to purchase through trade with the Soviet Union 20,000 tons of grain, 100,000 army coats, 200,000 sets of cotton clothes, 200,000 cotton caps, 200,000 shirts, a great deal of cotton cloth, 1,000 trucks with a carrying capacity of 4 or 5 tons, 100,000 kg of cottonseed, and 65,000 production tools.[19]

Peng Dehuai's conception and practice of the development and construction of the northwest fully demonstrated his foresight and sagacity. Although many of Peng Dehuai's proposals and plans were not fully realized during his tenure in Northwestern China, the remarkable achievements in the construction of the region today have proved the scientific nature and rationality of his notions.

(The author is working at Party History Research Office of Xinjiang Uyghur Autonomous Region Committee of the Communist Party of China)

17. Peng Dehuai's Report to Chairman Mao on Various Issues in Xinjiang Work, collected in the Archives of Xinjiang Uyghur Autonomous Region.
18. Peng Dehuai's Report to Chairman Mao on Various Issues in Xinjiang Work, collected in the Archives of Xinjiang Uyghur Autonomous Region.
19. The Central Telegram Volume (Volume 8), the General Office of the Regional Party Committee in 1950, collected in the Archives of Xinjiang Uyghur Autonomous Region.

Peng Dehuai and Ethnic Work in the Northwest Liberation War[1]

Mou Huifen

In July 1949, the First Field Army of the Chinese People's Liberation Army launched the Fumei Campaign on the northwest battlefield, the prelude to liberating the northwest. Northwestern China was an area where a large number of ethnic minorities were concentrated, especially the Hui people. To liberate this vast area in a short time, the first task was not only to wipe out the remaining Kuomintang troops, but also to settle the ethnic issues. As commander-in-chief of the Northwest People's Liberation Army, Peng Dehuai creatively employed the Party's ethnic policy and created a forward-looking strategy of national unity. He made outstanding contributions to the rapid liberation of the northwest, the consolidation of the border areas, the establishment of the people's political power, and the realization of ethnic equality and prosperity.

I

When the KMT troops of Hu and Ma attacked the Shaanxi-Gansu-Ningxia border region, Peng Dehuai had already planned and designed for the solution of ethnic issues of the liberation of the northwest, manifesting his broad mind and long-term vision of this proletarian strategist. In May and June 1947, after the three victories

1. This article was originally published in the *Collected Works on Peng Dehuai's Life and Thoughts, a Great General with Great Achievements*, Contemporary World Press, 1999.

in the three battles of Qinghuabian, Yangmahe, and Panlong, when the Northwest Field Army moved its troops to Longdong looking for opportunities to annihilate the enemy, it attacked Ma's troops in Ningxia and Qinghai, which had invaded the border region, and captured a number of Hui officers and soldiers. After the war, when General Peng was listening to the reports from the troops, some people mentioned that the captured Hui officers and soldiers refused to eat with the Han prisoners. General Peng acutely pointed out that "on the surface, it's a small matter in life, but in essence, it matters a lot. How should we give preferential treatment to prisoners? Our Party and army's current traditional policy of preferential treatment to prisoners is to avoid killing, beating, scolding, and physical searching for money, while ensuring that staying or leaving are voluntary, which is absolutely right and effective. However, a considerable proportion of the enemy forces captured by the Northwest People's Liberation Army were formerly forces of the five Mas' troops. Among them, the 82nd Corps of Ma Bufang in Qinghai Province brutally killed the prisoners of our West Route Army during the Long March. They are afraid we will take revenge, and thus are particularly stubborn. Given this, it is imperative to add a special regulation to the current preferential treatment of the Hui prisoners." General Peng assigned the task of drafting the regulation to Fan Ming, Director of the Liaison Department of the Northwest Field Army. Fan Ming then drafted a "special code" of preferential treatment of the captured officers and soldiers of the Hui people, which specifically stipulated that Muslim stoves, religious activities, passes, and tolls, among other things be made available to them. After receiving approval from General Peng, it was issued across the military for action.

In the battle of Jiangtai, Huachi, Longdong, Ma Dianbang, head of the 179th Regiment of the 81st Division of Ma Hongbin in Ningxia, was captured by our army. General Peng personally talked to Ma, treated him with courtesy, shared the vision of the National War of Liberation, and explained the Party's ethnic policy. Peng mentioned that when the Red Army reached Tongxin County in Ningxia during the Long March, the local people all said that Ma Hongbin was a good man, and Peng asked Ma Dianbang to convey his greetings to Ma Hongbin when he went back. Before Ma's departure, the army sent him travel expenses and horses and arranged a farewell banquet of Hui style. This greatly touched Ma Dianbang. When he went back to Ningxia, Ma Hongbin was moved by our sincerity and immediately released eighteen comrades detained in Zhongning. From then, Ma Hongbin's troops remained in the civil war, waiting for opportunities to stage an uprising.

Ma Bufang and Ma Hongkui, the reactionary Ma family warlords in the northwest, had long planned a political plot to take advantage of the ethnic minorities to oppose the PLA. They tried their best to instill in the masses feelings of hatred against the Communist Party, incited narrow national emotions by deception, spread the idea that "the Communist Party is coming to kill Islam," and preached that the public in the Linxia Mosque should "sacrifice their lives to protect their religious beliefs and to serve Ma Bufang, the military, and political officers of the Muslims in the northwest." This delusion left the PLA stuck in the minority areas. General Peng had long noticed this problem and thought that the best solution was to work with the captives.

After the Battle of Fumei, the First Field Army took the momentum of the victory to launch a pursuit against the two Mas' troops in Qinghai and Ningxia. In the Battle of Guguan Town, our regiment annihilated Ma's 14th Cavalry Brigade in Qinghai and captured the enemy's deputy brigade commander and a group of officers and soldiers. This troop was the strongest enemy of the KMT reactionary forces in Northwestern China, and also the most feudal, stubborn, and brainwashed troop. Demonstrating the Party's national policy through the prisoners and getting them to publicize to the masses with their own experiences was the most powerful tool for breaking through the reactionary deception. For the Hui prisoners, our army strictly followed the policy of offering them special preferential treatment. Those who were injured or ill were properly treated. Special meals were provided, and they were allowed to worship and recite their scriptures. When they were later released, each was given three silver coins for their transportation expenses.

Our army's special policy of preferential treatment for prisoners achieved positive results. When the People's Liberation Army entered Sanzigou, northwest of Ningding County (now Guanghe County), the Hui people did not flee, but took snacks and sheep to greet the People's Liberation Army, as if they were relatives. Ma Weifu, an old Hui man in the village, put it well, when he said that "before the PLA came, Ma Bufang's troop said that when the Communist army came, they would kill all the Hui people, rape the women, and force the Hui people to eat pork. We were very afraid. However, a couple of days ago, a soldier in Ma Bufang's 14th Cavalry Brigade came back to our village. He was wounded in a battle with the PLA in Guguan Town. The PLA doctors gave him medicine and bandaged his wounds, and when he was released, they gave him three silver coins for travel expenses. He said that he saw with his own eyes that the People's Liberation Army was kind to the public, with no forced recruitment and no demands for money.

Deputy Commander-in-Chief Peng Dehuai personally went to the front line to command the battle. Pictured is the artillery post on the front line of Guanjianao in Wuxiang County, just 500 meters away from the enemy.

Instead, they paid for everything they bought. Over the past few days, we saw that the PLA were truly admirable."

On August 9, Peng Dehuai also mentioned in his report to Chairman Mao Zedong that "in mid-July, hundreds of soldiers captured from Wang Zhiqi's troop were released. Recently, more than a hundred prisoners from Ma's troops in Qinghai were released, and each was given three silver coins to cover transportation costs. On their way back, they started to publicize that our army had given preferential treatment to the prisoners and the Hui people. When we went into Gansu, the Hui people welcomed us as much as the Han people. We plan to release another batch to return to Qinghai and Linxia, in hopes that this will expose Ma Bufang's misleading publicity over the years."

Most of the Ma troops were strong young men who had been captured or coerced to join the army. By publicizing the Party's ethnic policy, especially the ethnic policy toward prisoners, the PLA helped them feel the wisdom and greatness of the Communist Party's policy. When they returned to their hometowns, they spread the news of their own experience and shattered all the rumors spread by the Ma group.

II

Our troops did not disturb the people, instead we respected the customs of the ethnic minority groups, not entering mosques, not slaughtering pigs near the houses of the Hui people, and not borrowing their cooking utensils. In addition, the soldiers helped the masses solve their difficulties and engaged in other such activities. This was one reason the PLA was able to go into the ethnic areas and win the support of the ethnic minority communities.

When the PLA prepared to deepen its engagement in the ethnic areas, Peng Dehuai would study the customs of the local people in every aspect, and he specifically asked Lu Ruilin, Political Commissar of the 62nd Army (Lu was from Lujiagou, Linxia, Gansu Province) to have a detailed discussion on the subject. Linxia was a place where the Hui people lived together, and it was also the home of the two Mas (in Qinghai and Ningxia) of the KMT in the northwest. Most of the officers at the middle and lower levels in the two Mas' troops were from Linxia, where reactionary forces were relatively strong. Plus, with the historical barrier between the Hui and the Han, if we were not careful in liberating the ethnic areas, we would be utilized by the enemy. Under the leadership of Peng Dehuai, the PLA formulated a code governing how to respect the customs and religious beliefs of the Hui people when entering the Hui nationality areas, especially enacted the specific provisions on uniting the Hui compatriots. The army was required to give full play to the style of "being both a combat team and a working team" and do a good job with the masses in the newly liberated areas even as they engaged in fighting the enemy.

Upon entering Zhangjiachuan, where the Hui people lived together, the Fourth Corps of the Second Regiment conscientiously carried out the Fourth Army Discipline Order. The head of the army visited the Zhangjiachuan Mosque and held a small forum to publicize the Party's ethnic and religious policies. Soldiers posted slogans on the door of the mosque, such as "Freedom of religious belief, protection of the mosque," and "Eight codes of the Chinese People's Liberation Army." Some of the officers and soldiers of the company (the Hui people's company) shared their own stories with and publicized the policies to the Hui people, thus eliminating the doubts of the masses. Some companies preferred to sleep in the open than go into the Hui people's houses, despite the owners' absence. In a short period of time, the Hui people came to understand the Communist Party's policy toward ethnic minorities, and they were moved to say, "Only the Communist Party regards us as a people and respects our national habits. In the future, only by following the Communist Party can we live and work in peace and contentment." Some of the Hui people far away in Huining, Dingxi, and Linxia came to inquire about what happened to the Hui people and to the mosque. When they saw that the People's Liberation Army had done no harm to the masses, they all returned, feeling reassured.

Therefore, when the PLA entered the Linxia area, both Hui and Han people rushed to the streets to meet the army. At that time, Guo Peng, Commander of the Second Corps of the First Regiment, and Wang Enmao, Political Commissar, who had entered Linxia earlier, reported in a telegram sent to Peng Dehuai that "the Sixth Division entered Linxia at 14:00 today (August 22), and Han Qigong's bandit army fled to Xunhua in the morning. Then the people of Linxia came out to welcome the PLA. All the way from Sanshilipu, the Hui and Han people took to the streets to welcome the army, especially in the city and outside the city gate, with welcome slogans being visible everywhere. Groups of people clapped and fired their guns in salute. I had not seen such a grand welcome since I came to the west regions." On reading the telegram, General Peng was filled with excitement. He wrote below the telegram, "Our Second Corps was in Linxia, and the people in the hometown of the Ma's bandits in Qinghai and Ningxia were amazingly welcoming to the PLA." It was evident that the specific ethnic policies formulated under the direct leadership of Comrade Peng Dehuai played a positive role in the liberation of the ethnic areas.

III

To speed up the process of the liberation of the northwest and reduce the suffering of the people of all nationalities, especially when the PLA destroyed the reactionary rule of the KMT in the northwest in such an indomitable way, and to reduce the loss of lives among those deceived Kuomintang officers and soldiers, Comrade Peng

Dehuai creatively employed the Party's ethnic policy, united the ethnic and religious elites, and gave full play to their influence for the peaceful liberation. With the care of General Peng, before the PLA liberated Qinghai, Ningxia, and Xinjiang, they contacted the upper classes of the ethnic and religious people who had extensive contacts with and relatives in the Kuomintang troops in these places to form a peace delegation to appeal for the peaceful liberation of these areas.

When marching to Qinghai, Wang Zhen, Commander of the First Regiment, asked Ma Pilie, an open-minded person in Linxia, a relative of Ma Bufang, and a member of the Hui upper class, to liberate Qinghai. Ma Pilie had worked in Qinghai before and knew many people. Now that he was asked to contribute to the liberation of Qinghai, he happily agreed. At Ma Pilie's suggestion, Ma Liang, Ma Bufang's uncle, and two other Han representatives were invited to form a Linxia peace delegation to Qinghai (also known as a lobby group for surrender).

After Ma Pilie and others went to Xunhua with Commander Wang Zhen, they learned that there was a Ma Quanyi infantry troop defending the North Bank of the Yellow River. In order to protect the PLA from losses as they crossed the river, with the consent of Commander Wang Zhen, Ma Pilie and Ma Liang immediately wrote to Ma Quanyi, urging him to revolt on the spot and telling him to get out of the way instead of resisting. Upon reading the letter, Ma was surprised and said, "This is the handwriting of my uncle!" The next day, Ma Quanyi withdrew.

When Ma Pilie arrived before the first regiment to Xining, he went first to Shangwuzhuang and Sanjiaocheng, talked to Ma Bufang's army, division, brigade, and regiment leaders who were defeated in the Lanzhou campaign, introduced the situation in Linxia's liberation to them, publicized news of the PLA's westward advance, and introduced the Party's ethnic and religious policies. With Ma Pilie's patient persuasion, even some officers and soldiers who were ready to flee to Tibet had no more concerns, and they put down their arms to surrender to the PLA.

On the eve of entering Ningxia, General Peng was still concerned about my old contacts in Ningxia who might help with our work. One day, Peng told Fan Ming, "Now, the 19th Regiment is about to march into Ningxia. Although Ma Hongkui and Ma Hongbin are strong, they have ties with us. It is possible to strive for peaceful liberation when they see the irreversible trend and the approaching PLA. Your liaison department should take the initiative to contact them and invite them to cooperate with the 19th Regiment in this aspect."

After that, Peng decided to invite Guo Nanpu, an elderly man with great prestige among the Islamic elites in Lanzhou and Ningxia, to go with Ma Shouli and Ma Jikang to Ningxia for the peaceful liberation. For this reason, Yang Dezhi,

Commander of the 19th Regiment, and Li Zhimin, Political Commissar, visited Guo Nanpu's home multiple times. Guo gladly promised to go to Ningxia to inform Ma Hongkui and Ma Hongbin that, "Although I have different surnames from them, we are of the same family and have the same religious beliefs. I would like to convey to them your army's friendship with the Hui people and your goal of serving the country and the people."

On September 6, the peace delegation to Ningxia headed by Guo Nanpu left Lanzhou, went past Huajialing, Guyuan, Tongxin, and Zhongning, and arrived in Yinchuan on the night of September 14. In the process of fighting for the uprising of the 81st Corps of the Kuomintang, the peace delegation led by Guo Nanpu risked their lives and drove through the line of fire to do much work in Zhongning and Yinchuan. The uprising of the 81st Corps contributed to the disintegration of the Kuomintang corps and the rapid liberation of Ningxia. Afterwards, General Peng sent a congratulatory telegram, and Ma Hongbin replied with a telegram of thanks. As a token of gratitude to Guo Nanpu for his efforts in the peaceful liberation of Ningxia, the leaders of the 19th Regiment jointly presented him with a banner embroidered with the phrase, *Man of Peace*.

General Peng was also committed to the Party's national unity. As long as they stood on the side of the people and did good deeds for the people, General Peng saw them as the distinguished guests of the Party. Ma Quanqin, the grandson of Ma Zhan'ao, a renowned personnel in Northwestern China in the late Qing Dynasty, was from a family of generations of officials. At the time of our army's liberation in Linxia, Ma Quanqin took the initiative to send people to contact Commander Wang Zhen, and he did much positive work in appeasing the minority people in Dahejia and Xunhua, collecting provisions, persuading the enemy to surrender, and supporting the PLA to cross the Yellow River. Introduced by Wang Zhen, he was appointed by General Peng as the senior staff officer of the First Corps of the People's Liberation Army.

After the peaceful liberation of the Xiahe area in Gannan, General Peng sent special personnel to pick up Huang Zhengqing, the former Security Commander of the Xiahe Labrang of the Kuomintang, who had been in our camp, to take him to Lanzhou. General Peng invited Huang to have a long talk that lasted all night, and he patiently explained the Party's ethnic policies to Huang. Peng stressed that all ethnic groups should be united to take the socialist path and build a new China. Peng also encouraged Huang to work well with the Party and build the idea of serving the people, learning by doing, and doing by learning.

Huang Zhengqing.

After the peaceful liberation of Ningxia, Ma Hongbin returned to Lanzhou. General Peng visited Ma Hongbin in person and talked with him like an old friend. Peng hoped that Ma Hongbin could shift from a military to a political career, strengthen national unity, and build Lanzhou afresh.

Later, General Peng said, "In doing the United Front work, especially the National United Front work, we should be humble, prudent, and respectful, trying to make friends rather than being domineering. We should treat the ethnic people as our guests of honor rather than behaving like victors before them." After liberation, these personages became our Party's loyal friends who played an irreplaceable role in strengthening national unity and building the new China together. From this, Comrade Peng Dehuai's broad political vision of and dedication to national unity is evident.

IV

When our army went to Lanzhou, Comrade Peng Dehuai had already considered the peaceful liberation of Xinjiang. As early as July 23, in his telegram to General Peng, Chairman Mao pointed out that "as I see it, as long as the Pingliang Campaign can annihilate two main forces, the northwest war can largely be accomplished, and the future occupation of the four provinces of Gansu, Ningxia, Qinghai, and Xinjiang will simply be a matter of proceeding to take over." In accordance with the instructions of the Central Committee, General Peng frequently met with Xinjiang's ethnic minority communities and people from all walks of life in Lanzhou after the liberation of Lanzhou, despite his tight working schedule. He directly introduced the Party's ethnic policies and the Party Central Committee's policies on Xinjiang issues to them. He worked in all aspects, especially in multi-level ethnic unity, so as to realize the peaceful liberation of Xinjiang as early as possible.

On the third day after the liberation of Lanzhou, General Peng met with people from all walks of life of all ethnic groups in Xinjiang in the San'ai Hall, including Hou Ruichang, the son of the king of Mongolia, and his wife Shi Ruilan, Ahmad Wajidi, a Uyghur businessman, Usmayi, a Uyghur religious leader in Lanzhou, and some officers above the level of colonel in Tao Zhiyue's troop who were on vacation in Lanzhou. General Peng asked them to introduce Xinjiang, explained to them the policies of the Communist Party, and asked them to spread the concept that Xinjiang could only be liberated peacefully. During this period, General Peng appointed Fan Ming to set up the Xinjiang Research Association. With the support of General Peng, the Research Association did much good for the peaceful liberation of Xinjiang. At the same time, with the support of General Peng, Sun Zuobin and Fan Ming were put in charge of the establishment of the Xinjiang Working Group accompanying the army, with Ahmad Wajidi as the head and Wu Jianfu as the deputy head, and with the participation of the Xinjiang Hui and Uyghur people traveling in Lanzhou. After its departure from Lanzhou in mid-September, under the leadership of the Political Department of the First Corps, the Working Group did much ethnic work in Hami, Shanshan, Turpan, and other places. It made great contributions to stabilizing the situation in Xinjiang, consolidating the achievements of Xinjiang's peaceful liberation, uniting people from ethnic and religious circles around the Party, and jointly building Xinjiang. On September 24, General Peng was invited to attend the gathering of Xinjiang

Uyghur compatriots in Lanzhou. General Peng had a cordial talk with Uyghur compatriots, listened to their ideas about looking forward to the early peaceful liberation of their hometown, and encouraged them to do more to promote the peaceful liberation of their home.

In the process of peacefully liberating Xinjiang, General Peng directly organized Ma Fuchen (uncle of Ma Chengxiang, commander of the KMT's Fifth Cavalry Corps in Xinjiang), Ma Zhenwu (cousin of Ma Chengxiang), and Zhan Fushou to form the peace talk delegation along with some of the family members of the Fifth Cavalry Corps in the interior to do persuasion work in Xinjiang. After Ma Fuchen and his Party moved westward to Zhangye with the Second Corps of the First Regiment, he wrote a letter to Ma Chengxiang on September 17, informing him of the People's Liberation Army's wise policy and strict discipline and advising Ma Chengxiang to send important personnel or to personally welcome the People's Liberation Army.

In early October, when Ma Fuchen and his party completed their peace mission and returned to Jiuquan, Peng Dehuai and Wang Zhen, who happened to be in Jiuquan, hosted a feast of mutton at the local mosque to welcome Ma Fuchen and others. During the banquet, General Peng praised Ma Fuchen for his great ethnic righteousness and for his contribution in urging Ma Chengxiang, commander of the Fifth Calvary Corps of the KMT, to give up the resistance, which paved the way for the peaceful liberation of Xinjiang.

When the PLA was ready to go to Xinjiang after its peaceful liberation, General Peng once again urged the troops to "be loving toward the people of all ethnic groups in Xinjiang and united with the Xinjiang national army, to resolutely implement ethnic policies, respect the customs and habits of ethnic minorities, unite and help the people of all ethnic groups to establish their own happy life, and unite the people of all ethnic groups in the People's Republic of China into a big, united family."

All the officers and men of our army who entered Xinjiang resolutely carried out General Peng's instructions and the Party's ethnic policy. After entering Xinjiang, although Kuomintang secret agents and some separatist forces stirred up an uprising and incited rebellions, the people of all ethnic groups in Xinjiang hoped for peace and liberation, actively cooperated with the PLA, quickly quelled the rebellion, and stabilized society. As a result, the PLA went straight in within a very short time, panted the red flag on the Pamir Plateau and Hongqilapu Pass, and quickly liberated the entire occupied area of Xinjiang, one sixth of the territory of the country. Wherever the PLA went, people of all ethnic groups, young or old, sang and danced, welcoming them warmly. This fulfilled the goal of the PLA's takeover and peaceful liberation of the area. All of this, of course, was closely linked to much of the work our Party and army did, and the role of ethnic work was especially evident. During the liberation of Northwestern China, Peng Dehuai's specific ethnic policies for the army united the people of all ethnic groups, maintained the unity of the motherland, and rescued millions of oppressed and exploited people of all ethnic groups. General Peng's contribution to the Chinese nation and the war of liberation will continue to be cherished by the people of all ethnic groups.

(The author is working at the Investigation and Research Office, Party History Research Office, Gansu Provincial Party Committee.)

Peng Dehuai in Charge of Northwestern China[1]

HE LIBO

Peng Dehuai's Grand Blueprint for the Construction of the Northwest in the Early Days of Liberation

From the time the Central Red Army arrived in Northern Shaanxi in 1935, Peng Dehuai spent most of his time in the northwest. The people of the northwest supported and nurtured the people's army in the difficult war years, and the footprints of the soldiers were spread all across the Northwest Plateau. Peng Dehuai often went deep into the masses to understand the hardships of the people's lives in Northwestern China. Even in the war years, Peng studied the history of the northwest, local chronicles, historical materials, and even the collected works of Zuo Zongtang. He often told the officers and men of the army that they should "settle down and take root" in the northwest and work with their brothers and sisters of all nationalities to build the area.

After the basic liberation of the northwest, Peng Dehuai considered ways to quickly heal the war wounds in the northwest and restore industrial and agricultural production. On September 27, 1949, Peng Dehuai called Xi Zhongxun, Political Commissar of the Northwest Military Region, who presided over the daily work of the region in Xi'an, from Lanzhou. Peng proposed that there should be overall (five provinces) planning for all work, especially for economic construction, so that production, transportation, and marketing could be systematically planned.

1. This article was originally published in *The History of the Party*, Issue 10, 2008.

Peng Dehuai after the Red Army arrived in Northern Shaanxi in 1936.

Jia Tuofu, chairman of Northwest Finance and Economics Committee and Chairman of the Northwest Federation of Trade Unions.

Comrade Jia Tuofu (then a member of the Standing Committee of the Northwest Bureau and Director of the Northwest Finance and Economics Commission) was to immediately hand over the role of Mayor of Xi'an and the role in the Military Control Commission thereby devote all his energy to planning the economic construction of the northwest. Peng Dehuai clearly said that "after the war, financial expenditure must be within the limits of income, and the bank's issuance (currency) should be used to develop production as much as possible."

After a period of preparation, on November 15, 1949, Peng Dehuai reported to Mao Zedong the preliminary arrangements for production and transportation construction in Northwestern China in 1950, especially the resumption and development of oil production in theYumen Oilfield, the only oil field in China at that time. In the report, Peng Dehuai pointed out that "in order to rapidly develop industrial and agricultural production in Northwestern China, we should be particularly thrifty over the next five to ten years. Aside from building the necessary houses for factories, the government, Party, and military organs should not plan to build additional houses in the coming years, and the old houses should instead be renovated to protect them against cold and wind." On December 24, Peng Dehuai delivered a speech, calling on all the army and people in the northwest to live frugally and struggle diligently. "At present, we should focus on restoring and developing production and improving people's lives... developing and building the northwest with arduous effort and in the spirit of seeking truth from facts."

As for how to strengthen the construction of Northwestern China, Peng Dehuai proposed specific tasks. In January 1950, at the Fifth Meeting of the Central People's Government and the Northwest Military and Political Commission, Peng Dehuai made a report on the work of the northwest region and its tasks since then. He said that the overall task was to carry out democratic reform and develop production, improve literacy, and build a new northwest. He pointed out that the main task at the time was to "thoroughly eliminate bandits and secret agents, carry out democratic reform, mobilize all forces, economize on food and clothing, overcome difficulties, and resume and develop production... For a certain period of time, agriculture and animal husbandry should be the mainstay of economic construction in Northwestern China. At the same time, we should pay close attention to industrial and mining production and transportation as well as prepare to build new railways."

On September 24, 1950, Peng Dehuai brought forward the goal of building a new northwest at the Northwest Literature and Art Workers' Congress, saying that "our general task is to unite and educate the people of all ethnic groups, steadily and thoroughly eliminate all the old systems and ideas that hinder the development of productive forces, and build a prosperous, strong, and progressive new northwest."

Through a large number of investigations and studies, Peng Dehuai stressed that we should create a comprehensive plan for the development and construction of the northwest and give different tasks to different regions, so as to suit the actual situation of each province and give full play to their advantages and strengths.

The Economic Construction of Northwestern China Should Be Based on Agriculture and Animal Husbandry for a Certain Period of Time

On September 26, 1949, Lanzhou had just been liberated. When mapping out the tasks in the next step for the liberation of the northwest, Peng Dehuai suggested that "we have a plan, that is, a gun in one hand and a pick in the other. This year we must march into Xinjiang to make all the preparations for production next spring." He pointed to a map of the northwest and said to everyone, "Look what a big place the northwest is. It has a vast land and abundant resources, but it is sparsely populated, extremely poor, and desolate. We need to start the construction now...

The Northwest Field Army began to attack on the external front in February 1948. Pictured is Peng Dehuai delivering a battle mobilization report to the army.

We must liberate, build, and change the outlook of the northwest. This is the task entrusted to us by history, and it is a task we cannot shirk."

There were good natural conditions for the development of agriculture and animal husbandry in Northwestern China. Agriculture and animal husbandry accounted for a large proportion of the local economy. Before Liberation, agriculture accounted for 75% of the northwest's economy, animal husbandry for more than 20%, and modern industry and handicraft industry for less than 5%. However, due to historical and other reasons, Northwestern China had poor infrastructure and production conditions for agriculture and animal husbandry, which was highly vulnerable to natural disasters, and its production was quite unstable. Many places were "relying on nature for grain." In particular, in the autumn of 1949, many places in Northwestern China suffered from disasters, and more than 500,000 people faced various difficulties. The vast new areas were plundered and squeezed by the long-time KMT reactionary rule, resulting in a widespread spring famine.

In the meantime, after the liberation of the five provinces in Northwestern China, it took a large number of Kuomintang military and political personnel to set up political power at all levels. As a result, the number of military and political personnel reached more than one million, accounting for about 4.5% of the total population. The contradiction between supply and demand of food and other necessities became acute, which was fully illustrated by the situation in Xinjiang at that time.

Given this, Peng Dehuai advocated that the economic construction in Northwestern China should be based on agriculture and animal husbandry for a certain period of time. In January 1950, at the first meeting of the Northwest Military and Political Commission, he pointed out that "for a certain period of time, the economic construction of the northwest region should focus on agriculture and animal husbandry. In agriculture, we should boost farmers' enthusiasm for production, improve seeds and farming methods, restore and develop water conservancy works, highlight the protection and cultivation of forests and grasslands, and prevent and control disasters... Livestock production in Gansu, Ningxia, Qinghai, and Xinjiang should not be lower than that it was in 1949."

In the spring of 1950, the Ministry of Agriculture and Forestry of the Northwest Military and Political Commission failed to formulate a thorough research plan in advance, and the work also lacked specific guidance and in-depth inspection. As a result, more than 100,000 *mu* of cotton fields in Guanzhong were ridged and short of seedlings, causing serious losses to the people and state property. Peng Dehuai severely criticized this matter and announced in the newspaper the decision to punish the person in charge. From then, he frequently used this case as a reference to warn cadres that they must go into practice and go to the front line of production, instead of sitting in the office giving orders to guide production.

In production and construction, Peng Dehuai attached great importance to the role of the army and conveyed multiple times the instructions of the CPC Central Committee and Mao Zedong stating that the army was both a combat team and a working team. "It's a big issue that so many troops are supported by the state. We should engage in production," he said. "In peacetime, the PLA should inherit the tradition of arduous struggle, become the main force in production and construction, and be one of the major forces in building a new northwest." At the beginning of 1950, Peng Dehuai presided over a meeting of cadres at or above the commander level in the First Field Army in Xi'an, focusing on the issue of the army shifting to production practice. He said that because of the long-term war, the people had a hard life. To implement Chairman Mao's policy that the PLA was a combat team, a publicity team, and a production team, the PLA must to engage in agricultural production to reduce the burden on the people. The soldiers' annual grain yield should be 350 *jin* and the cadres', 250 *jin*. Of course, they should not occupy the fields of the farmers, but instead open up wasteland to grow grain; and the whole 64th Corps and part of the 63rd Corps could build the Tianbao Railway. In the spring of 1950, when inspecting the work in the northwestern provinces, on multiple occasions Peng Dehuai called on all cadres and local garrisons to "settle down and take root" in the border areas, and to work alongside their brothers and other nationalities to build the northwest. He said that now we had become the owners of the land, so we should do a good job in production. We should have a gun in one hand and a pickaxe in the other. We should be able to produce in peacetime and fight in wartime, so that we could be invincible in the world.

With the effort of the people's governments at all levels and all the people in the northwest, by the end of 1950, agriculture and animal husbandry in the northwest had made great progress, with 100 million *mu* of grain being sown in summer and autumn. In particular, hundreds of thousands of officers and men of the armed forces were engaged in agricultural production, which greatly increased the agricultural labor force that year. More than 2 million *mu* of land was reclaimed and 3.7 million *mu* of water conservancy irrigation area was restored. The government loan was equivalent to 4.8 million *jin* of wheat and more than 100,000 head of livestock were well treated. The recovery and development of agriculture and animal husbandry provided sufficient material guarantees for the development of Northwestern China.

Northwest Development with Transport as the Top Priority

The very first thing Peng Dehuai thought of when he was in charge of the Northwest Military and Political Commission was the construction of the western region of the motherland and of its thoroughfares as national ties. At the beginning of the founding of the new China, the backward traffic conditions seriously hindered the development and construction of Northwestern China. Peng Dehuai had a very clear understanding of the importance of transportation to the development and construction of the northwest, and he put forward the conclusion that vigorously improving transportation was a prerequisite for economic development.

The railway played an important role in transportation. Even before the founding of the new China, Peng Dehuai had the idea of building railways in Northwestern China. On September 28, 1949, he signed and issued an order of the Committee of the Communist Party of China for marching to Xinjiang, which pointed out that "we should liberate the frontier of the motherland to develop oil sources and build railways. This is of great significance to the development of the economy and the consolidation of border defense." After the liberation of Northwestern China, Peng Dehuai believed that the construction of the railway was the most important thing for the development of the regional economy. If we waited until the railways in the northeast and the north were completed, we would have to wait at least twenty years for the large-scale development and construction of the northwest to take off. It was thus better to strive to build the Northwest Railway as early as possible.

On November 15, 1949, when reporting to Mao Zedong about the restoration of the Yumen Oil Field, Peng Dehuai demanded that in addition to the Tianshui-Baoji Railway, the Tianshui-Lanzhou Railway should be built with the help of the Ministry of Railways of the Central People's Government to extend the Longhai Railway, the traffic artery across China, to Lanzhou, the capital of Gansu Province. On December 29, 1949, when reporting to Mao Zedong on various work in Xinjiang, Peng pointed out regretfully that "Xinjiang is a vast region with underdeveloped transportation. It is difficult not only to get help from the interior, but also to transport grain more than 2,000 *li* from Southern Xinjiang, where there is more grain, to Northern Xinjiang, where there is a food shortage. It costs more than ten *dan* of military expenses to transport one *dan* of grain to Xinjiang." Later, at the Fifth Meeting of the Central People's Government Committee, Peng Dehuai once again talked about the backwardness and difficulties of transportation in the northwest. On January 2, 1950, Peng Dehuai again asked Chairman Mao and the Central Committee to inquire if we could "work with the Soviet Union to build railways from Tacheng or Ili to Dihua and Hami." In March and April 1950, Mao Zedong instructed that the Northwest Railway should be built to Dihua within ten years, and if it could be done sooner, that was even better. On August 6, 1950, Peng Dehuai pointed out in his speech at the closing ceremony of the Third Northwest Youth Congress that the current issue was to improve transportation, build railways, and lay a solid foundation for industrialization. Now we were building the Tianbao and Tianlan Railways, which would be extended to Xinjiang in seven or eight years. Northwestern China was preparing to build three major lines and more branch lines. This arduous, long-term task needed to be carried on by the younger generation.

Peng Dehuai had fought in the northwest for years and was very familiar with the terrain and natural conditions of the region. He directly participated in technical discussions and research on the project, often studied the route with Soviet experts, went to the construction site to inspect the project, and solicited opinions from engineering and technical personnel. In April and May 1950, Peng Dehuai traveled all over Gansu, Ningxia, Qinghai, and Xinjiang. By the end of 1950, the original railways in Northwestern China had been rapidly restored and opened to traffic. On December 20, 1950, the Tianbao Railway project was successfully completed within 250 days. The Tianlan Railway not only started its construction smoothly, but also completed half of the total earthworks in 1950. On September 29, 1952, the Tianlan Railway was officially opened to traffic. Mao Zedong, Liu Shaoqi, Zhu De, Peng Dehuai, and others all wrote inscriptions for the opening.

Peng Dehuai also attached great importance to highway construction. In January 1950, he made timely arrangements to repair the main roads that had been damaged by the enemy. In April and May that year, he took great pains to set foot on the snow-covered Qinghai-Tibet Plateau, personally surveyed and determined the route for building the Qinghai-Tibet Highway, and organized human and material resources mainly from the army to go to the construction site. Peng Dehuai remained concerned about the traffic construction in Northwestern China after he left the post, and he made a point to share his experience in North Korea for reference. After returning from Korea in 1952, Peng Dehuai took over the daily work of the Central Military Commission from Zhou Enlai.

In discussing the Qinghai-Tibet highway, it is important to mention Mu Shengzhong, Director of the Organization Department of the Tibet Working Committee of the Northwest Bureau and Political Commissar of the Northwest Tibet Branch. In January 1952, Mu Shengzhong went to Beijing for a meeting, and visited Peng Dehuai and reported the idea for building the Qinghai-Tibet Highway. Mu Shengzhong believed that in the long run, only relying on human power was not the best way to transport grain to Tibet. Rather, a road should be built. Mu Shengzhong's proposal coincided with Peng Dehuai's own idea. Peng pointed at the map of China and said that, from Dunhuang to the south of Tibet, "it's still blank. In the long run, there needs be a major transportation artery." Peng Dehuai was determined to build the Qinghai-Tibet Highway, not only as a military thoroughfare, but more importantly, he believed that it was a road of unity between nations and a link between ethnic groups. On the same day, Peng treated Mu Shengzhong for dinner at his home and entertained him with wine the Soviet military delegation had given him. Before his departure, Peng Dehuai asked Mu Shengzhong to draft a road construction report, which he would hand over to Premier Zhou.

Peng Dehuai carefully studied the feasibility of building the Qinghai-Tibet-highway and drew a preliminary route map of it. The route Peng Dehuai drew was not only an economic route to Tibet, but also of great military significance. Peng directly reported to Premier Zhou Enlai to raise funds. Two days later, he asked Mu

Shengzhong to come to the office and told him that "Premier Zhou has approved your report. It's your turn to compose the next chapter." Zhou Enlai directly approved the road construction report of the Qinghai-Tibet highway, agreed to build the Golmud to Hoh Xil section first, and granted 300,000 yuan as the road construction fund. According to the minimum standard for road construction at that time, 300,000 yuan was only enough to build 5 kilometers, at most. Although it was only a drop in the bucket, it was precious to Mu Shengzhong. Peng Dehuai later transferred a large number of military and material resources from the Northwest Military Region to this project. After fully listening to the opinions of the engineering and technical personnel, Peng directly determined the route into Tibet for the Qinghai-Tibet Highway and decided that the construction of the road should be mainly carried out by the People's Liberation Army. On December 25, 1954, in Lhasa, the opening ceremonies of the Qinghai-Tibet Highway and the Kham Tibet Highway were held at the same time. Tibetan compatriots thronged to the celebration. Seeing hundreds of cars decorated with red flowers, they were extremely excited. They called the two roads "golden ribbons," "golden bridges," and "glamorous roads." Many years later, every time Mu Shengzhong spoke of Peng Dehuai, he would say, "Without Mr. Peng, there would be no Qinghai-Tibet Highway."

In January 1955, Mu Shengzhong went to Beijing for a meeting and visited Peng Dehuai. At lunch, Peng Dehuai took out a bottle of baijiu with ginseng and served it to Mu Shengzhong. "This is wine I've made myself. It's good for your health." He poured three cups of wine for Mu Shengzhong and said, "Today, I'd like to toast three cups of wine to the hero of road construction." Mu Shengzhong then invited Peng Dehuai to inspect the Qinghai-Tibet Highway. Peng readily agreed. In October 1958, Peng visited Golmud. When the plane landed at the Qarhan Salt Lake Airport, Peng Dehuai couldn't help but said excitedly when he saw cars running on the salt bridge, "This airport is very impressive, and the road is extraordinary!" Hearing the news about Peng's arrival, the road builders, officers, and soldiers all came to see him. He waved to everyone and said, "Comrades, I'd like to express my admiration for you. We must always have an uplifting spirit if we are to achieve something. You have built roads on the roof of the world and a new town in Qaidam. This is amazing. I hope our comrades will continue to fight and forge ahead."

Accompanied by Mu Shengzhong, Peng Dehuai visited the Qinghai-Tibet Highway and the Kunlun Pass. Poplars were planted in the Gobi Desert, adding a tint of refreshing green. Neat rows of houses were built in the wasteland where wild animals had lived. Seeing all this, Peng Dehuai was very pleased, saying, "We need to thank the road building heroes for their hard work in opening up the Qinghai-Tibet Highway, and we should write a book about them." Having left Golmud after the inspection, Peng Dehuai kept thinking about the plateau construction work and instructed the General Administration to assign more than 7,000 graduates of military academies to the Qinghai-Tibet Plateau for construction.

Peng Dehuai was also committed to the development of Northwest Airlines. At that time, it was very difficult for the newly established New China to develop aviation on its own. Given this, Peng suggested to Chairman Mao and the Central Committee on December 29, 1949, that "the northwest region is vast in territory and underdeveloped in transportation, which greatly affects the progress of the guidance work. It is thus necessary to negotiate with the Soviet Union to extend the civil aviation agreements with Almaty, Dihua, and Hami to Lanzhou, Xi'an, and Beijing." Chairman Mao and the central government adopted this proposal. After negotiations between the two governments, the *Agreement on the Establishment of Sino-Soviet Civil Aviation Joint Stock Company* was officially signed on March 27, 1950.

Advocating the Establishment of a Sino-Soviet Union Joint Venture in Xinjiang

In the northwest, Xinjiang was the last province to be liberated, and it had the most complicated situation. At the beginning of Liberation, there were serious financial and economic difficulties in Xinjiang. In the face of this serious situation, Peng Dehuai issued a timely report to the Central Committee, suggesting that based on self-reliance, China should actively strive for the Soviet Union's support for the development and construction of Xinjiang. At that time, Mao Zedong was visiting the Soviet Union. Peng Dehuai wrote a report on this situation and forwarded it to Mao through the Party Central Committee. Peng explained in the report that the current problem in Xinjiang was financial and economic. This was because Xinjiang itself could only handle about 30% of the expenditure of the Party, government, and army. It had a vast territory, with underdeveloped transportation and a shortage of food. In previous years, it had stopped trade with the Soviet Union, and it was too far away from the interior, resulting in shrinking production and economic depression. If we failed to resolve the financial and economic problems in Xinjiang, it would affect the army and national unity. "In order to address the current difficulties in

Xinjiang and the construction in the future, I think it is necessary to have the help of the Soviet Union," he wrote. Peng's specific suggestions were to ask the Soviet Union to help solve the equipment and transportation problems, to officially trade with the Soviet Union, to carry out local economic cooperation between Xinjiang and the Soviet Union, to incorporate oil companies, rare metal, and non-ferrous metal companies, and to extend the civil aviation lines to Lanzhou, Xi'an, and Beijing.

The Party Central Committee and Mao Zedong adopted Peng Dehuai's opinions. On March 27, 1950, China and the Soviet Union signed the *Agreement on the Establishment of the Sino-Soviet Union Non-Ferrous and Rare Metals Joint Stock Company* in Xinjiang, the *Agreement on the Establishment of the Sino-Soviet Union Oil Joint Stock Company* in Xinjiang, and the *Agreement on the Establishment of Sino-Soviet Union Civil Aviation Joint Stock Company*. In fact, Peng Dehuai's proposal was the forerunner of what we call today's practice of introducing foreign capital and establishing Sino-foreign joint ventures. When the news of the signing of this agreement was made public, many people in China did not understand it, and mistaken that it damaged China's sovereignty. Peng Dehuai firmly believed that his proposal did not damage the sovereignty of the country, but was instead conducive to promoting the economic construction of Northwestern China and the new China. He believed that the signing of the agreement was beneficial to the consolidation of national defense and the development of Northwestern China. "The major imports now are grain, cotton, and oil. Exploiting Xinjiang's oil can save a large amount of foreign exchange, which is of great benefit to the construction of industry and agriculture in Northwestern China... The two agreements have been concluded on the basis of absolute equality, and what's provided on our side is merely the land... The term of the agreement is thirty years. In thirty years, we will have trained cadres, and what remains of the project will be ours, while the Soviets will leave. Some of our comrades argue about the percentage of the share capital, which is what we call 'missing the forest for the trees.' It is like a small gain with a big loss, due to a lack of vision."

Peng Dehuai said, "The Sino-Soviet Union Civil Aviation Agreement stipulates that there is a route from Almaty to Beijing via Yining, Dihua, Jiuquan, Lanzhou, Xi'an, and Taiyuan, which is most beneficial to China's transportation, especially in the northwest, because transportation in the area is currently very inconvenient. Our share capital is nothing but the airport. Before the development of petroleum in the northwest, the civil aviation did not make any profit, as they needed to provide all the aircraft, petrol, and equipment. This is beneficial to China. We can train cadres and build our civil aviation. This is fundamentally different from the civil aviation agreement between Chiang Kai-shek and the United States. In the previous agreement, the American planes could go anywhere in China, but now, the Soviet Union has fixed routes, and any new route is subject to the approval of the Chinese people's government." To ease the disputes, the Party Central Committee specifically issued instructions within the Party, stressing that "in order to make use of foreign capital to facilitate China's industrialization, it is essential for certain undertakings and foreign capital to join hands and establish joint-stock companies. We may conclude such joint-venture contracts or even concession agreements under appropriate conditions, with the Soviet Union and other new democratic countries, or even some capitalist countries." The Party Central Committee fully affirmed and supported Peng Dehuai's proposition of introducing foreign capital and developing Xinjiang's mineral resources by means of Sino-foreign joint ventures, which was popularized widely as a valuable experience.

Vigorously Advocating the Anti-Corruption Campaign

Peng Dehuai paid special attention to requiring all cadres to uphold the principle of serving the people wholeheartedly, carrying forward a clean work style, and opposing any unhealthy tendencies. Since they had come to the city, some cadres had begun to feel proud and take credit for what they had done, and they were reluctant to keep working hard. They tended to live a more extravagant life or even take a path of corruption.

Given this tendency among cadres, Peng promptly sounded the alarm. In April and May 1949, Peng Dehuai came to Beijing from the northwest frontier to report on his work to the CPC Central Committee and study the issues to be settled. Peng went to Zhou Enlai's office and was received with a warm welcome. During the conversation, Peng reported to Zhou Enlai the situation in Northwestern China. He then expressed his views about some of the comrades who had started to work in the city. Having mentioned that there were usually sofas, carpets, tea tables, bonsai, fish tanks, and other items in a cadre's office, Peng told Zhou quite straightforwardly that "the cadres on the front are suffering extremely hard living and working conditions. What I'm concerned about is that they may not be pleased to see what's going on here, and what's worse, that the comrades coming to the city will feel detached and distanced from the working people in the rural and remote areas. I've noticed that those living in the city are becoming unfamiliar with the countryside, and this happens very quickly after they get to the city. What will happen if they stay longer?" Peng Dehuai's views were incisive and profound, in those circumstances. Zhou Enlai attached great importance to his views and said with approval that it was "well spoken and timely criticism. We must guard against this tendency. The Central Committee will pay particular attention to these problems. Currently, we should fight to eliminate the enemy and engage in production and construction work. We must take over and learn to do urban work, and we must do rural work well. In a word, we must settle both urban and rural issues."

In November 1949, Peng Dehuai raised the issue of opposing extravagance and waste at the expanded meeting of the Northwest Bureau of the Communist Party of China in Lanzhou. He said that leading organs and cadres at all levels should be particularly thrifty for another five to ten years. Apart from the houses constructed as factories, the government, Party, and military organs would not build other houses over the next couple of years. He called on all cadres in Northwestern China to live frugally and struggle diligently, to be role models in this regard, and to be ready to continue living a hard life. Peng Dehuai promptly noticed the emerging dangerous tendencies and constantly educated the cadres to carry forward the Party's fine revolutionary tradition and "strictly carry out a clean, simple work style." He clearly pointed out that we must put aside the identity of veterans, or it would confine us to death. "Individuals add and teams multiply. Without the working people, the leadership of the Communist Party, and the ideological weapon of Marxism and Leninism, we would have achieved nothing."

In late January 1950, when speaking at the meeting of the Northwest Military and Political Commission, Peng Dehuai proposed that extravagance and waste should be strictly prohibited. Some extravagance, such as entertaining, existed in our work. Necessary dinners should be simple, because it was the common people who were paying. It was important to save their money. To nip away the unhealthy tendencies and advocate the clean work style, Peng Dehuai delivered two long speeches in March 1950 at the Executive Council of the Northwest Military and Political Commission. They were entitled "Streamlining the Organization" and "Practicing a Clean, Simple Style and Opposing Extravagance, Waste, and Corruption." He pointed out that extravagance and waste resisted the building of a country with diligence and thrift, departmentalism resisted unified leadership, and guerrilla habits resisted legal orders. Extravagance, waste, and corruption were crimes against the cause of the people and the construction of the motherland. If the revolutionary comrades were infected with this shameful, abominable habit of thinking, they would be guilty of damaging the interests of the people and should be punished according to Party discipline and state law. If we did not resolutely oppose it, we would follow the style of the KMT reactionaries. Therefore, every government official should take "severely punishing corruption, prohibiting waste, and opposing bureaucracy divorced from the masses" as the motto and firmly act upon it.

According to the decision of Peng Dehuai and the Northwest Bureau, after March 1950, the Northwest Bureau, the Northwest Military and Political Commission, and the Party, government, military, and civilian organs and organizations of the Northwest Military Region launched a campaign against unhealthy tendencies. At the end of May, the Northwest Bureau of the Communist Party of China issued instructions to rectify cadres' work style, making the rectification work clearer, more planned, and widespread. By the beginning of September, those who took part in the Rectification Movement had written their personal inspections on the basis of the inspection work. On September 6, Peng Dehuai delivered a systematic summary at the Northwest Rectification Forum.

Peng Dehuai stayed in two sitting rooms linked by a corridor, east to a meeting room of Xincheng building of the organ. The two rooms served as his office, reception room, dining room, and quarters. The leading comrades of the Northwest Bureau intended to provide him with a bigger place, but he resolutely rejected. The staff wanted to install a flushing toilet in the room, which he rejected as well. Peng Dehuai suffered from gastroenteropathy because of his long, hard wartime life. When he was seriously ill, he ate little. The doctor told me to mix protein powder and fruit juice with water for him to drink. Peng Dehuai took it only after we explained that it was given on doctor's advice. At that time, the supply system was implemented. Peng often went to the Director of General Affairs to calculate meal costs to ensure it would not exceed the standard. He wore a military uniform all year round, a thin one in summer and a thick one in winter. He was dressed like the ordinary soldiers. No one could tell that he was a commanding officer of hundreds of thousands of soldiers.

On October 1, 1950, when celebrating the first anniversary of the founding of the new China, the *People's Daily* and the *Xi'an People's Daily* published a special article entitled "The Work in the New Northwest Over the Past Year," written by Peng Dehuai, which summarized the work of the Military and Political Commission since its establishment. It covered five aspects: military affairs, finance and economy, political power construction, national unity, and reform and development of education. As soon as the National Day celebration was over, Peng Dehuai focused on the implementation of the three-year construction plan. On October 4, the central government sent a special plane to take him to Beijing to attend the meeting of the Political Bureau of the Central Committee. The meeting discussed the issue of sending volunteers to support the Korean War against the United States. The CPC Central Committee and Mao Zedong decided to send Peng Dehuai to lead the Chinese people's Volunteer Army to the DPRK. Later, Peng Dehuai led the Chinese people's volunteers across the Yalu River and shouldered the glorious, arduous historical task of resisting US aggression, aiding Korea, and defending the motherland. Peng Dehuai remained concerned about the work in the northwest region during the war in Korea. He sent back messages whenever possible. His instructions and hopes greatly inspired and encouraged the leading cadres and facilitated the work in the northwest region.

(The author is working at Research Office of Party History, Hebei Provincial Committee of the Communist Party of China.)

On Xi Zhongxun's Religious Work Strategy[1]

Li Wenshan and Chen Yi'ou

Xi Zhongxun (1913–2002) was an outstanding proletarian revolutionist and a political leader of the Communist Party of China and the People's Liberation Army. Before and in the early days of Liberation, he worked in the northwest region, where ethnic and religious affairs were varied and complicated. After Reform and Opening Up began, he served as Secretary of the Central Committee and Vice Chairman of the Standing Committee of the National People's Congress, leading the Party's United Front and ethnic and religious work. In his leadership in religious work, he combined principle with flexibility, comprehensively and properly implemented the Party's policy on freedom of religious beliefs, actively guided religion to adapt to the socialist society, paid special attention to strategies and methods, creatively put forward ideas in line with the actual work, enriched the Party's theoretical wealth in religious work, and achieved positive results in practice.

Adopting the Policy of "Steady Progress with Prudence" to Deal with Complicated Issues in Ethnic and Religious Areas

Religion is a complex social phenomenon, and religious issues are complex social issues, especially in China, where they are often intertwined with ethnic issues. In

1. This article was taken from *Northwest Ethnic Studies*, Issue 1, 2009.

his long-term practice of ethnic and religious leadership, Xi Zhongxun realized that China's religious issues were complex, transnational, and long-standing, which were of concern to the masses and nationalities. Instead of implementing simple administrative orders, it was important to treat and deal with religious issues by means of education and guidance, so as to promote long-term, stable development in ethnic and religious areas. Xi especially emphasized that religious cadres should form a work style of "particular prudence," "preciseness," and "meticulous consideration," paying attention to strategies and methods rather than rushing into action.

In the *Biography of Comrade Xi Zhongxun*, the CPC Central Committee commented that when Xi presided over the northwest work, he "acted on principle with flexibility, boldly and properly resolved the complex ethnic and religious issues, united and won over a group of ethnic and religious elites, and laid a solid foundation for consolidating the new political power, establishing a new social order, healing the war trauma, and carrying out large-scale economic construction."[2] In the early days of liberation, he directly led the persuasion of Xiang Qian and ultimately won him over, which was a typical case of adopting the policy of "steady progress with prudence" to deal with complex issues in ethnic and religious areas. In December 1949, Xiang Qian, a member of the 12th generation head of a thousand households of the Nganglha tribe in Qinghai Province, together with Ma Bufang's bandits, organized the so-called Anti-Communist National Army and launched a rebellion. Xi Zhongxun, Second Secretary of the Northwest Bureau of the CPC Central Committee at that time, took into account the special complexity of ethnic and religious areas, and on multiple occasions, he instructed the leaders of the Qinghai Provincial Party Committee to properly settle the Nganglha rebellion, which was of great significance not only for addressing the relationship between Nganglha Tibetan compatriots, but also for our Party to gain a firm foothold in other Tibetan areas and ethnic minority areas in Qinghai and establish the people's power and carry out work in the Tibetan areas in Gansu, Sichuan, and Kham Tibet, and even Tibet. He stressed that we must adhere to the principle of political struggle based on full military preparation, let go of the impatience of blind military suppression, instead adopt a cautious attitude and a policy of constant struggle plus extra leniency, and strive to settle the problem by peaceful means. It took two years and seven months to win Xiang Qian over. Through persistent effort, Xi ultimately

2. "Life of Comrade Xi Zhongxun," *People's Daily* (May 31, 2002), p. 4.

achieved success in this regard, which greatly facilitated peace and stability in the northwestern region. Mao Zedong spoke highly of Xi Zhongxun, "You are truly powerful. Zhuge Liang captured and released Meng Huo seven times. You are more powerful than Zhuge Liang."[3]

After the founding of the People's Republic of China, carrying out land reform in ethnic and religious areas was a major challenge. Xi Zhongxun studied the issue in combination with the specific situation of ethnic and religious areas. In 1952, when he was in charge of the Northwest Bureau, in an effort to unite a large number of ethnic and religious elites, reduce resistance, and increase aid for land reform in ethnic and religious areas, Xi put forward the well-known notion of "uniting feudalism against feudalism" in his report to the Central Committee. In other words, it was necessary to first do a good job of uniting the ethnic and religious elites, and then mobilize the masses to carry out reform, to "resort to 'more peaceful' means and necessary compromises in exchange for better conditions to mobilize the masses, preserve part of feudalism, while destroying most of it...[4] we should adopt a lenient, compromising policy to these people to help them go through the land reform." This view respected the religious beliefs and customs of all ethnic groups and strove to unite the forces that might "help with (or at least not oppose) the land reform." It was the specific application, enrichment, and development of the Party's United Front concept in China's ethnic and religious areas in land reform, which was recognized by the Party Central Committee and appreciated by Mao Zedong. With the proper land reform principles and policies, the Party successfully carried out large-scale land reform in more than 170 counties and cities in five provinces and autonomous regions in Northwestern China, united and won over a group of ethnic and religious elites, effectively safeguarded the interests of the vast number of farmers and herdsmen, and laid a good foundation for consolidating new political power, establishing a new social order, and carrying out large-scale economic construction.

3. *Xi Zhongxun's Revolutionary Career* (CPC History Press, China Literature and History Press, 2002), p. 37.

4. *Collected Works of Xi Zhongxun* (Central Party Literature Press, 1996), p. 209.

Widely Win Over, Unite, and Educate Influential People in Religious Circles

Xi Zhongxun once pointed out that "to develop the patriotic United Front, we should engage in all parts of the country, educate all kinds of people, and unite all those who can be united."[5] To do religious work was to do the work of the United Front. It was necessary to win over, unite, and educate people in religious circles. He believed that the religious elites of ethnic minorities had a high social status in their own regions and played a great social role with much influence. If they were won over and united, they could become a bridge and link between the Communist Party of China and religious believers in ethnic minority areas and play a great role that our cadres and Party members could not replace. Therefore, he proposed that when working in religious minority areas, it was important to make friends with influential people in religious circles, so that we could go deeper into the masses.

In ethnic and religious areas, many people had religious beliefs and strong religious feelings, so religious leaders had a widespread appeal and important influence. Xi Zhongxun particularly emphasized the United Front work for religious leaders and their role, saying that "ethnic affairs are complex which require much research. It is necessary to figure out the situation of leaders so as to facilitate their work."[6] For example, he suggested in a written instruction on the Tibet issue in 1982 that "the key to the Tibet issue is that of the Dalai Lama and the Panchen Lama, that is a religious issue. Today, it involves the basic understanding of the two spiritual leaders. Only when we are certain about how we are going to treat the two can we make policies and guidelines for Tibet. Otherwise, we will be confused and lost in our policy-making, which will lead to inconsistency in policy and mistakes in our work."[7]

With the broad vision and magnanimous mind of a communist, Xi Zhongxun had long enjoyed strong ties with people in religious circles and made friends with a number of influential people in religious circles, including the leader of Tibetan Buddhism, the 10th Panchen Lama, Geshe Sherab Gyatso, the sixth Gungtang, Jigma Tenpai Wanchuk living Buddha, and the prestigious Islamic personages Bao Erhan and Ma Fuchen. Adhering to the communication principle of "unity and

---

5. *Collected Works of Xi Zhongxun* (Central Party Literature Press, 1996), p. 400.
6. *In Memory of Xi Zhongxun* (Chinese Communist Party History Press, China Literature and History Press, 2005), p. 85.
7. *Xi Zhongxun's Revolutionary Career* (CPC History Press, China Literature and History Press, 2002), p. 337.

cooperation in politics, mutual respect in belief, care in life, and improvement in ideology," Xi Zhongxun stayed in touch with them, helped them establish a correct understanding of the Communist Party of China and socialist society, won their trust and respect, and made them reliable friends for long-term cooperation with the Communist Party of China.

Xi Zhongxun once said in his article "The Truth of Making Friends" that "in dealing with friends, we should be humble, sincere, and honest, taking care of each other wholeheartedly."[8] With this attitude, Xi Zhongxun forged a deep friendship with the tenth Panchen Lama, who was 25 years younger than Xi. They often communicated and sent greetings frequently. When having difficulties at work, they talked to each other, trying to understand the situation and offering input and suggestions. Xi often inspired and guided the Panchen Lama to properly understand the Party's ethnic and religious policies, reminding the latter of his dual identity as a national leader and a religious leader and helping him to strike balance between the two roles. The Panchen Lama had great admiration for and trust in Xi Zhongxun, two of whom formed a deep friendship.

Geshe Sherab Gyatso, a master of Tibetan Buddhism, was Vice Chairman of the Mongolian Tibetan Committee of the national government before the founding of the new China. After the founding of the new China, Geshe Sherab Gyatso served as the President of the National Buddhist Association and Vice Governor of Qinghai Province. He was not moved by the temptation of the authoritative seal and the title the Kuomintang had offered. With the enthusiastic help and instruction of Xi Zhongxun, he developed a sincere admiration for the Communist Party of China.[9] Geshe Sherab Gyatso was appointed by Xi Zhongxun to help in the winning over of Xiang Qian, and he risked his life to make three visits to persuade the tribes to surrender, which played a great role in the victory of that struggle.

Preventing and Overcoming Leftist Thinking and Rightist Tendencies

Religion has always been a traditional cultural pattern with historical continuity and a social ideology with real-world application, especially in some minority areas. Chinese Communists were atheists, but it was important to respect and protect the people's freedom of religious belief. A few Party members and cadres

8. *Collected Works of Xi Zhongxun* (Central Party Literature Press, 1996), p. 427.

9. *Xi Zhongxun's Revolutionary Career* (CPC History Press, China Literature and History Press, 2002), p. 350.

did not have a correct understanding of the nature of religion and the objective law of its emergence, development, and extinction, so that they had a one-sided understanding of Marx's assertion that "religion is the opiate of the people," which led to leftist ideological tendencies. Classic Marxist writers have analyzed the harm of interfering in the freedom of religious belief. For example, Lenin once pointed out that "it is a foolish act to declare war on religion."[10] However, during the Cultural Revolution when the extreme leftist ideology was rampant, the Party's religious policy was seriously damaged, and many religious people were wrongly treated, which had serious consequences.

After the adoption of the Reform and Opening Up policy, Xi Zhongxun emphasized that to fully implement the Party's policy of freedom in religious belief, first of all, China's staff should guard against the leftist ideological tendency. In 1985, at the National Symposium on the Implementation of Religious Policies, Xi clearly suggested that "religion and people's belief in religion is a long-existing fact that does not change just because we wish it to. We need to approach the issue with prudence and appropriateness, rather than settling it with simple administrative orders."[11] To overcome the leftist ideology, it was necessary to fully realize the long-term, complex, mass, and transnational nature of religious issues under socialist conditions. Xi Zhongxun pointed out that "people with leftist ideas often doubt and negate the Party's policy of freedom in religious belief, and they set the implementation of the Party's religious policy against socialist material and spiritual civilization. They discriminate, suppress, or even crack down on religious groups, believers, and their normal religious activities. When dealing with normal religious affairs, they are narrow minded and impatient, and they employ simple and rough measures, resulting in a negative political impact."[12]

At the same time, due to the complexity of religious issues, some religious workers had a rightist tendency in the face of difficulties, and they dared not govern even illegal activities undertaken under the guise of religion. Xi Zhongxun believed that those people "often give in to the inappropriate demands of the minority people who are unreasonable and ignorant of the overall situation in religious circles, and neglect to do ideological and political work with them. They even turn a blind eye to illegal activities undertaken under the guise of religion, which has resulted in great confusion and loss."[13]

---

10. *Complete Works of Lenin, Vol.17* (People's Publishing House, 1988), p. 389.
11. *Collected Works of Xi Zhongxun* (Central Party Literature Press, 1996), p. 404.
12. *Collected Works of Xi Zhongxun* (Central Party Literature Press, 1996), p. 419.
13. *Collected Works of Xi Zhongxun* (Central Party Literature Press, 1996), pp. 420–421.

Xi Zhongxun analyzed the nature of these two erroneous ideological tendencies, and he held that "be it leftist or rightist, despite their different forms, the consequence is weakening the Party's leadership over religious work, hindering the correct, comprehensive implementation of the Party's religious policy, and thus breaking away from the majority of religious and non-religious people and giving opportunities to those who make use of religion for illegal activities and for the infiltration of the hostile forces of foreign religions into our country."[14]

He pointed out that we should manage religious affairs in accordance with the law. We should firmly guarantee all regular religious activities and resolutely crack down on those illegal criminal activities under the cover of religion. The struggle against the Shouters sect from 1982 to 1984 was a case in point. In 1982, the Ministry of Public Security reported that the Shouters sect emerged among small Christian groups in Zhejiang Province, which, under the control and sponsorship of foreign reactionary religious forces, incited religious fanaticism and encouraged believers to oppose the Party and the government. On reading the report, Xi Zhongxun promptly instructed the relevant departments to "study and formulate comprehensive management measures as soon as possible." Later, he systematically expounded the policies and measures to settle the problem of the Shouters sect at the relevant meeting, pointing out that "to solve the problem of the Shouters sect, we must carry out comprehensive management. In brief, we should make full use of legal weapons, resolutely crack down on the ringleaders, and seriously punish them. We should implement religious policies, do a good job in mass work, and strengthen the Party's leadership."[15] Under the direct guidance of Xi Zhongxun, the Party won the struggle and maintained the local social order and regular religious life. Guarding against and overcoming the leftist thought and the rightist tendency remained a major challenge in religious work even when we reached the stage of building an affluent society in all aspects.

The combination of firm principle and flexible strategy was an important policy and strategy of the Party. In leading religious work, in the spirit of seeking truth from facts, and with his "perfect" (to quote Mao Zedong) leadership and consideration of the characteristics of China's religions, Xi Zhongxun creatively applied and gave full play to this strategy. His ideas and experience were of great relevance and significance in properly implementing the Party's basic principles of religious work, handling religious hot spots, difficulties, and sensitive issues,

14. *Collected Works of Xi Zhongxun* (Central Party Literature Press, 1996), p. 421.

15. *Xi Zhongxun's Revolutionary Career* (Chinese Communist Party History Press, China Literature and History Press, 2002), p. 288.

fostering harmony in religious relations, guiding religion to adapt to socialist society, widely and fully mobilizing all positive factors in the religious community, and exerting the positive roles of religious personages and believers in promoting social development.

(Bio of the authors: Li Wenshan, Department of Political Science and Law, Hanshan Normal University, and Chen Yi'ou, Party School of Xiangqiao District Committee, Chaozhou City, CPC)

Postscript

I have known Mr. Shao Jiyao for more than twenty years. He is a learned, responsible teacher, composed and confident, and a role model for me. At the beginning of 2008, Mr Shao, then over 80, returned to the ancient city of Xi'an from abroad. As in the past, when talking to him and his wife, Ms. Ai, and listening to him talk about history and philosophy, I found that he often talked about the people and events of the Northwest Bureau, frequently repeating the stories. Later, he did a good deal of research to check his memory. Despite the hot weather and their advanced age, the couple went through the streets of the city to look for the remaining friends and places.

From what I know, Mr. Shao and his wife went overseas years ago to be united with their children and conduct their academic research. For a long time, they had little contact with their colleagues and friends at home. Every time they returned home for a brief period, they tried to make contact with old friends. It was not an easy job to locate the places and people from previous times, as a result of the rapid urban development in recent years. In our talks, when Mr. Shao took out some photos and books to share with me, with a childlike look and a smile, how he found the previous comrades who had worked and studied in the Northwest Bureau and were still alive, I was deeply moved by his laughter, his gestures, and his clear, flowing memories of the Northwest Bureau. I was also sad and touched as he sank into long silences with a deep sigh when talking about the familiar leaders and colleagues who had passed away.

Reviewing the ups and downs in history, we remain dedicated to what we have believed. In the following weeks and months, when we walked into the inner world of those surviving veteran cadres of the Northwest Bureau, we started to feel and understand the passionate years of the Northwest Bureau, as if we were among groups of young people who were simple, ambitious, idealistic, vigorous, and enterprising, and entirely typical of their times.

In 2009, I began to interview the veterans of the Northwest Bureau and began to record their oral narrations. "I was very happy to work in the Northwest Bureau." The 88-year-old Shi Hong sat quietly on a corner of the couch, holding a cane, staring at the portrait of her husband Huang Zhi as she told us about the glorious history of the Northwest Bureau more than half a century ago. Her thin face brightened as she spoke.

Before we arrived, 81-year-old Zhang Ke had been standing at the door, waiting to meet us. He had to be supported by his wife. Judging from his height and loud, strong northern Shaanxi accent, we could visualize what a strong, handsome, capable, and promising young man he was in the years of the Northwest Bureau. For over two hours, as he spoke, we confirmed our conjecture. He said affectionately, "the Northwest Bureau is my home and part of an unforgettable memory. I have deep feelings for her." Zhang Ke's strong northern Shaanxi accent still buzzes in our ears even now.

Zhang Zhenbang, 92, is a kind, wise old man. As he greeted us and asked us to try the Luochuan apples on the table, he gently rubbed his hands and recounted in a soft voice about the joy and hardships in the Northwest Bureau, when they tried to rescue themselves with grain production in the face of unprecedented difficulties. At the end of the interview, he wrote down the line, "unforgettable days, happy memories," in our notebook.

"I experienced real joy in my days in the Northwest Bureau. My tutors will always live in my mind, and I will always remember them." Shao Jiyao, 82, was formerly an underground worker for the Party, and he later worked in the Policy Research Office of the Northwest Bureau. He was graceful, poised, and articulate, with profound attainments in policy theory, but he suffered wrong treatment for 26 years. I had heard his experiences many times, but never as complete as this time. As usual, he spoke with gentleness and composure, but when he counted to talk about the familiar leaders and colleagues, he choked up.

These veterans, who were once strong and powerful, have gone through turbulent years. The past is gone and the dust settled, but when recalling the days in the Northwest Bureau, they seem to travel back to the era of pursuing faith and ideals, warm spring sunlight, and the bright sunshine.

The Northwest Bureau implemented the "triangular organization system" and carried out the construction of a new type of democracy and democratic regime. It advocated that the Party members should work closely with non-Party individuals and discuss important matters with them. According to Chairman Mao, the border region was a democratic anti-Japanese base area, where we should "improve ourselves and help others… to set an example for the entire country and serve as a role model" so as to "facilitate the democratization of the entire nation."

The Northwest Bureau established a broad National United Front, adopted effective policies, opposed both Han chauvinism and local nationalism, stabilized the situation in the northwest, and laid a foundation for the smooth development of land reform and suppression of bandits and despots.

Based on different historical conditions, the Northwest Bureau carried out the land reform in line with local conditions and corrected "the anti-Marxist, anti-Leninist ordering and tailism in the Party" with its "vivid and specific experience." After the Yihe Meeting, it promptly spotted and corrected the leftist tendency, which was affirmed by the Party Central Committee and Chairman Mao.

The Northwest Bureau stressed the need for regular training of cadres, as well as their self-disciplined learning and education. It employed various means to train a large number of cadres for the liberation of the northwest. More than half a century later, all this is still moving and inspiring.

Recalling the Northwest Bureau, we cannot help but remember Comrade Peng Dehuai for his unique contribution to the overall work as the First Secretary of the Northwest Bureau for many years. From military work to politics, from economic construction to cultural education, from principles and policies to working methods, he was always ready to offer his strategies and suggestions. He took the trouble to enlighten the cadres on the ethnic issues of special significance to Northwestern China and the issue of uniting non-Party personages. He had full trust in and support for Comrade Xi Zhongxun, who had great respect for him in return. This was another major reason the Northwest Bureau did such a good job.

Recalling the Northwest Bureau, we cannot help but remember Comrade Xi Zhongxun. He attached great importance to the study of Marxism, Leninism, and Mao Zedong Thought, and he was good at proceeding from reality and combining the central line, principles, and policies with the actual situation in Northwestern China. He adhered to the principle of seeking truth from facts, and his selfless dedication to the comrades and the people was a solid foundation for the Northwest Bureau to do well.

Recalling the Northwest Bureau, we also cherish the memory of Mr. Lin (Boqu) and Mr. Xie (Juezai), who presided over the work of the border region government, as well as Comrades Jia Tuofu, Li Zhuoran, Zhang Jiafu, Zhang Desheng, Wang Feng, and Zhao Boping, who were in charge of various aspects of the work. In the words of Comrade Ma Wenrui, former Director of the Organization Department of the Northwest Bureau, we have made due achievements in our work only through close cooperation, unity, adherence to the principle of the Party spirit, consideration of the overall situation, and selfless dedication.

At the end of the interview with Mr. Shao Jiyao, we couldn't help but ask what the comrades in the Northwest Bureau thought about and whether they had any worries or frustrations. He said that "at that time, those who took part in the revolution didn't feel afraid, aggrieved, bitter, or tired, and they didn't think much of the difficulties. They simply concentrated on the revolutionary work, thinking about how to complete the task and ignoring what might have happened to them. This was a common aspiration of all those working in the Northwest Bureau at that time."

Their ideals are truly noble and uplifting. To work hard, be courageous in overcoming difficulties and good at solving problems, be united and ready to help, and selflessly dedicate to the interests of the revolution and the goods for all, seek truth from facts and be down-to-earth as opposed to boasting and empty talk, remove the outdated and be innovative and revolutionary – all these is the legacy and inspiration the Northwest Bureau has left for us.

We need to embrace and carry forward the spirit embedded in that particular period of history that has been passed down to us. As He Zai, a 90-year-old man, said, "Proceeding from reality and seeking truth from facts was the most prominent feature of the Northwest Bureau… The Bureau made great contributions in the history of the Party." The Bureau remains our spiritual pillar, sustaining us to continue with its aspiration and fine tradition as we bear them in mind and carry them forward. This represents the greatness of the Northwest Bureau, and it also remains the ideal that every one of us living today is pursuing.

The People's Republic of China has celebrated its 60th birthday. Reviewing and summing up the glorious course and valuable experience of the Northwest Bureau is of far-reaching significance, enabling us to have a profound comprehensive understanding of more than sixty years of history, to thoroughly implement the spirit of the 18th CPC National Congress, to comprehensively promote the project of Party building at a new historical juncture, and to write a new chapter of building socialism with Chinese characteristics.

Today many veterans from the Northwest Bureau are no longer with us. Just before the publication of the book, I learned that Mr. Shao Jiyao passed away. I couldn't help but feel sorrowful.

In memory of the Northwest Bureau. In memory of the revolutionary pioneers of the Northwest Bureau.

Shi Jie
April, 2013